THE ROOSEVELT LEADERSHIP 1933-1945

BY EDGAR EUGENE ROBINSON

DA CAPO PRESS • NEW YORK • 1972

Library of Congress Cataloging in Publication Data

Robinson, Edgar Eugene, 1887-
    The Roosevelt leadership, 1933-1945.

    (The American scene: comments and commentators)
    Includes bibliographical references.
    1. Roosevelt, Franklin Delano, Pres. U.S., 1882-
1945. 2. U.S.—History—1933-1945. I. Title.
[E806.R722 1972]   973.917   75-146154
ISBN 0-306-70202-9

This Da Capo Press edition of *The Roosevelt Leadership,
1933-1945,* is an unabridged republication of the first
edition published in Philadelphia and New York in 1955.
It is reprinted by a special arrangement with
J. B. Lippincott Company, Philadelphia, New York.

Published by Da Capo Press, Inc.
A Subsidiary of Plenum Publishing Corporation
227 West 17th Street, New York, New York 10011

THE ROOSEVELT LEADERSHIP
1933–1945

THE ROOSEVELT LEADERSHIP

1933-1945

BY

EDGAR EUGENE ROBINSON

J. B. LIPPINCOTT COMPANY

PHILADELPHIA AND NEW YORK

To

The late J. Brooks B. Parker

who believed that the influence

of

Franklin Delano Roosevelt

upon this nation

was very great

and wished

for a contemporary appraisement

without fear, favor, or prejudice

CONTENTS

PART TWO

PREFACE

THIS BOOK is the story of the influence of one of the great leaders of the modern world. The story is the result of an inquiry into the nature and purpose of Franklin Delano Roosevelt's political leadership and its effect upon democratic government in the United States. This leadership was highly personal; its influence was felt throughout the world; and it brought into being the New America in which the American people now live.

Obviously, the soundest judgment upon what Mr. Roosevelt said and did is to be based upon as complete and as honest a record as can be found. Fortunately he was aware that someday this would be sought, and he prepared a record.*

It may well be that President Roosevelt felt that an adequate history of his administration could be written only by a statesman. Yet in the decade since his death, his own record has been amplified by the testimony of innumerable contemporaries, by the publication of memoirs of his advisers and colleagues, and by the interpretations of countless critics of varying degrees of competence and insight.

The present volume attempts to cut a path through masses of conflicting evidence already well known, and to reach a point of detachment from which to survey the forest of fact and fiction that already tends to obscure the figure of President Roosevelt.

Among historians and others interested in public affairs, no comment is more frequently heard in discussion of contemporary events than "It is too early to tell the story. There is not sufficient evidence to attempt an explanation. More perspective is needed to pass a judgment. Passions must cool before history is written."

This is nonsense, when viewed in the hard light of con-

---

* See Part Two.

9

temporary need. It may be attributed to the inheritance of an earlier time when the line between past and present was more clearly marked. Today the American people are forced to choose their leaders and determine their future policies in the light of what they know and think of the immediate past. In this swiftly moving world we cannot wait—unless history as a guide is to be completely abandoned.

Furthermore, legends are in the making as an event takes place, and evidence, unless nurtured in its own time, seems less and less important to the descendants of those who witnessed the event and contributed to the legend. To write about the career of Franklin Roosevelt within ten years of his death may be as helpful to posterity as it would have been to write of Lincoln in 1875.

Yet this is not a biography of Franklin Roosevelt, nor a history of his administration. A narrative history of the twelve years would call for several volumes. The reader will look elsewhere for minute and analytical examination of President Roosevelt's executive acts, and will seek elsewhere, likewise, the analysis and explanation of technical aspects of his legislative program, of his military decisions, and of his foreign policy. The philosophy underlying the New Deal is dealt with only in its broadest aspects.

The story presented in this volume is intended for the general reader who is concerned with President Roosevelt's basic purposes as well as his general methods, and for those who desire an interpretation of the era of his leadership, as well as for those seeking guidance in the vast array of manuscript and of published materials already available.

For the years 1933 to 1945 records exist as never before in the history of man. This volume is based upon a reading of the published materials available, in particular the writings of President Roosevelt himself, and the responses of informed commentators to his utterances and action at the time. Important manuscript sources pertinent to the issues considered have been examined in detail. Recent interviews and earlier associations with a number of the contemporaries of Mr. Roosevelt, who had an active part in the events discussed but whose views have not as yet been published, have been an important source of additional information.

Firm in the belief that the United States shelters opportunity for continuous functioning of the human mind, the author does not anticipate that the report of his findings will be acceptable to all who read it. As Mr. Dooley warned earlier in the century, "Th' further ye get away fr'm anny perryod th' betther ye can write about it. Ye are not subjict to interruptions be people that were there."

The chapters that follow in Part One are not all in narrative form. The story moves forward, but at times the material determined an expository approach, and again a descriptive account. From time to time it seemed well to pause and consider the results of the acts and utterances of President Roosevelt, not waiting for the summaries that appear in the final chapters.

The chapters in Part Two present the "record" as we know it now. The bibliographical materials, when presented in *chronological order,* tell the story. The historical development of these years was not in a placid stream whose movement could be easily timed. It might rather be likened to a whirlpool. The manner and time of emergence of much of the record were important factors in the development of the legend of the Roosevelt Leadership.

The title, *The Roosevelt Leadership,* refers to the period during which Franklin Roosevelt was President of the United States. The book ends in 1945, not because the influence of President Roosevelt ceased, but because with his death this influence entered an entirely different phase. The living figure was gone. The legend began to displace the fact. In the spring and summer of 1945, with a world war ended, United Nations launched, and new problems of world politics on the horizon, the American people entered upon a new phase of their history.

EDGAR EUGENE ROBINSON

December 1, 1954

INTRODUCTION

THE LEADERSHIP OF Franklin Delano Roosevelt is an outstanding fact of modern history. Others have seized power and dominated millions. Others have swayed the imagination of their fellow men for a longer time. Roosevelt was chosen by the people, repeatedly, against continued and growing minority protest, and, as the chosen leader of the American people, he represented their interests in the world when the United States was, by all tests, the determining power. Roosevelt by act and word determined in large measure the state of the world in which Americans live ten years after his death. In fact, as well as in legend, Franklin Roosevelt will rank as the most powerful of American Presidents.

Yet, as leader when he came to power in 1933, he was not placed there, as were Washington, Jackson, and Grant, because of a personal record that the people approved. Nor did he win a place as leader of the minds of men as did Jefferson, Lincoln, and Wilson. Nor did he come to his supreme opportunity, as did Herbert Hoover, because of the conviction of an overwhelming majority of voters that in his conception of the power of the individual citizen there might be a New Day for all mankind in a world of science, invention, and co-operation.

Roosevelt emerges, even now, as a leader identified with the aspirations of the common man and the hopes of democracy—as Americans have known it. He expressed the desires of a great popular movement in the United States which had been a half-century in the making. He expressed the weaknesses in the movement. In the end he symbolized the frustrations of all popular rule.

Throughout the years of majority support, there was opposed to Mr. Roosevelt a great minority who were convinced of his inadequacy in office, of the unsoundness of his program, and of the vital necessity of blocking him at every possible opportunity.

When he ceased to lead, the effect of his years in power was manifested in a weakened Constitutional system, in imperiled national security, in diminished national morale, in deteriorated political morality, and in an overburdened economy. Powerful beyond comprehension, because of the power of the American people, President Roosevelt had an important part in destroying dictators representing the entrenched totalitarianism of the few, only to leave his nation exposed at home and abroad to a totalitarianism of the masses more terrible than any foe yet faced by a free people.

If Americans are to see Mr. Roosevelt in the perspective of history, it must be first of all in an acceptance of the fact of his wide acclaim. But it is vital to honest thought that the legend of accomplishment be measured against the facts that explain continued support. We should examine in detail the development of this theme in the dozen fateful years in which President Roosevelt dominated the American scene.

Franklin Roosevelt prepared himself for the Presidency in ways quite unlike those used by contemporaries who were aspirants for the office. He acquired an extensive knowledge of the intricate machinery not only of politics as practiced in the United States, but also of government as operated by politicians. More than Jackson, Cleveland, or Wilson, Roosevelt embodied in his leadership the diverse elements that enter into the Democratic party. To millions his political personality came to mean superlative leadership. Facing the crisis of depression, he was affirmative in his program. Its immediate success seemed to justify the course taken.

In lands beyond the seas, this American figure became in his lifetime the symbol of hope to millions. This hope has come to be a legend. Franklin Roosevelt remains in world history the great champion of the masses. Identified by word and deed with compassion for all who were in need, this patrician—who had shared in all the opportunities that the United States had to offer—was hailed as their leader by those whose lives were less fortunate.

Thus, in a world in the throes of profound social and economic change, Mr. Roosevelt from the outset of his Presidency was thought of by many as a leader in a revolution. It might be his particular kind of revolution, but it was seen as a revolt against the *status quo*. And it seemed to the informed somehow inevitable, for the United States was itself the product of continuous change for the betterment of the common man.

To millions of people, at home and abroad, the historic figure of Franklin Roosevelt is one of undiminished brilliance. His voice, his smile, his gestures have been immortalized in recording, film, and photograph. His utterances have come to be a part of the American heritage.* His actions, as he appeared among the great of the earth, are vividly portrayed. His influence transcends all bounds of over-emphasis. What manner of man was he? What is legend, and how much is fact?

Those who seek a full explanation of human conduct and of national destiny dare not accept the "history" of the Roosevelt years as prepared by the supporters of Mr. Roosevelt. Led by Mr. Roosevelt himself and his group of immediate aides in preparation of the personal record, the participants have presented the narrative of these years countless times in the frame of reference prepared by themselves. In the decade since Mr. Roosevelt's death, this pattern has not changed in any marked degree.

It must be said that the majority of the American people have tended to accept this pattern inasmuch as they feel themselves, as was so often asserted by Mr. Roosevelt, to have had a very important part in the making of the story. But it is not the whole truth as posterity will find it. Nor is it the full record that the interested citizen can find, even today.

A realization that the Roosevelt followers have not told the whole story has led to an outpouring of highly critical works.

---

* Charles A. Beard on January 30, 1937, wrote Stephen Early, Secretary to the President: ". . . . As a life-long student of American history, I am convinced that no President, not even Washington and Jefferson, ever wrote state papers that went wider and deeper into fundamentals than President Franklin D. Roosevelt has written. As the great state papers of the past have furnished guidance and inspiration to the American people in maintaining institutions of popular government, so President Roosevelt's papers will, I feel sure, establish the framework of opinion and ideals in which the grave problems of the future will be solved according to our best traditions . . ." (President's Personal File 98, Franklin D. Roosevelt Library).

13710

These reflect the intensity of feeling of many who were opponents of the President during his lifetime. Few of them
have attempted to present or pretend to present a rounded picture. Their purpose has been to correct the record, and this has
given them the appearance of extreme partisanship, and has
tended to put them constantly on the defensive in that they
were attacking a record already made.

Now the truth that we seek is not to be found in a minute
examination of the record for its flaws and errors and false-
hoods. Of course they are there, and it will take a generation
or more to sift them out and to make sure what does stand the
test of careful examination. But the primary task is that of dealing with the existent pattern of Roosevelt's leadership and it
must be done now.

The task is this: To provide a frame of reference that expresses exactly and without partisanship the basic problems
faced by the people of the United States in these twelve years.
Upon these problems Mr. Roosevelt took action and gave his
opinion, and his opponents did likewise. Of primary concern to
us is the question of the relation of these problems to the daily
life of the people as they tried to determine their national
future.

The basic problems were those of *livelihood, co-operation,*
and *defense.* On each of these the President was called upon to
take a stand.

His position from the outset was that the livelihood of the
citizen was the concern of the government. Upon this he built
a vast structure of public works and of social security—each of
these to protect the citizen.

Likewise, co-operation was called for repeatedly by the President. It was a co-operation of citizens forced by necessity, not
by conviction, nor by belief in a basic philosophy. It was the
essence of social democracy as envisaged by followers of the
President.

And a people dedicated to the support of all and the co-
operation of all must defend itself at home and abroad from
those forces that denied these fundamentals. Herein lay dramatic foundation for leaders who as a matter of daily life were

satisfied with generalizations and who lived in a world of desirable objectives.

What then gave Roosevelt the transcendent power he undoubtedly had—in utterance and in action—in leading his fellow Americans? It must be concluded that he represented fairly well the level of conception, understanding, and purpose that characterized the mass of the American people of his time. In him there was a happy combination of elements that gave highest place to aspiration, compelling regard for simplicity of statement, and an abiding faith in the judgment of the common man.

This kind of democratic appeal fitted the mood of the time —and it had deep roots in American history. Franklin Roosevelt built upon the work of innumerable rebels that preceded him. This is true. But more important than the legacy of these earlier reformers is the heritage of the masses of Americans who have always been radical in outlook and aspiration, though infrequently in action. They have, however, wanted practical results. These Franklin Roosevelt could provide them, for a time, because of the crisis in which he first appeared, and because of the unusual combination of radical elements that repeatedly returned him to power.

When, in due time, the American people and their leaders realize that the hard realities of a mechanized world demand economics and politics of a superior order, it will be found that the record of these years is as barren of real understanding and accomplishment as it is rich in expressions of the promises that have always made America the hope of the world.

The significance of the twelve-year debate with former President Hoover was not realized by the American people because Mr. Hoover was a private citizen at the time. Yet there is every reason to accept R. G. Tugwell's phrase descriptive of Roosevelt and Hoover: "protagonists in an epic struggle of ideas." *

We shall see that in these years there were other "revolutionaries" at work. Roosevelt's leadership was the façade behind which a less understanding but profoundly convinced revolutionary leadership was provided in the Congress, in administrative departments, in the press, on the radio, and in the

---

* "The Protagonists: Roosevelt and Hoover," in *The Antioch Review*, XIII (Winter 1953-1954), 442.

colleges and schools. It was rarely a leadership pledged to doctrines alien to American soil.

Indeed, this other leadership arose directly from American experience, and many Americans found it to their liking for that reason. It was a revolutionary leadership in the sense that it was the work of fairly small groups dedicated to making over American society. And it used the slogans that found ready response in the hearts of Americans, in particular those associated with freedom of thought and expression. Eventually these advocates of fundamental change found their counterparts in other nations, and America was plunged into a world conflict of ideas, as well as of armies.

Franklin Roosevelt, possessing indomitable courage and will power, won the allegiance of innumerable enthusiasts, and by an incomparable sense of timing, he won continuing support of a huge body of voters.

This gave him control of a nation, and direction of the greatest striking force in the world. For a time he was the most powerful leader of the twentieth century, and in fact the most powerful in the history of mankind. A man of good intention cast in the role of hero, he was overwhelmed by the inexorable forces of his time. This was his tragedy, the tragedy of his people, and the tragedy of the world.

What was the political situation out of which such continued leadership arose? What were the methods by which President Roosevelt retained that leadership in peace and in war? What was the status of the United States, and what was the outlook of the American people when he gave up this power at the time of his death in April, 1945?

Answer to these questions must be found if we are to evaluate the nature and significance of Franklin Roosevelt's leadership, and to pass judgment upon the interests and skills of American citizens in maintaining self-government in a world of war, revolution, and uneasy peace.

Acknowledgments

MY INTEREST in the subject of this book dates from my studies on the political leadership of Franklin Delano Roosevelt which were published in 1947 under the title, *They Voted for Roosevelt.*

A full list of those to whom acknowledgment and thanks should be given would be a very long one. Few will expect a formal acknowledgment here, for they already know of the deep indebtedness felt by the author and have been given assurance of the fact. A few would prefer not to be named.

To my colleagues in the Department of History at Stanford University, I express my thanks for comments and judgments. To my graduate students in seminars on the Roosevelt administration I express appreciation for their development of many ideas.

During the preparation of this study I have profited from many a conversation with Dr. Frank Freidel. He generously placed at my disposal valuable information gathered in his research at the Roosevelt Library. He read the completed manuscript, but is in no way responsible for point of view or conclusions.

My knowledge of the work of the State Department, 1939-1945, owes much to conference and correspondence with the late Harley Notter, whose volume, *Postwar Foreign Policy Preparation 1939-1945,* I read in advance of publication.

Thanks beyond measure are due to Director Herman Kahn and the staff of the Franklin D. Roosevelt Library, and to Luther Evans, Librarian of Congress at the time of my research in the Library. David Mearns and Katharine Brand of the Manuscripts Division of the Library of Congress were of great assistance. Thanks are due the officials of the Hoover Institute and Library on War, Revolution, and Peace. In particular do I wish to express my deep indebtedness to Director Raynard C. Swank and the staff of the Stanford University Libraries. To President J. E. Wallace Sterling of Stanford University I owe much for assistance at the time of the launching of this study, and thereafter for hearty encouragement.

For more than a year Dr. Vaughn D. Bornet, formerly Research Associate in the Institute of American History at Stanford University, was my brilliant associate. He produced the critical Bibliography upon which Part Two is based. It reflects his creative insight, careful summary, and definitive comment.

Throughout this work, the Research Secretary of the Institute of American History, Lisette Emery Fast, has been my indispensable aid. Every aspect of the book bears the result of her indefatigable research, painstaking summary, and incisive criticism.

Joan Tocher, E. Carolyn Di Maria, and Theressa Gay have typed understandingly and most effectively.

Several of my close friends have read portions of the book. I thank them, but wish to avoid any responsibility that might be theirs if they were named here. My wife, Katherine Young Robinson, has listened to the repeated reading of the manuscript and I have profited from her illuminating comments. Dr. Cecilia Robertson Irvine read the manuscript and her criticisms were invaluable.

To George Stevens I wish to express deep appreciation for his editorial guidance.

The preparation and publication of this book at this time are due to a provision in the will of the late J. Brooks B. Parker of Philadelphia which reads as follows: "Believing as I do that the influence of the late Franklin Delano Roosevelt upon this Nation and its institutions as a whole, and upon the individual lives of its citizens, be such influence good or be it bad, was very great and, FURTHER, believing that, without fear, favor or prejudice of any kind whatsoever, a relatively contemporary appraisement of the Roosevelt influence should be made for the benefit of posterity before it is too late, I hereby direct, authorize and instruct my executors hereinafter named to engage the services of one or more, as they in their absolute discretion may deem best, of the Nation's outstanding historians who shall engage in a comprehensive study of the acts and deeds (acts of omission and acts of commission being included in said study) of the said Franklin Delano Roosevelt during the years he held high office as President of the United States, to the end that the findings be published. . . ."

Finally, I express hearty thanks to Thomas Hart and the late S. Leonard Kent, Executors of the will of the late J. Brooks B. Parker. They chose the author and acquiesced in his wishes at all times.

PART ONE

Chapter I

OUT OF AN OLD AMERICA

WHEN FRANKLIN DELANO ROOSEVELT on March 4, 1933, took oath of office as President of the United States, he was not the man he came to be in the ensuing twelve years of his administration. He had been chosen to lead at a moment of great crisis in national life. Known to the public at the time as Governor Roosevelt, he had served New York State through four years of depression. Not a Republican, as had been the other Roosevelts in public life, he was thought of as a Wilsonian Democrat. In 1932 Franklin Roosevelt appeared as an Eastern progressive who had attracted Southern conservatives and won support in the Middle West and Far West. Some remembered his campaign for the Vice-Presidency twelve years earlier.

The road he had traveled had been a hard one—and an easy one. At fifty he looked back upon a political career unique even in the United States, where in an earlier day "any boy" might become President. This was no longer true, and Franklin Roosevelt was aware of the drastic changes in the American scene in politics, in business, and in education. He had known the Old America at the turn of the century. To understand the course the new leader was to take is to understand the change that had come in the United States during his lifetime.

In his early years Franklin Roosevelt had lived a protected life and only later came to know, as he admitted, that poverty and misery were all around him. That he came to be the image that the majority of the American people liked to think of as their own is the more remarkable. Yet it is natural in times of swift change for men to yearn for the golden era of the past and to welcome its symbol. This past, this Old America, Franklin Roosevelt represented in more than his familiar name. He seemed to revive in his person the optimism, as well as the idealism, that was obscured during the years of mounting depression. He was a figure out of The Past, however much he talked of The Future.

The rejection of Herbert Hoover and the acceptance of Franklin Roosevelt as the nation's leader in 1932 was symptomatic of more than surface reaction on the part of Americans. In the light of the dreams of the American people, what program did they lose when they rejected Hoover in 1932? Such a question has pertinence for the consideration of the program that Roosevelt brought them. The divisions that developed in the outlook and the feeling of the American people were the result of the clash of an Old America with a New Day.

Underlying all American feeling in the early years of the century—and feeling was far more potent than thinking in the national consciousness—was insistence upon freedom. Instinctively felt as a resistance to tyranny of all kinds, it was not something to be taken for granted. Freedom was its own corrective among a people who lived it, valued it, and knew that it must be asserted. Roosevelt and Hoover had both experienced the freedom of life in their country. Like his contemporaries in school and college, Roosevelt knew he was by birth free to plan his life as he saw fit.

Of the freedom of newer community life in the West, and of frontier enterprise in the United States and abroad, from personal experience Hoover knew much, and Roosevelt, comparatively little. Political, social and economic fluidity, as familiar to Herbert Hoover in his youth as the air he breathed in Iowa, Oregon, and California, was novel and exhilarating to Franklin Roosevelt, rooted in Dutchess County along the Hudson River.

Acceptance of freedom and reliance upon it in the Old America did not rest merely in guarantees of protection in the law or in the Constitution. Indeed, the Bill of Rights and the protections provided in judicial procedure were not debated. They were taken for granted. They provided a free community within which lawyers and judges and juries pursued their independent ways, always within the proper functioning of the system. Not since the days of the Declaration of Independence and acceptance of the Constitution had there been any national tyrannical control of the lives of the people. Only local mob action from time to time, racial patterns inherited from the past, or the momentary ambition of a would-be tyrant in a local community—soon crushed—had marred the general pattern of freedom.

Enthusiastic proponents of the American way of life said the United States was the most revolutionary force in modern history. Its strength had grown mightily in the new land because it was at a distance from centers of world control.

Everywhere in the Old America, the sick and unfortunate were thought of as part of a burden to be carried, often reluctantly by individual or private aid, or ineffectually by public means. As metropolitan areas grew in population and problems of congestion and of social conflict became evident, the more alert and socially aware, even though few in number, took measures to organize relief and to work among the poor as an obligation that a free society placed upon its members. All of the inequalities that were known to be in existence emphasized the general conviction that it was man's duty to alleviate distress and to care for those in need. The environment could be improved, and here education was thought to be helpful. Moreover, in all of rural America it was the privilege of those who had, to help those who had not.

Both Hoover and Roosevelt were nurtured in this tradition and accepted it. In later life, however, the first remained faithful to the principle of voluntary community aid, enlarged in 1914 to 1917 to include whole peoples; whereas the second became familiar with government responsibility for the needy, be it the Navy caring for its personnel or the State of New York alleviating unemployment.

The builders of America of the generation of Hoover and Roosevelt had come to know that in the United States, the financial-industrial edifice had distinctive American foundations. The system was always in flux—not only because new blood constantly flowed into the channels of business, but because the locale of Big Business and the areas for new development of resource and enterprise were constantly augmented.

However much the centers of capitalism might tend to concentrate in certain cities of the nation, the actual operation of the capitalistic system appeared in due time to benefit every section of the nation. The increasing concentration of wealth in the hands of a few men resulted in the effort of these men to control both national and state governments, not only in protecting themselves in their special opportunities, but in the continuance of their activities in developing the national industrial and financial power.

On the fundamental acceptance of capitalism in the Old America, coupled with an abhorrence of imperialism, Roosevelt and Hoover were in general agreement. Spectacular to some was their parting, in thought and expression, over the implications of the American Constitutional system and on the significance of freedom in economic enterprise.

A man of the people and of the soil of the Middle and Far West, Herbert Hoover had made his own career, at first with more persistence than certainty. That opportunities had come to him to share in many of the great projects of his generation to make the earth serviceable to mankind was due to his basic humility, superior abilities, and willingness to undertake hard work.

In Franklin Roosevelt there came into the world the descendant of old established families who had already made their fortunes in a traditional American way. Divisions of the population into classes were freely accepted in the America in which he had grown to manhood, however much the outward manifestations of class were derided. If he followed the path early set before him, the star of Franklin Roosevelt as a prominent private citizen would be in the ascendant, but the blood of this Roosevelt was in revolt against his class.

Herbert Hoover, on the western side of the continent, acquiesced in the gradations of American society because he knew that everything was in process of change. Aspiration could thrive in a society that had already proved itself again and again capable of giving unlimited opportunity to so many. This society seemed to promise to keep the doors of opportunity open to youth and to the newcomer—indeed, to everyone who wished to "better" himself.

No shadow of enforced military service fell over the youth of Hoover or Roosevelt. It was the American practice of voluntary service when needed, by contrast with European practice, that assigned the military profession in the United States the inferior place it held in American feeling and thought at the turn of the century.

Yet here again Hoover and Roosevelt parted tradition. Quaker breeding and preoccupation with constructing rather than destroying emphasized Hoover's inherent abhorrence of war. All of Roosevelt's early experiences, including his vicarious view of the interest, exploits, and attitude of his cousin "Uncle Ted" emphasized acceptance of contests in which heroes participated.

It was in another field of strife that the two representatives of the Old America most emphatically differed. To the peace-loving Hoover, the acceptance of "politics" was a passive rather than an active role. His interests led him into the manipulation not of men's minds but of their resources for living.

The very fact that a century and more of experience had shown that the system of politics in America did work, and gave free reign to violent language and personal rivalry, came to fascinate Franklin Roosevelt as a young man. The American record was rich in expressions of ardor for an America that enabled men of no experience in government and with no backing of any large group or class, but moved by a sense of self-expression and self-advancement, to achieve a local and sometimes a national prominence.

Perhaps nothing in the Old America so clearly exemplified acceptance of rule of thumb and a prevailing tendency to improvisation as did the party system. For more than a century the party manager had succeeded in keeping the wheels of democracy in constant motion. Usually holding no public office, he had given elections their vitality and often had determined their true significance. Always speaking "on behalf of the people," he had in truth come to rule the United States in local, state, and national politics. He had less influence in regular machinery of government, although here too he often maintained a place of power that was essential to continuing party success.

To Herbert Hoover in his youth, manual labor was no novelty. Bred without class consciousness, he was thus never sufficiently detatched to regard "labor" romantically and was therefore without a political weapon of which Franklin Roosevelt made increasing use throughout his career.

Farming had been throughout the nineteenth century a "way of life" for millions of Americans. Only a few realized the changes that had taken place as the twentieth century advanced. The "farm" in the sense of physical occupation of the land, had been the agency that had built America. Yet the farmer had realized over and over that he was at a disadvantage in every market in which he was compelled to dispose of his product. The organization of society gave advantage to the buyer, and the organization of government was dominated by those who in finance, in construction, and in expansion were "building America."

As will later be evident, the opposing yet inter-active interests of the farm bloc and the labor bloc were viewed from different points of strategy by the two men who were to come into conflict in the national arena at the close of the third decade of the new century.

That the country squire, who never in a sense "left the farm," should in time come to a conclusion so different from that of the farm-bred engineer is a familiar American paradox. But it must be remembered that Mr. Hoover was "building America," although often in foreign lands and under another flag. Mr. Roosevelt, on the other hand, had leisure to turn over in his mind ways to "reform" the old crude American society in which both laborers and farmers had suffered at the hands of the "builders." Franklin Roosevelt early felt himself to be in the stream of historical American reform.

The last decade of the nineteenth century had witnessed a dramatic effort of the forces of labor and of the farmer to obtain control of the government in Washington. The Populists, an aggregation of many divergent interests including labor, but dominated by the farmer, had denounced the prevailing political power in violent terms. Winning, in 1892, a greater number of votes than any third party had hitherto been able to attract, they elected a considerable number of Representatives to Congress. They controlled several state governments. Although some of their proposals were extreme, everything was to be done within the American system of government and the American system of free economic enterprise.

The failure of this movement of "the masses" to achieve a national control, and the ensuing four years of panic and depression had resulted in a redistribution of major political forces in 1896. The Democratic party came into control of the radicals who proposed extreme measures on money and on the judiciary, and gave promises to labor, meanwhile denouncing monopoly. The Republican party by unusual effort was able to win a majority of the voters. They established in Washington an administration backed by a support in Congress pledged to sound money, a high tariff, and conservative policies in the control of business.

Meanwhile, by the opening of the new century, the tremendous increase of industry and commerce had brought about in the United States, as earlier in the more developed nations of western Europe, a modification of the hitherto dominant agricultural basis of society. As this change became apparent, not only were reasons for increased democratization of society emphasized, but all movements for social justice had increased appeal. Some asserted that the United States of America had now passed through its period of frontier-making only to arrive at the economic status of more developed European states.

Yet it must be insisted that the American people had reached this familiar impasse in industrial history with a century of entirely different experience. Not only had it produced thousands of leaders who had won their way to success in America by their own efforts, but it had produced millions of followers who were firmly convinced that the opportunities in this kind of enterprise were widely distributed whenever the rules of fair play were in force. Reliance could be placed, so felt Americans, upon the process of the government bringing justice to the common man, because the masses of the common men controlled that government.

Nevertheless, with the election of William McKinley and the triumph of the Eastern capitalists, a temporary brake was put upon demands for more democratic procedures. As the new century opened, the alignment in politics and in society became clearer. There were those who held to the view that the American system, *as then constituted,* gave protection to those who controlled the business and economic development of the nation. Others, like Bryan and presently La Follette, called for greater protection of the masses not only in equality of opportunity but in their access to the suffrage and their redress to the courts.

The call for programs that would enable the people to capture their own government had a general appeal resting in fundamental beliefs and in dominant misconceptions, as well as in a desire to participate and to further individual self-interest. It was an appeal to return to the earlier practice of democracy. It did not essay new patterns. It had the appearance of true conservative doctrine: "Maintain your heritage." That the claim for that heritage was historically inaccurate did not weaken its general appeal to a people who did not know the full story of the American past. They fervently believed that the United States belonged to the people.

All supporters of democratic government held it to be fundamental that they could lose their freedom by indirect control of government and by disloyal representatives in office.

A vivid expression of the meaning of the conflict between old prejudices and new aspirations was found in the career and pronouncements, in the appeal and final failure of Theodore Roosevelt. His years in the Presidency witnessed the battle in which the divergent purposes of the Old America contended for control of the direction of the New America. The collapse of political parties as they had existed was seen in the defeat of reform measures during the Taft administration. The ensuing Presidential campaign and the candidacy of Woodrow Wilson gave the Democratic party opportunity to support his New Freedom rather than the New Nationalism of Theodore Roosevelt. The Wilson administration in its domestic program pointed the direction that the New Freedom would take, not only in measures passed by the Congress in the first year, but in the nature of Republican opposition and the collapse of the progressive movement as a national party. The basic issue was to be fought within each of the dominant parties and this would take many years. It was thus within the American practice. Meanwhile, the growing strength of the Socialist party pointed to the possibility that a more radical program might appeal to the increasing number of Americans who doubted that the American system could be maintained.

Only very gradually did the people of the United States and their leaders come to recognize that the economic and social bases of the nineteenth century had been finally destroyed by World War I and its aftermath. The immediate political effects of the war were obscured by the struggle in the United States over adherence to the League of Nations. Resurgence of a blatant and undiscerning Americanism was followed by reappearance of the former alignment within domestic politics. The elements that had brought progressivism to both political parties went down in 1920 before the arguments of the old familiar conservatism.

With increasing emphasis, the term "liberal" came to be applied to those who—disillusioned but not disheartened—were prepared to question almost anything that had previously been taken for granted. They found some hope in the "insurgent" tradition in American politics of La Follette, Wheeler, and Norris and in the attitude of Socialists who questioned the economic bases of the prevailing government. But for the most part the liberals let politics alone [1] and, using the press, the journal, and the public forum, questioned the bases of American society.

Meanwhile, two streams of influence that were to become national had arisen at the dividing line between the Old and

---

[1] Notable exceptions were the editors of the *New York World,* and William Allen White in the *Emporia Gazette.*

the New America. One of these was definitely political and in direct line with previous American hopes. At Chicago on May 29, 1919, to the members of the Democratic National Committee, Franklin Roosevelt, then serving as Assistant Secretary of the Navy, sketched for his hearers the struggle within each of the great parties between forces of reaction and of progress.

He found that the battle for progressive reform, once so promising in its results within the Republican party, had been lost by that party. But the Democratic party, true to its tradition, had done wonders under Wilson. "During its first four years, it has carried through more great measures for the good of the whole population than any other party in any similar period," asserted Roosevelt. He was certain that the majority of the wealthy were Republican, and that the newspapers and magazines were Republican, although this was comparatively unimportant, he thought. For he saw:

> Deep down beneath the daily actions of a man's life lies a something which is the true man—call it what you like, his principles, his conscience, his spirit. Nearly always it is possible to see this inner spirit through the facts of life, through his expressed personality. So it is with parties. "By their acts ye shall know them." Place side by side the two great political parties and judge them by their acts of the past ten years, in other words by that period during which their present leaders have been to the fore. I see in one of them a soul, hesitating, groping, self-seeking, narrow, material. And in the other, I see a clean soul, clear thinking, straight living, humbly proud to have been and to be of service, unselfish in its devotion to the great ideals of a great people—a soul proven worthy of trust —the spirit of the Democracy of America.[2]

The following year Franklin Roosevelt was the Vice-Presidential candidate when James M. Cox of Ohio was the Presidential candidate of the Democratic party. Whereas "the election was an overwhelming defeat which was accepted very philosophically by my husband," later wrote Mrs. Roosevelt,[3] the campaign was of course a priceless political experience for

---

[2] Franklin D. Roosevelt, Address, Banquet of the Democratic National Committee, Chicago, May 29, 1919, in Woodrow Wilson Papers, File VI, 21 (Box 40), Library of Congress.

[3] Eleanor Roosevelt, *This Is My Story*, p. 320.

him. It meant as well that a second Roosevelt had entered
national politics and would remain a spokesman for the Democratic party of future campaigns.[4]

Unnoticed by the majority of the American people, another
stream of interpretation of American democracy had developed.
Traceable to the shattering of traditional thought by the shocks
of World War I, both before and after American participation,
it appeared in journalism, in thoughtful literature, and even
in the discussions of a considerable number of experienced
financiers and business men.

Not clearly identified with any special group within the
population, the exponents of this new idea were not content
with the Old American tradition. They saw an opportunity for
development in the United States—and it was to be hoped, later
in the world—of what may be termed a scientific approach to the
problems of politics.

Recognizing, as did most of its adherents, the reality that lay
back of the protest of radicals and the real causes which gave
progressive programs such wide appeal, nevertheless they were
not satisfied that mass action in dealing with such matters really
solved the problems that had to be dealt with. On the other
hand, they were convinced that the underlying philosophies of
conservatism were quite inadequate to meet the problems in
finance, industry, or politics that were created by the New
World brought into being by the advances of science.

So it was that they proposed a different line of action than
had been customary. This new approach called for careful examination and analysis of existing maladjustments in society. It
called for wide use of modern efficiency methods. Indeed, it
called upon the electorate for a more mature task of thinking
than had yet been undertaken by the most developed and
thoughtful of American leaders.

Valiant service in the cause of informed criticism had been
performed by the editors of the *New Republic* in the earliest
years of that journal.[5] An outpouring of critical writing from

---

[4] It was in the course of this campaign that Theodore Roosevelt, Jr., in supporting the Republican National ticket spoke of his cousin Franklin as a
"maverick" not having the "brand of our family." Cited by T. A. Bailey, *Woodrow Wilson and the Great Betrayal*, p. 324.

[5] See also Herbert D. Croly, *The Promise of American Life* (1909).

those who might be termed social workers emphasized this new approach to politics.

A notable expression of an attempt to formulate the new approach appeared in a little book by Herbert Hoover. Closely identified with humanitarian efforts in World War I, he was, as many years later his *Memoirs* were to show, a prime example of the accomplishments of an earlier age in America and in the world. The heart of the message contained in his book, *American Individualism,* was little understood in 1922.

As the event proved, the new approach to politics came to a point of decision, although it was not recognized at the time, in the nomination of Herbert Hoover as Republican candidate for the Presidency in 1928. The candidate was not acceptable to either of the elements so clearly identified in the struggle of the previous thirty years within the Republican party. He certainly did not satisfy the progressive elements from the western states. He represented, rather, the progressive attitude associated with the leadership of the late Theodore Roosevelt. Despite the support of his candidacy by many persons high in the financial world, at no time was Mr. Hoover felt to represent fully the convictions of those who held that American conservatism had proved itself the builder of America.

It was the man and *not his program* that was accepted both by his party and by the electorate. Hoover's triumph in the election of 1928 was held by the more discerning to be an opportunity for trial of the new approach to the problems of government. This in turn necessitated the education of the American electorate to a new attitude toward the popular will.

In his campaign speeches, Mr. Hoover developed the program to which the name "New Day" was given. He was suggesting that the New Day was neither the "day" envisaged by the progressives nor that pictured by the conservatives. It was to be a period in which, by the application of science, intelligence, and great good will, poverty was to be abolished. Aided by the guiding hand of public officials, private enterprise was to be fostered and additional opportunity offered to more and more persons in the field of competition.

Based fundamentally on a firm belief in the virtues of the Old America and in the proofs of its accomplishment, this new program held the hope of those who saw in widespread economic well-being the future of a better America. This program concentrated on two objectives—prosperity and well-being for the masses, and social justice and greater opportunities for all. Honesty, hard work, and efficiency would insure a better future. To some it was later to seem to merit the title "Planned Economy" as distinguished from "Managed Economy." An age of waste of resources in men and material was to give way to an age of efficiency.

The election of Herbert Hoover placed a stamp of popular approval on the opportunity to have in the Presidency a man who combined the qualities of administrator and humanitarian, who had a reputation for public service not only in time of war but in time of peace, and who was neither a military leader nor a politician. To have a President above the strife of party might have advantages. He might build more stately mansions for the men and women who loved the freedom of Americans.

How unrealistic such a conception was, came soon to be revealed. Yet it emphasized at the time the remoteness of the world of orderly and efficient relations from the world of partisan discussion and strife. For never were parties more uncertain, nor more disorganized—the prey of forces within society producing disunity and disintegration.

Within three months of the advent of the new administration the dream faded. The powers of the Congress involved in tariff revision and farm relief stood across the path of intended Presidential action. It became apparent that the Senate would not provide a Republican majority because there were three and sometimes five factions in the Republican membership. More important, revealed to the public and to the Democratic opposition, was the failure of the President to conciliate the Republican rebels in the Congress.

This meant that Herbert Hoover was not to have the opportunity to lead the nation in building new patterns of economic and social organization that the demands of the new financial and industrial age made imperative. Moreover, the hysteria of wild speculation came to a sudden climax not long after Mr. Hoover assumed office. Confidence disappeared and Americans admitted that they had not yet found their way in the New World habitat. Thus President Hoover's New Day was to end before sunrise.

Chapter II

A CRISIS IN LEADERSHIP

FRANKLIN ROOSEVELT IN 1920 had thought well of Herbert Hoover as a possible President.[1] They had both been in Washington in the second Wilson administration and had met occasionally. In 1928 Roosevelt thought differently of Hoover's candidacy, and said so. Out of an Old America yet lingering on the banks of the Hudson River, Franklin Roosevelt had been drafted by the friends of Alfred E. Smith to make the campaign for the governorship of New York. Roosevelt had won the governorship—as Smith lost the Presidency. The gubernatorial victory was not overwhelming. It was won by 25,564 votes, less than 1 percent of the votes cast.[2]

In this campaign, Mr. Roosevelt had discussed national politics, giving particular attention to the candidacy of the Republican Presidential nominee. Roosevelt challenged Hoover

---

[1] Mr. Roosevelt wrote Hugh Gibson on January 2, 1920, "I had some nice talks with Herbert Hoover before he went West for Christmas. He is certainly a wonder, and I wish we could make him President of the United States. There could not be a better one." Quoted by Frank Freidel, *Franklin D. Roosevelt: The Ordeal*, p. 57.

For an interesting account of a suggested Hoover-Roosevelt candidacy on the Democratic ticket in 1920, see L. B. Wehle, *Hidden Threads of History*, pp. 81-88. Mr. Wehle, a friend of Mr. Roosevelt, states that on January 10, 1920, he suggested it to Roosevelt, and on January 16, 1920, to Hoover. Roosevelt, according to Wehle, said, "You can go to it so far as I am concerned."

[2] For an analysis of the vote and hypothesis as to the meaning of Roosevelt's victory and Smith's defeat, see H. F. Gosnell, *Champion Campaigner: Franklin D. Roosevelt*, pp. 81-90, 226.

on a fundamental issue of the century, namely, the "masses" versus the "individual." Mr. Hoover had said in his little book on *American Individualism:*

> Acts and ideas that lead to progress are born out of the womb of the individual mind, not out of the mind of the crowd. The crowd only feels: it has no mind of its own which can plan. The crowd is credulous, it destroys, it consumes, it hates, and it dreams—but it never builds. It is one of the most profound and important of exact psychological truths that man in the mass does not think but only feels.[3]

Quoting this extract from Hoover's book, Roosevelt said to his listeners in a campaign address at Yonkers:

> I know the gentleman well, and have for many years; and that, in my judgment, is the best insight that you can possibly find into the personality of Herbert Hoover, into his approach to every public and private question. It is characteristic of the man. . . .

> Now, Mr. Hoover's theory that the crowd, that is to say, 95 percent of all the voters who call themselves average citizens, that the crowd is credulous, that it destroys, that it hates, that it dreams, but that it never builds, that it does not think, but only feels—that is in line with the training, the record and the methods of accomplishment of the Republican candidate for the Presidency.

> It is another way of saying, and I say this as an analyst and not as a candidate, that there exists at the top of our social system in this country a very limited group of highly able, highly educated people, through whom all progress in this land must originate. Furthermore, that this small group, after doing all the thinking and all the originating, is fully responsible for all progress in civilization and Government.[4]

As we have seen, Hoover and Roosevelt spoke out of their individual experience of what has been termed an Old America. Their difference in view is indicative of the divisions in public

---

[3] Quoted here from the original in *American Individualism* (Doubleday, Page, 1922), pp. 24-25. Governor Roosevelt's version, given in *The Public Papers and Addresses of Franklin D. Roosevelt, 1928-1932* (cited hereafter as *Public Papers*), p. 68, is inaccurate.

[4] *Public Papers, 1928-1932*, pp. 68-69. See also letter of Roosevelt to Wehle, October 13, 1935, in Wehle, *op. cit.*, pp. 91-92.

opinion that had become increasingly evident in the new century, particularly after World War I. These differences were intellectual as well as economic and political; differences perceptible in attitude toward the future of the nation, as well as in concept of the nature of citizenship in the new age. Mr. Roosevelt saw little future justification for the "individualism" that had in the past furnished leaders in the professions, in business, and in government. In Mr. Hoover's view, this was to be, as it had been, the outstanding contribution of the American system.

Yet Mr. Roosevelt, whose advantages in family position and economic well-being were conferred by birth, placed his faith in native ability. Mr. Hoover, in the American tradition of the self-made man, put his faith in developed processes. Mr. Roosevelt entered the forum of political debate; Mr. Hoover raised his eyes from graphs and columns of figures to contemplate the constructive possibilities of the new scientific age.

Much was made, at the time of Roosevelt's nomination for the Presidency, of the fact that he was serving as Governor of New York. This conspicuous position, in itself, gave him a leading place in any race for the Presidency. In the public view it meant a preparation for the Presidency. Such a view justifies examination.

A successful term as governor of a state has been, in the American public mind and in the planning of party managers, a proper preparation for the Presidency. Just why this might be so, on careful analysis, is difficult to explain. The problems of even the largest of the states do not include foreign affairs, and certainly do not partake of the intricacies of national policy on any major economic problem. Neither do the states as a rule carry the burden of sectionalism, which demands careful balancing on the part of a national government which is to affirm and carry out a unified policy.

Ten governors had been nominated for the Presidency since the opening of the century. Alfred E. Smith had been the latest one. That he was defeated did not alter the legend.

Much more than minute knowledge of special fields of government, of administrative, legislative or judicial service, or specific knowledge of political and economic realities in the world outside the United States, has been demanded in preparation for the Presidency. Moreover, the demands of the office, as well as the expectation of the people, have asked of every President since George Washington more and more emphatically the attributes of a monarch.

Yet there has been no sure keynote to studied preparation for such a task—except the man himself. Nor could this voluntary preparation rest on ambition alone. The candidate must give his attention primarily to the need of accommodation, of painstaking compromise, of faithful service to party organization in an effort to be available, that is, to be chosen, first, by a party organization and, second, by a vast electorate that might be well aware of its desires but wholly incompetent to judge of the qualities of a would-be President.

The man who would prepare himself adequately to be President must first be of the people, in the sense of real understanding of their limitations as well as their hopes. He must devote himself wholly to their interest. To do this, he must, however, periodically rise above all of them in his thinking, if not in his feeling, and particularly above their representatives in the Congress.

In this situation, the opportunity for the political leader has been determined in largest measure by the identification of his career and his cause with the interests of the average citizen. Even though belonging to, or responsive to a party organization—which has been all-important—it must appear that he was independent of it in ultimate interest.

Moreover, it must be clear that he was a leader who could be expected to deal with special interest groups as realities, not only in government but in politics as well. This situation has made it clearly apparent that a successful leader must have his own organization quite apart from party, group, and government. No one man could cope with the gigantic problem of public relations. He must be supported by a group of devoted personal followers.

Lack of a real tradition of preparation for the Presidency doubtless accounts for the fact that few men of national vision, mature outlook, and superior competence devote themselves to public affairs. They turn rather to business, to the professions, and to "elegant leisure" in a highly organized society.

A growing appreciation of the high calling of public service has led many men to forsake private pursuits and enter government service. Occasionally such a man has caught the vision of creativeness in the public service. Unaccustomed to the practical politics of party organizations, however, most of these devoted public servants have found difficult the adaptation of vision to reality.

This was true of Theodore Roosevelt, of Woodrow Wilson, and of Herbert Hoover alike. Each qualified for highest office; each gave ample evidence of superior competence in the greatest of callings; and each left to the nation a legacy of accomplishment for the public good. But the failures of each cast a vivid light on the supreme challenge that is daily faced by the chief of a great people.

It was abundantly evident, even early in the century, that American society was so divergent in basic needs, so thoroughly organized by special interests, so fragmentary in procedure, response and demand, that only as there could be fully developed the leader of public outlook who devoted all of his life to the public service, was there hope of having Presidents in the image of this new prospect in American life. Yet, on the whole, Presidential leadership remained a task outside formal preparation.

Such a task Franklin Roosevelt, consciously or unconsciously, undertook at a fairly early age. Despite the trivial occupations of his protected boyhood,[5] the failure to excel in intellectual pursuits,[6] and the immaturity of his early political utterances, the design of his life is marked by a growing sense of the urgency of influencing those immediately surrounding him and of understanding their needs and desires.

Franklin Roosevelt in 1928 might well be thought of as a veteran among public servants. He had entered politics in 1910, being elected to the New York State Senate in the election in which Theodore Roosevelt failed to capture control of the Republican party organization in that state. During his political

---

[5] The story appears in Sara Delano Roosevelt, *My Boy Franklin,* to which critical commentary has been added by Eleanor Roosevelt in her memoirs.

[6] See Frank Freidel, *Franklin D. Roosevelt: The Apprenticeship,* pp. 72-73, on the record at Harvard: ". . . while Roosevelt learned much at Harvard, most of it seems to have come from his social and extracurricular activities, not his studies," and ". . . it never occurred to him to be one of the scholars or to accept their standard of values."

service in Albany, Franklin Roosevelt became identified with the movement that resulted in the nomination of Woodrow Wilson for the Presidency. And it was Wilson, rather than his cousin Theodore, whom Franklin Roosevelt supported in the ensuing election of 1912.

Furthermore, he early attached supreme importance to whatever he was doing at the time. On his wartime mission abroad he wrote of his observations and of his concerns with the genuine excitement of one who was making history.[7] His family relationship with "Uncle Ted," his admiration of Woodrow Wilson, and his eight years of association with official Washington—no less than his activities as a public servant since 1910—quickened his natural love of country and sharpened his interest in the Democratic party.

Eight years of administrative service in Washington as Assistant Secretary of the Navy; the campaign for the Vice-Presidency in 1920 during which he traveled eighteen thousand miles from coast to coast; and his prominence as a convention leader supporting Al Smith in the campaigns of 1924 and 1928 —gave ample opportunity for the expression of Franklin Roosevelt's views as to what the United States of America meant to successful men and women who wished to participate in public life.[8]

Yet, when he took the oath of office as Governor of New York State in January, 1929, Roosevelt had been out of public life for eight years. During this period, which was the only time in his life after his election to the New York Senate that he was a private citizen, he continued to have such interest in public affairs as would be expected from one who felt it part of the obligation of the citizen to participate. In private correspondence he did much to emphasize the importance of party harmony. In this correspondence the politician was uppermost.

During the years 1920-1928 the Democrats had been a mi-

[7] See letters of Roosevelt to Daniels, Josephus Daniels Papers, 1913-1932, Library of Congress.

[8] The years to 1928 have been given minute factual treatment by Frank Freidel in *Franklin D. Roosevelt: The Apprenticeship* and *The Ordeal*. By 1920, certainly, the intimates of Mr. Roosevelt thought of him as a Presidential candidate at a later time. Other studies of special value are the 1932 campaign biography by Ernest K. Lindley, *Franklin D. Roosevelt, A Career in Progressive Democracy*, and the antagonistic but often thoughtful, and well-documented volume by Mauritz A. Hallgren, *The Gay Reformer*, especially chapters I-VI.

nority party in the nation. The Democratic party favored American acceptance of membership in the League of Nations with reservations, advocated repeal or at least modification of the Prohibition Amendment, and proposed strong measures to deal with such organizations as the Ku Klux Klan. In the popular mind, however, the Democrats had ceased to be the militant party of progressive democracy that much of the time from 1913 to 1921 had responded to the leadership of Woodrow Wilson.

In the campaign of 1924 the Democrats had attempted to merge the divergent elements of which the party was composed. The party had offered in this year of the La Follette-Wheeler "third party" revolt, the candidacy of John W. Davis and Charles W. Bryan. In this Presidential election year, as in 1928, Franklin Roosevelt was identified with the political ambitions of Governor Smith of New York.

Both before and after he was stricken with infantile paralysis, Roosevelt had been active in the formation of the Woodrow Wilson Foundation. Undoubtedly his vigorous advocacy of the League of Nations while he was a Vice-Presidential candidate in 1920[9] furnished some of the reason for the warmth of the correspondence that developed between the former President and his Assistant Secretary of the Navy.[10]

Apparently the driving force of insurgency in both major parties in 1924, resulting in the ticket of La Follette and

---

[9] In 1923 Mr. Roosevelt prepared, for submission for the consideration of the committee on the Bok Peace Award, "A Plan to Preserve World Peace." It is printed as Appendix I in Mrs. Roosevelt's *This I Remember*, pp. 353-366, and contains the following note in a summary: "The basis of this plan assumes, first, no plan to preserve world peace can be successful without the participation of the United States; second, the United States will not now or probably for many years to come join the existing League of Nations." At this time Mr. Roosevelt suggested the creation of a permanent and continuing international conference to be known as the "Society of Nations." He later made a memorandum and attached it to a copy of this plan on January 19, 1944. (See *F.D.R.: His Personal Letters, 1928-1945*, II, 1488. Edited by Elliott Roosevelt. Subsequent references appear as *Personal Letters*.) He referred to it again in a memo prepared at Quebec on September 15, 1944. (*Ibid.* pp. 1540-1541.)

[10] The relationship between Wilson and Roosevelt is revealed in the Woodrow Wilson Papers, Library of Congress, covering the years, 1921-1923. Roosevelt as Chairman of the National Committee on the Woodrow Wilson Foundation had addressed a message to Woodrow Wilson on his birthday, December 28, 1921. On the back of the telegram under date of January 5, 1922, Wilson had written: "Your own friendship and unselfish devotion to its objects give me, as I hope you know, peculiar gratification."

Wheeler, led to no pronouncements or activities on the part of Roosevelt, other than those expected of a loyal and active party member.[11] Late in 1924 he attempted to bring together national leaders in a harmony conference. He continued his efforts the following year. That he was aware of the continuance of a serious schism in the Democratic party, arising out of pressure in favor of modification of the Volstead Act, was revealed in a letter written to William Jennings Bryan in 1923.[12] Roosevelt later became convinced that it would be the part of political wisdom not to revive the issue of the League of Nations.[13]

The continuity of the thinking of Mr. Roosevelt during the period of his retirement from public life may be found in a comparison of two addresses, the one delivered in Chicago in 1919, to which reference has already been made,[14] and the other delivered in the same city ten years later, when he said:

> Progressives in the right sense of the word mean those who realize that a government must grow and change as its people grow and change; that what is wise government today may be foolish government tomorrow. The Conservatives are those who believe that things are good enough as they are and should be let strictly alone lest ruin and destruction follow in the wake of any alteration.[15]

Neither of these addresses advocate, beyond the usual general proposals of revision and party action, specific programs of reform in either local or national affairs. They emphasize party harmony.

From the outset of his career in politics, Mr. Roosevelt had as state senator favored such progressive measures as civil service reform, conservation of natural resources, and social legisla-

---

[11] In a letter to his wife dated October, 1924, Mr. Roosevelt said: "I have a hunch that Davis' strength is really improving, but I still think the election will go into the house. Anyway, I am philosophic enough to think that even if Coolidge is elected we shall be so darned sick of conservatism of the old money-controlled crowd in four years that we [will] get a real progressive landslide in 1928." (*Personal Letters, 1905-1928*, p. 566.)

[12] Roosevelt to W. J. Bryan, June 20, 1923, Bryan Papers, Library of Congress. See also Wehle, *op. cit.*, p. 101, as to division between Roosevelt and Smith on the issue of repeal.

[13] See Roosevelt to Robert W. Woolley, February 25, 1932, Woolley Papers, Library of Congress.

[14] Chapter I, p. 34.

[15] Quoted in Lindley, *op. cit.*, p. 322.

tion. As Governor, his recommendations continued to stress what in the language of the time were termed progressive measures.

In the perspective of later years there was much in the action, utterance, and experience of Roosevelt at this time that seemed to confirm a pattern of preparation for the highest office in the land.

Examination of responses to the utterances of Mr. Roosevelt in this period amply show the reason for the general thought that he was an engaging personality, a fairly young man as politics go, and of wide experience as an administrative officer in the national government before becoming governor of an important state. In word and in action, he had placed himself definitely in the progressive tradition of American politics.[16]

In advance of the campaign of 1928 he had written to a friend:

> . . . I am very sure the situation prevents and will prevent even the suggestion of my name as a possible compromise choice between the existing warring factions. I do not think that we can *elect* any compromise choice, but on the other hand, I think that we would stand an excellent chance of electing Governor Smith if we could nominate him. . . .[17]

In view of the fact that Mr. Roosevelt did become President, and one of the most controversial figures of modern times, unusual emphasis has been placed upon meanings to be drawn from the earlier period for an explanation of later developments. This is natural, but it is a procedure to be used with caution.

---

[16] Guides to Governor Roosevelt's words and deeds as state executive, 1929-1933, include the news columns of the *New York Times* and its *Index;* Volume I of the *Public Papers* covering the years 1928 to 1932; the four volumes of the *Public Papers of Governor Franklin D. Roosevelt,* published by the State of New York; and a typed compilation of 1928 campaign speeches in the Franklin D. Roosevelt Library, as well as the official gubernatorial papers and private papers housed there.

[17] In a letter to Josephus Daniels, June 23, 1927, (Josephus Daniels Papers, Correspondence with Roosevelt, 1913-1932, Box 15, Library of Congress) Mr. Roosevelt admitted: "I am very doubtful whether any Democrat can win in 1928. It will depend somewhat on whether the present undoubted general prosperity of the country continues. You and I may recognize the serious hardship which the farmers in the south and west are laboring under, but the farmers in the south will vote the Democratic ticket anyway and I do not believe that the farmers of the west will vote the Democratic ticket in sufficient numbers even if they are starving."

When as President, Mr. Roosevelt looked back upon these years, he realized that his background and that of his contemporaries would be of vital interest to the historians of his Presidency. Writing on January 24, 1938, Mr. Roosevelt said:

> In this generation the people of the United States have been facing two major problems, the solution of which seems more and more vital to the continued functioning of what we call the requirements of modern civilization . . . . the maintenance of that ideal of government known as the democratic process . . . . and the necessity of social justice.[18]

It was not as a private citizen, but as Governor of the most populous state in the Union, that Roosevelt had viewed the financial debacle of the autumn of 1929.

As he looked back upon it nine years later he felt that:

> . . . during the twenties of this century, control of government was allowed to slip back, in large degree, to the hands of small groups representing big finance and large industry. . . . Let me say with complete frankness that during the twenties, I, in common with most liberals did not at the start visualize the effects of the period, or the drastic changes which were even then necessary for a lasting economy. . . . It required the depression itself and my experience as Governor during that period to bring home to me the more fundamental, underlying troubles which were facing all civilization. . . . The 1929-1933 period was well fitted to serve as an education in social and economic needs . . .[19]

Those who, as Mr. Roosevelt saw it later, had created the depression, could not be entrusted with the task of recovery and would obviously ignore the needs of reform. The Democratic party, on the other hand, recognized that the ideals of democracy and social justice would build a new America.

Just before Herbert Hoover's election to the Presidency, Franklin Roosevelt wrote to a friend:

> Mr. Hoover, in spite of his many fine qualities, has such a passion for investigating and tabulating everything under Heaven, and particularly such a penchant for calling all kinds of busi-

---

[18] *Public Papers, 1928-1932*, General Introduction, ix-xii.
[19] *Ibid.*, x-xii.

ness groups to Washington and telling them how they ought to conduct their personal affairs, as to make him in my judgment an exceedingly dangerous man to have at the head of our government.[20]

A year later, when both men were launched in public office, the "dangerous" Hoover was engaged in an attempt to halt an orgy of stock speculation and gambling that had seized the country. Speculation was not confined to Wall Street, located within the state of which Roosevelt had been Governor since January. The boom was nation-wide. Public opposition to the curbing of speculation through the instrumentality of the Federal Reserve System contributed to the whirlwind of factors that finally resulted in the stock market crash of October, 1929.[21]

This catastrophe brought revision of the prevailing political mandate to further prosperity, and thus ended an era in the history of the United States. This, however, was not immediately apparent to the American people, to the President, or to the Governor of New York.

Nevertheless, a divided Republican party which had taken possession of the government in 1928 on the high tide of prosperity was weakened to the point of ineptitude by an economic recession reflected in the Congressional elections of 1930.

In 1930 Democratic governors displaced Republicans in both the East and the Middle West, notably in Ohio and in Massachusetts. As a result of the elections, the Seventy-second Congress would include in the House 218 Republicans, 215 Democrats, 1 Farmer-Laborite; and in the Senate, 48 Republicans, 47 Democrats, 1 Farmer-Laborite. About a dozen Republican Senators could not be counted on to follow the President.

Governor Roosevelt meanwhile had campaigned for re-election, in addition making over fifty addresses to business, farm, and labor groups, Legionnaires, county Democratic organiza-

---

[20] Roosevelt to Samuel Sloan, September 29, 1928. Franklin D. Roosevelt 1928 Campaign Correspondence, Box 17, Roosevelt Library. Three weeks earlier, in a campaign address, Mr. Roosevelt was quoted as saying, "There will be no fear of Depression under Smith, for if there was anything to fear, Governor Smith wouldn't be receiving the support of the major business interests of the United States in this campaign." (*New York Times*, September 9, 1928.)
[21] Mr. Hoover's account of his struggle with the directors of the Federal Reserve Board from March 4 to October 29 appears in his *Memoirs: The Great Depression, 1929-1941*, pp. 16-20.

tions, leading Jewish groups, state fair meetings, and firemen.[22] Water power, prison reform, and Tammany corruption occupied the Governor's time repeatedly during the year. A contest over the control of state finances between Roosevelt and the Republican-controlled legislature of New York was a leading issue of the day.

If the Governor spent any time in efforts to curb stock speculation or to reform the New York Stock Exchange, news of such endeavor did not reach the public. He did not take a leading part in the tariff dispute that tied up the Congress. He stated his own views on the subject to a Nebraskan in a letter of March 11: "I am inclined to think," he wrote, "that the Democratic Party will be able to make it perfectly clear that we are not for free trade; that we are for protection but that protection does not mean the right for manufacturers to sell their goods here at a higher price than they sell the same goods in other countries." [23]

At the Governors' Conference at Salt Lake City, in the summer of 1930, the Governor of New York received, it was reported, a "demonstration of greater warmth and volume" than any of the others at the opening session.[24] Roosevelt urged unemployment insurance based on "contributions from public treasuries, employers, and the workers themselves." He predicted the coming of a five-day working week to check unemployment and attacked those who, he said, distorted the facts about that controversial subject. He urged more general and generous old age insurance. As on several other occasions during the year, he paid his respects to what he called the old law of supply and demand, saying that those in Washington violated it by their reliance on high wage campaigns. He told the governors in another speech that the fields of federal taxation should be limited in order to aid state taxing units.[25]

On his way home, Governor Roosevelt predicted that state home rule would become an issue in 1930 and 1932. He was termed by a reporter "a consistent contender for States'

---

[22] Speeches reported in whole or in part by the *New York Times,* 1930.
[23] Roosevelt to A. N. Mathers of Gering, Nebraska, March 11, 1930. *Personal Letters, 1928-1945,* I, 108.
[24] *New York Times,* July 1, 1930.
[25] *Ibid.*

rights." [26] In this he was consistent with his nation-wide radio address of March 3 warning of a dangerous drift toward disregard of states' rights.

While referring particularly to prohibition enforcement, he generalized on the subject of federal powers at some length. "The doctrine of regulation and legislation by 'master minds,' in whose judgment and will all the people may gladly and quietly acquiesce, has been too glaringly apparent at Washington during these last ten years," he charged.

Reviewing the provisions of the Constitution giving powers to the Congress, he then said: "On such a small foundation have we erected the whole enormous fabric of Federal Government which costs us now $3,500,000,000 every year; and if we do not halt this steady process of building commissions and regulatory bodies and special legislation like huge inverted pyramids over every one of the simple constitutional provisions, we will soon be spending many billions more." [27]

The Governor of New York acknowledged at this time that government must protect the weak against the strong, and this meant that local and state governmental units must be safe against the national government. "There are many glaring examples of where exclusive Federal control is manifestly against the scheme and intent of our Constitution," he said. [28]

In June, Governor Roosevelt had asked in an address to a Syracuse University graduating class how much further the extension of government should go. Continuing the process might increase the burden of taxation to the breaking point. Yet demands on government to branch out into new activities were insistent. [29]

In late August, Roosevelt attacked the 1928 "Boston" speech of Hoover for its "prosperity prophecy" economics. Again the Governor paid homage to the law of supply and demand. "We are now paying the penalty for a wild spree based on uneconomic, unscientific, and unbusinesslike foundations," he charged. [30] If this seemed to echo statements of the President, so too did a letter in which Roosevelt wrote later in the year: "As

[26] *Ibid.*, July 4, 1930.
[27] *Ibid.*, March 3, 1930.
[28] *Ibid.*
[29] *Ibid.*, June 10, 1930.
[30] *Ibid.*, August 23, 1930.

a matter of fact, while I am much opposed to extension of Federal action in most economic-social problems, nevertheless the Federal government has a very distinct function as a fact-gatherer for the whole nation.[31]

Governor Roosevelt gained much national publicity in 1930, although he publicly disclaimed all thought of candidacy for national office in 1932. By September 13, 1930, however, the *Literary Digest* had little difficulty in assembling enough nation-wide newspaper quotations on him to fill a page, its anonymous compiler declaring, "Governor Roosevelt's silvery oratory reminds many of his hearers of the speeches of Woodrow Wilson, who wove such a spell over his audiences when Governor of New Jersey that he won the nomination for President." [32]

A week later the Governor of New York gained additional national attention when, in an open letter to Senator Wagner, he declared himself for the outright repeal of the Eighteenth Amendment and restoration of real control over intoxicants to the states.[33]

A plurality of 725,000 votes in the 1930 New York gubernatorial election was given the man who had spoken highly of the rights of that state and who had sought broadening of its social legislation. Both the Republican *Herald-Tribune* and the Democratic Philadelphia *Record* saw in him the probable Democratic nominee in 1932. "I am going back to the business of the State," said Roosevelt,[34] but there was certainly no question in his mind as to what the future probably held for him.

Meanwhile, the year 1930 was one of increased awareness of Communist party activity in the United States. On March 5, Congressman Hamilton Fish, Jr., of New York introduced in the House a resolution calling for an investigation into the activities of the Communist party. Later in the month he was named chairman of a special committee whose subsequent hearings provided much factual data on party methods, personnel, and plans. Fish was severely criticized by some "liberals" for allegedly Fascist tactics, a charge which a reading of the hearings

---

[31] Roosevelt to Mrs. Caspar Whitney, December 8, 1930, *Personal Letters, 1928-1945*, I, 161.
[32] *Literary Digest*, September 13, 1930, p. 7.
[33] *Ibid.*, September 20, 1930, p. 8.
[34] *Ibid.*, November 15, 1930, p. 7.

after two decades in no way substantiates. Communist witnesses told their plans and hopes readily, without marked fear or restraint.

In New York City numerous minor clashes between Communists and city police gave the former much publicity, while arrest of the leader, William Z. Foster, and others brought the Communists allies from those fearing infringement of civil liberties.

The link between the Amtorg Trading Corporation, the Soviet government of Russia, and the Communist International received publicity and general denunciation. Despite the fact that such an American as Matthew Woll, vice president of the American Federation of Labor, could spearhead anti-Sovietism in the United States in 1930, there were those who pondered the stock crash and slackening economy of a free enterprise, capitalistic United States and wondered whether Russia had found something new and better.

In this atmosphere the Socialist party of the United States under Norman Thomas worked vigorously to spread its doctrine of government ownership to be arrived at, assertedly, through democratic political means. During the year 1930, the League for Industrial Democracy sponsored 258 talks before 45,000 college students and more than two hundred addresses before 55,000 other persons, plus radio and political campaign speeches. About ninety-two college clubs were associated with this group, which declared its goal to be "education toward a social order based on production for use and not for profit." [35]

In the autumn elections, the Socialist candidate for governor of New York made good gains. The candidate, Louis Waldman, attacked his Democratic opponent, Franklin D. Roosevelt, as an ally of Tammany but drew only 200,000 votes. The leader of the Socialist party meanwhile had repeatedly pointed out examples of government activity which seemed to him to contradict the idea of "rugged individualism," asserting that the whole trend of modern life was toward collectivism.[36]

President Hoover struck back vigorously, though belatedly, as he lost support in this crucial year of 1930, and in an address

---

[35] *New York Times,* December 28, 1930.
[36] *Ibid.,* January 11, 1930, and May 2, 1930.

at Kings Mountain, South Carolina, defended the American system and resisted any threat of dictatorship or of socialism. No class or group, in his view, should be supreme. "Any practice of business which would dominate the country by its own selfish interests is a destruction of equality of opportunity," he said. "Government in business, except in emergency, is also a destruction of equal opportunity and the incarnation of tyranny through bureaucracy." [37]

Herbert Hoover saw himself in the tradition of the men who founded the Republic and who guided it in the early years. Many Americans in his era had let their devotion to democracy blind them to the reality that, throughout a hundred and sixty-odd years, they have been guided in business and in government by a comparatively small number of leaders who have thought in continental terms. Mr. Hoover represented the "very limited group of highly able, highly educated people" whom Mr. Roosevelt had satirized just two years earlier.[38] Here was reflected the basic division between the two great political parties of the American republic—the party of emphasis upon leaders, and the party seeking to enlarge the powers of "followers." [39]

In retrospect, Herbert Hoover termed the seventeen months from October, 1929, to April, 1931, "a period of a comparatively mild domestic readjustment, such as the country had experienced before." The nation was "convalescing" by the close of 1930.[40] Yet on December 11, 1930, a firebell was heard when the Bank of the United States, a private bank with sixty offices and 400,000 depositors, failed in New York City. Bankers elsewhere shuddered. By the end of the year, a total of 1,352 of the 24,079 banks in the country had failed—twice the total for 1929.[41]

The session of the Congress, meanwhile, had developed into a quarrel with the President over the amount to be spent for drought relief. The summer had been visited by one of the

---

[37] *Ibid.*, October 8, 1930.

[38] p. 39.

[39] Edgar E. Robinson, *The Evolution of American Political Parties*, chapter XVIII, "Realities in Party Life."

[40] *Memoirs: 1929-1941*, p. 38.

[41] *Historical Statistics of the United States, 1789-1945*, pp. 262-273. These figures are for "suspensions" and include "banks which closed and were later reopened or taken over by other institutions."

most terrible droughts in the history of some middle western states. Farmers looked to Washington for the help their states seemed incapable of giving.

In 1930 the federal government in Washington spent 1.4 billion dollars for what are called "goods and services," by contrast with 6.2 billion dollars that were to be spent in 1940. If the program President Hoover had recommended to Congress was not tailored to crisis conditions, it was because the nation was thus far refusing to believe that catastrophe lay beyond the panic of 1929. The President did urge increased public works. Banking reform, an expanded merchant marine, railroad consolidation, increased public health service, government reorganization for economy, and additional regulation of the inter-state distribution of public power—were among his recommendations. The President made it abundantly clear in succeeding months, however, that increased appropriations were unthinkable, and a balanced budget an essential.

Meanwhile, economic distress aside from the drought had been signalized early in the year 1930. A drop in building construction contracts had been an ominous portent, and steel output was at 50 to 60 percent of capacity. The Department of Labor reported that manufacturing employment was at its lowest since 1922. Automobile output for the last month of 1929 had been the smallest for any month since February, 1922. Yet this shocking downward trend in the national economy, if anticipated, was not emphasized in January, 1930, either in business or governmental circles. Nor did William Green, spokesman for American trade unions, foresee any such dismal destiny for the months that lay ahead. Whether the American people knew it or not, the great era of post-war prosperity was over by the winter of 1929-30.

If the assurance of inevitable prosperity had operated to minimize the responsibilities, duties, and obligations of the President of the United States, the possibility of economic disintegration was to create in time an opposite effect. Gradually throughout the months following October 24, 1929, the demand for Presidential leadership in time of crisis was heard in the land.

But in two branches of national government this change in

national psychology was not productive of results. President Hoover was reluctant to depart from what he considered the Constitutional and historic role of his office. Gradually he came to sense that dynamic and aggressive leadership was expected of him, even though such vigorous action might bring justifiable criticism that the executive was infringing legislative prerogatives.

In Congress, meanwhile, throughout the year 1930 "blocs" were reluctant to surrender their separate ways to a new rule—be it party responsibility or Presidential leadership. Minority leader John Nance Garner said he thought Congressional Republicans were bewildered at the lack of dynamic and forceful leadership from the White House.

Yet a number of Republican and independent papers thought the stubbornness of the Senate, especially its progressives, more at fault than the President. Mr. Hoover himself wrote some years later: ". . . it is not given even to Presidents to see the future. . . . We could have done better—in retrospect." [42] Yet in the President's view, the fundamental causes of the depression lay in the world outside the United States. As the nation entered a second downward movement under the influence of the European economic collapse of 1931, the President expressed this view:

> As we look beyond the horizons of our own troubles and consider the events in other lands, we know that the main causes of the extreme violence and the long continuance of this depression came not from within but from outside the United States. Had our wild speculation; our stock promotion with its infinite losses and hardship to innocent people; our loose and extravagant business methods and our unprecedented drought, been our only disasters, we would have recovered months ago.

> A large part of the forces which have swept our shores from abroad are the malign inheritances in Europe of the Great War—its huge taxes, its mounting armament, its political and social instability, its disruption of economic life by the new boundaries. Without the war we would have no such depression. Upon these war origins are superimposed the overrapid expansion of production and collapse in price of many foreign

---

[42] *Memoirs: 1929-1941*, p. 29.

raw materials. The demonetization of silver in certain countries and a score of more remote causes have all contributed to
dislocation.

Some particular calamity has happened to nearly every country
in the world, and the difficulties of each have intensified the
unemployment and financial difficulties of all the others. As
either the cause or the effect, we have witnessed armed revolutions within the past two years in a score of nations, not to
mention disturbed political life in many others. Political instability has affected three-fourths of the population of the
world.[43]

As the nation sank deeper and deeper in gloom; as the bread
lines grew longer; as a real sense of despair for the future as
well as the present gripped masses of the population—the political instability that the President had seen spreading over the
world threatened the United States. American liberalism, as
interpreted by President Hoover and a portion of his party, had
failed to establish the view that moderate and orderly progress
was equal to the economic crisis.

In such a situation, advocates of the abandonment of traditional and orderly forces, had their supreme opportunity.
These were the radicals, whose prospects were at the time similar to those of radical outlook among other peoples who had
experienced the industrial revolution—but who had not experienced America's freedom.

Protest literature that was frankly revolutionary made its appearance. As was to be expected, spokesmen for this view appeared in politics, in the pulpit, in the press, and on the radio.
The American pattern of thought and action was subjected to
the poison of an approach to governmental procedures hitherto
little considered in the United States. To some, this appeared
to have its origin in foreign influences, particularly those that
were termed Fascist or Communist.

The unusual flexibility of American political procedures has
made agitation in politics easy, and organization of groups to
push policies and candidates at the polls seems a normal path
of activity for Americans. Their history is strewn with the slogans of politics and the names of candidates of minor parties.

---

[43] Address before the Indiana Editorial Association, June 15, 1931, in *America
Faces the Future* (edited by Charles A. Beard), p. 387.

Yet, despite the fact that the subsequent record has often shown their policies incorporated into major party platforms and later enacted into law, it would be a mistake to suppose that, in any considerable measure, these represent an acceptance of the philosophies underlying these approaches to public policy.

As long as the depression continued, there was much public interest in the activities of Huey Long, Senator from Louisiana. In 1928 he had been elected Governor of Louisiana. Prior to this, he had been a stormy petrel in state politics, and his career as Governor focused national attention upon his methods, his objectives, and particularly upon his success in winning a popular following all over the country. He attacked conservatives and rival political leaders in violent terms; he spent vast sums on public improvements in Louisiana and especially on the public schools; he outwitted, outmaneuvered, and outtalked all opposition that in time charged him with wholesale bribery, widespread corruption, and personal violence.

Elected to the United States Senate, in 1930, Huey Long until his death by assassination five years later, was to carry on a campaign in the nation for a program that in its appeal to popular cupidity and acceptance of bizarre economics was well represented in his slogan, "Every man a king." [44] Appearing first in the Senate at the bottom of the depression, through the first two and a half years of the Roosevelt administration Long was to represent a threat to orderly procedures in business, politics, and government. In dark days of uncertainty, he won high place in the imagination of millions of Americans. One commentator referred to him with truth in 1933 as "one of our conquerors," for Long had become dictator in Louisiana.

Having taken over all of the machinery of elections and government in the state, Long aspired to national leadership. He presented to the nation, in critical years, a Share-the-Wealth program. As the shadow of world revolution lay over the continental United States, it was the threat of a rising dictatorship spearheaded by the Senator from Louisiana that concerned many discerning Americans. Of this threat, Franklin Roosevelt would become fully aware.

---

[44] Huey P. Long, *Every Man a King: The Autobiography of Huey P. Long.*

Another view of the economic crisis found expression in the *New Republic* of January 14, 1931, when Edmund Wilson wrote:

> . . . . May we not well fear that what has broken down, in the course of one catastrophic year, is not simply the machinery of representative government but the capitalist system itself? —and that, even with the best intentions, it may be henceforward impossible for capitalism to guarantee not merely social-justice but even security and order? May we not fear lest our American society, in spite of its apparently greater homogeneity, be liable, through sheer inefficiency, the heritage of political corruption, to collapse in the long run as ignominiously as the feudal regimes of old France and Russia? . . . it may be true that, with the present breakdown, we have come to the end of something, and that we are ready to start on a different tack. . . . It may be that the whole money-making-and-spending psychology has definitely played itself out, and that the Americans would be willing, for the first time now, to put their traditional idealism and their genius for organization behind a radical social experiment.[45]

For men who held such views, and they were increasing in number, the painstaking efforts of those in office received less and less attention. Officials who were technically in power were indeed voices "crying in the wilderness." It was advocates on the outside who were on the march. When suggestion of aid and support for the property-owning classes was made, it seemed indeed, relatively unimportant. Millions were without work and called for direct aid from the national government. Talk of extended credits and of increased taxation seemed a mockery when this was urged in an effort to balance the national budget.

There was, here, a political impasse, but it was of vastly greater importance that issues long in abeyance because of national prosperity were now to be brought forward at a time of national depression. The most dangerous aspect of the situation was a widespread feeling, natural to Americans, that the people could succeed where their leaders had failed.

---

[45] Quoted in Edmund Wilson, *The Shores of Light: A Literary Chronicle of the Twenties and Thirties,* pp. 522-530.

Chapter III

1932: THE PEOPLE DECIDE

THE AMERICAN PEOPLE—disillusioned by the collapse of their dreams in the stock market crash of 1929—welcomed three years later the most reassuring characteristic of their political system, a Presidential election. Here was an opportunity for the voters to state their will not only on the Presidency, but on the membership of the House of Representatives and a third of the Senate. At this time, students of politics familiar with the rhythm said to create the cycle of American experience, foresaw a decided change in political direction.

Such a change had taken place in 1912, when Theodore Roosevelt, seeking a renewal of power, had been the means of breaking the Republican party and bringing back to national dominance the Democratic party under the leadership of Woodrow Wilson. Those with long memories recalled that in 1892 the radical Populists had polled more than a million votes of protest. What species of revolt would result in a seizure of power in 1932? The Democrats, divided and defeated in 1924 and overwhelmed in 1920 and 1928, thought they had the answer this time.[1]

In the years 1929 to 1932, the people, deeply disturbed by voices of despair among them, gradually relaxed their initial

---

[1] For summaries of Presidential elections in the twentieth century see Edgar E. Robinson, *The Presidential Vote 1896-1932* (1934), and *They Voted for Roosevelt* (1947).

support of Herbert Hoover and the Republican party. The program of the President had been stricken by revolt in his own party, particularly in the Senate in 1929. The party had lost ground in Congress in the elections of 1930,[2] and for two years a divided government had grimly carried on the increasingly burdensome work of the nation. In the perspective of years, this was done with remarkable success, but in the eyes of the people at the time it appeared more and more unsatisfactory.

Split in three divisions of conviction, the Republican party was prepared for defeat in the Presidential election of 1932. But how could the Democrats win, and with what candidate, and for what declared purposes? No possibility of a decision by the electorate upon any major specific proposal in foreign or domestic affairs presented itself, unless it might be the repeal of the Eighteenth Amendment. Even on that, the issue was blurred in over half of the states of the nation.

Herbert Hoover was the first President in the history of the United States to offer national leadership in mobilizing the economic resources of the people. In calling upon individual initiative to accept definite responsibility for meeting the problems of the depression, he was unable to stem the tide of economic gloom that engulfed the country. This failure was definitely related to the task of the Presidency as he envisaged it. The office to which he was elected in 1928 was not the same office for which his successors would be chosen. Nor was the federal government centered in Washington, D.C., in 1929-1933 the same instrument of official action that Americans subsequently accepted.

Indeed President Hoover occupied an office which had prestige rather than power. From the day of his inauguration on March 4, 1929, he encouraged economic investigation, fact-finding, and exploration into the hidden resources of the nation he headed, seeking to find ways to leave it better than he had found it—without necessarily invoking the power of government to accomplish his ends.[3]

---

[2] On Congressional elections, see Cortez A. M. Ewing, *Congressional Elections, 1896-1944* (1947).

[3] See *Recent Social Trends in the United States; Report of the President's Research Committee on Social Trends* (1933).

At the time, neither the President, his advisors, nor other acknowledged leaders in or out of office in the United States were in fundamental agreement on the extent to which the powers of the government should be used to combat a depressed economy. Historical precedents lent little aid, for previous Presidents had not taken vigorous affirmative action at such times. In each previous economic crisis, recovery had come without much if any intervention by the federal government.

Had the Republican party in the Congress solidly supported Mr. Hoover, public distrust would have been lessened. It is possible that the nation would have been able to ride out the depression. As Mr. Hoover saw it, there was an "economic upswing from the bottom of the depression in July, 1932." [4]

But the Republicans, suffering the final stroke of a disunity which had first appeared in 1912, were hopelessly divided. Their progressive spokesmen continued to be suspicious of Wall Street. They were therefore disinclined to support Mr. Hoover's measures for co-operation with various groups in business and public affairs.

Had the Republican party been a unit, there would have been no opportunity in the opposing party for a candidate whose primary qualification was his "political availability." Such a candidate, at the time, was Franklin Roosevelt!

In 1932 the devoted supporters of Alfred E. Smith wished to give him another chance at the Presidency. Critics had agreed that decisive elements of weakness had defeated him in 1928. Certain events of the Hoover administration, beginning with the revolt in Congress in 1929, had made it clear that many progressives might actively support Smith if he were nominated.

But there was a division among the Democratic party leaders in Smith's own state of New York. Democrats had succeeded in electing Franklin Roosevelt governor in 1928 and had re-elected him to the governorship in 1930. His administration had encouraged the support of prominent leaders of labor, and had appealed to progressive elements in both parties. It was thought by personal followers of the Governor that a well-organized campaign in the state and in selected states of the

---

[4] *Memoirs: 1929-1941,* p. 267.

nation would result in strong convention support for this successful executive of the largest state in the Union.

Roosevelt was not threatened by the weaknesses of the Smith candidacy. He had won in New York in 1928 when Smith had lost his state in the Presidential race.[5] In fact, there appeared . to be no outstanding weakness in Roosevelt's candidacy, particularly in so good a year for the party of the "outs." If the nation, by November of 1932, should demand a crusading leader, it was not so clear that Roosevelt would qualify. Apparently there was to be no third party of importance.

Governor Roosevelt had come to be favorably known wherever energetic administration of state affairs was of interest. His activities as Governor had furthermore attracted national attention. A segment of those interested in politics had been impressed by his leadership on behalf of Smith in the Democratic National Conventions of 1924 and 1928. There was no doubt of Roosevelt's personal appeal, and it had been exercised on behalf of the man he had actively supported in the state for nearly a decade.[6] Governor Roosevelt's previous political career seemed—to a limited number of friends who in later years had much to say—to indicate a man of destiny. In 1932 the candidacy of Roosevelt appeared to be, as has been said, a clear case of availability. He was a "natural" candidate and one apt to win a "usual" campaign.

In the course of the depression years, Democrat Franklin Roosevelt had on occasion the usual things to say of the Republican party and its obvious deficiencies, and of the hopes to be realized if the Democrats could be brought to power. But aside from very good housekeeping in state affairs, and pledges long associated with Democratic campaigns, his was a routine political appeal and certainly presented no call for heroic action.

The campaign of Governor Roosevelt for the Presidential

---

[5] Writing on November 18, 1928, to Newton Baker, who was to be a rival for the nomination in 1932, Mr. Roosevelt said, ". . . we must do everything to carry on the organization work during the next three years without a discussion of presidential candidates." (Newton D. Baker Papers, Library of Congress.)

[6] Bernard Faÿ in *Roosevelt and His America* argues, though unconvincingly, that it was Roosevelt who forwarded Smith's political fortunes in New York State from 1920 to 1928 rather than vice versa.

nomination in 1932[7] was marked by features to which careful attention should be given by all who would understand his subsequent campaigns for the Presidency.

Formal announcement of the Governor's candidacy was made in January of 1932.[8] Following the announcement of Smith's candidacy two weeks later, it was generally agreed that the race was between the two New Yorkers. There were, as well, favorite sons in a half-dozen states. In seven states in which Democratic primaries were held and in which both men were candidates, Governor Roosevelt won in four and former Governor Smith, in two. In California both had fewer votes than were cast for Congressman Garner, favorite son of the state of Texas.

Roosevelt support was widely scattered over the nation. Smith's was concentrated in the Northeast. It was therefore felt that Smith's control of national party machinery might be a determining factor in producing a stalemate that would prevent the nomination of Roosevelt. Holding a majority of the delegates, Governor Roosevelt would nevertheless fall short of a two-thirds vote when the convention met.

The pre-convention campaign of Governor Roosevelt was fought on a national scale. There was widespread response from progressive Democrats. But careful planning of a small group of personal advisors did not result in more than an anticipated majority support when the convention met. There were a number of favorite sons, as well as former Governor Smith and Speaker Garner. The year previous to the convention had been marked by an intensive campaign on Roosevelt's behalf by James Farley.[9]

Roosevelt was opposed by Tammany, and in the support of delegates from every section of the country could be seen reflected his appeal to the average citizen at this time in his liberalism, his availability, and his probable support by the

---

[7] In a letter dated December 8, 1930, to Mrs. Caspar Whitney, cited on p. 51 Governor Roosevelt had written: ". . . quite frankly I mean what I have said—that I am not in any sense a candidate for 1932, partly because I have seen so much of the White House ever since 1892, that I have no hankering, secret or otherwise, to be a candidate. . . ." *Personal Letters 1928-1945*, I, 161-162.

[8] Note the cautious tone in the campaign biography by Ernest K. Lindley, *Franklin D. Roosevelt, A Career in Progressive Democracy*, which apparently enjoyed both the co-operation of the Governor in its preparation and a close review by his associates before final publication.

[9] See James A. Farley, *Behind the Ballots*, chapter II, "The Pre-Election Campaign of 1932."

middle-of-the-road voter wanting a change. Several narrow escapes in pre-convention maneuvers made it clear that the candidate might be expected to play politics to win. Party leaders saw reassurance in this, in that it seemed to promise a united party when the nominations had been made.

On the first ballot of 1,154 votes, Governor Roosevelt had 666; Smith, 201; Garner, 90; the remainder were scattered among favorite sons. Following the first ballot, Farley attempted to reach William Randolph Hearst, who was in California at the time and who controlled the votes for Garner in the California delegation at the convention.[10] Failing to reach Hearst directly, Farley then telephoned a close friend of Hearst and urged him to intercede with Hearst. This was done, Hearst's friend pointing out that a deadlock in the convention might result in the nomination of Newton D. Baker who had been known as an active supporter of American adherence to the League of Nations to which Hearst was strongly opposed. Hearst then let it be known that he favored switching the Garner votes in the California delegation to Roosevelt,[11] assurance being given that Roosevelt would take a position in opposition to United States membership in the League.[12]

Roosevelt's nomination was thus achieved by gaining the votes pledged to Garner from California and Texas. The selection of Garner as a running mate was a result. This combination appeared to emphasize the union of North and South —New York and Texas—as the ticket of Smith and Robinson had done four years earlier. Moreover, Garner was Speaker of the House. This meant recognition of the Southern Democrats

---

[10] In a letter to Josephus Daniels from Warm Springs on May 5, 1932, Roosevelt wrote that if California and Texas could be induced to swing from Garner to Roosevelt, it "would cinch the matter." (Cited by Carroll Kilpatrick, *Roosevelt and Daniels*, p. 115.)

[11] Confidential source, but see Farley, *op. cit.*, pp. 131-151. Of interest is Franklin Roosevelt's letter to Josephus Daniels on August 24, 1914 (Josephus Daniels Papers, Library of Congress), in which Mr. Roosevelt said, "I hear very little political news, but certainly hope the report that Hearst is to run against me is true [in the New York senatorial campaign]. It raises my fighting and sporting blood to think of a campaign against that person."

[12] Governor Roosevelt had written on January 29, 1932, to Robert Woolley (Woolley Papers, Library of Congress): "Let me know what people in Washington say about Newton Baker coming out against our entry into the League. He has—of course—said the right thing." On May 12, 1932, Governor Roosevelt wrote Daniels (Daniels Papers, Library of Congress) of the opposition that had developed to the nomination of Newton D. Baker, saying, "All this seems a pity— because Newton would make a better President than I would!"

so entrenched in chairmanships of committees of House and Senate due to their long service and seniority.

Continued careful planning, clever use of rival antagonisms, a keen sense of the popular mood—were to characterize the ensuing campaign.[13] In his first nomination, as later, Mr. Roosevelt sharpened the fact of personal leadership by unprecedented action. In this case, he flew from Albany to Chicago to accept the nomination from the convention directly. His address,[14] when read in conjunction with the Democratic platform [15] drawn up by the convention, prepares the way for an understanding of the campaign that was to follow, although not of the administration that came into being in 1933.

The platform had been prepared to meet the particular needs of an opposition party in time of depression. But Mr. Roosevelt called for followers to a crusade for all the nation. He called for a "New Deal." [16] It was a call to arms addressed first of all to the people. He was to lead in this effort to "restore America to its own people." What echoes were awakened of the declarations of the past fifty years! [17]

The ensuing campaign was characteristic of those that were to follow in subsequent elections. Roosevelt set out to inspire the confidence and then to win the support of the people.

[13] Roy V. Peel and Thomas C. Donnelly collaborated in a volume of contemporary observations on *The 1932 Campaign: An Analysis.*

[14] The acceptance address appears in *Public Papers, 1928-1932,* pp. 647-659. Raymond Moley states that this address was in preparation for three months. (*The Commonwealth,* Official Journal of the Commonwealth Club of California, August 25, 1952, p. 152.)

[15] Governor Roosevelt discussed the national Democratic platform in a radio address from Albany, New York, on July 30, 1932, published in *Public Papers, 1928-1932,* pp. 659-669.

[16] S. I. Rosenman (*Working with Roosevelt,* p. 71) claims credit for the phrase, "the New Deal," as does Raymond Moley (*After Seven Years,* p. 23). See Cyril Clemens in *St. Louis Post Dispatch,* May 31, 1952, in which Mr. Clemens records an interview with Mr. Roosevelt on December 8, 1933, during which, at Mr. Clemens' suggestion of a possibility that "New Deal" came from Mark Twain in *A Connecticut Yankee in King Arthur's Court,* Mr. Roosevelt said, "Yes, certainly, I am well aware of that fact, for it was there that I obtained the phrase."

[17] Note the words of the Populist party platform, adopted July 4, 1892: ". . . we seek to restore the government of the Republic to the hands of 'the plain people,' with whose class it originated. . . . We believe that the powers of government—in other words, of the people—should be expanded (as in the case of the postal service) as rapidly and as far as the good sense of an intelligent people and the teachings of experience shall justify, to the end that oppression, injustice, and poverty shall eventually cease in the land." (Cited in John D. Hicks, *The Populist Revolt,* p. 441.)

There was general agreement that no clear pattern of policy emerged.[18] It was easy to emphasize that the chief strategy of the Democrats was attack upon the record of the Republicans.

This was not new, but the distress of the country seemed in greater measure than usual to warrant it. Mr. Roosevelt did not until late in the campaign join in personal attack upon Mr. Hoover. Yet, as was the custom of an opposition candidate, he at once attacked the record of his rival and pointed out failures to meet the needs of the people in years of depression.

Franklin Roosevelt recognized party bosses as essential to success, and this was known.[19] He made moves to improve relations with powerful individuals within the party, and this was known.[20] In speech and statement, he obviously aimed to reach the voters; to speak directly to the people.

It is completely to misread the career of Mr. Roosevelt to suppose that he entered upon the race for the Presidency reluctantly and in response to a call of duty. He sought the people; he made the people the object of his regard; he wooed them that he might lead them. It was, to a supreme degree, an opportunity for self-expression that he had found. His extensive campaign served to reassure any who might feel that his health had been seriously impaired by the attack of infantile paralysis from which he had made a slow but definite recovery. During the eleven months preceding his inauguration, Mr. Roosevelt traveled approximately twenty-seven thousand miles and visited all but seven of the states.

What was referred to as the Roosevelt record was made in the years when he served as executive of the largest state in the Union. Of this record, it may be said that he fought the Republican legislature of the state of New York and won, and that his direct appeal to the voters was an important factor in this victory. He defied and antagonized some of the forces in Tammany, and won national recognition in so doing. He emphasized leadership within the state on matters of child welfare

---

[18] Based on an examination of the periodical literature of the period of the campaign.

[19] He was widely criticized, for example, for his hesitancy in moving against Tammany corruption in New York City in 1931-1932.

[20] The effort to achieve better relations with William Randolph Hearst is described by Charles A. Beard in *American Foreign Policy in the Making, 1932-1940*, chapter V.

and conservation. There were few changes in governmental method or in political device during his administration. He made many speeches, a number of them to national audiences by radio. He was clearly advocating greater participation of the people in government. He favored economies, and he was suspicious of what he called special interests.

During the campaign for the Presidency, Governor Roosevelt's approach did not greatly change. Increasing were the indications of the influence, upon his conduct as candidate, and sometimes upon the content of his speeches, of a group of personal advisers. Of these, Raymond Moley, Adolph A. Berle, Jr., Rexford G. Tugwell, and Ernest K. Lindley are to be given first consideration.[21] Tugwell later wrote, "Mr. Roosevelt sometimes spoke with the voice of a learning we made available. . . ."[22]

From the point of view of the campaign managers, effort was to be made to win a national vote by bringing to the voters a candidate with a platform that would deal aggressively with problems of unemployment, relief, and conservation. Viewed in retrospect, the utterances of the candidate in many speeches bore this emphasis.[23] But it is to be noted that the platform adopted by a convention that was confident of winning the election in November called for a drastic cut in actual expenditures and for a balanced budget. It defended private enterprise and promised a sound currency. It called for reform of abuses in the field of finance and the public utilities, and it promised national relief for the unemployed.

More than a hint of a candidate who would appeal in terms of compromise was given in Roosevelt's statement by telegram to the editor of *Collier's* just before the convention:

---

[21] Writing to Newton D. Baker on August 30, 1932 (R. G. Tugwell, "The Preparation of a President," in *Western Political Quarterly*, I (March, 1948), p. 22, Roosevelt said, "Professor Raymond Moley of Columbia University, an old friend who is assisting me in many ways, is acting as a sort of clearing house for me. This part of my task has nothing to do with those who are engaged in strictly political management of the campaign. . . ."

[22] *Ibid.*

[23] According to Tugwell (*op. cit.*, p. 20), "He had to make speeches, and they had to be carefully done; but although they dealt with economic subjects, their interest was to carry to the country, without much specification, a sense of the new possibilities growing without disaster, of a prosperous future which should replace a dismal past."

This nation needs progressive leadership. We must recognize two parts of the problem:

First, adequate immediate national, state and local aid to prevent actual want in the present and immediate future.

Second, a comprehensive plan covering all phases of our economic and social difficulties.

. . . The farming interests represent half our population. They have lost buying power and this has been largely responsible for depressing industry. We must . . . try out a new plan to insure getting surplus crops out of the country without putting the government in business, and set up machinery to save the mortgaged farm by cutting down amortization and lowering interest rates.

These immediate steps must be followed by a land utilization survey in order to eliminate marginal lands and start a very large reforestation and flood control program.

Finally we must give assistance to those families in cities who may wish to return to good land.

I use these as illustrations of the broad planning and active leadership which must extend to all the other problems because it is clear that the solution lies not in opportunism or in last minute remedies but in going to the sources of the trouble.[24]

Insisting that he was going to the sources of trouble was a familiar practice for Mr. Roosevelt. He referred to it repeatedly as Governor of New York. Later he wrote of his own thought in this period as follows:

It required the depression itself and my experience as Governor during that period to bring home to me the more fundamental, underlying troubles which were facing all civilization. . . . The 1929-1933 period was well fitted to serve as an education in social and economic needs for those who were willing to search out all the underlying causes and not merely symptoms on the surface.[25]

This simplification is a clue to Mr. Roosevelt's continuous procedure in politics.

---

[24] Quoted in W. L. Chenery, *So It Seemed*, p. 238.
[25] *Public Papers, 1928-1932*, General Introduction, xii.

Those who would examine in detail the record of this campaign might well ask three questions: How much did the mass of the people know of Roosevelt as Governor? How much did they know of his program as developed for the purpose of the election? How did the nominee reconcile his speeches to his view of the needs of the national crisis? The answers give basis for a conclusion that there was little reason for confidence that the people understood, or that the nominee understood the full nature of the economic crisis.

Nothing that clearly foreshadows the later New Deal takes form in the "new deal" promised in the acceptance speech. Three charges, often to be repeated, were: The depression was a home-grown, not a foreign product. The administration spent too much money and yet did not meet the public needs. Public works were only a temporary remedy; it was low purchasing power that brought the depression. No definite program was proposed except to cut expenses, to balance the budget, and to remove special privilege.

There was, in the best known of Roosevelt's campaign speeches, a clear indication of the dilemma he would face. He did face it in words. After stating the well-known theory that material construction of the nation was complete and that government action must now take the place of earlier natural forces such as the frontier, he advocated trade restrictions and state-guided monopolies. On the other hand, he called for social justice and conquest of poverty.

There was general agreement that in his Commonwealth Club address in San Francisco on September 23, 1932,[26] Mr. Roosevelt outlined more exactly than in any other address a program for building a new America. But in this address appear the words:

> Our industrial plant is built; the problem just now is whether under existing conditions it is not over-built. Our last frontier has long since been reached and there is practically no more free land. More than half of our people do not live on the farms or on lands and cannot derive a living by cultivating their own property.[27]

---

[26] *Ibid.*, pp. 742-756.
[27] *Ibid.*, p. 750.

The mood of the country in October, 1932, was receptive to the Roosevelt appeal because his flair for combination and compromise was at its best in political terms. The economic difficulties inherent in his promises to different economic interests were not apparent except to those elements in the population who were already opposed to his candidacy.

Perhaps the clue to Mr. Roosevelt's "fears" for the future of the United States is to be found in the following reflection in the midst of his San Francisco address:

> Where Jefferson had feared the encroachment of political power on the lives of individuals, Wilson knew that the new power was financial. He saw, in the highly centralized economic system, the despot of the twentieth century. . . . The concentration of financial power had not proceeded so far in 1912 as it has today . . .[28]

One of the most revealing addresses of the campaign was delivered in New York City on November 3 at a meeting under the auspices of the Republicans-for-Roosevelt League. In this address, Mr. Roosevelt attacked the Republican administration and President Hoover in bitter terms:

> There are ten million or more reasons embodied in the blighted hopes of the ten million or more of the unemployed. No doubt seeking to extend the campaign of fear so foolishly as well as so wickedly put in motion, the present Republican leader, the President, the other night referred to the fact that if the policies he had so valiantly developed be not continued, "the grass would grow on the streets of the cities." Well, the grass has little chance to grow in the streets of our cities now. It would be trampled into the ground by the men who wander these streets in search of employment.[29]

After stating that President Hoover had called for a continuance of faith and hope in the American system, Mr. Roosevelt went on to say:

---

[28] *Ibid.*, p. 749.
[29] *New York Times,* November 4, 1932. See bibliographical note, p. 423. On October 25, attacking the President, the Democratic candidate had charged: "The crash came in October, 1929. The President had at his disposal all the instrumentalities of Government. From that day to December 31st of that year, he did absolutely nothing to remedy the situation. . . ." Mr. Hoover had replied on October 28: ". . . It seems almost incredible that a man, a candidate for the Presidency of the United States would broadcast such a violation of the truth." (Hoover, *Memoirs: 1929-1941,* p. 260.)

This expression is another example of the old gambling spirit of the speculative boom that has so sorely mismanaged the country for the past few years. . . . As you who have followed the nation-wide campaign which I have conducted for the past three months will fully appreciate, both my political philosophy and my chart of action for the country's future differ widely from those of the President himself.[30]

The full force of Mr. Roosevelt's view of political means and political parties is found in the following:

This system, the American government itself, was founded on the principle that many men from many states with many economic views and many economic interests might, through the medium of a national government, build for national harmony, national unity and independent well-being. This is the American system. And if the President will turn from his made-to-order statistics, which he so sadly misrepresents and misinterprets; if he will turn his eyes from his so-called "backward and crippled countries" and turn to the great and stricken markets of Kansas, Nebraska, Iowa, Wisconsin, Illinois and the other agricultural states; if he will cease his utopian dreaming of inventions hidden in the "locker of science" that are going to make us rich, and turn to the true lessons of American history and the real words of the founders of this Republic, he will know what the American system really is.[31]

Four days before the election, in a speech at a rally in the Brooklyn Academy of Music, Governor Roosevelt pledged himself unmistakably to certain policies in language that cannot be written off the record of the ensuing years; though it was not included in the *Public Papers:*

One of the most commonly repeated misrepresentations by Republican speakers, including the President, has been the claim that the Democratic position with regard to money has not been made sufficiently clear. The President [Hoover] is seeing visions of rubber dollars. But that is only a part of his campaign of fear. I am not going to characterize these statements. I merely present the facts.

The Democratic platform specifically declares, "We advocate a sound currency to be preserved at all hazards." That, I take it, is plain English.

[30] *New York Times,* November 4, 1932.
[31] *Ibid.,* November 5, 1932.

In discussing this platform on July 30, I said, "Sound money is an international necessity; not a domestic consideration for one nation alone." In other words, I want to see sound money in all the world.

Far up in the Northwest at Butte I repeated the pledge of the platform, saying "sound currency must be maintained at all regards."

In Seattle I reaffirmed my attitude on this question. The thing has been said, therefore, in plain English three times in my speeches. It is stated without qualification in the platform and I have announced my unqualified acceptance of that platform in every plank.[32]

Despite the long and strenuous campaign of Mr. Roosevelt, it was evident at the close that there was less knowledge and understanding of his career and his proposals than had been seen in the estimates of the Democratic candidate four years earlier. But the Democratic party was more of a unit than it had been in 1928. And in no section of the country was there doubt that it would poll a great Democratic vote.

It was recognized as well that the Republican party would not, as in 1928, poll its full party vote. Too many progressives were in open revolt, some of them prominent and long thought of as national leaders. There was no such widespread independent Republican movement as in 1912 or in 1924. But the weakness of the Republican appeal was nevertheless a great advantage to the Democratic candidate and was an important element in his success. *How* important this was, it is impossible to say.

Full understanding of the deep impression that was to be made upon the public mind by the early developments in his first administration must rest in a remembrance of the enthusiasm that was contributed in the campaign of 1932 by those who already saw in Mr. Roosevelt a hero to match their dreams. Attractive, courageous, high-minded, and possessed of capacity to "see visions and dream dreams," this New Yorker was to realize for them the America that had been called for over and over by Bryan the militant crusader, by La Follette the dogged fighter, and by "Theodore the Great."

[32] *Ibid.*, November 5, 1932.

On the whole, it is clear that the electorate wished above all else a two-party contest and a clear cut decision. This is seen in the small number of votes cast for third party candidates. In a time of distress it would seem probable that a great vote of protest was to be expected. As measured by third party votes, this "protest" was in fact three times that of 1928, although it was less than in 1920. It was of no political significance in the final outcome. The temporary "protest" vote came from those who, all over the nation, voted for Franklin Roosevelt.

The heaviest vote ever cast in a Presidential election up to that time was polled in November of 1932. And the largest vote ever cast for a candidate up to that time was polled for Franklin Roosevelt—22,809,638—representing 57.4 percent of the entire vote cast. It was, however, a smaller *percentage* of the total vote than had been cast for Hoover in 1928 or for Harding in 1920. Yet emphasis must be given the fact that it represented a national sweep, for Roosevelt carried more counties (2,721) than any candidate had ever carried. Of these, 282 had never before gone Democratic. And in 3,003 of the counties of the nation (all but 93) the Democratic vote had increased.[33] It was an impressive victory, well reflected in the fact that Roosevelt carried 42 states and won 472 electoral votes, including every section of the country.

The Seventy-third Congress would have in the Senate 59 Democrats and 36 Republicans; in the House 313 Democrats and 117 Republicans.

The collapse of the Republican party in 1930, symbol of the closing of an era, was thus followed two years later by the end of Republican rule. The majority had turned out the Republicans who had ruled for ten years in the period 1921-1931. Rejected as well was Herbert Hoover, a man of proved integrity: an excellent administrator who had a developed philosophy of government, a grasp of European problems, and a plan for American leadership in the world.

Yet, in the combination of discordant and obviously "protest elements," the vote of 1932 was neither a clear cut victory for a national Democratic party, nor a personal triumph for the

---

[33] See Robinson, *The Presidential Vote, 1896-1932*.

Democratic party nominee. True, he had been overwhelmingly elected. And the immensity of the victory was attributed only in part to the weakness of the Republican appeal. In that a number of prominent Republican Senators had even left their party to support Mr. Roosevelt—most of them having presented for some time a political program that placed them more in harmony with the declared purposes of the Democratic party than with those of the Republican administration—it was a coalition victory. At the same time, the Democratic candidate had won the full Democratic support of the southern states, including those areas that had gone to President Hoover four years earlier. As the Democratic ticket had also had the support of city machines, it seemed obvious that all elements recently associated with Democratic appeal had united in electing the Democratic ticket.

Yet the Presidential contest of 1932 was fought in unreal terms. In opposition to the prevailing Republican administration was formulated a program that was based upon the challenge of widespread distress, upon promises of reformers of the preceding generation, and upon the device of locating a scapegoat in Mr. Hoover.

In taking this road and securing the mandate of the people to follow it, Democratic leaders were not utilizing the advances that had been made toward more effective government. They said merely, in effect, "Let the people rule, for the people have been thwarted by evil, immoral, and selfish interests who have sought to govern the United States for the benefit of a minority. Let the majority take possession of its household." [34]

In waging this type of campaign at this time, Mr. Roosevelt had brought business men and financial leaders into increasing disfavor. In labor organizations, in farm organizations, indeed in all areas in which progress had been made in light of the discoveries of the twentieth century, opportunity for influence was given those who were to rule in the name of the masses. This was the basis of discrimination.

The outstanding victory somewhat minimized the fact that the vote revealed Mr. Roosevelt had won to his standard the

---

[34] Democratic party campaign literature was filled with appeals to "dirt farmers," "city laborers," and the "man in the street." They were all promised a fair deal.

elements in the population—the farmer and the laborer—that had an urgent interest in his possible victory. At the same time, the support of the South—though given—was of relatively less importance than that of the new elements won to the Democratic party. In the final record the city machines and all old line Democratic organizations were in support.

For some aspects of the campaign of 1932, Franklin Roosevelt warrants eulogy as "champion campaigner." He did tour the country. He spoke many times. He vigorously attacked the administration. He appealed with great skill and adroitness to various special interest groups.

But he won the huge vote because he had the Solid South, the active support of all Democratic machines, the support of progressive Republicans, and finally, the great vote of those who wished for a change.

In the heat of the Presidential campaign of 1932, it was charged by conservatives that a Democratic victory would open the door to repudiation of the old American system of government. It was charged that the Democrats were Socialistic. It was charged that they would introduce alien doctrines of foreign origin. Such charges had been heard many times before 1932. They had been made against Republicans—such as Robert M. La Follette and Theodore Roosevelt—as well as against Democrats who had followed William Jennings Bryan.

Yet in this election it was clear that Democrats and progressives, if successful, would be in a position to promote doctrines and plans long associated with American radicals. That was clear to close observers, even though the majority of those voting for change scarcely thought of such a possibility. Revolution was not in the air in the summer and autumn of 1932. But there was deep resentment against "Wall Street," "Business Men," and all those termed "Reactionaries."

The successful Democratic candidate needed to be more than a progressive Democrat supported by progressive Republicans. For this role, his utterances and actions throughout his life had prepared Mr. Roosevelt. Furthermore, the New Day of Herbert Hoover compelled Franklin Roosevelt to chart a yet "newer" course to meet the challenge of the crisis. It was to be the New *Deal* that emerged from the election.

It is commonly thought that the depression forced the American political pattern to change. Yet old forms were used, as well as old slogans, and many experienced Democrats and Republicans appeared to be successful in the election of 1932. But the changes in physical and mental habitat of the nation had by the end of the third decade of the century made it absolutely essential that every man calling for leadership declare himself upon new issues. On this Herbert Hoover had led, and made clear his view, which had been repudiated. As yet Franklin Roosevelt had not met this challenge, except in old-fashioned terms that led to divergent interpretations. Would he go the way of socialism? Would he put his reliance upon the state?

Of political decisions made by Mr. Roosevelt prior to the outcome of the election, two need emphasis at this point. One carried into every activity the primary task of organizing and leading the Democratic party organization—local, state, and national. The other was the determination to stress every proposal and platform associated with progressive politics in the states and the nation. The result of such decisions upon his part placed the newly elected President in a position to use all of the power of Democratic party organization and to appeal to the widespread public interest in progressive programs.

It followed logically that there could be, in the President-elect's plan of activity, no co-operation on domestic or foreign problems with the outgoing administration. Likewise, as soon became evident, it was natural that the conservative forces not only in the Republican party but in the Democratic party should organize to oppose the new administration. That there would be widespread support of this opposition was to be presumed from the fact that forty-two percent of the electorate had voted against Mr. Roosevelt.

Strong, bitter, and violent language has long been the custom in American politics. In concluding his campaign, Mr. Roosevelt had remarked, "It may be said, when the history of the past few months comes to be written, that this was a bitter campaign. I prefer to remember it only as a hard-fought campaign." But the language and mood of others were bitter in 1932 and this was in an American pattern.

When Franklin Roosevelt was a boy of ten in 1892, the Populists had declared that selfish political and economic interests had brought the country "to the verge of moral, political, and material ruin." When in 1912 he was eight years out of Harvard and already a beginner in politics, the Progressive party platform of Theodore Roosevelt had asked "the people of the United States, without regard to past difference, who through repeated betrayals, realize today the power of the crooked political bosses and of the privileged classes behind them is so strong in the two party organizations that no helpful movement in the real interests of our country can come," to support a program of social justice. In 1924, the party of La Follette had outlined the basic struggle in politics in terms not unlike those used by Roosevelt in 1932.

Now many Americans agreed on the value of such protest as they voted in 1932; many more than in any previous election. Many were Democrats, but many were Republicans. Their spokesmen campaigned for Roosevelt, and in view of the small minor party vote, as has already been seen, it is reasonable to assume that most of the normal third party vote went to him. The insurgents expected more of the Roosevelt administration in fulfillment of their aspirations for the very reason that never before had they won a majority in a national contest—not in 1892 nor in 1912 nor in 1924.

Consequently, if some of the promises of the Roosevelt administration did not materialize, it would be certain that advocates of more extreme measures would receive wide support. In time of depression, promises of more democratic processes and of greater social justice, as well as of economic well-being, would be at a premium.

There is no doubt that the depression seemed to progressives to justify all they had long said of need of control of business; care of the impoverished; political change; social justice. Franklin Roosevelt was to inherit not only the crisis but the explanation of it! More was involved than turning the rascals out. It was a long-term indictment which the Democrats as a party had had only a share in preparing.

Coming to power in 1932, Mr. Roosevelt was in truth less a "Democrat" than the leader of a revolt that had been cutting party lines for thirty years. Woodrow Wilson had no such support twenty years earlier. His support was from Democrats. The Progressives had voted for Theodore Roosevelt in 1912. Understanding of Franklin Roosevelt's development of a personal following requires that it be seen how long in preparation, outside the Democratic party, was the road he was called upon to take.

As has been seen, since the opening of the century, American politics had turned upon proposals for "reform" in the government of the United States. Both of the great parties had been subjected to an agitation moving their members, and both had campaigned in terms of change. In thirty years many such platform proposals had been transformed into law. Some of the responsibility for this had been upon the shoulders of third party leaders in campaigns that had forced the governing party to provide a legislative program to meet their demands. The American public had been accustomed to proposals for economic change, political reform, and social justice—all within the American system—although some proposals, not adopted, had asked for fundamental changes in the system.

During these three decades neither the Democratic nor the Republican party was wholly radical and certainly neither was conservative. On the whole, Democratic organization and leadership was more advanced in its proposals, although Eastern leadership and Southern support were definitely conservative. At the same time, although Republican leadership had been basically conservative, the most salient facts in the politics of the period had been the revolts within the Republican party organization for a more advanced program in economic, political, and social fields, and the enactment by Republican leadership of a reform program of regulation and control of economic life.

Twice, insistence upon reform had broken party lines even in a Presidential campaign. The revolt of progressive Republicans in the Taft administration had eventually forced a split of the party. The short-lived Progressive party had presented a more advanced program in the campaign of 1912 and polled sufficient votes to bring about a Democratic victory. Although the party disappeared, much of its program was at the center of discussion for the ensuing twenty years.

Again in 1924, the more advanced elements in the Republican party left again—and were joined by the more radical Democrats in supporting an independent candidacy. This program was more radical than that of 1912, and was formally supported by the Socialists and some elements of organized labor. It, too, prepared the way for the alignment in 1932. Yet neither Theodore Roosevelt nor Robert La Follette had answered the call to provide the New Day. Both were content to call for the *repudiation* of an Old America.

Herbert Hoover in 1932 was still calling for a New America. For the time being, no one was speaking for the conservative Old America. Yet "dissent" certainly provided the background for Franklin Roosevelt's advent to the Presidency.

More important than all else in the public mind was the patent fact that Mr. Roosevelt was inevitably to inherit a great tradition when he entered upon the Presidency. What appeared to be the political impasse of thirty years had well prepared a large number of public-spirited citizens to look with critical eyes upon political party organizations, yet to realize anew that the way of achievement in politics or in government was to be found in the leadership of a President within one of the great parties.

The American people remembered that in this period of thirty-two years the Democratic party had been in absolute control by popular mandate only six years. With a minority backing in popular votes for the years 1913-1915, the Democrats had been responsible for the Presidency of Woodrow Wilson, who had had popular backing only in the election of 1916.

The twenty-two years of complete Republican control, as well as two additional years of control of the House, had been provided by impressive national victories. The Presidencies of Theodore Roosevelt and of Herbert Hoover had been marked by brilliant and effective personal—rather than political—leadership.

The founders of the Republic near the close of the eighteenth century had created a new office, carrying with it many of the powers of a king, but subjecting its incumbent to a vote of the electorate at stated times. The American people had, year by year, found in Presidents of varying view and capacity a new type of leader in the modern world.

Increasingly in these first three decades of the twentieth century had the American people seen embodied in the Presidency their conception of the American leader. This tradition of the Presidency explains much, but the changing views of the tradition tended always to emphasize the flexibility of the office. With all their deep-seated devotion to their Constitution, Americans had repeatedly found it necessary to adapt themselves to new types of leaders. They were soon to have another opportunity.

Chapter IV

INTERREGNUM

A NEW ERA was in sight when on November 8, 1932, 57 percent of the American voters chose Franklin Roosevelt President of the United States. That this era should commence at once was their intention. The people wanted an administration that would deal quickly and effectively with the domestic and foreign problems that according to their belief had brought panic and depression. They asked leadership of the newly chosen President, and they wished for immediate evidence of it.

Yet during the following four months no exercise of direct power was possible. The inauguration of President-elect Roosevelt, under Constitutional procedure,[1] had to be deferred until March 4, 1933. "In the interval prescribed by eighteenth century deliberation in order to permit the post-chaises and berliners of legislators to reach Washington from outlying points," as a British observer noted, "the whole economic fabric of the United States collapsed." [2] Of course this was an extreme view. Life did go on and the surface revealed no collapse. But in the hearts of multitudes was doubt—if not of the power of political recuperation in the nation—of the basic soundness of the Amer-

---

[1] Despite legislation already passed by the Congress, calling for the first session of a newly elected Congress in January and the inauguration of a President on January 20, this "lame duck amendment" was not yet in effect.

[2] Philip Guedalla, *The Hundred Years*, p. 347.

ican system. Confidence had been shaken by three years of depression, and it had not been restored in the course of the Presidential campaign.

As will be seen, due to the desire of Herbert Hoover to face the pressing problems in collaboration with the President-elect, more than a promise of leadership from him would have been possible had Franklin Roosevelt been ready and willing to act with the President. This Mr. Roosevelt would not do, and afterwards said that, under the circumstances, he could not do.[3]

The first interchange between Mr. Hoover and Mr. Roosevelt furnishes some evidence of the President-elect's early resolve "not to co-operate." In response to Mr. Hoover's telegram—

> I congratulate you on the opportunity that has come to you to be of service to the country and I wish for you a most successful administration. In the common purpose of all of us I shall dedicate myself to every possible helpful effort.

Mr. Roosevelt returned the following—

> I appreciate your generous telegram for the immediate as well as for the more distant future. I join in your gracious expression of a common purpose in helpful effort for our country.

But on the back of the telegraphic form on which President Hoover's message was recorded is written, in the longhand familiar as that of Franklin Roosevelt, the following: "I appreciate your generous telegram. I want to assure you that subject to my necessary executive duties as Governor during the balance of this year, I hold myself in readiness to cooperate with you in our common purpose to help our country. . . ." The phrases "during the balance of this year" and "in readiness to cooperate with you in our [common purpose]" are, however, crossed out, and in place of the latter is written "ready to further in every way."[4]

President Hoover had to carry on the administration of the government without the collaboration he sought during four months of unremitting crisis. As in 1860-61, the change of administration was of grave importance not only in compounding domestic problems but in imperiling foreign commitments.

---

[3] *Public Papers, 1928-1932*, p. 871. See p. 101, this book.
[4] President's Secretary's File, 1933-1935, Box 8, Roosevelt Library.

Every statement and action of the government in control was tentative unless the President-elect could be brought to cooperate, and the public to approve.

That President Hoover had been without Congressional support since the mid-term elections of 1930, when a Democratic majority had been elected to the House, was of course a further cause of governmental paralysis during the four-month interval. Even within his own party, due to factional disputes, as has been noted, Mr. Hoover had not received adequate support in the Senate at any time since September of 1929.

Obviously, Hoover had to have Roosevelt backing in any move made if it were to be accepted. Pending the transition of power in the period between November 8, 1932, and March 4, 1933, the nation drifted and was pushed by force of circumstances toward deeper financial crisis. The President was without power, except in law, and the President-elect could not under the law assume power.[5]

Whatever Mr. Roosevelt might say or do would be of inestimable importance, however, because of the vague nature of his campaign utterances, the divergent elements supporting him, the impressive vote given him—and finally, because he was to be President. In this particular set of circumstances, in the interval commonly known as "interregnum" in the United States, was to take place a test of the President-elect's conception of leadership. Possibly a foreshadowing of the ultimate direction he would later select, and a pattern of his policy, program, and personality in office, would be revealed. Franklin Roosevelt could not escape this test.

A President, whoever he may be, is set apart from other men, and the circle of protective officers set about Mr. Roosevelt, as soon as the election returns were conclusive, was a symbol of this fact. They accompanied him as he left the Biltmore Hotel at two o'clock in the morning of November 9 to go to the house in Sixty-fifth Street which was his home in New York City. From that moment until he took the oath of office at 1:08 P.M. at the Capitol in Washington on the following March 4, he was,

---

[5] The economic and political uncertainties of the entire Hoover administration had made imperative a re-examination of the Constitutional and party structure that had made such a mockery of efficient administration, of the popular will, and of the division of powers under the well-accepted democratic process. But that was a long-term problem.

although still only President-elect even after the meeting of the Electoral College on December 15, in fact already the chosen leader of the American people.

As leader in this period, Roosevelt worked within certain well-defined areas in each of which there was a test of his leadership. That his influence, even in this interval, was impressive lay in the character and conviction of the man, and especially in the salient fact that he, and only he, could determine the future. Of this he was fully aware.

The personality the people as a whole now saw for the first time and measured as their accepted leader, was winning in manner and reassuring in announced intention. The fact that Franklin Roosevelt radiated power not, as in the case of the usual "popular" leader by ceaseless physical movement, but by drawing others within the radius of his smile and of his voice, produced a feeling among the people that here was in spirit, as was soon to be in fact, the appropriate center of all executive action.

Meanwhile, President Hoover had to act. Before considering Mr. Roosevelt's responses to this leadership of Mr. Hoover—responses which cast long shadows down the future—it may be well to summarize the movements of the President-elect and his steps in preparing to take office sixteen weeks later.

During the remainder of the year and until January 2, when his successor, Herbert Lehman, took office, Franklin Roosevelt continued to serve as Governor of New York. He spent a portion of the month of November at Warm Springs, Georgia, where he was for the most part during the second half of January. Following eleven days at sea on Vincent Astor's yacht in early February, the President-elect was in New York City and at Hyde Park throughout the three-week period preceding his inauguration.

Naturally these months were marked by public discussion of what the President-elect would do. There was general agreement that, on the basis of campaign utterances, no clear cut course was certain. Much conjecture arose over his problems in organization of the Democratic party. Little consideration—except such as was forced by action of President Hoover—was given the Roosevelt position on domestic or foreign policy.

Surprisingly little attention was accorded Mr. Roosevelt's probable position on the proposed stabilization of world currency. On the whole, what was thought to be the general attitude of the President-elect was reflected in a comment of the day: "We will have to wait until March 4."

As a matter of fact, careful examination of the record of these weeks shows that no waiting was possible. The "party" had to be organized before it took office; the questions raised by Mr. Hoover had to be answered; some assurance had to be given the representatives of foreign nations. Routine matters could be postponed during this period of waiting. But the widespread unemployment, the financial uncertainty, and the general public unrest—all called for action. As yet, action was the responsibility, increasingly impossible, of Mr. Hoover.

Moreover, pressing problems in international relations had to be met. The fact that "foreign affairs" had not been an issue in the Presidential campaign should not blind one to the fact that throughout the campaign international problems pressed constantly upon the President. Some of these problems had to be acted upon in the period prior to the inauguration. Stabilization of currency and adjustment of war debts were closely interwoven with disarmament proposals and the whole question of the extent of American participation in world economic affairs. Yet impending change in the outlook of the incoming administration was not, however, suspected at the time.[6]

Immediately following the election, Mr. Hoover had given thought to what he has called the possibility of constructive action within the area outside of conflict between the incoming and outgoing administrations. President Hoover had taken preliminary steps in assuring the attendance of representatives of the United States at the World Economic Conference

---

[6] Louis B. Wehle (in *Hidden Threads of History*, pp. 118-121) states that on November 16, 1932, at Albany, Roosevelt reviewed with him the problems of the war debts and Wehle suggested that William C. Bullitt might take a trip to Europe to obtain information for the use of the President-elect. Mr. Roosevelt said he could see no harm in Bullitt going over "purely on his own for a look-see." Bullitt did go, reported his findings to Wehle by cable, and returned just before Christmas. Bullitt reported to Roosevelt on December 27. Roosevelt conceived the idea of himself making a trip to Europe prior to inauguration, and had Bullitt work out "an itinerary for their projected swing among some of the capitals." Roosevelt abandoned this idea, but Bullitt did make a second trip—sailing on January 13 and returning on February 15.

which had been in prospect for more than a year.[7] He assumed
that the new administration would wish to appoint a delegation, and, indeed, to make plans at once to provide its own
program. In addition, he had before him information that the
European debtor governments wished to postpone their December fifteenth payments on loans from the United States. The
President brought these matters to the attention of Mr. Roosevelt on November 12 and, having outlined his own view, invited the President-elect to a conference at the White House
the following week.

In his telegram to Mr. Roosevelt, President Hoover referred
not only to the problems growing out of the expiration in
December of the moratorium on war debts, but also to steps
necessary in preparation for the World Economic Conference,
to the question of American representation at the meeting of a
forthcoming World Disarmament Conference, and to international problems involved in the Japanese invasion of Manchuria.

Mr. Hoover had frequently made it clear that in his mind
any possible peace in Europe absolutely required some common
action on the matter of war debts, and a continuation of effort,
including our own, toward agreement as to limitation of armaments. But he had been careful to reassert his belief that, although the United States would not recognize violation of
treaties, it would not in his opinion use force to preserve peace.

Writing of this later, Mr. Hoover summed it up: "For on the
foreign front my positive influence was ended, as no foreign
government would come to an agreement with me unless they
knew that Mr. Roosevelt approved it. As he had not criticized
my foreign policies during the campaign, I naturally expected
that we could cooperate in that field.[8]

Any period of transition of political power is packed with uncertainty. In 1933 it was aggravated by increasing tensions in
every part of the world. The coalition government in Great
Britain was an uncertain factor in all calculations for the future.
The French government was unusually unstable. The rising
power of Hitler was to be dramatically emphasized almost at

---

[7] W. S. Myers, *The Foreign Policies of Herbert Hoover*, 1929-1933, chapter XI.
[8] Herbert Hoover, *Memoirs: 1929-1941*, p. 177. But see Roosevelt, *Personal
Letters, 1928-1945*, I, 209.

the moment of Roosevelt's accession to the Presidency. Soviet Russia, unrecognized by the United States, was still suspect among Americans. In the Far East, Japan was a threat to every interest that the United States had previously felt to be imperative to international understanding. The foreign policies of the new administration would be formulated in the light of this tense situation.

The President-elect accepted President Hoover's invitation to confer with him, and suggested that "the immediate question raised by the British, French, and other notes creates a responsibility which rests upon those now vested with executive and legislative authority." [9]

The conference of the President and President-elect was held on November 22. It was attended as well by Secretary Ogden Mills of the Treasury and by Mr. Raymond Moley, one of Mr. Roosevelt's advisers at the time. Of this meeting Mr. Hoover later said, "Of course, neither Roosevelt nor Moley could be familiar with the background of these complicated matters; worse still, they were obviously suspicious that we were trying to draw them into some sort of trap. Moley took charge of the conversation for Roosevelt. I, therefore, directed myself to primary educational work upon him, as he would influence the action of the President-elect." Mr. Hoover outlined the whole situation as he saw it at that critical time, and proposed joint action by Mr. Roosevelt and himself. "I did my best to disabuse both of them of the idea that we might have any other purpose than cooperation for the good of the country. I pointed out the urgency of furthering the general world recovery which had started in July," wrote Mr. Hoover.[10]

Mr. Roosevelt had brought with him to the White House a list of questions concerning the nature of the debt agreements and other agreements which might have been made with foreign governments by the Hoover administration. In describing the preparation of these questions, Moley remarked later, "But we were agreed that the heart of the recovery program was and must be domestic. We believed that the program would be jeopardized by the reaction in and out of Congress if F.D.R.

[9] Hoover, *Memoirs: 1929-1941*, p. 179.
[10] *Ibid.*, p. 179.

became involved in complicated negotiations with foreign nations." [11]

Mr. Hoover then presented his visitors with a summary of actions and commitments before the nation. His proposals included joint consultation by Mr. Roosevelt and himself with Democratic Congressional leaders in order to secure Congressional action on his proposed reactivation of the Debt Commission. Hoover was under the impression that Roosevelt was in general accord with him on this matter, and "was astonished to find later that Mr. Roosevelt had not communicated with the Democrat members [of Congress]." [12]

That President Hoover's first effort to secure the co-operation of Mr. Roosevelt had failed was clearly revealed in a press statement by the President-elect which was, said Moley later, "of profound importance because it was the first spectacular step Roosevelt took to differentiate his foreign policy from that of the internationalists. . . . It was a warning that the New Deal rejected the point of view of those who would make us parties to a political and economic alliance with England and France—policing the world, maintaining the international *status quo*, and seeking to enforce peace through threats of war." [13]

Roosevelt's statement to the press on November 23 concurred in the four points made by the President that the debts were actual loans made with the understanding that they would be repaid; the debts of each foreign government should be considered individually rather than collectively; debt settlements in each case should take into consideration the capacity of individual nations to pay; and these indebtednesses of European nations to the United States government had no relation to reparations payments made or owed them.

In disagreement, Mr. Roosevelt said:

Once these principles of the debt relationships are established and recognized, the methods by which contacts between our government and the debtor nations may be provided are matters of secondary importance. My view is that the most convenient and effective contacts can be made through the existing agencies and constituted channels of diplomatic intercourse.

[11] Raymond Moley, *op. cit.*, p. 70. See also *Personal Letters, 1928-1945*, I, 202.
[12] Hoover, *Memoirs: 1929-1941*, p. 181.
[13] Moley, *op. cit.*, pp. 78-79.

No action of the Congress has limited or can limit the constitutional power of the President to carry on diplomatic contacts or conversations with foreign governments. The advantage of this method of maintaining contacts with foreign governments is that any one of the debtor nations may at any time bring to the attention of the Government of the United States new conditions and facts affecting any phase of its indebtedness.[14]

President Hoover again on December 17 approached Mr. Roosevelt on the problem of the foreign debts and the pending World Economic Conference, modifying his original request for joint action to co-operation in exploring the situation through a personal representative who would "sit" with the officers of the Hoover administration. Mr. Roosevelt again declined to bind the incoming administration in any way. The President-elect wrote Mr. Hoover: "However, for me to accept any joint responsibility in the work of exploration might well be construed by the debtor or other nations, collectively or individually, as a commitment—moral even though not legal, as to policies and courses of action." [15]

Personal negotiations between the President and President-elect had reached what Henry L. Stimson later termed an "impasse." Roosevelt in conversation with a mutual friend suggested that Secretary of State Stimson come to talk with him. Stimson was agreeable, but when he took up the possibility with the President, Mr. Hoover was opposed to the meeting.

However, early in January Stimson reopened the matter with the President, stressing the importance of informing the President-elect on foreign affairs, and the President yielded, suggesting that Mr. Roosevelt request of the President that the Secretary of State come for conference with the President-elect. This was done, and a conference was held at Hyde Park on January 9.

The occasion was the first meeting between Roosevelt and Stimson. They surveyed the entire international situation, and the following week Roosevelt issued a statement to the effect that American foreign policy must uphold the sanctity of international treaties. He stated, as he had hinted before, that there

---

[14] Hoover, *Memoirs: 1929-1941*, p. 183. *New York Times*, November 23, 1932.
[15] W. S. Myers and W. H. Newton, *The Hoover Administration: A Documented Narrative*, p. 296.

would be no change in the Far Eastern policy of the Hoover administration as Stimson had explained it. Unusual care is necessary in interpreting the exact meaning of the Roosevelt-Stimson conference, particularly with reference to the Far East.[16]

The fact that, on all matters involving foreign relations, Secretary Stimson played a "personal part" is one of the greatest significance. For it was clear from the outset to Secretary Stimson, as well as to President-elect Roosevelt, that the two were in fundamental agreement in their general attitude. They met several times prior to the inauguration, and after Stimson returned to private practice they met frequently in 1933 and 1934. For the period October, 1934, to June of 1940, there was correspondence, but no meeting until Stimson was appointed Secretary of War by President Roosevelt.[17]

Secretary Stimson had consulted with President Hoover on January 4 regarding Japanese aggression in Manchuria. "Meanwhile," it has been reported, "certain nations that were members of the League of Nations demanded that economic sanctions should be imposed upon Japan. This idea seemed to have the support of the State Department and was especially appealing to the judgment and ideals of Secretary Stimson, who continually advocated this policy. Hoover not only strongly opposed this policy but placed his personal veto upon it on the ground that such a policy would lead directly to war." [18] On February 23, 1933, in a memorandum to Secretary Stimson, President Hoover wrote, "As you are aware, I have all along been inflexibly opposed to the imposition of any kind of sanctions except purely public opinion." [19]

---

[16] See H. L. Stimson and McGeorge Bundy, *On Active Service in Peace and War*, pp. 289-293; Moley, *op. cit.*, pp. 94-95; and W. S. Myers, *The Foreign Policies of Herbert Hoover*, chapter XII.

[17] Richard N. Current, *Secretary Stimson: A Study in Statecraft*, pp. 123-124.

[18] Myers, *The Foreign Policies of Herbert Hoover*, pp. 162-163. The long story of Stimson's attitude and of successive proposals with reference to the Far East is succinctly presented by Richard N. Current, *op. cit.*, in particular, chapters 4 and 5.

[19] Myers, *The Foreign Policies of Herbert Hoover*, p. 168. That Secretary Stimson was fully aware of the difference between President Hoover's view of the Japanese case and his own is clearly indicated by Current, (*op. cit.*, pp. 80-81) for Mr. Hoover had stated to his Cabinet, in opposing sanctions in the Manchurian crisis, that "The Japanese never could successfully 'Japanify' China, and they had some justification for their course in Manchuria, since the disorder there hurt them economically and exposed them to danger from a 'Bol-

The way had been paved during the Roosevelt-Stimson conference for another conference at the White House of the President and the President-elect, which was held on January 20,
but without any change in the position of Mr. Roosevelt that
"Debts" and "Economic Conference" were matters for separate
discussion.[20]

Mr. Hoover's subsequent summary of the situation was to
the effect that "Roosevelt's refusal to cooperate, in view of
which negotiations and Congressional approval were impossible, prevented the re-erection of the War Debt Commission and
postponed the World Economic Conference indefinitely. Apprehensions and fears over the country were greatly increased.
In the end the Economic Conference failed. The debts were
repudiated." [21]

Defenders of the President-elect put it this way. Holding the
views of the cause of the crisis and the remedies proposed by
the administration that Mr. Roosevelt did, it was not to be expected that he would co-operate freely with political opponents
in an atmosphere of common purpose. If the common purpose
was relief of distress—yes—but in anything that touched upon
banking procedures, upon foreign debts, upon manipulation of
the currency—no. In short, any easy transition of power was
not to be expected, and no considerable number of the American people expected it to be so. The gulf was too deep.[22]

Just how Mr. Roosevelt had been preparing for his task can
be seen in a detailed examination of his movements, his words,
his decisions. He had conferred repeatedly with Raymond
Moley, at the time Professor of Public Law at Columbia University. Bernard Baruch, financier and long an adviser of Presidents, was a frequent visitor. James A. Farley, as Chairman of

shevist Russia to the north and a possible Bolshevist China' on their flank."
Sanctions, in Mr. Hoover's view, would lead to war.
    [20] Moley, *op. cit.*, pp. 96-101. Full summary of the President's position is
given in a memorandum prepared by him on January 20, as quoted in Myers,
The Foreign Policies of Herbert Hoover, pp. 229-236; also a memorandum pre-
pared on January 21, pp. 237-238.
    [21] Hoover, *Memoirs: 1929-1941*, p. 191.
    [22] See editorial, *Boston Herald*, January 19, 1933, "A Danger and a Duty,"
See also Arthur Krock in Hanson W. Baldwin and Shepard Stone (eds.), *We
Saw It Happen*, p. 8.

the Democratic National Committee deeply concerned with patronage problems, was with Roosevelt many hours.

In Washington and at Warm Springs the President-elect was visited by numerous Democratic Congressional leaders. On December 7 in New York he conferred with "bankers and industrialists." In mid-December it was reported that there was serious criticism by Senate leaders of the President-elect's lack of consultation on a legislative program. On December 19 it was reported that he spent several hours with Owen D. Young at Hyde Park.[23] On December 27, he had Bullitt and their mutual friend Wehle as dinner guests at Albany.[24] At the end of this period, it was announced that at a forthcoming conference with Senate and House Leaders there would be discussion of the proposed legislative program.

When he reached his home in New York City on January 3, Mr. Roosevelt said, he found eight hundred letters awaiting his attention. In New York and at Hyde Park, until he left for Washington on January 19, he continued his conferences including an important meeting with Congressional leaders on January 5. It was reported that at this time he took a more vigorous leadership than heretofore in matters before the Congress. On January 9, as has been said, Mr. Roosevelt conferred for several hours with the Secretary of State, Mr. Stimson, and a week later issued a statement on the Far East.

On January 18, the president-elect attended a dinner at the Harvard Club in New York City, where he said, ". . . . I've been called a radical, because I advocate change."[25] At this dinner President Lowell of Harvard, "Turning directly to Roosevelt . . . said that the most important principle for the Chief Executive is that he must always take and hold the initiative in his dealings with Congress, with his Cabinet, and generally with the public." Lowell asserted that if, as President, Roosevelt

---

[23] Following Roosevelt's consultation with Young, Huey Long telephoned Roosevelt and said: "If I had not stood by you in Chicago you could not have been nominated." He warned Roosevelt against consorting with Young, Davis, Baker, etc. Mr. Roosevelt said at the time, "Huey is one of the two most dangerous men in the United States today. We shall have to do something about him." (Tugwell, "The Progressive Orthodoxy of F D R," in *Ethics, XIV* (October, 1953), 18.

[24] At this dinner Wehle suggested to Roosevelt, "Well, if we should recognize Russia, he [Bullitt] would by all odds be your best man as the first ambassador." Wehle, *op. cit.*, pp. 119-120.

[25] *New York Times*, January 19, 1933.

would follow this principle he would undoubtedly succeed.[26]

The next day, as has been seen, the President-elect made a second visit at the White House and, although refusing to make a joint statement with President Hoover on the war debts, Mr. Roosevelt let it be known publicly that he planned to take up the war debt problem immediately after inauguration. Later in the month he conferred with the British Ambassador. Summarizing in 1938, Mr. Roosevelt wrote:

> At no time did I discourage the President from making the necessary surveys and obtaining practical proposals from other Nations. I felt, however, that the world economic situation at that time would prevent any proposal to the United States which could possibly receive the approval of the Congress, and that a wholly different line of action should be initiated—the emphasis being placed on practical steps on a wide front at home, supplementing a broad domestic program with protection for the American dollar in international exchange. When the whole machinery needed overhauling, I felt it to be insufficient to repair one or two minor parts.[27]

This summary, written with a perspective of five years, well presents the complete separation of the view of Roosevelt from that of Hoover as to the position of the United States in the world of nations. In Mr. Hoover's view, a continuity of policy was possible in matters of deepest concern—debts, disarmament, and plans for peace. Mr. Roosevelt apparently viewed these matters as subject to the changing interests of the United States. He seemed to take the position, furthermore, that the change in administration, although primarily of interest in domestic affairs, was of vital importance in our foreign relations as well.

Prior to Roosevelt's departure for a short respite at sea on Vincent Astor's yacht, widespread discussion of the Cabinet took place. Mr. Roosevelt stated that no invitations had yet been issued. In this period he conferred with such progressive Republicans as Senators Hiram Johnson and Bronson Cutting, and toured Muscle Shoals with Senator George Norris.

At Montgomery, Alabama, on January 21, after inspecting Muscle Shoals, the President-elect gave utterance to a plan of

---

[20] Wehle, *op. cit.*, p. 134.
[27] *Public Papers, 1928-1932*, p. 868.

his administration in these words: "I am determined on two things as a result of what I have seen today. The first is to put Muscle Shoals to work. The second is to make of Muscle Shoals a part of an even greater development that will take in all that magnificent Tennessee River from the mountains of Virginia down to the Ohio and the Gulf." [28]

On February 4, Mr. Roosevelt sailed on his vacation, and on his return landed at Miami, Florida, on February 15. Declaring that he had been away from the news and free of conferences, he had taken the opportunity for a rest. In that period his aides, particularly James Farley, had been busy on matters of patronage. Others had been working on preliminary arrangements for Cabinet appointments.

To a crowd gathered at Bayfront Park, Miami, President-elect Roosevelt spoke briefly, and afterwards conversed with Mayor Anton Cermak of Chicago. It was then that Guiseppe Zangara fired several shots in the direction of the President-elect, mortally wounding Cermak. Several others, including one of the bodyguard, were wounded less seriously.

Attempted assassination of the President-elect fixed the attention of the nation on Franklin Roosevelt as a person. Had Mr. Roosevelt been killed, it is clear that he would have had little place in American history. His career as Assistant Secretary of the Navy, 1913-1919; his candidacy for the Vice-Presidency in 1920; his service as Governor of New York, 1929-1933—these had left little impression on national development.

No action of his up to this time and no statement of policy previously made had produced such a result as this escape from death. Mr. Roosevelt's very evident courage in response to this attack gave him an acclaim that strengthened him with all elements in the population, now aroused to appreciation of the dangers of violence. At the same time, the incident emphasized the nervous uncertainty of a baffled and distressed people. It put a premium on action—any action—and discounted discussion of causes or niceties of treatment in matters of finance, foreign relations, and relief.

Resumption of the task of organizing the incoming administration began on the train carrying the President-elect from

---

[28] *Ibid.*, p. 888.

Florida to New York City, where he arrived at 4 P.M. on February 17. En route he conferred with Cordell Hull, whom he
was to appoint Secretary of State; and with Carter Glass, who
declined the Secretaryship of the Treasury because the President-elect would not give satisfactory assurances on maintaining
the gold standard.[29] Roosevelt also conferred with Senator Cutting, and on the eighteenth saw sixty or seventy persons including William H. Woodin, who was to become Secretary of
the Treasury. He talked with Henry Wallace, who was to be
appointed Secretary of Agriculture. Mr. Roosevelt talked on
the telephone with Secretary Stimson and that evening attended
a dinner of the "Inner Circle" at which he received from President Hoover a private letter appealing for concerted action to
meet the growing danger of a complete financial collapse.

The President stated in his letter that he had been
attempting to get in touch with Mr. Roosevelt since February 6. Despite the failure of previous attempts to obtain the
co-operation of the President-elect, Mr. Hoover felt that conditions were so serious that another attempt must be made. He
wrote:

> A most critical situation has arisen in this country of which I
> feel it is my duty to inform you confidentially. I am therefore
> taking this course of writing you myself and sending it to you
> through the Secret Service for your hand direct as obviously its
> misplacement would only feed the fire and increase the dangers.

> The major difficulty is the state of the public mind, for there is
> a steadily degenerating confidence in the future which has
> reached the height of general alarm. I am convinced that a very
> early statement by you upon two or three policies of your Ad-
> ministration would serve greatly to restore confidence and cause
> a resumption of the march of recovery.

> It would steady the country greatly if there could be prompt
> assurance that there will be no tampering or inflation of the
> currency; that the budget will be unquestionably balanced,
> even if further taxation is necessary; that the Government
> credit will be maintained by refusal to exhaust it in the issue
> of securities . . .[30]

[29] Hoover, *Memoirs: 1929-1941*, p. 204.
[30] In the President's Secretary's File, *1933-1935*, Box 8, in the Roosevelt Library is the long-hand letter of Mr. Hoover (on White House stationery) and

Too little attention has hitherto been given this attempt of President Hoover to obtain support from the President-elect. In view of the failure of all previous attempts to obtain co-operation, it is not strange that Mr. Hoover should have tried by private letter to bring home to the President-elect the gravity of the crisis, and to use this final means of persuasion.

On March 1, "after an elapse of twelve days," Mr. Roosevelt's reply to Mr. Hoover's letter was received at the White House.[31] The delay has never been satisfactorily explained, although Mr. Roosevelt offered an excuse for his failure to reply to a handwritten letter from the President of the United States:

> I am dismayed to find the enclosed which I wrote in New York a week ago did not go to you, through an assumption by my secretary that it was only a draft of a letter.

The inclosure stated:

> I am equally concerned with you in regard to the gravity of the present banking situation—but my thought is that it is so very deepseated that the fire is bound to spread in spite of anything that is done by way of mere statements. The real trouble is that on present values very few financial institutions anywhere in the country are actually able to pay off their deposits in full, and the knowledge of this fact is widely held. Bankers with the narrower viewpoint have urged me to make a general statement, but even they seriously doubt if it would have a definite effect.
>
> . . . . frankly I doubt if anything short of a fairly general withdrawal of deposits can be prevented now.[32]

The President-elect's secretary, Grace Tully, wrote later: "Reading the Hoover letter from a distance of sixteen years, it remains, as Roosevelt felt it to be, a 'cheeky' document. By im-

---

with it the plain envelope addressed to Mr. Roosevelt as President-elect. On the envelope is written "Delivered to me at the 'Inner Circle' Dinner in N. Y., at 11 p.m. Feb. 18, 1933. F.D.R." Included with this is a second letter from Mr. Hoover dated February 28 and received at Hyde Park on March 1; also a carbon copy of a reply to Mr. Hoover's first letter written at "49 East 65th Street" on February 20, but mailed from Hyde Park on March 1.

[31] Myers and Newton, *The Hoover Administration*, p. 344.

[32] *Ibid.*, 344-345. Myers and Newton recall (p. 345) that "Mr. Roosevelt's statement . . . that 'the real trouble is that on present values very few financial institutions anywhere in the country are actually able to pay off their depositors,' he obviously learned later to be untrue."

plication it asked Roosevelt to abandon his own program and accept that of a discredited administration." [33]

Meanwhile, Mr. Hoover's second appeal to Mr. Roosevelt on February 28, referred to the situation as "even more grave," and claimed that "lack of confidence extended further" than when he wrote to Mr. Roosevelt ten days before. Stating that he felt a declaration from Mr. Roosevelt would restore confidence and that an early meeting of Congress would make for stability in the public mind, Mr. Hoover warned that "There are contingencies in which immediate action may be absolutely essential in the next few days." He closed the letter with the declaration: "I wish to assure you of the deep desire of my colleagues and myself to cooperate with you in every way." [34]

Mr. Hoover wrote later:

. . . up to the day I left the White House, more than 80 per cent of the banks in the country, measured by deposits, were still meeting all depositors' demands. I, therefore, refused to declare a holiday but constantly proposed, up to the last moment of my Presidency (eleven P.M. of March 3rd), to put into effect the executive order controlling withdrawals and exchanges if Mr. Roosevelt would approve. That would have effectively prevented practically all the banks from closing and given time for the panic to subside. At this last moment I called Roosevelt on the telephone, and he, in the presence of Senator Glass, again declined.[35]

In the interval between Mr. Hoover's appeal of February 17 and his own reply, the President-elect continued his conferences in New York City and at Hyde Park. Mr. Roosevelt saw British, French, and Canadian government representatives. Appointments announced were inclusive of Hull, Woodin, and George Dern, who was appointed Secretary of War. After his return from Florida there is increasing evidence that, despite denials and perhaps disinclination, the President-elect was conveying decisions in conversation and otherwise that indicated

[33] *F.D.R., My Boss*, p. 63.
[34] Herbert Hoover to Franklin D. Roosevelt. February 28, 1933. Hoover Archives.
[35] Hoover, *Memoirs: 1929-1941*, p. 213.

he was already thought of by his associates as the President. It could hardly be otherwise.[36]

At the opening of the final week before his inauguration, Mr. Roosevelt announced the expected appointment of James A. Farley as Postmaster General and of Henry Wallace as Secretary of Agriculture. There followed quickly the designation of Claude A. Swanson as Secretary of the Navy; of Harold Ickes as Secretary of the Interior; and then the appointments of Thomas J. Walsh, Attorney General; and of Frances Perkins as the first woman Cabinet member in the post of Secretary of Labor. Daniel C. Roper was to be appointed Secretary of Commerce.

These appointments confirmed the speculations of previous news stories that the Cabinet would include representatives of the party organization, of the Congress, and of the non-Democratic supporters such as Wallace and Ickes. On Monday, February 27, at Hyde Park, Mr. Roosevelt began composition of his inaugural address. By this time it was an accepted fact—accepted by all save Mr. Hoover, perhaps—that Roosevelt would not join the President in a statement to ease the existing financial crisis.

Mr. Hoover wrote later:

> The election by its determination of an abrupt change in national policies naturally brought a break in the march of confidence and recovery. This hesitation quickly transformed itself into alarm among an enlarging circle who were convinced that under the new policies the gold standard would be abandoned, that inflation and enormous government outlays and borrowing would be undertaken.[37]

Throughout this period of personal struggle, President Hoover was interested in "recovery"; [38] President-elect Roosevelt, in "reform." There can be no other conclusion. By March 1, it was apparent that any effort to deal with the immediate crisis would depend upon action that President Hoover

---

[36] Wehle (*op. cit.*, p. 123) makes much of the Bullitt relationship as indicating: the amount of information that Franklin Roosevelt had of the foreign situation; and the need of a greater assumption of power by the elected but as yet uninvested President.

[37] Hoover, *The Challenge to Liberty*, pp. 170-171.

[38] Hoover, *Memoirs: 1929-1941*, p. 40.

was prepared to take by himself. He nevertheless persisted in his appeals to the President-elect.

The latter arrived in Washington on the morning of March 2, holding conferences all day and again on March 3. At four o'clock that afternoon his courtesy call on the President was utilized by the latter for yet another appeal; Mr. Hoover could not believe that Mr. Roosevelt could not be moved by the urgency of the crisis. To the end, however, the President-elect maintained an independent position.

Mr. Moley, in describing the events of this period as a whole, wrote:

> Roosevelt went serenely through those days on the assumptions that Hoover was perfectly capable of acting without his concurrence; that there was no remedy of which we knew that was not available to the Hoover Administration; that he could not take any responsibility for measures over whose execution he would have no control; and that, until noon of March 4th, the baby was Hoover's anyhow. . . ." [39]

Subsequently Mr. Moley provided another explanation of the final struggle between Herbert Hoover and Franklin Roosevelt.[40] Roosevelt had successfully asserted his will over that of Hoover. The latter afterwards wrote:

> It is not difficult to explain why we had a panic of bank depositors during the few days before March 4, 1933. It was simply because the bank depositors were frightened. Their fright had mounted steadily for two months. What were they afraid of? Surely not an outgoing administration with but a few days to run. Certainly not of the foreign countries, for they were steadily recovering. It was fear of the incoming administration.[41]

It is perhaps of some significance that on February 27 the President-elect wrote the first draft of his inaugural address. The phrase "the only thing we have to fear is fear itself" does not appear in this draft. But the full force of the Hoover appeals was based upon the fear that was increasingly apparent among the people of the nation because, he believed, of a lack of any statement from the President-elect. In a subsequent

---

[39] Moley, *op. cit.*, p. 143.
[40] Hoover, *Memoirs: 1929-1941*, p. 215.
[41] *Ibid.*, pp. 215-216.

draft of the inaugural address—just when, is not known—appeared the statement on "fear."

That the incoming and outgoing Presidents held irreconcilable views on foreign and domestic policies should by this time have been apparent to both. They had long expressed basic differences in doctrine. Roosevelt perceived this; Hoover apparently did not.

The moves of the President-elect; his repeated refusal to accept either the foreign or the domestic policies of the government he was to take over; his utterances given the press—all indicated that the new administration intended to start, as they said, a "new deal." [42] In short, perhaps the most stupendous decision made by Mr. Roosevelt after the election, was *not* to co-operate, not to give reassurances at home or abroad that the present measures or anything like them should be continued.

Yet it would seem that the President-elect was torn between two impulses—to co-operate with President Hoover, and *not* to co-operate. That the latter impulse prevailed is the theme of the interregnum. The story is complicated by the pressure of events on the international as well as on the national scene.

Many who had examined his record as governor had asked for particulars and had felt uncertain because they did not foresee, as they said in public and in private, the emergence of a leader powerful enough to deal with the crisis. They agreed that only a powerful leader could succeed where so powerful a leader as Mr. Hoover had failed with the Congress and now with the electorate.

In this situation, a leader with a generally known program would have been at a disadvantage. A successful leader would be one who would be accepted by the people in the belief that he would have a solution for problems after he assumed office. How limited was the President-elect's vision of opportunity for political reformation may be seen in the summary made of his views as expressed to George Creel just before his departure for Washington. There was certainly nothing strikingly new in this statement.[43]

---

[42] See Moley, *op. cit.*, illustration facing p. 146.
[43] George Creel, *Rebel at Large*, pp. 271-273.

The influence of the President-elect, which was very great at the time, was to be exerted to make the utmost possible use of the effect of "expectation."

So long had Democrats and Progressives been thwarted in their attempts to make plans for a new America, that the great opportunity which would be theirs after March 4 gave rise to a very lively expectation of success. This shines through the temporary despondency of the financial crisis. After all, the newcomers and their supporters reasoned, that had been caused by the outgoing administration! It would soon be disposed of and America would resume her progress.

Subsequently, Mr. Roosevelt, in the first volume of his *Public Papers*, published in 1938, provided an explanation of his action and lack of action during the interregnum. He wrote:

> It is well to remember that during the trying days of January, February and the first three days of March, prior to my Inauguration, I was a private citizen wholly without authority, express or implied. The Congress of the United States was Democratic by a narrow margin in both Houses. For me to have taken part in the daily relations between the Executive and the Congress would have been not only improper, but wholly useless. On only one occasion was my opinion asked by Congressional leaders. It had been suggested that a general sales tax be imposed to meet the great and growing deficit in the Treasury. For many years I had expressed my opposition to a general sales tax, on the ground that such a tax bore inevitably far more heavily on the poor than on the rich. This I told to the Democratic Congressional leaders. The proposed tax was not pressed.[44]

He then revealed a far more urgent reason for maintaining independence of the outgoing administration:

> For the President-elect to dabble with superficial remedies would have been to impair or destroy the efficacy of the drastic, far-reaching actions which were put into effect in the "One Hundred Days" immediately following March 4th. To attack one symptom by weak methods would have impaired the broad attack on a score of fronts which came later. No participation by me as a private citizen would have prevented the crisis; such

---

[44] *Public Papers, 1928-1932*, p. 871.

participation in details would have hampered thoroughgoing action under my own responsibility as President.[45]

This, then, was the leader who drove with Mr. Hoover to the Capitol on March 4 to take oath of office as President. Of course few saw him as he has been depicted in the foregoing account of the previous four months. Certainly he, himself, has left no analytical view of what he had said and done. No memory, however powerful, could have accomplished that feat.

Although some commentators attempted at the time to show the pattern, they were lamed by lack of knowledge of the record later revealed in letters, interviews, and telephone calls. As for the public at large, they understood little that was taking place, and for prophecies of exactly what was to happen they cared less. A ruler had come to power. They liked him. He inspired confidence. Finally, he seemed now to have an opportunity to act. Would he do so?

Franklin Delano Roosevelt was fully aware of the national crisis when he took office. Every aspect of the crisis had been brought to his attention. He had prepared the way for action to the extent possible to him by his conferences with party leaders, by his selection of his Cabinet, by his ceaseless conferences with advisers, and by the organization of his thought in the preparation and revision of his inaugural address.

In its very nature, the inaugural address provided no detailed program for either Executive or Congressional action. It did state the view of the author as to the exact nature and precise cause of the crisis. It did reflect his determination of the extent to which he would act. It clearly indicated that risks would be taken, that unusual powers would be used, and that the executive intended pronounced leadership. Such a courageous and optimistic attitude expressed by any President would have heartened many. Back of the words stood a record, known to some; an assurance of party support, known to all; and a growing body of personal supporters who would help to interpret his acts to the country and to the world.

---

[45] *Ibid.* This summary completely ignores the danger of such an approach to foreign affairs because, notwithstanding the lack of debate upon them in the Presidential campaign of 1932, it was a fact that action on disarmament (by conference agreement at Geneva) and on "debts" and on currency stabilization (by conference planned for London) could not be postponed.

Franklin Roosevelt had spent nearly eight years in Washington as a minor but influential official—in six years of peace and two years of war. In a sense he was prepared for the atmosphere of Washington and the "place" of the President.

The influence of this President upon developments of the next few years would be very great. How far it would be beneficial would depend upon the immediate results in restoration of confidence, business activity, production in farm and factory, and in providing buying power to insure resumption of employment for millions. In the meantime, there were still a sufficient number of critics to make it certain that every view of his actions would be presented to the people.

What evidence appears in this period as to the nature of the power Franklin Roosevelt was to exert throughout the remainder of his life as President of the United States? An answer to this question may be briefly summarized now, and expanded as the narrative develops. There was revealed a leader who would consult with many, discuss with a few, and act with decision. Decision would carry with it ample evidence of finality, yet always include as well a promise of readjustment upon later review.

This leadership was appealing to the people as a whole, yet reassuring to specialists of more knowledge and interest. Little had appeared to indicate a leadership of doctrinaire view; nothing at all to indicate a thoughtless agitator; and much to indicate a public man devoting himself wholeheartedly to politics rather than to statesmanship—but nevertheless always "playing for the verdict of history." Permeating everything Franklin Roosevelt said and did at this time was a mood of supreme self-confidence born of a personal elation that was evident to everyone.

Chapter V

AN ECONOMIC PROGRAM

SINCE THE BIRTH of the nation in 1789 there had been but one crisis comparable to that of 1933. Just seventy-two years after Washington's inauguration, Lincoln took the oath of office on the eve of a rebellion born of dispute over the status of the Negro in the American democracy. Another seventy-two years had gone by and again the nation was in the grip of a crisis that threatened revolution over the status of the masses of all men in the American democracy.

On March 4, the day of inauguration, the mood of the country was emphasized by flags at half mast—honoring Senator Walsh whose recent death brought a vacancy in the new Cabinet. Before Franklin Roosevelt took his oath of office, the flags were run up, and a new outlook was embodied in the inaugural address—delivered under leaden skies as a chill wind snarled among the leafless trees before the Capitol.

The address, written by the President-elect in longhand at Hyde Park on February 27, had passed through several revisions.[1] Before he went from the Senate Chamber to the plat-

---

[1] The manuscript copy in the President's papers at Hyde Park has attached a typed memorandum of the President, dated March 25, 1933, stating "This is the original manuscript of the inaugural address. . . . A number of minor changes were made in subsequent drafts, but the final typewritten draft is substantially the same as this original." But the phrase "the only thing we have to fear is fear itself," is in the final (typewritten) draft at Hyde Park. As to its origin, there has been much speculation. See Rosenman, *Working with Roosevelt*, p. 91.

form overlooking the inauguration crowd Mr. Roosevelt inserted at the opening, "This is a day of consecration." In speaking, he added the adjective "national," [2] and said: "The people of the United States have not failed. In their need they have registered a mandate that they want direct, vigorous action." [3]

The financial crisis was real; no one could doubt it. The financial life of the nation was in a state of inanimate suspension. In the view of the outgoing administration, this condition was the result of the unwillingness of the incoming administration to co-operate in measures to restore confidence. The mass of the people were in a mood of despair. The millions of unemployed had yet to see any system of relief at the hands of the national government. For the able-bodied and the healthy there were no precedents for government aid.

President Roosevelt believed that the first of his problems was the restoration of confidence. His own words at the time embody his view of the necessity facing him.

> Values have shrunken to fantastic levels; taxes have risen; our ability to pay has fallen; government of all kinds is faced by serious curtailment of income; the means of exchange are frozen in the currents of trade; the withered leaves of industrial enterprise lie on every side; farmers find no markets for their produce; the savings of many years in thousands of families are gone. . . . More important, a host of unemployed citizens face the grim problem of existence, and an equally great number toil with little return. Only a foolish optimist can deny the dark realities of the moment.[4]

Yet a radio commentator had noted that on his way to the Capitol, Mr. Roosevelt looked "magnificently confident." According to his wife, the new President "believed in God and His guidance. He felt that human beings were given tasks to perform and with those tasks the ability and strength to put them through. He could pray for help and guidance and have faith in his own judgment as a result. The church services that

---

[2] Rosenman, *op. cit.*, pp. 90-91.
[3] *Public Papers, 1933*, p. 15.
[4] *Ibid.*, p. 11.

he always insisted on holding on Inauguration Day . . . and whenever a great crisis impended were the expression of his religious faith." [5]

Mr. Roosevelt felt that the inaugural address contained all the elements in his program.[6] It was the conviction of those who formulated this program that his addresses in the campaign had foreshadowed every important element in the New Deal. Viewed in perspective, no such pronounced result as emerged had in fact been envisaged.

As one of his closest advisers at the time saw it, "We stood in the city of Washington on March 4th like a handful of marauders in hostile territory . . . the Republican party had close to a monopoly of skillful, experienced administrators. To make matters worse, the business managers, established lawyers, and engineers from whose ranks top-drawer governmental executives so often come were, by and large, so partisan in their opposition to Roosevelt that he could scarcely be expected to tap those sources to the customary degree." [7]

During the early phases of the first administration, conspicuous as personal advisers were Raymond Moley, Rexford G. Tugwell, Adolph Berle, Hugh Johnson, and of course Louis Howe and Henry Morgenthau, Jr. The work of each of these men in contributing to the determination of public policy deserves extensive examination. As the administration moved into its second year, the influence of Secretary Ickes became very important. The contribution of such close associates as Henry Wallace, James Farley, William Woodin and Frances Perkins had become well known. Harry Hopkins was in a different category than any other adviser, as events were to show. Not coming to Washington until May 22, he became almost at once—in the eyes of eager commentators—the embodiment of the New Deal as it related to relief.

It was not clearly apparent at the time, even though much public attention was fixed upon these men, how important they were in the emerging pattern of government in the

[5] Eleanor Roosevelt, *This I Remember*, p. 69.
[6] *Public Papers, 1933*, p. 5.
[7] Moley, *op. cit.*, pp. 128-130.

"progressive" spirit.[8] The people as a whole had voted to take over their own government. That was Mr. Roosevelt's view. But they had to have men in government to do this work. Experts, not elected to office, were to aid the President in his task.

To identify Franklin Roosevelt with the attitude of these experts who seemed, during the years 1933-1937, to speak for the nation, is to misunderstand him completely. It is possible that the time may come when a product of professional training in the social sciences will be elected to the Presidency. By inclination or experience, Mr. Roosevelt was not of such a group, however much he valued and used their services and however often, on occasion, he used their language. When he spoke of the American people he meant, as he visualized them, a people with somewhat the same attitude toward democracy, toward party, toward progress, toward reform, that he had. He conceived of reformers as men of action, rather than as men of thought. Roosevelt and the People were one.

Clearly, semi-dictatorial powers had been granted the President. The Fascist press in Italy, commenting on the inaugural address, commended the cutting short of "the purposeless chatter of legislative assemblies."

The President was fortunate in being able at once to assert positive leadership. Meeting with his Cabinet on Sunday, March 5, he issued a proclamation at eleven o'clock that evening ordering a bank holiday from March 6 to 9. This he did under a war enabling act passed during the administration of Woodrow Wilson. It was plain that this "negative" action would be followed at once by affirmative action in providing more rigid governmental control of banking. This the President initiated in a message to the Congress, which he called into session on March 9.[9]

Congress responded to Presidential leadership with speed, but in a manner to cause much misgiving that such conduct

---

[8] The most exhaustive revelation to date of the continuous and effective influence of "progressives" upon the President is found in *The Secret Diary of Harold L. Ickes.*

[9] It is important to remember that the Democratic party organization dominant in the Congress since the elections of 1930 had no plans for dealing with financial disaster and economic chaos, although many measures had been proposed by individual Congressmen.

was necessary even in time of crisis. Representative Snell, Republican Leader of the House said, "The situation is so terrible at the present time that we must accept the Administration's recommendations aimed to open the banks and pass the legislation without delay."

Within eight hours and a half, Congress had rushed through the emergency banking legislation giving the President power to reopen banks with qualifications as to solvency. The Senate vote, after three hours of discussion, was 73 to 7. The House passed the bill unanimously, it was reported, after forty minutes. But because the Treasury Department had to make certain regulations, the President had to proclaim an extension of the bank holiday.

The so-called Economy Bill, which the President had requested to enable him to make certain cuts in the Budget, passed the House only because 69 Republicans (62%) voted for it along with 197 Democrats (68%). In the Senate the vote for passage was 62-13, 19 Republicans voting affirmatively. In this Congress were approximately one hundred and fifty representatives serving their first term of office.

The President had explained his point of view at his first press conference on March 8 and "delighted" the press with his candor. On Sunday evening, March 12, Mr. Roosevelt outlined the banking situation to the nation in a fifteen-minute radio address. The commentator Will Rogers wrote, "Well, he made everybody understand it, even the bankers." [10] When the "Beer Bill," amending the Volstead Act, passed the House 316-97, Rogers was saying, "I don't know what additional authority Roosevelt may ask, but give it to him, even if it's to drown all the boy babies. . . . It just shows you what a country can do when you take their affairs out of the hands of Congress."

The response of the country to the new leadership was immediate, and on the whole favorable. The vigorous support in definite Congressional action was proof that the President had successfully asserted aggressive leadership.

---

[10] "The draft of this address had been submitted to us at the Treasury for suggestions, thus insuring full harmony with Treasury ideas." (Arthur A. Ballantine, Under-Secretary of the Treasury until May, 1933. "When All the Banks Closed," in *Harvard Business Review*, March, 1948, p. 140.)

President Roosevelt saw the nation's emergency as long in the making. In amplifying his view of this in 1934, he wrote:

> After the World War, a wholly unplanned pyramiding of production and of speculation had left the country in such condition that methods of recovery used in previous periods of depression were useless.[11]

He had seen it as

> . . . an emergency that went to the roots of our agriculture, our commerce and our industry; it was an emergency that had existed for a whole generation in its underlying causes and for three and one-half years in its visible effects. It could be cured only by a complete reorganization and a measured control of the economic structure.[12]

Yet, as he faced the tasks of the coming months, the country was still divided on his general policy as on no political issue since 1861. The proposals it was feared he would make were so divergent from the action of previous administrations and had been so lacking in development in his campaign utterances that the atmosphere of fear, in being dispelled, was followed by one of constant suspense and growing distrust.

Although Mr. Roosevelt did not publicly plead for the repeal of the Eighteenth Amendment, the President had on March 13 quoted to Congress what he termed "almost literally the language of the Democratic Platform," in recommending "immediate modification of the Volstead Act, in order to legalize the manufacture and sale of beer . . . and to provide through such manufacture and sale, by substantial taxes, a proper and much needed revenue for the Government." [13]

The President's aim now, as expressed to Congress on March 16, was to restore purchasing power to farmers. This was to be accomplished by the reduction of acreage for certain basic crops, thus lowering the market supply; and by relief of the farmer from the pressure of mortgages on his farm and his home. The Agricultural Adjustment Act (AAA) of May 12 was in time the outcome of this request.

---

[11] *On Our Way*, p. 85.
[12] *Ibid.*, p. 35.
[13] *Ibid.*, p. 37.

Then followed the President's recommendation of the Civilian Conservation Corps, the fruition of a long-cherished idea.[14] This measure made it possible to employ 300,000 young men in relief work on forest conservation, flood control, and the prevention of soil erosion.

Further measures for unemployment relief by the federal government, for grants to states for relief work, and for a broad public works labor-creating program were requested. The Federal Emergency Relief Act, which became law on May 12, provided financial aid to states. Harry L. Hopkins was appointed Federal Relief Administrator. Public works were authorized on June 16, a Federal Works Administration was appointed on July 8, and on August 19 its functions and powers were authorized by Executive Order.[15] Secretary of the Interior Harold L. Ickes was placed in charge.

Protection of investors in the purchase of securities was requested by the President in a recommendation to the Congress for legislation for federal supervision of "traffic in investment securities in interstate commerce," in order to "protect the public with the least possible interference to honest business." [16] The Securities and Exchange Act of May 27 was the result.

Suggestion was made on April 10 that Congress create a Tennessee Valley Authority to develop national planning of power development, flood control, soil erosion, afforestation, withdrawal of marginal lands from agricultural use, and control of industry throughout the area served by the Tennessee River. Mr. Roosevelt envisaged in this great project "a return to the spirit and vision of the pioneer," and hoped for "a like development of other great natural territorial units within our borders." [17]

Of this period in the development of the New Deal, President Roosevelt wrote:

Every day that went by not only brought before me and the Cabinet and the Congress some new emergency need which

---

[14] See Eleanor Roosevelt, *This I Remember*, p. 135.

[15] One cannot write of the Roosevelt domestic policy, 1933-1938, without giving a large place to the work of Harry Hopkins. Much that is associated with the name of Franklin Roosevelt in terms of *relief* was the work of Hopkins. Nor in judging Roosevelt can one ignore the fact that he came to look upon Hopkins as a possible successor.

[16] *On Our Way*, p. 45.

[17] *Ibid.*, pp. 55-56.

cried out for action, but it gave us the opportunity to sift out
the more distressful of the depression conditions and to move
forward to the attack.[18]

Meanwhile, in view of the alarming shrinkage in gold re-
serves, the President had called into the banks all outstanding
gold, whether coin, bullion, or gold certificates, and by Executive Order of April 20 proclaimed an embargo on shipments of
gold. He was gratified by the result, almost immediate, by
which, as he saw it, "American exchange weakened in terms of
foreign currencies; and the price level at home went up substantially." [19]

As President Roosevelt in the spring of 1933 viewed the
financial situation, one course was liquidation through bank-
ruptcies and foreclosures. The other was a deliberate increase
of property values.

But the President insisted that "When the United States
went off the gold basis in April, 1933 . . . the country understood that the dollar was just as good a dollar as it had been
before, and that, in fact, we proposed to make it a more honest
dollar than it had been during the three and one-half years of
constant and growing deflation." [20]

Said the President of the significance of the embargo on gold:

> Many useless volumes could be written as to whether on April
> twentieth the United States actually abandoned the gold stand-
> ard. In one sense, we did not because the legal gold content of
> the dollar was unchanged and because the Government and the
> banks retained all gold as the basis for currency. On the other
> hand, gold here in the United States ceased to be a medium of
> exchange.[21]

In a message to Congress formally outlined on May 17, the
President called for "a great cooperative movement throughout
all industry in order to obtain wide re-employment, to shorten
the working week, to pay a decent wage for the shorter week
and to prevent unfair competition and disastrous over-produc-
tion." Mr. Roosevelt wrote, "As far back as the autumn of
1930, I had begun to discuss ways and means for the relief of

---

[18] *Ibid.*, pp. 58-61.
[19] *Ibid.*, p. 62.
[20] *Ibid.*, pp. 62-63.
[21] *Ibid.*, p. 61.

unemployment and for the reconstituting of our economic machinery." In applying to industry "a concept new in our history," the President hoped that through the co-operation of employees and of labor in developing "codes" for each industry, "wide re-employment would result through the shortening of the working week, that child labor could be eliminated and that a decent minimum wage could be guaranteed to every worker." [22] This new venture in the industrial life of the United States was to take form eventually in the National Recovery Act.

"Before leaving Washington on June seventeenth," said Mr. Roosevelt in description of the events of this time, "I gave out the following statements about the Recovery Act, which I think are worth reprinting because so much of our future history will date back to this moment":

> History probably will record the National Industrial Recovery Act as the most important and far-reaching legislation ever enacted by the American Congress. It represents a supreme effort to stabilize for all time the many factors which make for the prosperity of the Nation, and the preservation of American standards.[23]

In reporting to the nation by radio on May 7, the President had reviewed the accomplishment of eight weeks in a crisis that "did not call for any complicated consideration of economic panaceas or fancy plans." As the President saw it, "We were faced by a condition and not a theory." That condition the President called "deflation." In dealing with this situation, the Congress "still retained its constitutional authority and no one has the slightest desire to change the balance of these powers. . . . The only thing that has been happening has been to designate the President as the agency to carry out certain of the purposes of the Congress. This was constitutional and in keeping with the past American tradition." [24]

Said the President, further:

> . . . The people of this country have been erroneously encouraged to believe that they could keep on increasing the output

---

[22] *Ibid.*, pp. 84-89.
[23] *Ibid.*, p. 97.
[24] *Ibid.*, pp. 71-72

of farm and factory indefinitely and that some magician would find ways and means for that increased output to be consumed with reasonable profit to the producer. . . . We are working toward a definite goal, which is to prevent the return of conditions which came very close to destroying what we call modern civilization.[25]

A *New York Times* editorial on the May 7 Fireside Chat was highly favorable, the only criticism centering on the idea of the flexible dollar: "The President himself did no boasting, indulged in no flamboyant prophecies, and confined himself to telling the people modestly in everyday language what he and Congress have been driving at the past two months," was the comment, with the reflection that "from it all the country cannot fail to take courage. Perhaps the spirit shown by the President counts more than any one thing which he said. To think of him as an ambitious dictator is ridiculous. He steps forward merely as a leader and a fellow-worker in the effort to bring the nation through an unprecedented emergency." [26]

The New Deal that was thus launched in the first hundred days of his administration was, as the President saw it, "a satisfactory combination of the Square Deal and the New Freedom . . . the fulfilment of the progressive ideas expounded by Theodore Roosevelt of a partnership between business and government and also of the determination of Woodrow Wilson that business should be subjected, through the power of government, to drastic legal limitations against abuses." [27]

The President felt, furthermore, that:

In any event, the overwhelming majority of the business men in May, 1933, were entirely willing to go along with a great cooperative movement directed by the Government and working towards the elimination of the costly practices of the past.[28]

There had been a swing of a large number of conservatives to the Roosevelt standard. They were being hospitably received and legislation of importance had been revised "in the light of the experience and opinion of men who work in the

[25] *Ibid.*, pp. 75-77.
[26] *New York Times*, May 9, 1933.
[27] *On Our Way*, Foreword, p. x.
[28] *Ibid.*, p. 86.

financial districts of the great cities." [29] The boom support and stock market speculation of the 'twenties was thus in a way matched by the "risks" taken on the New Deal by the American people as a whole.

The financial and industrial groups were actually the first to be rescued by the New Deal, which in the perspective of history must stand as the substitution of "government inflation, risk, experiment, and, indeed, speculation, for almost complete private responsibility in this respect . . . substitution . . . initiated and progressively developed at the request, or with the connivance, of powerful leaders in banking, industry, agriculture, and labor organizations. . . ." [30]

Ultimately a day by day—not to say hour by hour—account of the events of 1933 will bring to the reader as near a reproduction as it is possible to furnish. It will be false to the truth, however, if it does not convey the sense of emergency, the feeling of desperate need, the determination that the will to live should be expressed in ceaseless activity.

By June 16, a Congress that had done the President's bidding toward relief, recovery—and reform—adjourned. That the response to this program had been varied was to be expected. On the whole, however, the country gave approval of action in all of these fields while waiting the degree of success that would attend it. Irrespective of the effects to be seen in labor, farming, and industry, it was clear—even in June—that the government of the United States had taken an advanced position.

In this, the aides to the President had been far more aggressive than any group in the Congress, even though individuals in both Senate and House—some of long experience in legislation of this kind—gave enthusiastic support. The President's personal advisers, who played an important part in the early months of the administration, were clearly working toward legislative and administrative action in three fields of great interest to elements that had given support to the Democratic ticket—the farmer, the laborer, and the small business man so dependent upon loans and an active market.

Even as early as mid-April there was, however, restiveness among the more experienced members of Congress, who de-

---

[29] Arthur Krock, in the *New York Times*, April 15, 1933.
[30] C. A. Beard, and G. H. E. Smith, *The Old Deal and the New*, p. 277.

clared that speed had already resulted in ill-considered legislation. A group of Republican members of Congress issued a statement to the effect that the administration's inflation legislation "violates the most elementary principles of sound monetary credit and financial policies. It is better designed to defeat than to promote business recovery." [31]

The battle over monetary policy was thus launched early in the new administration. Disagreement among the President's advisers was particularly acute. "It was a battle not so much of men as of two conflicting schools of thought," commented James P. Warburg, one of the advisers, adding that the President acted "as a tireless, serene, and often amused referee." [32]

"The President listened patiently to what I had to say" against further depreciation of the currency, said Mr. Warburg of a conference with Mr. Roosevelt on September 20, 1933, "but when I was all through, he smiled and told me that all that was very pretty, but meantime how were we going to keep prices advancing? How were we going to relieve the debt burden? What were we going to do about the farmers?" [33]

Significant, in view of the fears expressed during the "interregnum," was the action of the President in this matter of currency manipulation. Although he felt justified in taking steps to control and direct what he perceived would be inevitable inflation in the hands of speculators, he said himself that the problem of the depression could best be solved by a policy that would encourage domestic inflation.

The first step in this process was the raising of commodity prices, but this was to be accomplished by raising the purchasing power of consumers by providing work for the unemployed. The cost of public relief, in the President's original plan, was to be met partly from diversion of funds allotted to the veterans' program, partly from taxes which would eventually be replaced by revenue from the sale of liquor, and partly by the issue of bonds to be paid off in the future.

When Mr. Roosevelt had asked for authority to obtain drastic retrenchment in government expenditure early in March,

---

[31] *New York Times,* April 22, 1933.

[32] Warburg, *The Money Muddle,* p. 133.

[33] *Ibid.,* p. 147.

he had not contemplated "billions" for relief. The burden on the future came in time to be a heavy one, but in the first year of the New Deal emphasis was not on financing the program of relief, but rather on the machinery by which these benefits to the people might be distributed.

In his radio address of October 22, the President, reviewing the national situation for the fourth time during the year, announced:

> When we have restored the price level, we shall seek to establish and maintain a dollar which will not change its purchasing and debt-paying power during the succeeding generation. . . . [34]

The reader must conclude from the President's summary that, as far as he was concerned, traditional economics might well give way, under pressure, to experimentation.[35]

The primary result of what his critics called "tinkering" with the currency was the furtherance of a "profound monetary revolution" [36] by which, under cover of necessity, President Roosevelt was able to accomplish what radicals for generations had demanded. The devaluation of saved income, both of institutions and of individuals, Bryan had called for, as had the "silverites" up to 1930. Roosevelt's was revolutionary action under cover of law and was a blow intended to alter, in a fundamental way, the financial structure which had been built up by those who had hitherto dominated finance in the United States, not only in private but in public life.

This, accomplished as part of the recovery program, was in fact an evidence that the reform purposes of the President and his liberal advisers were dictating the new national policy. Control of the nation would be taken out of the hands of the bankers and placed in the hands of those who had seized con-

---

[34] *On Our Way*, pp. 182-183.

[35] Wehle, who has been justly termed an expert in law, engineering, and finance, (*op. cit.*, p. 116) writes, "He instinctively avoided sustained effort or attention. The field in which this disability was most unfortunate was economic, fiscal, and monetary policy. There intuition is at a discount, because understanding causes or visualizing results calls for mastery of complex facts and arduous abstract thinking unaided by human-nature considerations. This seems to account for his selection of some inexperienced but cocksure advisers and for some of his ventures in short-cut boomerang solutions."

[36] In the words of Alvin Hansen, *Monetary Theory and Fiscal Policy*, p. 205. See also Hoover, *Memoirs, 1929-1941*, pp. 390-407; and Arthur W. Crawford, *Monetary Management under the New Deal*, especially pp. 330-352.

trol of the government under cover of a general mandate from the people. The President, guided and advised by groups convinced of the necessity of remaking the financial structure of the nation and backed by subservient Congressional majorities, was in truth remaking by executive order this financial structure not only in his own time but for the future.

Yet it was argued twenty years later that President Roosevelt compromised too much in meeting the financial crisis of 1933. The nationalization of the banking system could have been tried, had not "practical" men opposed.[37] Thus, the President compromised on "reform" in order to win "recovery." Mr. Warburg had remarked, shortly after the eventful period of President Roosevelt's first months in office that "Franklin Roosevelt will get more credit, when the final page is written, for having resisted inflation than for the steps he took in its direction." [38]

On the whole, despite the setbacks, uncertainties, and utter confusion of the summer and autumn months, the year 1933 witnessed a restoration of confidence in the future of the United States. All proposals that had been adopted were presented in a light to relate them in some degree to approved American practice and long-term improvements urged by American progressives.

It had been pointed out early in the spring that the President had done more "to start the nation toward a socialist order . . . than all the agitation carried on by all the avowedly socialist agents in our national history. . . . It is a new United States toward which Mr. Roosevelt is directing the nation." [39] Much was made by critics of the fervent declarations of New Dealers that they were at last "rearranging existing society."

A thoughtful reader comes to an amazing conclusion in considering the rapid establishment of the new program. A group of intimates of the President, although changing personnel from time to time, is seen to have exercised tremendous power in a government, not of laws or of men but of ideas. Under

[37] R. G. Tugwell, "The Compromising Roosevelt," in *Western Political Quarterly*, June, 1953.

[38] Warburg, *op. cit.*, p. 158.

[39] *Christian Century*, 50 (March 22, 1933), p. 383.

cover of the President's name and backed by all of the power residing in the executive office, these men for a time not only formulated an economic program but imposed it, in all its ever-changing aspects, upon the people of the United States.[40] Those who still say, "It can't happen here," should re-examine what happened to the United States when President Franklin D. Roosevelt and his well-meaning advisers took over in 1933. The President who had exercised his power was to be given repeated endorsement by the people in whose name he had done it.

Opinions will continue to differ on what would have been the course of domestic recovery had the President's policy in international relations been otherwise than it was. Whether the inconsistencies of his policy are to be attributed to the tremendous pressure of events upon his thinking, or to his lack of comprehension of the fundamental principles of international trade and international finance must always remain in question. Certainly there is ample evidence to support both explanations.

The unbelievable concentration of power of decision in the first weeks of the administration may easily be thought of as sufficient explanation. It must have driven all but the most immediate ideas from the mind of the President. That he was sometimes aware of the gulf between thinking and action appears again and again in his personal correspondence, as in a letter he wrote to Josephus Daniels on September 28, 1940:

> About fifteen years ago I attended one of the famous luncheons in the French mahogany carved sanctum of "The New York Times." In that rarefied atmosphere of self-anointed scholars, I had the feeling of an uneducated worm under the microscope. But the America of the satisfied professors will not survive, and the America of you and of me will.[41]

Although many minds had contributed to the origin and development of the policies which were embodied in the administration's acts and the legislation of the "hundred days," the program for the crisis came to be thought of as the Presi-

---

[40] The establishment of the Civil Works Administration and the work of Harry Hopkins as Federal Emergency Relief Administrator represents this completely.

[41] *Personal Letters, 1928-1945*, II, 1068.

dent's. A minute examination of the record of these events will
not change that primary fact. It is of unusual importance to
know what the President thought of his leadership, how he related it to the preceding events, and to what extent he used it
as a basis for subsequent action. Writing of this period in 1938,
the President said:

> From the first day of my Administration permanent security
> was just as much in the front of our minds as the temporary
> bolstering of banks, the furnishing of immediate jobs and the
> increase of direct purchasing power.[42]

The New Deal in the eyes of its sponsor embodied an active
participation of government in a promise of new benefits for
masses of workers, farmers, and business men who had been
exploited by supporters of special privilege. How completely
the President saw himself as the inheritor of the tradition of
progressive reform is seen in the words:

> Because the American system from its inception presupposed
> and sought to maintain a society based on personal liberty, on
> private ownership of property and on reasonable private profit
> from each man's labor or capital, the New Deal would insist
> on all three factors. But because the American system visualized
> protection of the individual against the misuse of private eco-
> nomic power, the New Deal would insist on curbing such power.

> A frank examination of the profit system in the spring of 1933
> showed it to be in collapse; but substantially everybody in the
> United States, in public office and out of public office, from the
> very rich to the very poor, was as determined as was my Admin-
> istration to save it.[43]

In acting for the American people, which was constantly his
declaration of purpose, Mr. Roosevelt was aware that the crisis
that was so evident in banking was duplicated in industry, in
labor, and in farming. From his point of view it was a crisis
"in the spirit and morale of our people." They were in a mood
to try extreme measures.

> . . . . Millions of people . . . had begun to feel that the machin-
> ery of modern American economics and Government had broken

---

[42] *Public Papers, 1933*, p. 4.
[43] *Ibid.*, p. 5.

down so completely under the strain of the new demands placed upon it by modern civilization, that an entirely new type of mechanics for existence would have to be invented.[44]

From this point of view, the radical and reactionary approaches were alike unsatisfactory. There must be *immediate* relief, but there must also be reform of the existing system of private property and private enterprise.

The President's view had perspective.

The task of reconstruction . . . did not call for the creation of strange values. It was rather finding the way again to old, but somewhat forgotten, ideals and values. . . . America was privileged to show the world in that year of crisis that democracy can find within itself the elements necessary to its own salvation.[45]

This was his challenge to radicals and reactionaries—at home and abroad.

In contemplating the results of the recovery program in 1933 and 1934, the President found advancement in every area in which statistics were available. He felt that reform had been strengthened as well, and pointed with particular pride to "the beginning of our whole program of social security through the appointment of a Committee to devise and recommend a Federal system of Old Age assistance, unemployment insurance, and other forms of help to underprivileged groups." [46]

The President always stressed the need of co-operation. As he said at Green Bay, Wisconsin, August 9, 1934:

It is just as hard to achieve harmonious and cooperative action among human beings as it is to conquer the forces of nature. Only through submerging of individual desires into unselfish and practical cooperation can civilization grow.[47]

As was natural, this extensive program of recovery and reform brought down upon the President charges of executive

[44] *Ibid.*, p. 3.

[45] *Ibid.*, pp. 9-10. The obvious, not to say gleeful, expectancy that animated much of the public discussion was well stated by Unofficial Observer in *The New Dealers* (p. viii): "We are having a revolution and the revolutionary process will take from ten to twenty years."

[46] *Public Papers, 1934*, pp. 3-5.

[47] *Ibid.*, p. 372.

usurpation, of unconstitutional legislation, of stifling debts and taxation and, of course, certain national bankruptcy.

This brought into sharp focus the basic assumption of the President that the causes for maladjustment and weakening of democracy were to be found in the intention and philosophy of selfish groups who had ruled in the business and governmental life of the nation, and would do so again if the President were not upheld. These groups, in turn, made plain their opposition to his program of recovery and reform—even though they reluctantly accepted most of the measures for relief. Even these were preludes to socialism—in the eyes of most of his critics.

The heart of the opposition was found among the American business men who expressed more clearly than anywhere else in the world the view dominant among industrial and financial classes. The business man knew that he was no longer favored by a government that gave increased benefits to laborers in factory, farm, and mine. And unorganized labor was favored also because it was from its ranks that came the majority of the unemployed. If the purpose of the President was to bring into "better balance," as he so often said, agriculture, labor, and industry, then it was evident that he had succeeded—to the great advantage of wage earners and consumers—that is, if the capitalistic system could stand such transformation.

Chapter VI

A FOREIGN POLICY

THE PRESIDENT, in his inaugural address, had said: "I favor as a practical policy the putting of first things first. I shall spare no effort to restore world trade by international economic readjustment, but the emergency at home cannot wait on that accomplishment." [1] Mr. Roosevelt did not believe that the depression in the United States could be conquered by international measures.[2]

Yet on foreign affairs it had not been thought in the campaign of 1932 that there was a serious issue between Mr. Roosevelt and Mr. Hoover. Nor did President-elect Roosevelt's refusal to co-operate with President Hoover on international issues during the interregnum appear at the time to have special significance apart from the refusal to co-operate on domestic affairs.

Nevertheless, roots of the later Roosevelt foreign policy are to be found in the first year of the administration and, indeed, as has been seen, in the period of the interregnum.[3] But in his annual message to Congress in January, 1934, he disposed of foreign affairs in two brief paragraphs introduced by the

---

[1] *Public Papers, 1933*, p. 14.
[2] Moley, *op. cit.*, p. 88.
[3] How important were the relations of Roosevelt with Secretary of State Stimson between January 9 and March 4, 1933, is revealed in detail in Richard N. Current, *op. cit.*, pp. 117-130.

words, "I cannot, unfortunately, present to you a picture of complete optimism regarding world affairs." [4]

In 1932, so fixed upon the domestic crisis had been the attention of the American electorate that, despite the uncertain relationships that existed in every part of the world, parties in their pronouncements had postponed discussion of basic differences over foreign policy. Had the nation been concerned in a critical way with relations with other nations, unquestionably many voters would have given thought to the fact that Mr. Roosevelt in 1920 had campaigned in favor of American adherence to the League of Nations. As has earlier been stated, at the time of his nomination for the Presidency, Franklin Roosevelt was committed *not* to favor United States participation in the League of Nations, in which he had in fact notably lost interest since the death of Woodrow Wilson.

It is of the highest importance that the Secretary of State, Cordell Hull, in whom the President had great confidence, was devoted to the cause of international co-operation. Moreover, unlike the President, Mr. Hull had the innate capacity and intuitive impulse to co-operate with persons in the United States, in and out of official life, who were repelled by the attitude and utterances of Mr. Roosevelt. This was true of Mr. Hoover, with whom Mr. Hull conferred frequently. It was also true of the "isolationists" in the Congress who, although misguided, Mr. Hull felt, were on the whole patriotic Americans believing themselves to be in the American tradition.

Shortly after the inauguration, the stage was set for the International Economic Conference, which was finally held in London from June 12 to July 27. In response to Mr. Roosevelt's invitation, many leaders representing foreign nations came to Washington in April and May for the purpose of discussing common economic problems prior to the opening of the conference. Among these representatives were Prime Minister MacDonald of Great Britain, Prime Minister Bennett of Canada, Monsieur Herriot of France, Finance Minister Jung of Italy, Ambassador Le Breton of the Argentine Republic, Finance Minister Schacht of Germany Finance Minister Pani of

---

[4] Hull, *Memoirs*, I, especially pp. 170-177; 222-280

Mexico, Finance Minister Soong of China, Senhor Brasil of Brazil, Viscount Ishii of Japan, and Señor Torres of Chili.

The President wrote later that the conversations with these representatives were "on broad lines, relating to many subjects . . . in no sense confined to stabilization of the pound, franc and dollar . . . related far more to the breaking down of trade barriers by reciprocal and other methods, and the visualization and application of world remedies to world problems." [5]

Of these talks, Secretary Hull later wrote: "Each of the conferences was without particular controversy, whatever may have been in the back of the minds of the leading participants. . . . The sum total of them all was almost precisely nothing. Moreover, the time taken up in talking to and entertaining these foreign delegations cut down the time available for the careful preparation of our Government's policies for the coming world conference and the instructions for carrying out these policies." [6]

The President had stated, at his press conference on March 13, that he did not yet know how many delegates would go to the Economic Conference, whether it would be "three or twenty-three." Party politics would not enter into the consideration of its membership. [7]

Mr. Hull noted that "The truth of the whole pre-conference situation was that nations were extremely active in discussing the important topics on the agenda, but with an astonishing amount of confusion and lack of system or orderly procedure . . . the proceedings prior to the conference grew increasingly unstable and almost chaotic. It was in this state of turmoil, cross-purposes, and frequent changes of positions by Governments that the Conference was to meet." [8]

Early in May the President, fearing, as he said at the time, a breakup of the Disarmament Conference then in session in Geneva, sent a message to the heads of governments throughout the world in which he said:

The World Economic Conference . . . must come to its conclusions quickly. The world cannot await deliberations long drawn

---

[5] *On Our Way,* p. 114.
[6] Hull, *op. cit.,* I, 247.
[7] *New York Times,* April 1, 1933.
[8] Hull, *op. cit.,* I, 247-248.

out. The Conference must establish order in place of the present chaos by a stabilization of currencies, by freeing the flow of world trade, and by international action to raise price levels.[9]

But by June it was clearly evident that events in the United States forced upon the President a leadership that put solution of internal problems on a national rather than an international basis.[10] This was a reversal of decision by the President, but it should be considered against his view of the background of economic crisis, accompanied at the moment by signs of possible recovery.

"In judging this turning of the presidential coat," wrote a British critic,

> . . . a European observer . . . must remember that in this age a President of the United States might attain his tremendously powerful office without ever having held a post of national responsibility before. Mr. Roosevelt, indeed, was well trained in public affairs; but the administration even of a state the size of England involved no concern with such questions as external trade or monetary standards. . . . Small wonder that he tended to follow the finger of changing circumstance, privy counsel, and popular emotion. To these guides he added his own rooted opinions, which included—for no light reasons in that period of American financial history—a vigorous dislike of bankers and monetary magnates. He suspected the policies they urged, and he would not choose his economic advisers from among them. The natural radicalism of his mind caused him to listen more readily to those who taught that a cheaper dollar must mean higher internal prices, and who whispered that plans for stabilization were only a European gambit to secure American gold, than to those who praised the economic security of stable exchanges and appealed to the more old-fashioned principles of economics.[11]

Nevertheless, from President Roosevelt's own account of the London Conference, as well as from the accounts of such participants as Secretary Hull, James P. Warburg, financial adviser of the American delegation, and Raymond Moley as the President's "liaison" representative whom he sent to London while

[9] *Public Papers, 1933*, pp. 185-186.
[10] *Ibid.*, pp. 245-246.
[11] H. V. Hodson, "Adjustment and Revival," in Part 1, World Economic Affairs, *Survey of International Affairs, 1933*, Arnold J. Toynbee (ed.), pp. 79-80.

the conference was in progress—a pattern of procedure emerges. This is of more importance in understanding Franklin Roosevelt's leadership than any of his pronouncements of the time.

The initial approach to the matter of the conference was, during the interregnum, a cautious one. But it was affirmative. Indeed, "The President conceived of the Conference," according to Raymond Moley, "not as a place where immediate and definitive decisions were to be made but as a study group out of which might come a crystallization of many points of view and many national aspirations. He had in mind developing through the Conference a new kind of international exchange." [12] As has been noted, Mr. Roosevelt's interest in an international society of nations had deep roots.[13]

The appointment of the American delegation from those deserving political recognition by the new President was a compromise of the kind he would continue to make. That the members of the delegation did not understand or agree on the questions for discussion is not the strangest of the circumstances of their appointment. Mr. Hull remarked that "Few mistakes can be more unfortunate than for the official head of a delegation to a world conference not to have a chance to consult with the President on the selection of the entire personnel, or at least let the personnel have that distinct impression. Otherwise there is little sense of loyalty or teamwork on the part of some, and open defiance from others." [14]

The President cabled Secretary Hull in London, "I am squarely behind you and nothing said or done here will hamper your efforts. There is no alteration of your policy or mine." [15] Yet Mr. Roosevelt had to confess that he could not lead Congress to pass the tariff legislation that he had agreed with Mr. Hull was required to sustain the bargaining position of the United States at the conference.[16]

The President sent to London a declaration, known as the

---

[12] Moley, *op. cit.*, p. 240.
[13] See chapter II.
[14] Hull, *op. cit.*, I, 254.
[15] *Ibid.*, p. 252.
[16] *Ibid.*, p. 251.

"bombshell," [17] decrying "basic economic errors that underlie so much of the present world-wide depression . . . the specious fallacy of achieving a temporary and probably an artificial stability in foreign exchange. . . . So, too, old fetishes of so-called international bankers. . . ."

Singularly lacking in the language of persuasion characteristic of the President was the jibe:

> When the world works out concerted policies in the majority of Nations to produce balanced budgets and living within their means, then we can properly discuss a better distribution of the world's gold and silver supply to act as a reserve base of national currencies.[18]

Further, said the President, "The sound internal economic system of a Nation is a greater factor in its well-being than the price of its currency in changing terms of the currencies of other Nations." [19] If this was the declaration of a reformer, the following was surely the confession of an experimentalist: "Let me be frank in saying that the United States seeks the kind of a dollar which a generation hence will have the same purchasing and debt-paying power as the dollar value we hope to attain in the near future." [20]

"It was fantastic, of course," wrote Raymond Moley, "that Roosevelt, who had let himself seem so eager, back in April and May, to have the Conference, should have put himself into the position of striking it down. He had made himself, first, when he agreed to let the Conference be held in June, the victim of his own enthusiasm. He had made himself on July 1st, when he rejected the harmless declaration [of the Conference] on the grounds that it was a stabilization agreement, the victim of his own lack of knowledge. He had made himself on July 3rd, when he sent 'The Bombshell' which he considered a way of scolding the Conference into a consideration of the problems he thought important, the victim of his own clever-

---

[17] A Wireless to the London Conference Insisting upon Larger Objectives Than Mere Currency Stabilization, July 3, 1933, *Public Papers, 1933*, pp. 264-265.
[18] *Ibid.*, p. 265.
[19] *Ibid.*, pp. 264-265.
[20] *Ibid.*, p. 265.

ness. He had thought that he . . . understood the psychology of the conferees better than those who were in London." [21]

Most of the newspapers extolled Mr. Roosevelt as a national hero and declared that his message of July 3 was a "second Declaration of Independence." [22] The President himself remarked to Moley upon his return: "My statement certainly got a grand press over here!" [23]

That the conference "did not break up in a state of chaos and anger at President Roosevelt was due to the patient determination of one man, Cordell Hull," reported James P. Warburg. "The American Secretary of State—his lifelong dream of international economic understanding shattered—his policies thrown into the discard—fought for three weeks for no other purpose than to keep the blame for having wrecked the hopes of the world from falling too heavily upon his President." [24]

On July 6 Mr. Warburg tendered his resignation as financial adviser of the American delegation, saying in his letter to Mr. Hull:

> It is clear from the President's messages of the last few days that he now has in mind a monetary and currency program which differs quite radically from that which formed the basis of his original instructions to us . . . it seems clear to me that this new thought has not been sufficiently developed at the moment to enable us to proceed here at the Conference to preach the new gospel. . . . No matter how good the plan may eventually be, it will in its very nature be an experiment and I do not feel that we can urge such an experiment upon other nations at the present time and under the present circumstances. . . . I must ask you to accept my resignation . . . on the very simple ground that we are entering upon waters for which I have no charts and in which I therefore feel myself an utterly incompetent pilot.[25]

---

[21] Moley *op. cit.*, p. 267.

[22] Bernard Faÿ, *op. cit.*, p. 337.

[23] Moley, *op. cit.*, p. 270.

[24] Warburg, *op. cit.*, p. 121.

[25] *Ibid.*, pp. 121-123. See also the conclusion of Jeannette P. Nichols, "Actually, in view of the attitude of all of the nations from the outset, there is much room for doubt whether the conference would have accomplished anything even if Roosevelt had accepted the final and weakest draft of an agreement." "Roosevelt's Monetary Diplomacy in 1933," in *American Historical Review*, LVI, (January, 1951), 317.

President Roosevelt's preoccupation with domestic affairs throughout the year 1933 is indicated not only by his treatment of the London Economic Conference,[26] but by the tone of his few public messages and statements on the world situation in whole or in part. International co-operation had received a body blow, from which it was not soon to recover.

It will be remembered that the day after Franklin Roosevelt was inaugurated President of the United States, Adolf Hitler and his bloc won a Reich majority. By March 23 Hitler achieved the triumph for which he had been fighting for fourteen years and became the master of Germany. For the Reichstag, by a vote of 441-94, had given the Cabinet power to make laws by decree for four years. This enabling act meant that the Weimar Constitution had ceased to exist "for a long period, probably for good," [27] and that much of President von Hindenburg's authority had passed to Hitler. "What we wanted in that distant Spring of 1919 is today Italian reality and will tomorrow be European reality," [28] prophesied Premier Mussolini in a message addressed to the Italian nation on the fourteenth anniversary of the founding of fascism.

Widespread agitation in the United States on behalf of German Jews, reported to be suffering persecution, was the most conspicuous indication of American reaction at the time to what Consul General George S. Messersmith in Berlin called "a real revolution . . . and a dangerous situation." [29] As Secretary Hull saw the situation at this time, "The world . . . never more nearly approached economic and financial catastrophe domestically, and anarchy internationally." [30]

In mid-October, on the eve of Germany's withdrawal from the Disarmament Conference [31] and notice of withdrawal from the League of Nations,[32] Mr. Roosevelt said, in a radio address:

---

[26] W. L. Langer and S. E. Gleason were to say many years later (*Challenge to Isolation*, p. 16): "[Roosevelt's] handling of the London Conference of 1933 was certainly a case of almost unpardonable bungling."
[27] *New York Times*, March 24, 1933.
[28] *Ibid.*
[29] *Peace and War: United States Foreign Policy 1931-1941* (Department of State Publication No. 1983), pp. 191-192.
[30] Hull, *op. cit.*, I, 172.
[31] *Ibid.*, I, 222-231.
[32] *Ibid.*, I, 241.

The danger to world peace certainly does not come from the United States of America. As a Nation, we are overwhelmingly against engaging in war. As a Nation we are seeking no additional territory at the expense of our neighbors. . . . It is this . . . complete lack of a national desire for territorial expansion—which makes the rest of the world begin to understand that the United States is opposed to war. I will go one step further in saying that the very great majority of the inhabitants of the world feel the same as we do about territorial expansion or getting rich or powerful at the expense of their neighbors. It is only in the case of such people in the world as still have imperialistic desires for expansion and domination in their minds or in their hearts that threats to world peace lie. And, finally, it seems clear to me that it is only through constant education and the stressing of the ideals of peace that those who still seek imperialism can be brought in line with the majority.[33]

Looking abroad for possible alliance in such a world, was it not natural that President Roosevelt sought to open the door to the recognition of Soviet Russia? To Mr. Roosevelt's worldwide appeal of May 16, Michail Kalinin, President of the All Union Central Executive Committee of the Union of Soviet Socialist Republics, had responded with a conciliatory statement to the effect that the "Soviet Government also proposed and supported measures aiming at preventing or at least impeding any kind of aggression or any attempt on the part of any State to enlarge its territory at the expense of others." This historic statement recalled to the President of the United States that "The Soviet Government has concluded non-aggression pacts with most of the countries with which it is in official relations and can therefore only welcome your proposal for the conclusion of a pact of non-aggression by all countries." [34]

The President's views on recognition of the Soviet government of Russia may be inferred from the account of Mr. Hull that:

"I favor recognizing Russia," I said, "although our correspondence reveals that great numbers of people are opposed to it. Russia and we had been traditional friends up to the end of the World War. In general, Russia has been peacefully inclined. The world is moving into a dangerous period both in Europe

[33] *Public Papers, 1933*, p. 394.
[34] *Ibid.*, p. 201.

and in Asia. Russia could be a great help in stabilizing this situation as time goes on and peace becomes more and more threatened."

The President, without a moment's hesitation, replied, "I agree entirely." He then added: "Two great nations like America and Russia should be on speaking terms. It will·be beneficial to both countries to resume diplomatic relations." [35]

The subsequent negotiations were, it seems, conducted by the President.[36] Secretary Hull, in describing the interchange later, remarked: .

Numerous occasions were later to arise when the President preferred thus to communicate directly with the heads of other governments instead of having the governments communicate through their respective foreign offices. In many instances I doubted the wisdom of this course.[37]

It would appear that American business interests concerned with the falling off of trade with Russia after 1930 were disposed to look with favor upon recognition. It is also to be noted that there were discussions among public men concerned with diplomatic relations as to the desirability of using Russia as a counterbalance to the growing·power of Japan in the Far East.

A letter of November 27, 1933, from his Ambassador to Germany, William E. Dodd, an historian trained in Germany, must have confirmed Mr. Roosevelt in his Russian recognition policy as a "peace" move as far as Europe was concerned, for Mr. Dodd wrote the President:

Your remark in your letter of the 13th about the eight per cent of the world's population defeating ninety-two per cent in their peaceful objectives leads me to think that you might possibly profit from this summary [of the Hitler-Goebbels-Goering triumvirate]. . . .

You have, therefore, a unique triumvirate. . . . I do not think there has ever been in modern history such a unique group. There was such a group in ancient Rome, and you probably

---

[35] Hull, *op. cit.,* I, 297.
[36] The steps in the negotiations have been traced carefully and clearly in R. P. Browder, *The Origins of Soviet-American Diplomacy.* See especially page 218 and the Preface.
[37] Hull, *op. cit.,* I, p. 298.

recall what happened. You may see, therefore, something of the
problem you have to deal with. . . .[38]

A salient aspect of President Roosevelt's foreign policy becomes clearer at this time. Like many another American political leader, he had carried the imagery of the battlefield into his
domestic campaign, attacking his adversaries in violent terms
and calling them enemies of the people. Early in his public
career, he had found enemies to attack, that is, enemies of the
people. Inasmuch as he was *for* the people, these enemies were
his as well. They might be representatives of Tammany, presidents of power companies, speculators on the Stock Exchange,
or, most offensive of all, a selfish few who manipulated the
government of the nation to their own advantage, leaving the
masses of the people without economic opportunities or social
justice in the measure to which they were entitled.

In the campaign of 1932 it had not been difficult to describe
these enemies of the people. The atmosphere of distrust and
uncertainty growing out of financial panic, industrial depression and, it must be admitted, the revelation of downright dishonesty of some prominent leaders in the financial world made
this appealing. The insistent drive in the matter was furnished
by denunciation in terms that suggested battles and enemies
and victories and the triumph of heroes.

Had Mr. Roosevelt limited this approach to the period of
the campaign, before entering upon the responsibilities of
office, it might be dismissed as merely a familiar method in
politics. But twelve years in office were to follow, and three
later campaigns were to be characterized by a continuance of
battle cries and insistence upon the dangers that flow from the
machinations of enemies of the people.

Easily the President transferred this pattern to his campaign
to arouse the American people to the dangers of enemies beyond our borders, where it was even easier to insist upon the
virtue of the American view. Even in the period of the "hundred days," when the enemies of the people were put to rout
at home, it seemed clear to him that the enemies of our best
interests were plotting our destruction in attempts of foreign

---

[38] William E. Dodd to President Roosevelt, November 27, 1933. Roosevelt
Library, President's Secretary's File, 1933-1935, Box 10.

representatives to control the London Conference. Disagreement as to financial stability and stabilization of the currency did not constitute the issue at stake. The United States must protect its own national interest. An extreme isolationist could not but applaud.

Mr. Hull later said he believed "that the collapse of the London Economic Conference had two tragic results. First, it greatly retarded the logical economic recovery of all nations. Secondly, it played into the hands of such dictator nations as Germany, Japan, and Italy. At that very time this trio was intently watching the course of action of the peace-seeking nations." [39]

Yet, as Mr. Hull added, "At London the bitterest recrimination occurred among the United States, Britain, and France. The dictator nations occupied first-row seats at a spectacular battle. From then on they could proceed hopefully: on the military side, to rearm in comparative safety; on the economic side, to build their self-sufficiency walls in preparation for war. The conference was the first, and really the last, opportunity to check these movements toward conflict." [40]

In the case of the Good Neighbor Policy, a promise of reciprocal trade was not emphasized so much as a policy indicating that we were not at war, even economic war. Again, this was an oversimplified view of what constituted peace. The United States would live in the world—but on Uncle Sam's own terms! [41]

At the Seventh International Conference of American States held late in 1933 at Montevideo, Secretary Hull, although reacting to fears of other states, was nevertheless rigidly emphasizing the view of the United States in endorsing a resolution which declared that "No state has the right to intervene in the internal or external affairs of another." [42]

At the end of the year President Roosevelt declared that "the definite policy of the United States from now on is one opposed to armed intervention." [43]

---

[39] Hull, *op. cit.*, I, 268.
[40] *Ibid.*
[41] C. A. Beard, "President Roosevelt Adheres to an Isolationist Policy in 1933," in *American Foreign Policy in the Making, 1932-1940*, pp. 117-156.
[42] Hull, *op. cit.*, I, 333.
[43] *Public Papers, 1933*, p. 545.

Among Americans of informed view on international affairs were some openly distrustful of Soviet Russia. Many of these were Republicans identified with the government in office from 1921 to 1933. The basic religious opposition to recognition was very great, as was that of the upholders of isolation at any cost. The opposition of many labor leaders was expressed. Thus, when anti-war, anti-Communist, isolationist forces set about opposition, their common target was "internationalism." Co-operation with the British did not in itself constitute internationalism, but the acceptance of Soviet Russia did. Furthermore, recognition of Russia meant acquiescence in the method—or at least the results—of revolution!

Thus, an acceptance of Russia—and of its declared objectives —which was of such interest to American liberals, began with formal recognition of the Soviet regime by President Roosevelt in November of 1933. But this acceptance did not end with formal recognition. In the struggle against fascism, Soviet Russia continued to appeal to some liberals, and this finally led to acceptance of Russia as an ally in 1941, and ended with Russia's victory in 1945. The road from November 16, 1933, which Secretary Hull found a rough road from the beginning,[44] had many turnings, but at each one, additional reason presented itself for maintenance of the avenue of original choice.

Against a background of habit and practice based, it is evident, in a firmly held conviction on the part of the President as to the effective way to lead a people and to govern them—the foreign policy of the President at this point was built upon elements that in time would make for certain conflict.

Pursuing, as he so often said, the pattern of pacific intention and stating always that peace was the goal, nevertheless the practical man who torpedoed the London Conference and who recognized Soviet Russia in order to emphasize American belief in self-determination of *peoples,* was the leader who ultimately found the basic cause of conflict to be not the maladjustment of economic forces but the sinister purposes of selfish men!

Sinister forces were at large in the world. Of that there was no longer, in 1933, any doubt. But they were merely symbolized by the leaders envisaged by the President. Here again was

---

[44] Hull, *op. cit.,* I, 302-307. See also Browder, *op. cit.,* pp. 218-222.

the pattern of strife that so often has deluged the world in blood when whole peoples have been convinced by misinformation that their "enemies" were the cause of warfare.

Into this maelstrom of iniquity the President was to plunge in his Quarantine Speech four years later.

The incoherence of international economic relations was partially accountable for the President's view of the world and of his responsibilities in it. The conviction of those who wished to refrain from international agreements, even from embargoes of war material against "aggressor" nations,[45] guided the President in his belief that he was acting for the people. Thus the President found no way to prevent almost complete default on the war debts owed the United States by European nations.[46]

Increasingly evident was Mr. Roosevelt's tendency to play by ear, his independence in utterance of officials and others, and his dependence for knowledge, though not for advice, upon the group of advisers with whom he was consulting at the time.

Furthermore, President Roosevelt was constantly asserting his position as President, believing in "the beneficial effects of communications directly between the heads of Governments rather than through the foreign offices," notwithstanding the consequent weakening of strategy.[47]

If Franklin Roosevelt felt that it was essential at this time to make perfectly clear that he was not going to be governed by the wishes of foreign nations, he had succeeded at the outset of his administration. The recognition of Soviet Russia was in the general pattern of rejecting the plans and programs of western European nations and receiving the outsider, as later became apparent, on Russia's terms.

Thus, the failure of the United States government, through its President, to assume international responsibility in any form in the crucial year 1933 not only lessened national security through estrangement from other nations of liberal political outlook and practice, but brought nearer the day when it would

---

[45] Hull, *op. cit.,* I, 229-230.

[46] Beard, *American Foreign Policy in the Making,* pp. 118-123.

[47] Hull, *op. cit.,* I, 297-298. Yet Secretary Hull recalled, as well, that "During his first term in office President Roosevelt was so immersed in an avalanche of domestic questions that he left me in almost full charge of foreign affairs." (p. 194).

be necessary to recognize, as Secretary Hull at the time warned, that "A general war during the next two to ten years seems more probable than peace." [48]

In formulating a judgment upon the foreign policies of Franklin Roosevelt during his first administration, the reader must bear in mind the existence of major factors in the President's previous decisions—which have not been discussed. Each of these factors involved forces beyond the President's control.

A great majority of his own people were on the whole desirous of isolating themselves as far as possible from other peoples.[49] He could not reach them with an affirmative program on foreign relations; he could only hope to restrain them from renouncing their support of his domestic program. As he said, in writing of this period eight years later:

> It is a little difficult, in 1941, to look back upon the days of 1933 and fully appreciate the danger which then faced the United States. The grave threat which today faces our democracy and our independent existence comes from an alien philosophy and an alien military machine, both of which have overrun the world about us. That threat is physical; it is imminent; it draws ever closer. It crowds out recollection of that other threat of destruction which faced us in 1933. Besides, the great recovery in business, in agriculture, and in employment which has come since then—the great increase in our security and physical well-being—have dimmed somewhat our memory of the hazards of those days.[50]

Furthermore, in Europe the threat of a continental conflict of arms was such as to make abortive any effort on his part to play more than the role of a disinterested onlooker. Finally, in Asia the advances of Japan seemed to threaten the position of Americans as distant but interested participants in international co-operation. Because of these major factors, any presentation by the President of an affirmative policy would force

---

[48] *Ibid.*, I, 231.

[49] A significant quotation from Stimson's diary appears in Current (*op. cit.*, p. 130). In pointing out how Stimson and Roosevelt had conferred frequently March 4, 1933 to October 30, 1934, Current writes: "Their estrangement was increased by the fact that as Stimson later put it, after 1934, bowing to the overwhelming opinion of his countrymen, Mr. Roosevelt for some years pursued a policy in foreign affairs which seemed to Stimson not sufficiently positive or active."

[50] *Public Papers, 1937*, Introduction, L-LI.

him into open conflict at home and abroad. For this he was not yet prepared in conviction or intention.

However, the President was talking of an international conference to further the cause of peace. On August 26, 1936, Arthur Krock stated that the President was thinking, in case he was re-elected, of meeting with Edward VIII, Stalin, Hitler, Mussolini and others, using the Pan-American agreements as a model. No treaties were to be called for, and no commitments; merely personal declaration by rulers.[51]

The President wrote Ambassador Dodd on January 9, 1937: "That story by Arthur Krock was not wholly crazy. If five or six heads of the important governments could meet together for a week with complete inaccessibility to press or cables or radio, a definite, useful agreement might result or else one or two of them would be murdered by the others!" [52]

Meanwhile, the United States must protect its own interests. Abstaining from joint action, it must prepare to defend itself— if necessary. Maintaining neutrality in the law, the President could eventually request billions for expanding the defense of the United States.

The time will come when a full and meaningful analysis of the foreign policy of the first administration of President Roosevelt may be made. All attempts by participants and commentators thus far have been limited by lack of full information. But tentative conclusions may be stated at this time.

The public record—in every field of expression—had emphasized the friendly attitude of the United States toward other peoples. This public record showed innumerable moves that indicated that this function meant co-operation with like-minded peoples. Friendliness and co-operation would presumably lead the United States—in days to come—to further participation in some form of world organization, economic and political.

This definite possibility brought into increased opposition to the President not only the forces at home that were isolationist or nationalistic, but all forces abroad that found in nationalism—not internationalism—their supreme opportunity for advancement—peaceful or otherwise.

---

[51] *New York Times*, August 26, 1936.
[52] *Personal Letters, 1928-1945*, I, 649.

Chapter VII

PATTERN OF LEADERSHIP

IT WAS WIDELY ASSERTED that the surrender of Congress to the President throughout the first year of his administration had upset the division of powers between legislative and executive branches of the government. The gradual substitution of administrative drafts for legislative proposals was said to constitute the most serious source of danger. Assertions of power by administrative agencies greatly enhanced executive powers. The contention that this had been a necessity did not diminish criticism.

Had the Constitutional system been changed? This in turn raised another question. Was the administration policy, in planning for national public works, a serious threat to private enterprise? Did the policy of the administration in relief spell bankruptcy and an endless drain upon the Treasury?

Perhaps the question on which there was most discussion arose out of the assertion of a new role of government in caring for the interests of labor, of the farmer, of industry, and indeed of finance. Was it possible to plan for a continuance of capitalism under such an assumption of control and responsibility by the government? It appeared that in a world much concerned with the appeals of fascism and communism, a major modification of capitalism, in any important respect, was a serious matter.

Despite continued interest in domestic recovery, earnest discussion took place, at least among informed elements of the people, as to American relations with other nations. No issue was concisely presented, for matters were very much in flux.

Much was made by the administration of what it termed the Good Neighbor Policy; [1] of resumption of relations with Soviet Russia; of plans for limitation of armament; and of the advantages of reciprocal trade.

But what of such objectives and their possible attainment in a world still suffering, tragically, the results of the war; wholly unbalanced in trade; and eagerly listening for voices of would-be saviors? Could America continue to follow a policy of occasional co-operation, or must America return decidedly to a policy of isolation?

A long-standing query emerged more and more distinctly in discussions of the people at large. Were the traditional practices of American democracy going to survive the crisis of panic-depression followed by the administration program of recovery? Judging by the assurances of the President, Americans were to have a greater democracy and more extensive care for the masses of men.

Many thought and said, however, that the proposals made by the President were too slight to affect seriously the appalling deficiencies in social and economic democracy that had been revealed. Change must go much further than had been proposed. Move quickly, they said, for the old American system is dead!

Amid the loud assertions of advocates of all brands of radicalism and the subdued protest of those who still felt that a conservative approach was now possible because the immediate crisis had passed, scant attention was given a question which in the long run was to have more significance than any. It was this: Could a program, based upon an appeal for increasing

---

[1] "Generally associated with the name of Franklin D. Roosevelt, the real beginning was made both in name and deed by Herbert Hoover," according to Graham H. Stuart in Foreword to Alexander de Conde, *Herbert Hoover's Latin-American Policy*.

democratic process and greater social justice—relying upon widespread belief in the soundness of the popular will—be harmonized with the demands and needs of the modern industrial world? Could a program long called for, demanding experts in government and a truly informed electorate, be salvaged from the emotionalism that accompanied the early experiments of the New Deal?

In a reasoned survey of the status of the New Deal, Charles A. Beard found that, inasmuch as a long democratic tradition put first of all care for and interest in the people, the American background for the actions of the administration was clear enough. He concluded, however, "The tradition has been altered, of course, by an influx of ideas imported from the Old World." [2]

The President, in addressing the nation on October 22, 1933, in what he called the fourth Fireside Chat, defended the results of the New Deal as he saw them at that time. Of ten million citizens seeking work when he was inaugurated, 40 percent had by this time found employment. Said the President:

> How are we constructing the edifice of recovery—the temple which, when completed, will no longer be a temple of money changers or of beggars, but rather a temple dedicated to and maintained for a greater social justice, a greater welfare for America—the habitation of a sound economic life? We are building, stone by stone, the columns which will support that habitation. Those columns are many in number and though, for a moment, the progress of one column may disturb the progress on the pillar next to it, the work on all of them must proceed without let or hinderance. [3]

As a practical gesture, the President had publicly asked that:

> ... foreclosures on farms and chattels and on homes be delayed until every mortgagor in the country shall have had full opportunity to take advantage of Federal credit. I make the further request which many of you know has already been made through the great Federal credit organizations that if there is any family in the United States about to lose its home or about to lose its chattels, that family should telegraph at

---

[2] *American Political Science Review*, XXVIII (1934), pp. 2-14.
[3] *Public Papers, 1933*, p. 421.

once either to the Farm Credit Administration or the Home
Owners Loan Corporation in Washington requesting their
help.[4]

Claiming that "the farmers of the United States will receive
33 percent more dollars for what they have produced than they
received in the year 1932," the President said that it was a part
of his policy "to increase the rise and to extend it to those products which have as yet felt no benefit," for, he added, "If we
cannot do this one way we will do it another. Do it, we will." [5]

Of the N.R.A., the President said:

It has abolished child labor. It has eliminated the sweat shop.
It has ended sixty cents a week paid in some mills and eighty
cents a week paid in some mines. . . . The secret of N.R.A. is
cooperation. . . . We know that there are chislers. . . . Ninety
percent of complaints come from misconception.[6]

Thus the President saw the pattern of his leadership, and as
was his custom, he asked popular approval. As the nation
moved into the second year of the New Deal, Mr. Roosevelt
felt that the restoration of confidence throughout the country
had continued as a result of the fact that the executive and
legislative arms of the government had proved themselves willing and able to take care of pressing problems. These problems
continued to appear to him as the care of the suffering in the
depression; second, erection of means whereby recurrence of
this situation would be prevented; and third, steps to rebuild
the bases of social justice. To substantiate this point of view,
the President felt that statistics proved his contention, and he
was proud of the legislation comprising reforms.

Those who opposed the President in his interpretation of
what had happened repeatedly pointed out that reform tended
to jeopardize recovery, in that it upset previous ways of thinking and acting and led to uncertainty as to the future. The
President retorted that permanent recovery would demand a
real readjustment of the economic system, which had tended to
"concentrate power in the hands of a few." He was eager to
assert that reforms would destroy control by a few, and cited

[4] *Ibid.*, p. 422.
[5] *Ibid.*, p. 423.
[6] *Ibid.*, p. 424.

speculation in securities and exploitation of labor as examples of the evils residing in such control.

Franklin Roosevelt did not originate attacks on selfish interests. There was a long line of practitioners of this method of political advancement. Yet at the conclusion of a review of legislation initiated by the executive and of his own more conspicuous utterances, he said:

> I do not indict all business executives, all labor leaders, all editors, all lawyers. But I do indict the ethics of many of them and I indict those citizens whose easy consciences condone such wrong-doing. . . .

> Vision is an essential in all service—some quality of the mind which is never satisfied with things as they are—some quality that achieves an immediate objective and proceeds forthwith to gain the next. It is only the cynic whom I have just described as a poor citizen who will suggest that the man or woman of vision is "impractical." The idealist is not of necessity a wretched executive. Some of the greatest administrators are people who are constantly seeking better things for mankind.[7]

The President at this time stated that he was "fortunate in the unselfish loyalty and help given me by those like Howe and McIntyre and Early and Moley whose varied services I call upon at any hour of the day or night." [8] Widespread rumor as to who was included in this group or trio of groups [9] occupied the minds of many who at the time failed to perceive that the President's was a "personal" government which was certainly not new in the world, and which transcended even formal Presidential appointments.

Mr. Hull was the "idealist" whom the President had placed in the State Department, but it was not even the Secretary of State on whom the President relied for his foreign policy. Nor were the President's advisers chosen from any body of "experts" that would have been recognizable as such in the preceding administration. Nor was the Democratic party organization the

---

[7] *On Our Way,* pp. 250-251.
[8] *Ibid.,* p. 252.
[9] Moley in *Today* (I, April 14, 1934, No. 25), wrote that the original group of advisers that included Samuel I. Rosenman, Basil O'Connor, and Raymond Moley—who had aided in the first campaign—had given way to "three brain trusts."

source of Presidential advice. No progressives of either party were continuously influential in Presidential decisions.

A new element had come to power in the United States. It was vaguely termed a "brains trust" [10] yet it included men of such diverse interest that a practical concern for "results" was perhaps the only unifying element in what Raymond Moley called the "card file" in Franklin Roosevelt's memory. Ideas and imagination were the qualifications for those who were associated with the President in any advisory capacity.

Although his associates changed constantly, the President moved, as most of the powerful leaders of the world have always done, through personal avenues of accomplishment. Much has been written of the men who surrounded the President and of their conjectured influence upon him. The evidence indicates that, though seeking the knowledge and views of countless individuals, the President made his own decisions and did not reveal to anyone what piece of information, expressed view, or attitude of others turned the scale.[11]

The "feeling" of the period when the New Deal had passed its early crisis and there was a growing conviction that the greatest opportunity ever offered social reformers was in the grasp of those in office, is revealed in theater director Eva Le Gallienne's second autobiographical volume, *With a Quiet Heart*. Here is included the record of a conversation with Harry Hopkins following a dinner at the White House at which President Roosevelt and Miss Le Gallienne had discussed the possibility of her heading a National Theater Division of the W.P.A.

"Dear Miss Le Gallienne," said Mr. Hopkins, "you should learn to play politics." After Miss Le Gallienne had replied that she had never learned to do this and was not sure that she wished to, Hopkins continued, "If you would just learn to play politics, you could get millions out of the old man." [12]

Mr. Roosevelt's problem, throughout 1933 and 1934, was to direct the current of relief legislation in such a manner as to

---

[10] Moley, *After Seven Years.* Index items on "Brains trust," and especially pp. 83 and 182.

[11] *The Secret Diary of Harold L. Ickes* (1933-1936), is a mine of evidence on this point (pp. 585-610).

[12] P. 63. In the winter of 1933, Hopkins explained to the President his plans for relief. "Let's see," said Roosevelt, "four million people—that means roughly four hundred million dollars." Robert Sherwood, *Roosevelt and Hopkins*, p. 51.

withstand attacks from extremists. But as he "gave in" to win support of the radicals, he faced full attack from the conservatives of all parties. The masses of the people—neither radical nor conservative—had for a long time demanded national solution of national problems heightened by the depression, and they submitted to the regulatory features of the President's recovery program because it seemed to be the result of their own demands.

In his basic conception of his function, the President had long since made clear that he thought of himself as representing all the people. But this in fact meant, in terms of policy or vote getting, reaching certain segments of the people. It was obvious that some he could not reach or did not wish to reach.

These included the lawbreakers either great or small, of whom in the circumstances of a speculating, bootlegging era there were thought to be many. The President did not address himself to the "privileged classes." Nor could he persuade the much larger number habitually adhering to the Republican party. Large numbers of conservative Democrats, particularly in the South, likewise refused to fall under his spell.

It followed that the President could attack many elements and in doing so would be acting for "the people." Surely *they* would be united in favor of the prosecution of lawbreakers. *They* would agree on restrictions upon privilege. *They* would enthusiastically support change of the rules making for wider use of the resources of the nation on behalf of the masses. In the very circumstances of the case, although President of the United States, he appeared to the people primarily as a fighter, a crusader—rather than as administrator and executive.

Yet in his relations with the Congress, particularly in matters of patronage but also in moves concerning legislation, the President displayed increasingly the adroitness of an experienced politician.[13]

In judging the means he used, as well as his purpose, the distinction between recovery and reform is unreal. It is clear from both his statements and his actions that he would "re-

---

[13] On October 3, 1934, the President wrote William Randolph Hearst: "Dear W. R. I am delighted to hear from Joe [Joseph P. Kennedy] that you are coming down to see me on Monday. If you have not made other arrangements, I hope you will stay with us Monday night at the White House." *Personal Letters, 1928-1945*, I, 424.

cover" and "reform" by attacking abuses. His entire approach was based upon the proposition that the government, that is, the people, was strong enough to do anything necessary.

The government, in their name, could close the banks; it could reopen the banks for business; it could prosecute law-breakers; it could build public works. If the government were to do these things and were to be all-powerful and able to plan for the future, as well as act from day to day, it must be supported. The government in this conception was the *people*.

Thus, the government, that is, the people, must keep private enterprise actively and vigorously at work. In short, the economic life of the nation must be productive in order that taxation would be possible to pay the costs. It was therefore quite right to assert, as was so often done, that the administration, the President, and the people believed in private enterprise.

The tasks envisaged by the administration, in recovery and in reform, could not be accomplished by private agencies. It was inconceivable that national recovery and national reform could be accomplished by any other means than by a powerful, aggressive government backed by the people. Moreover, a careful distinction was made that in the United States the people chose to do this. The American people, through their representatives, did it willingly.

Why was Franklin Roosevelt able to do what others, so-called radicals, had not done and in all probability could not do? In seeking an answer to this question, there needs to be full treatment of the responses to his leadership. In the Congress and in the courts existed, as had always been the case under powerful Presidents, a frequent disapproval. The expression of this disapproval, not only on specific proposals but on general policy, had been the clearest indication of the functioning of our democratic procedures as measured in political terms.

Responses from leaders in the financial world, always interested in the policies of the national government, on the whole were in violent opposition.[14] Responses from industrialists and from the business world generally were adverse.

---

[14] In the autumn of 1934 the American Bankers' Association met in Washington, D. C. Jackson E. Reynolds of the First National Bank of New York

In addition, came the positive responses of organized labor, of various organizations of farmers, of party organizations including the Republican party, and leaders of minor parties. To an unusual degree, because of the nature of the President's personal leadership throughout the period, continuous and critical response came from an increasing number of political commentators. American newspapers carried much editorial response, as well, and made frequent use of foreign comment upon administration action.

Not only at campaign time, but between campaigns, as the years passed, prominent political leaders, such as Elihu Root and Alfred E. Smith, declared themselves upon the policies of the administration. After the middle of the first administration the critical comment of former President Hoover became increasingly pronounced. Finally, the response to which primary attention has quite properly been given in measuring contemporary judgment, was that of the votes cast by the people in elections in which the President's policy was the dominant issue.

The results of administrative action, facilitated by Congressional agreement in the first year of the new administration, thus produced varying response from the American people. Unquestionably a growing sense of assurance and of confidence activated the workers of the nation. This brought public realization, as well, of the vast number of the so-called underprivileged in so large a nation. Many of the would-be leaders had perceived a way out of their distress, and the extremists among them saw that perhaps this was the time to make fundamental changes not only in the political structure but in the social bases of American life.

At the same time, a revival of doubt as to the wisdom of much that had been done in 1933 was particularly evident among those who had been defeated in the Congressional elections of 1932. After all, many of these representatives of the people had been in power for a long time. They felt that they represented sections of the population that had led in the

City, in an address to the convention, made a highly conciliatory approach to the President of the United States. Arthur Krock in the *New York Times*, September 25, 1953.

building of America. They represented now the gigantic power that rested in potential industrial and financial might.

Neither convinced followers of the New Deal nor those who had for a time acquiesced in it but were now convinced that it was filling but a temporary need, were much interested in the significant events taking place in western Europe. So concentrated upon the American scene was popular attention that most commentators agreed that the advocates of isolationism were expressing a deep and widely felt conviction of masses of the people.

As the campaign for members of the Congress developed in the late autumn of 1934, proposals for social security were an issue. The Democratic organization and most of the Democratic candidates actively supported administration proposals on this matter. Although the President was not personally a candidate, to an unusual degree the campaigning of 1934 was done in terms of the issues raised by his Presidential leadership. He was charged with unconstitutional action, with general usurpation of power, with a shifting policy on both taxation and debts, and with a general willingness to push the nation into later bankruptcy in his vigorous desire to build broader bases for political action through public expenditure.

It was remarked, as the campaign came to occupy general attention, that despite some significant state conflicts, no clear cut national decision was possible because the Congressional elections were, as usual, fought at random in terms of persons as well as issues. The outcome, nevertheless, strengthened the Democratic party in the Congress. This in turn, as usual, enlarged the problem of party control for the President, and decisions made by the Congress were, paradoxically, less clear cut.

As long as the President had loyal following in the Congress, the way of executive-legislative action was clear. Long-term results could not as yet be measured. Of course each new departure in legislation would in time be brought into the courts for judgment on Constitutional grounds.

Had Mr. Roosevelt ceased to be President in 1934, it is safe to assume that the New Deal would have disintegrated rapidly. Both the great party organizations were controlled by men who were disposed to move slowly and not take too seriously the demands of radicals for drastic reform of the whole system. Progressive programs had risen to widespread influence in this year of change.

This was not because the people had elected progressives to Congressional office in 1932. With the coming to the Presidency of Mr. Roosevelt, a union of forces for a time gave to his leadership a semblance of realization of the demands of such forerunners as the Populists and the Progressives and insurgents within both of the great parties.

A test of this in the elections of 1934, without the appeal of Mr. Roosevelt himself, would have brought prompt division of the Democrats into three if not four factions; of the Republican party into at least two factions. A strong popular movement, under the leadership of Huey Long, thus might have taken minority control of the Congress. It was the leadership of Franklin Roosevelt which prevented the development of this dangerous possibility.

Moreover, under his leadership in preparation for the tests of 1934, the call was continued for action on problems of agriculture and labor and, particularly, on social security. As the event proved, the main issue in the Congressional elections of 1934 came to be proposals for social security. The dominant public feeling was one of deep gratitude to Mr. Roosevelt for his leadership in what appeared to be national recovery in the spring and summer of 1933.

This first national opportunity for a record of popular response, which was afforded by the Congressional elections of 1934, brought from the President's point of view an overwhelming endorsement. The 60 Democrats in the Senate were increased to 65, thus reducing the Republicans to 25 with 2 Independents. The gain of a dozen Democrats in the House brought their number to 322, as against 102 Republicans and 10 Independents.

Despite the attack within his own party membership, as well as from the Republicans, the vote did seem to show that a great majority of the people supported the President in his conception of his duty to them. If so great a majority be given to a program already in action, was it not clear that the majority favored the next step in the program proposed?

The President had prepared the way for this view when he wrote:

> Apart from phrases and slogans, the important thing to remember is, I think, that the change in our policy is based upon a change in the attitude and the thinking of the American people —in other words, that it is based upon the growing into maturity of our democracy; that it proceeds in accordance with the underlying principles that guided the framers of our Constitution; that it is taking form with the general approval of a very large majority of the American people; and finally, that it is made with the constant assurance to the people that if at any time they wish to revert to the old methods that we have discarded, they are wholly free to bring about such a reversion by the simple means of the ballot box. An ancient Greek was everlastingly right when he said, "Creation is the victory of persuasion and not of force." The New Deal seeks that kind of victory. . . .[15]

It follows that the President's leadership was essential—and that everyone accepted the fact. It followed also that, if he were to hold together the movement that he had led thus far, he would turn not right, but increasingly left. Such a development would insure success in the Congress—and probably in the nation in the election of 1936.

"That he is entitled to full credit for inducing recovery" could be said by Walter Lippmann in early 1934 as "demonstrably certain." [16]

Yet a British critic observed that "In thus pinning their faith to the hem of the garments of a superman, the American people in 1933 were reacting to the World Crisis in somewhat the same fashion as their German and Italian and Russian contemporaries." [17]

But an American publishing *The New Dealers* under the pseudonym of "Unofficial Observer" wrote with keener insight

> The essence of the peaceful revolution which has begun under Roosevelt is that it is a new deal and not a free-for-all. . . .

---

[15] *On Our Way*, Foreword, xi.

[16] *Interpretations, 1933-1935*, p. 250.

[17] *Survey of International Affairs, 1933*, Arnold J. Toynbee (ed.), Introductory to Part 1, World Economic Affairs, p. 7.

For the New Deal is a laughing revolution. It is purging our institutions in the fires of mockery, and it is led by a group of men who possess two supreme qualifications for the task: common sense and a sense of humor.[18]

It was said by the President that the people had nothing to fear but fear itself. This was primarily a call upon the individual to reassert his manhood. As the event proved, however, it was a suggestion that he might be saved by efforts other than his own. Presently he was assured that he *need* not fear, because his government would take care of him.

In this atmosphere of dependence, the American people easily gave over powers to the President. Millions were voted for the unemployed. Men co-operated in caring for themselves as they cared for their fellow citizens! This attitude of dependence—of itself working incalculable harm to the sturdy mind of America—was accompanied by cynicism and crass materialism. Much has been made of the iniquities of the industrial and financial world. Less has been said of the general attitude of distrust, envy, and disillusionment among the American people as a whole at this time. Too little, furthermore, has been said of the underlying feeling that enabled a people emerging from serious financial crisis to acclaim the repeal of the Eighteenth Amendment.

Whereas renewed confidence among those who were guiding the destinies of the country came to be for the time being the mood in which Congress resumed its function in January of 1935, many of the more extreme elements in the population still looked for drastic changes. Leaders representing these elements had wide appeal—particularly within a half dozen states of the Union—and there were representatives in the Congress as well.

The fact that the extremists were not satisfied with what the administration was doing is in itself clear evidence, if further evidence was necessary, that the President was succeeding in his role as conciliator of the organized units of the American economy. Whatever may be thought of his qualities in economic statesmanship, his program for labor, agriculture and industry,

---

[18] Pp. 403-404.

as well as for finance, indicated how easily in fact, if not in appearance, he took the middle road. As long as the country felt that it was returning to normal ways of living and working, such a middle road would have great appeal.

A considerable number of business men and industrialists had taken the lead in the formulation of the National Industrial Recovery Act, whereas the reforms proposed in dealing with agriculture and with labor were reforms that had been foreshadowed in much of the agitation of the previous fifty years.

Let it be repeated that, except for the first days of the administration, there was continuous criticism of the actions of the President. This was a natural outgrowth of the arguments that had been given free rein in the campaign of 1932, and that had not abated to any considerable extent in the period prior to the inauguration.

Moreover, this criticism was continually given new reason for existence by the increasing tendency of many, after the immediate crisis had passed, to give fulsome credit to the leadership of the President. From any point of view the center of the controversy was the conduct of the President himself. There was disagreement, and will be for many years to come, as to the extent of the President's influence in the formulation of policies, bills, and pronouncements. Yet however diverse their origin and even their written formulation, it was the President who took responsibility and was held responsible.

In one year of administration he had so completely held the center of the stage that there was agreement by advocate and opponent alike that he was in the line of "strong" Presidents. This was far from the expectation of friends and opponents alike when he had been elected. Thus, increasingly, the issue in politics was the President himself.

The fact that, as a result of the 1934 Congressional elections, the Democratic party maintained its control in both House and Senate meant that through that party organization the President would continue to work his will and that of his advisers. The party membership was of divergent view on the issues before them. It was noted as well that although the Republican membership was on party principle opposed to everything in the President's program, some Republicans in Senate and House were in reality supporters of the President's policies.

Had the President chosen, now that the crisis was past, to turn "right," in the phrase of the day, it is absolutely certain that no leadership existent in the Congress could have commanded a national following for a program of social reform or economic change. If the President did not push reform, no one in Congress would do so. There were aspirants for opportunity to *lead*, but none of real competence. No one, not even Huey Long, Senator from Louisiana, had the power.

Despite Mr. Roosevelt's apparent stand for a policy in advance of Mr. Hoover's, when the President now turned to dealing directly with the problem of insecurity in finance and the problem of social security, he found himself less eagerly followed.

The continuance of a program of government help for unemployment was apparently the most unorthodox of all his plans. It reflected the point of view and purpose of great numbers of social workers, but it certainly did not reflect the convictions of those who felt that government must pay its own way.

In due time, when all the materials are available and when years of research and analysis have carefully arranged the narrative of events, it will be possible to see with reasonable finality how the program of the New Deal was formulated, and why it was planned thus. At present this much can be said:

The President placed himself actively at the head of those who held that government is all-powerful; that it must act for the interests of the people as a whole; that it must convince them it so acts; and that the way to do this is to recognize divergent economic interests, and by arrangement, compromise, and even authoritarian control, to compel them to work together.

Such an approach ran counter to the view and action of the preceding administration; it ran counter, as well, to the prevailing economics of the American system. Within this system, by following an entirely different method of political action, remarkable results had been attained under free enterprise.

But the New Deal did embody a new force to meet a new

emergency. It appeared to fulfill the general point of view which had been held by progressives and liberals and radicals in politics for a half-century.

In seeming, however, to follow a familiar road, that is, in retaining the outward appearance of unlimited private enterprise, the administration was assured of a popular backing. Just so, Mr. Roosevelt was assured of the active opposition of all those who still held to the view that the chief duty of government was merely to hold the balance for a competitive system of free enterprise.

Much has been made, and properly, of the weakness of Mr. Roosevelt's knowledge of economics.[19] Fortunately, his primary task was not in the field of economics. It was in the field of politics. And here he was well informed and by nature interested. Information and interest, together with growing experience, gave him great power.

The President appeared to his fellow citizens in the years 1933-1935 as their symbol of recovery and of promise for the future. His pace of action and of utterance was vigorous. Everywhere he went and before many audiences, he appeared no longer as the advocate of a particular program. He appeared as a new kind of President, and he was given wide acclaim.

Most of his critics present his position unfairly. They condemn his policy because it does not fit into an economic theory, or because it does not give proper protection to some particular group. Yet he was faithful to his idea that he was acting for the American people as a whole. He wanted to protect their liberties and give them opportunities, and he chose measures and men to bring this about.

Much has been said of his use of radio. It lent itself readily to his conception of the role of President. It enabled him to bring within the sound of his voice the masses of men that he repeatedly said were his first concern. He explained to them directly what he was doing and why he was doing it.

---

[19] Banker James P. Warburg, in *Hell Bent for Election*, pp. 67-68, says: ". . . . I am perfectly certain that [Mr. Roosevelt's] mind is capable of delving deeply into a subject. I have seen him delve into subjects in which he was interested. . . . On the other hand, he is undeniably and shockingly superficial about anything that relates to finance. This is not, I think, because he is incapable of grasping these subjects, but because he does not like them and therefore refuses to make any great effort to understand them."

The pattern was a simple one and it rarely varied from the principle underlying his personal approach. He pointed out that all were engaged in a common enterprise, and that he was but voicing enthusiasm and giving expression to the common hope. Moreover, although the problems were national, they were personal. It always appeared that those who opposed the program were not aware of the reasonableness of the solutions offered. They were even enemies of the public welfare. Were it not for these opponents and their views, the common purpose would be easily achieved!

Such a pattern, simple and natural, was readily accepted by the average human being as expressing his view of what he would like to do and would do in public affairs if he were not thwarted by those who united to undo the work of the children of light. It provided a basis upon which the President proposed solutions and argued in favor of their acceptance by his fellow countrymen.

This pattern, followed by the President on the radio and often in personal appearance when impromptu speeches were made, became very persuasive. It could of course be used most effectively by a man who was actually the President, speaking from the exalted position of that office to his constituents. It was an approach used somewhat less effectively in addressing the Congress, or in campaigning, where the President appeared as either a joint ruler in the one case, or as a candidate although in office at the time.

For the Congress there was, in fact, another pattern—in addition, it is true, to a gesture of co-operative understanding. The President, in facing the Congress, was acutely aware that many in his audience were not to be persuaded, and with them he was not disposed to argue. He could and did present his case, but even in the most aggressive mood he always preserved the gentleman's acceptance of the fact that his listeners too had constituents.

Still another pattern prevailed in press conferences. Rarely could a member of the conference feel that he was taken at his full stature, for he was always at a disadvantage. Despite outward cordiality and often much banter, nothing could change the fact that the President was master and would and did refuse to answer, naming his own terms. His constant assumption that, as he often said, he was "writing the story," was an indication of his superior position.

Mr. Roosevelt's conception of political leadership had been seen in his early treatment of the Congress. Here, by general consent, he displayed political adroitness. At a time when he came, in truth, to be the chief lawmaker and was exercising the functions of a prime minister, he was operating in a political atmosphere in which inaction was considered not only politically inept but even worse.

His incisiveness in exercising the powers of a leader had been seen in the procedures by which he was enabled to obtain from the Congress in record time the Emergency Banking Bill, followed by the Economy Bill, and in the midst of final action on this bill, the passage of the first bill to modify the Prohibition Amendment.

Having obtained from the Congress his immediate objectives, the President had then proceeded to deal with agricultural distress and long term unemployment. Securing from the Congress enactments dealing with refinancing of farm mortgages and provision for farm relief by the control of agricultural production, he asked and obtained as well federal grants to the states for direct relief, and the establishment of a federal relief agency with a fund of $50,000,000. The United States Employment Service was established in the Department of Labor, and a much discussed Civilian Conservation Corps was urged upon the Congress and authorized in record time.

A careful reading of the arguments in favor of these enactments convinces one that measures for immediate relief were almost always joined with far-reaching plans for subsequent action. The debate over the establishment of the Tennessee Valley Authority is a case in point. The President had made it very evident, even before he took office, that he had definite plans reaching into the future for the expansion of such powers as had been set up in this initial legislation.

It is to be noted that it was the practice of the President to hold meetings with Congressional leaders of his own party. He worked in close touch with committee chairmen, and when a message was read to the Congress it very soon appeared that a member of the Congress, and sometimes more than one member, was prepared to explain and elaborate upon the proposal.

All this served to emphasize the fact that the President was the unifying force in lawmaking. He spoke with persuasion to the public, and he dealt with great skill in his negotiations with the Congress. This was particularly true when it was evident that blocs were appearing in the Congress representative of veterans, labor organizations, farm organizations, and inflationists. Within a year of the taking of office, it was apparent that there was general acceptance of the fact that under Mr. Roosevelt's leadership the President had become the vital co-ordinating unit in the American system.

Charges of dictatorship were made, arising out of the pressures exerted by Mr. Roosevelt upon the Congress, which were resented by many Congressmen. Such charges were naturally of interest to commentators, who were quick to see that although the formalities of the Constitutional system were being observed, the actualities were quite otherwise.

It must be said that an examination of the comments of the period reveals that the President's control of the patronage was an important factor in his influence upon individual members of the Congress. The forms of legislative enactment were observed. This was possible because the President unerringly chose and maintained the initiative. Buoyed up by unmistakable evidences of popular backing, advised closely by men who were experts in the matter of legislation, the President had a partisan control of the Congress. As has been seen, no Constitutional change had been asked, except for the preliminary steps that had led to the rescinding of the Eighteenth Amendment.

Even though the American system worked through a combination of popular support, Congressional acquiescence, and Presidential initiative, the great test would in the end be what is termed Presidential leadership.

The sessions of the Seventy-third Congress, which concluded in June of 1934, had made amply apparent to all who would see that two aspects of the legislative program associated with the New Deal were now coming to stand forth as all-important. One of these was full acceptance of the idea of vast federal expenditures contributing speedy recovery. The other was the growing satisfaction, at least among those in public office, at the large amount of patronage available and the increasing number of persons dependent upon federal subsidy.

The programs of relief and recovery would in the nature of things cost billions. Inasmuch as no steps had yet been taken to deal effectively with the tax structure, it was apparent that this method of conducting government must rest upon the broad basis of borrowing. The free acceptance of this fact, not of particular interest to the public as a whole, was of vital concern to all those engaged in private enterprise.

A sense of insecurity and uncertainty as to the future was of course particularly felt by those interests in the financial and industrial world concerned with public utilities. The program of the administration embodied in the T. V. A. and the explanations of its purpose clearly foreshadowed extension of governmental activity in this field.

Mr. Hoover repeatedly warned that the greatest danger in planning and regimentation lay in decline of the representative body and undue reliance on bureaucracy. "We cannot extend the mastery of government over the daily life of the people," Mr. Hoover contended, "without somewhere making it master of people's souls and thoughts." [20]

It was clear by this time that the American people had set forth upon an unaccustomed and dimly discerned road to the future.

---

[20] *The Challenge to Liberty*, p. 203.

Chapter VIII

A MASTER PLAN

As the President saw it, the New Deal program was of one piece. It was relief and recovery; it was reform; and it was of vast importance in rebuilding the American system. "It is childish," said Mr. Roosevelt, "to speak of recovery first and reconstruction afterward. In the very nature of the processes of recovery we must avoid the destructive influences of the past." [1] He suggested that there was a master plan, although he did not use that phrase.

Taking such a general view of the President's program, an economist who had observed it closely wrote:

> . . . to appraise the New Deal it is imperative that it be viewed as a whole. No single phase of it can be taken by itself as an accurate sample by which to judge the total. This is equally true regardless of which part one may consider—the monetary manipulations, the enormous spending program, the regulation of business through the National Recovery Administration, the agriculture experiment, the banking and security reforms, or the social legislation. . . . Individually, they are the groundwork

---

[1] *Public Papers, 1934,* p. 287. Mr. Roosevelt later wrote in the Foreword to his gubernatorial papers for 1932 that the New Deal "was not really completely new" in view of his administration as Governor of New York.

for reform; collectively, they are the foundation for social revolution. . . . Unfortunately many people fail to distinguish between the significance of the component parts of the New Deal and the New Deal as a whole. This accounts in no small measure for its widespread appeal. For regardless of whether one's leanings are conservative, liberal, or radical, he can find something that he likes.[2]

In assessing the attitude of the people toward the New Deal, Mr. Roosevelt found that:

In the great national movement that culminated over a year ago, people joined with enthusiasm. They lent hand and voice to the common cause, irrespective of many older political traditions. They saw the dawn of a new day. They were on the march; they were coming back into the possession of their own home land.[3]

In the Seventy-third Congress, the President had found, on the whole, support of his program. In his first Fireside Chat of the year, on June 28, 1934, he remarked that:

It has been well said that while there were a few exceptions, this Congress displayed a greater freedom from mere partisanship than any other peace-time Congress since the Administration of President Washington himself. The session was distinguished by the extent and variety of legislation enacted and by the intelligence and good-will of debate upon these measures.[4]

This was the Congress that, said Mr. Roosevelt, "reorganized, simplified and made more fair and just our monetary system, setting up standards and policies adequate to meet the necessities of modern economic life, doing justice to both gold and silver as the metal bases behind the currency of the United States." [5]

The Gold Reserve Act signed by the President on January 30, 1934, was "rushed through Congress more quickly than seemed justified in a measure which altered monetary practices of a century." [6]

---

[2] Ralph Robey, *Roosevelt versus Recovery*, p. 3.
[3] *Public Papers, 1934*, p. 372.
[4] *Ibid.*, p. 312.
[5] *Ibid.*, p. 313.
[6] A. W. Crawford, *Monetary Management Under The New Deal*, p. 79.

Although a movement toward creation of a system of currency management by the federal government had started prior to Mr. Roosevelt's election in 1932,[7] continuous experimentation with the monetary system throughout his first ten months in office served to identify him with a revolution in the financial system. And so it was. Indeed, "a managed currency system became a definite objective as part of a comprehensive scheme of economic planning." [8]

Yet the President could say, five months later:

A few timid people, who fear progress, will try to give you new and strange names for what we are doing. Sometimes they will call it "Fascism," and sometimes "Communism," sometimes "Regimentation," sometimes "Socialism." But, in so doing, they are trying to make very complex and theoretical something that is really very simple and very practical.

I believe in practical explanations and in practical policies. I believe that what we are doing today is a necessary fulfillment of what Americans have always been doing—a fulfillment of old and tested American ideals. . . .

All that we do seeks to fulfill the historic traditions of the American people. Other Nations may sacrifice democracy for the transitory stimulation of old and discredited autocracies. We are restoring confidence and well-being under the rule of the people themselves. We remain, as John Marshall said a century ago, "emphatically and truly, a government of the people." Our Government "in form and in substance . . . emanates from them. Its powers are granted by them, and are to be exercised directly on them, and for their benefits." [9]

The President, viewing the situation as he saw it in December of 1937, recalled the exercise of Executive power to meet the critical needs of 1933 and 1934:

There was of course uppermost in our minds from the very beginning the question of the extent to which these powers could be exercised. We had to consider not only constitutional provisions and principles, but judicial interpretations and precedents as well.[10]

---

[7] *Ibid.*, p. 13.
[8] *Ibid.*, p. 1.
[9] *Public Papers, 1934,* pp. 317-318.
[10] *Public Papers, 1935,* p. 3.

As the President saw it in 1937:

> For nearly a half century the tendency of the Supreme Court arising from these economic and social predilections has unfortunately been to place a narrowing construction on the powers of Government. The rights of Government to protect individual citizens from aggregations of private economic power were being gradually whittled away. The rights of economically powerful individuals and corporations to pursue activities free from Government restraint, were being continuously extended and glorified.[11]

Moreover, Mr. Roosevelt noted that "commencing in 1935, and running down to the election of 1936, there came a line of decisions from the Supreme Court (and also from lower Federal Courts) which so limited the powers of the Federal Government and the powers of the State Governments to obtain the legitimate objectives for which the people voted at the polls in 1932 and 1934, that all real progress toward those objectives began to appear impossible." [12]

Specifically, the President charged:

> . . . in the year and a half commencing with the "hot oil" case and ending with the New York Minimum Wage case [June 1, 1936], it became quite obvious that the *Advance of Recovery and Reform* begun by the Congress and the Executive in the *Year of Crisis,* which its opponents could not stop by the election of 1934, was being nullified by a barrier which read *"The Court Disapproves."* [13]

Yet Mr. Roosevelt's proposals in the field of reform by no means met the demands of extremists who, particularly in 1935, had a wide field for their talents. Moreover, the fact that the President and his group were not out and out Socialists led to widespread dissatisfaction among doctrinaire radicals. It could be said, notwithstanding, that an "excellent record" in fulfillment of the first twelve planks in the Socialist party platform of 1932 had been made by the Democrats.[14]

On the other hand, the President's pressure for action led to immediate opposition from the conservatives in and out of

---

[11] *Ibid.,* p. 5.
[12] *Ibid.,* pp. 6-7.
[13] *Ibid.,* pp. 12-13.
[14] Warburg, *Hell Bent for Election,* pp. 3-6.

Congress. His insistence, when by the end of 1934 it became evident that he would press forward with undiminished momentum, seemed to make clearer than ever the revolutionary character of the New Deal.

From the point of view of his critics, the nation had never voted such a course of action; had indeed never favored what so often had been offered them. It seemed to follow that if the President's program could be revealed for what it really was, it would be rejected by the electorate in 1936.

Viewed in this light, the political events of 1935 and the first half of 1936 fall into place. The administration reiterated its program of ideas and achieved some important legislation. The opponents prepared a case that appeared to meet their need of emphasizing the revolutionary character of the objectives now revealed by the administration.

Socialists who hitherto had been skeptical of what the administration had accomplished now subdued their political agitation, and it was evident that more radicals would support the President in 1936.

Moreover, the conservative Republicans were now more closely united in opposition, and were joined by some outstanding Democrats as well. A realignment was in the making.

Unreal though this new distribution was in terms of political parties, it was clear enough in the claims of political support made by the President. The President's procedures and his success had in effect destroyed "parties" as they had existed for more than two generations. Party designations lingered on, and the party records of the election of 1936 were to appear in familiar terms. But in fact the President emphasized not a victory for the Democratic party or against the Republican party, but *for* the People—against their selfish and powerful opponents. No demagogue could have stated this more clearly than did the President, when, in addressing the American people on June 28, 1934, he said:

> But the simplest way for each of you to judge recovery lies in the plain facts of your own individual situation. Are you better off than you were last year? Are your debts less burdensome? Is your bank account more secure? Are your working condi-

tions better? Is your faith in your own individual future more firmly grounded? [15]

Those who opposed him, the President said, were

... not the overwhelming majority of the farmers or manufacturers or workers. . . . The most vociferous of the Doubting Thomases may be divided roughly into two groups: First, those who seek special political privilege and, second, those who seek special financial privilege. . . . It is well for us to remember that humanity is a long way from being perfect and that a selfish minority in every walk of life—farming, business, finance and even Government itself—will always continue to think of themselves first and their fellow beings second.

In the working out of a great national program which seeks the primary good of the greater number, it is true that the toes of some people are being stepped on and are going to be stepped on. But these toes belong to the comparative few who seek to retain or to gain position or riches or both by some short cut which is harmful to the greater good.[16]

However, it should not be forgotten that not only within the Democratic party, as represented in the Congress, but within the President's own official and unofficial circle of advisers, there was no unity on program when details were discussed. The "liberals" were divided and presently the original group was broken by resignation, withdrawal, or dismissal. The more "radical" remained with the President.

As has been seen, the Congressional elections of 1934 had brought a great triumph to the President, his personal supporters, and the program associated thus far with the New Deal. A careful examination of the campaign leads to the estimate that of the 561 members of the Seventy-fourth Congress that met in January of 1935, nearly two-thirds had been elected on their pledge to back the purposes of the New Deal.

Perhaps nothing summed up better the general opinion than the assertion of the leader that the fundamental purpose of government was to give security to the people. To the new Congress the President addressed himself first of all on the subject of security:

---

[15] *Public Papers, 1934*, p. 314.
[16] *Ibid.*, p. 315.

We find our population suffering from old inequalities, little changed by past sporadic remedies. In spite of our efforts and in spite of our talk, we have not weeded out the overprivileged and we have not effectively lifted up the underprivileged. Both of these manifestations of injustice have retarded happiness. No wise man has any intention of destroying what is known as the profit motive; because by the profit motive we mean the right by work to earn a decent livelihood for ourselves and for our families.

We have, however, a clear mandate from the people, that Americans must forswear that conception of the acquisition of wealth which, through excessive profits, creates undue private power over private affairs and, to our misfortune, over public affairs as well. In building toward this end we do not destroy ambition, nor do we seek to divide our wealth into equal shares on stated occasions. We continue to recognize the greater ability of some to earn more than others. But we do assert that the ambition of the individual to obtain for him and his a proper security, a reasonable leisure, and a decent living throughout life, is an ambition to be preferred to the appetite for great wealth and great power.[17]

The President said that he was ready to submit to the Congress a program which would "ultimately" provide security of a livelihood through the better use of the national resources of the land in which we live, security against the major hazards and vicissitudes of life, and the security of decent homes.[18]

Calling for an extensive program in public works, the President sought to implement this by a development of plans for the conservation of the natural resources. This was symbolized in the plans for the Tennessee Valley Authority. For here was included a means of providing a yardstick for costs of utilities to the common man, and a definite move to develop the resources of men as well as of nature in a backward section of the nation.

Yet by the close of the first session of the Seventy-fourth Congress in late August of 1935, it had become apparent to all who followed the development of Presidential leadership that the frantic drive which had characterized the early months of the

---

[17] *Public Papers, 1935*, pp. 16-17.
[18] *Ibid.*, p. 17.

year had diminished; that there had been a decided change in the personnel of those closely associated with the President; and that the various elements in the Congress were so at variance in their objectives that even Congressional leadership in matters of legislation could not be expected.

In a very real sense, therefore, the American people had reached a point where, if initiative should be lacking in the administration, and pressures of a "crisis" should no longer disturb the nation as a whole, proponents of extreme measures would have to renew their appeal.

Perhaps the extremists could make it appear that—despite the talk of long term planning and despite the fact that certain legislative proposals had resulted in reforms as distinguished from mere recovery—the great movement for wider political participation and deeper social justice was at a standstill. To those who saw "government" as, above and beyond the people of the United States, an agency that took care of the citizen, this was a situation that must be altered.

It was this point of view that was expressed by a Montana banker who wrote the President urging acceptance of the program of Huey Long, saying Long was "the man we thought you were when we voted for you." [19]

A consideration of the political strategy of Franklin Roosevelt in 1935 must be based in considerable part upon his methods in dealing with the extremist threat exemplified by Huey Long. It was a real danger to orderly government in the United States. For Long was dictator in Louisiana. His appeal on a national scale was that of a dictator. A considerable national following was in existence.[20]

The danger to Roosevelt lay not in the possibility that Long might succeed in capturing control of the national government, nor in Long's direct influence upon national policy,

[19] President's Secretary's File, Box 17, Roosevelt Library. See also memo of L. Howe to F. D. R. February 21, 1935, "It is symptoms like this I think we should watch very carefully. In a letter to Robert Woolley on January 29, 1932, (Woolley Correspondence with Franklin Roosevelt, Library of Congress), the President had written, "Someday when you get a chance, try to have a talk with Huey Long. I want your impressions of him, for I get all sorts of contradictory angles."

[20] In the spring of 1935 a flood of letters on the activities of Huey Long poured into the White House.

legislation, or administration. The danger to the Democratic party lay in the evident fact that an extreme movement—nationally developed in 1936—would take from Roosevelt a large vote and thus would improve the chances of a Republican victory.

Long's vicious attacks upon men in public life, particularly on Democrats in 1935, served to reveal the gulf between the world of politics envisaged by Franklin Roosevelt and that seen by Huey Long. The former worked in a world of accepted political procedures and practices; the latter, in a world of constant stress, turmoil, and terror. "In personal force, ability, resourcefulness and daring he is twenty times the peer of any of the demagogues who have piled up votes in this country since the Populists and Free Silverites captured the rural American imagination," [21] wrote Arthur Krock of Long.[22]

But Raymond Moley deprecated the danger of such demagogues, saying at the time:

> The joy of those opponents of President Roosevelt who have anticipated that Senator Long and Father Coughlin, representing the most articulate and strongest elements on the radical side, could, if united, bring about his defeat in 1936, is destined to be short-lived. The programs of the two men are fundamentally inconsistent. Their background and sympathies, methods, essential purposes and ambitions are totally different. There is no alliance between them, as Father Coughlin himself has stated, and I do not believe there can be.[23]

The great threat, but not the underlying cause for such threats, was removed by the assassination of Huey Long in September, 1935. But, as will be seen, the Presidential contest of 1936 witnessed an attempt to unite such opposition votes as adhered to candidates of his general outlook and character.

As a whole, the American people were beginning to feel in 1935 that they were again in the mainstream of American development. The objectives of the administration appeared to be the following: To continue to reduce unemployment; to de-

[21] *New York Times*, March 27, 1935.
[22] See note, 23, p. 92.
[23] "Madness in March," in *Today*, 3 (March 23, 1935), p. 13.

velop the purchasing power of the people as a whole; [24] to embark upon government projects; to develop reciprocal trade; to deal effectively with the problem of farm prices and farm mortgages; and to develop programs of social security.

These policies, it was thought, would meet pressing economic needs and, as well, contribute to the establishment of greater social justice. Such a program called for procedures associated with an American way, which would provide a wider basis for public welfare.

If this was to be accomplished under the leadership of the executive, it called for action by Congress and, subsequently, for approval by the courts. Methods for its accomplishment must also be developed, because this program demanded of the federal government many functions not before recognized as governmental.

And the program must be convincingly presented to the people, for it was recognized that it would meet the vigorous opposition of opponents of such changes. This need for explanation and for advocacy meant that the forces in favor of change must be marshaled and adequate machinery organized to unify effort.

One might rightly inquire what driving forces were active in this movement which came to be thought of as revolutionary change. There was continued evidence not only of unemployment, but of serious maladjustment of the financial and economic system. Need was in itself an impetus. Yet neither the unsettled condition of the country nor the proposals of the party in power could completely explain the direction taken. Demands of progressives of both parties over the previous half-century were also responsible.

It is significant that Mrs. Roosevelt, at the time viewing the developments of the preceding two years as of deep interest to the people as a whole, was reported in the *New York Times*

---

[24] Robert L. Owen Papers, Library of Congress: The President wrote on November 8, 1935, "As you know, I have long felt that a more generous availability of bank credit could materially assist our business recovery. I have been pleased to note, therefore, that the total of loans and investments of all important banks of the Federal Reserve System has been expanded almost without interruption ever since the middle of 1933, though not at as fast a rate, perhaps, as you desire. The gains of $4 billions in the aggregate of loans and investments, and of $6.16 billions in total deposits, of member banks during that period, have been substantial."

as stating that "The big achievement of the last two years is the great change in the thinking of the country." After listing the accomplishments of the period, she named desirable future achievements as follows:

> . . . complete realization by both labor and industry and capital of their responsibility toward each other and the public . . . a willingness [on the part of industrial leaders] to realize that labor must share to a greater extent and receive a fairer return for its part in the world's work, and that capital shall accept the fact of a more limited and reasonable return . . . a greater understanding [on the part of organized labor] of their responsibilities to the people at large and a recognition of the necessity that they look upon problems not only as problems of organized labor but as problems of the country as a whole . . . a greater realization of our international interdependence and our responsibility toward the rest of the world . . . [realization of] the problem of youth and . . . a more determined effort to be helpful to the rising generation . . . a security program really launched . . . which will include old-age pensions, a permanent ban on child labor, better unemployment insurance, better health care for the country as a whole, better care for mothers and children generally . . .[25]

It is obvious that the momentous developments of these years were associated with statements and actions of the President. That this was not always given adequate emphasis is explained by the fact that, in the period between 1929 and 1935, extreme proposals of numerous groups for changes in the American system were given constant and vigorous presentation in the radical press, on the rostrum, and over the air. The President said of his program:

> The Administration and the Congress are not proceeding in any haphazard fashion in this task of government. Each of our steps has a definite relationship to every other step. The job of creating a program for the Nation's welfare is, in some respects, like the building of a ship. At different points on the coast where I often visit they build great seagoing ships. When one of these ships is under construction and the steel frames have been set in the keel, it is difficult for a person who does not

---

[25] March 3, 1935.

know ships to tell how it will finally look when it is sailing the
high seas.[26]

As was natural, the opposition took many forms and never
ceased to influence methods as well as objectives. It is to be
noted that the attitude of the United States Chamber of Commerce and numerous other organizations of business men was
expressed most emphatically in calls for economy in government and for retrenchment in many of the services provided
by the government. They fought throughout the administration against imposition of a sales tax and against providing
huge sums for relief of unemployed workers.

The attitude which best expresses the conservative view toward every ambitious program of the administration was one
which drove all opponents of the President's program into the
position of those desiring weak government. The conservative
view assumed that the proper method of dealing with the problems of agriculture or of labor or of industry was to let private
agencies—which were said to express American life best—work
out their various problems without undue interference by the
government.

This would leave government in the position of umpire,
which is precisely where the conservatives have always conceived of it in the United States. Such a solution of course
would also take care of the mounting costs of administration.
The realism of such an approach rested in the fact that men of
experience in business and in government knew that the widespread belief that the people in the mass could conduct their
intricate economic life rested upon a fallacy. Experts must do
it.

As the second half of the year 1935 unfolded, the question
repeatedly arose whether the extremists divided the electorate
in such manner as to take away any possibility of the power of
decision. In short, might the presidential power be shorn of
its basic popular support? On the surface, extremists of all
kinds called for a strong Executive, and pushed for more and
more strong action by the President.

Despite growing dependence upon strong executives to deal

---

[26] *Public Papers, 1935*, p. 132.

with the problems of the modern world, those who tended to be conservative gathered strength in opposition to the call for dictatorial power.

The President answered, in speaking to the Young Democrats on August 24, 1935, that thirty years before, men had talked as if the people of this country would never be haunted by the grim specter of insecurity, for this was a land of plenty. "I did not know then of the lack of opportunity, the lack of education, the lack of many of the essential needs of civilization which existed among millions of our people," he confessed, and expressed the belief that the depression had taught the American people that they were not "immune." Whereas he pointed at the new need for new devices in economic, social, and political life to protect people under modern conditions, he said, "I do not believe in abandoning the system of individual enterprise." [27]

But in preparing for the election that was to come in 1936, the Administration had to face the harsh fact that the Public Works Administration had not "solved" the problem of vast unemployment. "Practical" men within the administration, notably Harry Hopkins, were prepared to deal with this as a political as well as an economic problem. It meant the expenditure of millions in the Works Progress Administration.[28]

What really emerged, as preliminary to the Presidential contest of 1936, was a familiar battle line—yet one that had disappeared in the course of the depression and remained in obscurity for a time even during the days of recovery. Could an old-fashioned conservative win against an acknowledged progressive?

Many of the conservatives who entered into the campaign professed to believe that it would be possible to defeat the Democrats. First, they reasoned, the depression had passed; second, elements within the Democratic party opposed to the newer elements had achieved a veto power upon further action.

[27] *Ibid.*, pp. 338-341.
[28] It was this struggle coming to a head in the early spring of 1936 that gave the public an example of the fighting within the administration, in this case between Ickes and Hopkins. As always, the personal struggle interested millions; the real issue at stake, a very few. And it was not until the publication of two books, Robert Sherwood's *Roosevelt and Hopkins,* and Harold Ickes' *Secret Diary,* that it was evident how completely Hopkins had won and why.

But so divided was the Republican party, owing to older divisions within it prior to the Roosevelt administration, that no direct challenge was made to the state socialism implicit in the development of the New Deal at this time. It is doubtful whether a majority of the electorate would have supported such a challenge. The American voters had long been fed upon the food of the progressives and were pleased enough with what had thus far been done without too carefully examining its implications.

No study of Mr. Roosevelt's leadership as President in this period would be complete without analysis of the responses made to executive action at this time by the other branches of the American system—the Congress and the Court. Visualizing both branches as composed of human beings—to be led, to be conciliated, to be overcome on occasion—Roosevelt found that they, too, could initiate as well as respond. They not only voted or gave opinions; they moved in opposition. And they revealed, in their various responses, the great body of voters they represented.

The President had compelled the Congress to remain in session until August of 1935 to enact the proposals in legislation which had been made to them. This was done in order that the second session of the Seventy-fourth Congress meeting in January of 1936 would be brief. Sporadic debate upon the separation of powers meanwhile had continued. At the same time, dissent was indicated in the decisions of the Supreme Court.

However, after the Court had invalidated the Agricultural Adjustment Act, two new bills dealing with the problem were introduced into the Congress and passed.

As it became clearer that decisions of the Court were to stand across the path of much New Deal legislation, discussion arose in the Congress, among both Republicans and Democrats, of what they termed judicial tyranny. To meet this in its simplest form Senator Ashhurst proposed that a Constitutional amendment be provided granting to the Congress "power to make laws to regulate agriculture, commerce, industry, and labor."

Two evidences of the atmosphere in which the legislation of an election year was considered were found in the fact that the substitute farm bills were prepared not in Congress but by Secretary Wallace in consultation with farm advisers, and that the revised tax bill was prepared by officials in the Treasury. The clearest evidence of the persistent attitude of the President toward his place in the government was found in the fact that the annual message to the Congress of January 3, 1936, was delivered at an hour chosen by him in order that it might be broadcast by radio to the people of the United States.

But the President now seemed less aggressive, both in the proposals he had made to the Congress and in the assertions made in his annual message. No specific requests for legislation were made in the annual message. By some it was felt that the President intended to give less guidance than in the previous three years. Even on the question of a bonus to veterans, the President was less inclined to oppose vigorously the majority sentiment of the Congress, which passed the Bonus Bill over his veto.

Dealing with the Congress, or dealing directly with the people, the President could push, as he so often did, the idea of "evil forces" and of "selfish interests." But in dealing with his immediate advisers, and particularly with the Court, all proposed measures must be presented as workable, efficient, and Constitutional. Herein was revealed the President's weakness, which was presently to come to judgment.

The new view of government must embody a strong appeal to the electorate. The scientific approach to legislation by experts, and to interpretation by jurists, had little to do with political pressures or with the will of the people. Thus, the use of patronage by the President and the spreading of public works for the purposes of relief and security were arguments used to overcome those who would deal more exactly, and therefore more slowly, with all proposals for remaking the American system.

Perhaps in the perspective of time, the greatest contribution of Franklin Roosevelt to the welfare of the American people will be seen not in his insistence upon political freedom and social justice for all men, but in his assumption on occasion that the increasing enlightenment of more and more people would bring a heightened sense of individual responsibility.

Insisting, as he did, upon ideas of reform, he used new agencies in government. Being a representative of the highest development of individual opportunity for the privileged in American society, he could not but envisage for the future an American society in which the truly representative individual would be one who, like himself, embodied a deep sense of obligation to do his part.[29]

The opportunism so often evident in Franklin Roosevelt's leadership, the experimentation which came to be thought of as an integral part of his procedure arose perhaps as much out of the opportunity he had experienced in American life as it did out of the necessities he faced in office. His influence, which was sufficient to win a wide response, was found in what he appeared to embody.

In a world—including the United States—deeply moved by crisis in war and in peace, masses of men felt and thought in terms of strong leadership. The protections provided in the American electoral system and in widespread economic opportunity explain why the American people did not follow, as did so many other peoples, "the man on horseback." Perhaps another fact however, has been overlooked. From American society emerged not the military leader, nor the special interest tyrant, nor even a representative of the submerged millions, but a man who embodied the kind of life that Americans liked to call their own.

It would seem improbable that at this stage of American development a man of the people, or a successful practitioner of his own business or profession, or the officeholder however devoted to the public need—would quite meet the demands of this dream of an all-sufficient American. Of course he must in a sense stand apart from business or profession or office. He must not be too occupied with the demands of social life. He must be a man who had some freedom and who liked to use it because he liked to live with the people.

Surely there was in this widespread acclaim given Franklin

---

[29] Some such view was taken by Secretary Ickes in his comments—written at the time. Although he had various disagreements with the President, and he could believe that the President often worked without a definite plan, yet he concluded, "I told him there wasn't another man in the United States who could lead the country at this time along the paths that it ought to tread." *Secret Diary* (1933-1936), p. 104.

Roosevelt something more than a response to his actions or to his utterances. Back of these and explaining them is the man himself, or perhaps more exactly, the man the people felt existed. And he was a man who had experienced, through inheritance and contact, the best that American life could give his generation.

For it appeared to masses of his fellow citizens that Franklin Roosevelt had dealt effectively, if not efficiently, with the problems of relief born of widespread depression. He had also led in developing a program that appeared to provide for a road to economic recovery on familiar American lines. What was more natural than to suppose that such a leader was dealing with relief and recovery in such a manner because he believed that in the American system there were, as Americans had always said, great capacities for reform.

Chapter IX

1936: MANDATE OF THE PEOPLE

IN THE CONGRESSIONAL ELECTIONS of 1934, the American people had in their first opportunity, expressed their reaction to the leadership of Franklin Roosevelt. The electorate had seen effective government in action, for President and Democratic majorities in the Congress had worked together.

The voters had seen the pledges of the Democratic platform repudiated. They had seen erected a vast structure of "recovery and relief" legislation. They had seen full confirmation given to the progressive pronouncements of many years.

The people had, in 1934, returned enlarged Democratic majorities to the Congress. Thus, for the years 1935 to 1937 the President was enabled to continue his earlier course of action and to meet effectively the calls of radicals for measures that far outdistanced all proposals that had earlier been made by the Democratic and Progressive parties.

Mr. Roosevelt's foreign policy had held the support of the vast majority of the people because of its adroit combination of conflicting views.

By the spring of 1936 there was no doubt as to the case President Roosevelt would present to the nation. Yet grave doubt was expressed at times by members of the Democratic "high command" as to whether he could win the election.

This Presidential election was the first of the three tests of the whole electorate on the leadership of President Roosevelt. It was a national test—not of groups, organizations, leaders, or parties—but of the entire body of voters, a possible forty-five million. Approximately one-half of the vote would be cast in the eight states of the Middle Atlantic and North Central sections of the United States.

The opponents of the President comprised elements well recognized by all commentators: The primary opposition was of course the national Republican party organization and its chosen nominee, former President Herbert Hoover. Those who followed him in his interpretation of events in speech, magazine, and book represented a hazard of uncertain proportions. The Democratic conservatives were now formally organized in opposition to the New Deal, most conspicuously in the American Liberty League.[1] There were, as well, extremists fighting at random outside of the two major parties, but particularly against the existing government.

All of these had one objective in common: to defeat the re-election of President Roosevelt. They knew this to be necessary in order to obstruct the kind of changes associated with the New Deal, which was repugnant to all of them.

To meet this opposition, Mr. Roosevelt must promise continued advancement on the road of reform. Aside from this, his chief claim would have to be that the country had recovered from economic distress.

Of the arguments used by the opposition, aside from those that were always present, two stand forth: First, that the costs of recovery as supervised by the administration were too great for the country to bear; and, second, that the administration proposals for reform, especially because of the way in which they were being developed, meant destruction of the American system of private enterprise. In short, the two charges most frequently pressed were summed up in the assertion that the administration was not what it claimed to be.

The elements of strength in the Democratic appeal for the

---

[1] Organized in 1934, this group came to include Alfred E. Smith and John W. Davis, both of whom had been nominees of the Democratic party for the Presidency.

Presidential election included, of course, control of the Democratic party organization; active support and sure votes of all the southern states; the support of progressives, some of whom had been won to Roosevelt's program four years before; and the vote of radicals who saw in the new administration a surer realization of their hopes than had attended any previous leader, even Theodore Roosevelt or Woodrow Wilson. These elements did not include the Socialist leaders although some habitual Socialist voters were included.[2] A new element of voting strength was derived from the fact that millions of persons were now and had been for some time dependent upon the national government either for wages or unemployment relief.[3]

It would seem that nothing could possibly defeat Mr. Roosevelt in his second campaign if he could succeed in polling all of these elements. Arguments as to the cost of the New Deal, or its radicalism, would fall on deaf ears. It would appear to millions of Americans that the President had saved the country, that he had provided a strong government, that he had pushed measures of social justice. Through it all, he had stressed the strengthening of political democracy. His program, as has been seen, had something for labor, something for the farmer, something for industry. It perhaps could be ignored that the "elite" opposed him.

Even the representatives of the "elite" had to admit that the country seemed restored to confidence in its future; that amid a world toying with machinery of totalitarianism, the American forms of government had been maintained; that the existence of private enterprise had remained fundamental; that even though the cost of government had risen, the rights of the people had been strengthened. It could be argued that the ex-

---

[2] Norman Thomas, in *Is the New Deal Socialist?*, answered that it was "state capitalism" (p. 7). He said further: "Mr. Roosevelt did not carry out the Socialist platform, unless he carried it out on a stretcher. . . . His slogan was not the Socialist cry: 'Workers of the world, workers with hand and brain, in town and country, unite!' His cry was: 'Workers and small stockholders unite, clean up Wall Street.' That cry is at least as old as Andrew Jackson. What Mr. Roosevelt and his brain trust and practical political advisers did to such of the Socialist immediate demands as he copied at all merely illustrates the principle that if you want a child brought up right you had better leave the child with his parents and not farm him out to strangers" (pp. 4-5).

[3] This was expressed most vigorously in the increasing activities of Harry Hopkins and enlarged sums spent on the W.P.A. projects in the spring of 1936.

tremists were finding it less easy to gain adherents. The success of the administration seemed to indicate that it had effectively taken a middle road.

What, then, could be said against continuance of such an administration? The whole enterprise had been too costly; it had been shot through with appalling inefficiency; it contained threats of additional legislation which were undermining confidence; and it was not anything more than a temporary solution. It was pointed out that the huge costs and the army of dependents made the government weaker when it claimed to be stronger. Could a people's government assume, under the American system, such burdens, such costs, and such powers?

The strength of established leadership needs to be recognized. Mr. Roosevelt was in office. He was not a contender for office. He was the executive, and he personified the administration. This of course meant that he, personally, was under attack. But he did not envisage himself in office as either *executive* or *administrator*. This became particularly evident as he entered actively upon the campaign for re-election.

He envisaged himself as the *representative* of the people. He was leading them in a crusade. Constantly he saw, and said he saw, the forces of evil taking rights and powers and opportunities away from the people. In assuming this position, he made it abundantly clear that his critics were quite right. He was fighting against them, and he was taking power from them, taking privilege from them, taking money from them. He was their enemy.

Had Mr. Roosevelt seemed to be a less intelligent man, had he emphasized in manner the traits of a demagogue, and in particular had he risen from the people, it would have been clearer to all that he was, as he said near the close of the campaign, envisaging himself as "master" of the forces that hated him so profoundly. Having such a conception of his leadership, he could quite naturally use the phrase "economic royalists" in description of his opponents.

Yet it is true that Franklin Roosevelt did not hold the view that, because the people had the power to decide, their decisions were necessarily right. He had said in 1932 in Georgia and again in San Francisco, that it is the duty of the statesman to educate. He took upon himself when in office to organize such agencies as would provide solutions for the problems of government. He believed that, placed in office by decision of the people, leaders of the people were bound by duty to formulate and provide the right outcomes of those decisions. This conception placed upon President Roosevelt and his government great burdens. It fitted well the idea of a strong government, yet one always backed by the people.

The President had put himself at the head of a general movement, long in the making, to provide national solutions for national problems in industry, labor, and farming. In the period of the crisis—to save time—the formulation of these programs were not left to the Congress.

Again and again, a small group of continually changing personnel worked with the President in composing plans. The administration pressed the programs; Congress prepared, or at least passed, the bills. An administrative agency was then provided to carry out the purposes of the enactment. This was seen, for example, in the Agricultural Adjustment Act and in the National Industrial Recovery Act.

This procedure was by some designated an American form of fascism. The basic point of view of the proponents and of the critics was, however, the same. Nothing effective could be done to deal with problems of employment or of marketing except on a national scale, whether it be done by public or by private means. It would seem to follow that if the problems were national and not to be dealt with by the states, such problems called also for unity of action by the economic interests involved.

Only economic agencies could deal effectively with such problems as production, prices, and wages. If no group of private interests could proceed to do this on a national scale, then government must do it. Moreover, so intricate were these matters that the Congress could not legislate, except in the most general terms, nor could the courts interpret, except on general principles. The solution must be the work of administrative agencies that could effectively deal with the intricacies of the problem and the niceties of personnel, each of these within the general framework of a legislative statute.

Mr. Roosevelt as candidate was in a position to emphasize his role as an evangelist. He spoke with authority and what was believed to be deep understanding of the problems of government. He specialized in expression of hope for the future. He did not need to discuss doctrine nor did he need to emphasize unity of forces. As an experienced leader of the people, he could rightly take the highroad of the crusade for righteousness. He need not counsel caution, and he need not appear humble.[4]

It is a common practice of American political campaigning to make extreme statements and to apply violent terms to the opponent, whoever he may be. Yet it is doubtful whether, in American practice, there has been a clearer example of unfair campaigning than that of Mr. Roosevelt in 1936. It can be justly retorted that the opposition was violent. Mr. Roosevelt, however, was President of the United States.

Repeatedly he insisted, early in the year, in his Jackson Day address and later in his campaign speeches, that he represented *all* the people. Then, in doing so, he singled out elements in the population as antagonists who were declared to be small in number, self-seeking, and ill informed.

It must be emphasized that campaigning as he did, not only in the autumn of 1936 but in his addresses to the Congress during the year, President Roosevelt was attacking the basic assumption of an effective system of government by *laws* rather than by *men*. He repeatedly singled out men in groups as opposed to the administration, however, and intimated and later asserted that he would master them. In both cases he accepted the less desirable practices in American politics. In truth, he was not the first national leader to follow this course of action.

In attacking groups as he did, the President asserted that they were enemies of the masses of the American people. He would dignify the contest at times by pointing out differences of opinion as to measures and as to policies. But again and again his opponents were singled out as enemies of the people, and

---

[4] The "acceptance" speech at Franklin Field, Philadelphia, on June 27, 1936, is an outstanding example of his appeal. It contains denunciation of "economic royalists" and envisages a "rendezvous with destiny." It was this speech which Moley said finally caused him to leave the service of the President, because after Moley had a part in preparation of the speech the President "incorporated passages that seemed to be designed to inflame class feeling and bitter antagonisms." (Moley, *How to Keep our Liberty,* p. 98.)

appeals were made to the people to support *him*. What, surely, could a people do except vote against their enemies? And the President added for good measure that the people were not only ill informed, but that the truth was kept from them by their leaders and particularly by their newspapers. From his high point of influence, the Presidential office, he could assert such partial truths without fear of effective denial.[5]

It may be said that he was riding the storm. For, although the immediate crisis for the United States seemed past, the demands of extremists were not abating. And all the world seemed about to burst into flames.

Many American radicals who were actively interested in extreme measures had long held the support of Socialists or of Communists. Mr. Roosevelt was neither. But in his emotional appeals, he was depending upon the support of widespread discontent to further strengthen his own particular program of revolutionary control.

Unlike theorists among the intellectuals, and unlike the advocates of structural change operating within the minor parties, Mr. Roosevelt would continue to lead in accomplishing a revolution of his own.

That this point of view was held by the President not only during the campaign but subsequently, as he reviewed events and was conscious of his overwhelming victory, is seen in his summary written early in 1938. In this there was still an indication of the violence of his attitude toward the opposition and his insistence upon his own way. It appeared in his identification of his program with the interests of the masses of the people. His charge against the selfishness of opposing interests grew in intensity. Writing on January 17, 1938, he said:

> Looking back on the year 1936, I consider it a period in which the American people began to think more than before in specific terms. In the three previous years . . . we had been thinking rather generally in terms of "business," "agriculture," "industry," and "labor."
>
> In 1936, however, we commenced to discriminate in our public thinking. . . . For example, the public began fully to under-

---

[5] The drafts for the acceptance speech of 1936 were militant in tone. Some —but not all—of the militancy appeared in the final speech. (See Drafts of Acceptance Speech of 1936, Roosevelt Library.)

stand that the efforts of the Administration and the Congress to close loopholes in the tax laws which had been taken advantage of by a few rich men and corporations, were not an attack on all rich men and corporations; and, in the same way, that efforts to end abuses perpetrated by some public utilities were not a campaign against successful private ownership of utilities.[6]

The completeness of the change that had come over the political scene in four years may be seen in the comparison of Mr. Roosevelt as leader with all would be competitors. The Republican showing in the campaign of 1936 had been feeble, although the Republicans in convention had drawn up a telling indictment of the New Deal and declared "America is in peril." Governor Landon had proved to be no match for the successful Roosevelt.[7]

Within the Democratic party no national leader had a substantial following in his opposition to the President. It was not that the President-in-office created this situation, although outwardly this appeared to many to be the case. In fact, no one in the Democratic party had the national stature to compete in such a contest as took place in this second campaign.

Dictator he might not be—as some judged the President was —in intention or in method or in manner. But to have only one real competitor in the realm of debate—and that one competitor still under the cloud of misunderstanding that had covered him when he left office in March of 1933—gave any contest an air of unreality. Mr. Hoover, as he continuously opposed the President, was in fact his only experienced and informed antagonist.

As Walter Lippmann had said:

Our political customs accentuate the difficulty of organizing the opposition. For those most competent to lead it—namely, those who have held responsible posts in the previous administration—are forced into complete retirement. It is a wasteful and inherently absurd arrangement which deprives the nation

---

[6] *Public Papers, 1936*, p. 5.

[7] A caustic note on Landon's real place was indicated by Carter Glass when he said to the President, who had asked him to speak for the ticket in '36: "Since I must vote for a New Dealer, I prefer to vote for a first-rate one rather than one who is distinctly second-rate. That means I will vote for you." (R. Smith and N. Beasley, *Carter Glass*, p. 369.)

of the services of those most able to criticize, and produces such spectacles as the attempt of Republican Senators to debate the money bill though they do not understand it, while Mr. Hoover and Mr. Ogden Mills, who have the equipment to understand it, are not heard in the debate.[8]

To interpret the outcome of the election of November, 1936, in the light of a simple comparison with the election four years earlier would be a mistake.[9] The comparison is easy and patent to the eye in terms of declared issues, campaign utterances, and the result in votes cast. Considering the latter, it is obvious that the electorate endorsed the administration of President Roosevelt and did so in decided terms, measured either by his proportion of the Presidential vote, or by the vote cast for his supporters in the Congress. The American people had accepted the Roosevelt regime and asked for more of it.[10]

The situation—economic, political, and social—at the opening of the year 1937 was quite unlike the situation four years earlier when Mr. Roosevelt, newly elected, was during the interregnum composing his program, selecting his advisers, and refusing to cooperate with his predecessor. Notably, in 1933 prior to the inauguration, there was real uncertainty as to the administrative capacity of Franklin Roosevelt, and real doubt whether he had an integrated program and an overwhelming concern with the vital functions of government.

In 1937 Mr. Roosevelt could present a record of utterance and action; of mode of conduct and use of the tremendous powers of the Presidency. This record gave all discerning ob-

---

[8] *Op. cit.*, p. 300.

[9] "The general impression of the overwhelming nature of the victory for the Democrats is drawn from the fact that Landon carried only two states, Maine and Vermont, and won eight electoral votes. In forty years only Taft's defeat in the three-cornered contest of 1912 had produced such a Republican record in state control. . . . Although the percentage of the total vote of 1936 which went to Mr. Roosevelt was 60.2 percent, as compared with 57.4 percent of the total vote in 1932, this was slightly less than the percentage cast for Harding in 1920." (Robinson, *They Voted for Roosevelt*, pp. 36-37.)

[10] "So overwhelming was Roosevelt's 1936 victory that its political decisiveness is often overlooked. . . . But 1936 was also the year of realignment in which the Democrats became the nation's normal majority party. The traditional dominance which the Republicans had enjoyed since the Civil War was washed away and a new era in American politics began." (Samuel Lubell, *The Future of American Politics*, p. 43.)

servers a sense of impending change far greater than feared in 1933, and also warning of a revolutionary movement to achieve objectives often stated but never achieved.

The endorsement of the President in 1936 meant that for the first time in all the history of movements for reform in the United States, a leader who had been in office with intention to promote reform was given a mandate to achieve results, even though by so doing he was in the process of changing the government of the United States.

So long had reform proposals been advocated by pioneer insurgent and minor parties—thereby furnishing a tinge of danger to all electoral contests—that urging reform was commonly regarded as inherent in the functioning of American democracy. But now many of these long-urged reforms were embodied in the plans of the administration in power.

The contest between those favoring plans of the administration and the advocates of extreme measures did not now seem so important as it had prior to the death of Huey Long in 1935. As radicalism came to be less important, in view of the electoral decision in November of 1936, so, too, the progressives of various shades of opinion in both major parties attracted less attention. They appeared unnecessary to the Democrats in view of Mr. Roosevelt's control of the party machinery, his mastery of the various economic elements giving him support, and his declared purposes.

The plan of campaign and its appeal to various elements is clearly seen in the titles given the President's major campaign addresses: "Never Has a Nation Made Greater Strides in the Safeguarding of Democracy"; "This Administration Is Determined to Continue in Active Support of the Ever-Growing Farm Co-operative Movement," "The American Farmer Living on His Own Land Remains Our Ideal of Self-Reliance and of Spiritual Balance," "We Have Sought and Found Practical Answers to the Problems of Industry, Agriculture, and Mining," "It Was This Administration Which Saved the System of Private Profit and Free Enterprise," and "The Interest of Every Business Man Is Bound to the Interest of Every Wage Earner." [11]

---

[11] Titles of addresses as published in *Public Papers, 1936*.

The record of President Roosevelt's first administration had placed him beyond competition for office. His program had eliminated the need of radicalism other than his own. It had made parties of doctrine, long time rivals in national contest, seem pathetic and beyond real discussion.

It was also true that his accomplishments had given the President powers in office and in his relations with the Congress far outreaching any hitherto asserted by any leader of the American people. No one of his predecessors at any time had had endorsement for a revolutionary program.

President Roosevelt had asked for just that. He had said in the campaign that he wished to master the forces that opposed him. Throughout his administration, he had said repeatedly —and confirmed in action—that he was working on behalf of the people and protecting them from the evil forces that stood between them and their desired objectives.

President Roosevelt's wide acclaim had been often stressed. Yet many thoughtful citizens, careful scholars, experienced men of affairs, and many holding Socialistic views—did not share in this acknowledgment. This fact cannot be dismissed by the assertion that resistance was due to selfish personal reasons or lack of fundamental understanding. The matter is not so simple. It cannot be said that the mass of men and the minorities among them vote as they do simply because it is to their self-interest to do so.

No leader having the kind of support given Franklin Roosevelt could have seemed satisfactory to the doctrinaire Socialist, the trained scientist, or the experienced man of the world. The program and the conduct of Mr. Roosevelt were opportunistic and experimental—in a word "political"—in a sense understood by the *mass* of men in the American democracy. Rising not too far above the crowd in his comprehension, the President at this time seemed to voice very well what they thought and felt. So this patrician was thought of as a man of the people.

It was said, in this campaign in particular, that Mr. Roosevelt's leadership had an appeal for young people. It did, and he spoke of this frequently. There was reason for this eager response, in that he had done so much for youth in the opening years of the administration. His approach to public problems placed emphasis on the brighter future that youth would have, for this future would ensue for all those who were then taking their places in the world of work.

Moreover, youth in these years had turned in an even greater degree than usual to programs of reform, and had been unusually interested in suggestions for fundamental change. There were some who saw in communism a natural development, so they said, of American democracy.

The President, as he looked back upon the year 1936, felt that lip service had been given by his opponents to many of the accomplishments of the first administration, and that this had led to emphasis on minor errors and to a tendency to increase personal attacks. He felt that the opposition of at least 85 percent of the press was a serious deterrent to full understanding of what had been accomplished.

It was the Supreme Court, however, that had actually struck down many of the legislative enactments of the Congress, and obviously something must be done to deal with this obstruction of the popular will. For the New Deal had been endorsed by the people in November of 1936. As the President wrote in January, 1938,

> It was hoped that, in the election, a great popular majority would express itself in favor of the New Deal objectives. This hope was abundantly fulfilled. The overwhelming popular and electoral approval followed the clear-cut statement of our objectives in our platform and in many of my campaign speeches, especially in my Madison Square Garden speech where I made a definite promise that the fight for them would go on with unabated vigor. . . . The election results permitted no doubt whatsoever to remain that, so far as the policies and goal of the New Deal were concerned, *The People Approve.*[12]

But how to rule for the people? All the movements for better government, or provision for superior civil service, have been advanced on the assumption that the essential of good government is a sound program and honest administration. When Mr. Roosevelt called upon experts to prepare bills and lawyers to explain programs, he was in line with approved procedure.

---

[12] *Public Papers, 1936,* p. 5.

But when he denounced men for disagreeing with his proposals, not because they argued against efficiency or soundness but because they represented selfish interests, he was leaving the area of scientific government for the forum of the demagogue.

In using the methods of the demagogue, Franklin Roosevelt was doing nothing new. In that sense, his revolutionary procedures were closely akin to those of a long line of American radicals. But *his* revolution consisted in making over the government itself: first, in a tremendous concentration of power in the Executive; second, in building up a vast system of bureaucratic control of private business; and third, by destroying the idea that much could be achieved for the people, by the government as umpire, through a careful adjustment of conflicting economic interests.

It is not possible to get at the heart of the Roosevelt revolution by confining attention to Mr. Roosevelt's wide support by masses of the population. The revolution consisted, rather, in a complete shift of the American view of the *role* of government. Government, and particularly the Executive, was to be all-powerful.

The defense of this—if there was a defense—was that the people freely and frequently could pass judgment upon it. As long as free elections persisted at stated times, no danger was embodied in such a government.

Protection against the action of a powerful government was assured by the strong weapon in American practice—free speech and the free press. Of course any suppression of absolute freedom would limit criticism.

It is perhaps significant that, like all popular leaders, the President was highly critical of those who freely criticized him. It is perhaps also significant that the masses did not fail to support him, and that except for a minority of extremists they failed to criticize him. Support based upon absence of criticism shelters the seeds of disaster. Had there been at any time a mere suggestion of suppression of the newspapers and commentators who vigorously opposed him, it would have been clearer to all how great a claim to absolute power the President's utterances and acts embodied.

To sum up the effect of Mr. Roosevelt's leadership at the time of his first re-election, it might be said that it was altogether "good" in arousing the public conscience to evils which had been observed by generations, but which had never moved any group in power to a comprehensive program of change. It might be added that it was "good" that he was able to formulate changes and to write them into law.

On the other hand, that his leadership aroused intense antagonism on the part of the more thoughtful members of society, was a direct effect of the basic *methods* used by the President. That is, in declaring that championship of a program on behalf of the people was in itself an indication of the virtue of the program, the President allied himself with the oldest enemies of democracy, in scorn of careful and sustained thought.

It cannot be said that in the long run the Roosevelt leadership was "good" in weakening greatly the powers of Congress. It must be admitted, however, that the events which followed the end of the Roosevelt years would tend to suggest that Congress has returned to somewhat the same position and function that it occupied prior to 1933.

It cannot be said that the attitude of the masses of the people on the Roosevelt leadership at this time was altogether healthy. That the place of careful planning was weakened is notable. In short, Mr. Roosevelt's experiments worked the greatest harm to the very people they were intended to benefit.

Yet, in the perspective of the intervening years, the emotional drive back of many of the violent charges against the President seems as unreal as the emotions of men a hundred or five hundred years ago. That Franklin Roosevelt was destroying private enterprise, was providing financial ruin, was substituting for a people's government a vast unmanageable bureaucracy; that there was in existence an electioneering agency that could not be beaten,[13] that the administration was in fact Socialistic and Communistic—criticisms that won plaudits from conservatives in 1936—seem unreal in 1955.

---

[13] Harold Ickes, in his diary entry for September 8, 1936, wrote: "The President approved a number of new PWA projects totaling something in excess of $7 million. He spoke with great enthusiasm of some PWA projects that he had seen in Indianapolis [housing projects]. . . . His picture was in the window of every house. . . . He thought these projects would be of great advantage politically. . . . *Secret Diary* (1933-1936), p. 673.

The fundamental reason the changes brought about in the New Deal were not permanent was the absence of an integrated and substantial opposition program against which this social revolution could be measured. The revolution was understood clearly neither by its proponents nor by the opposition. This is to be borne in mind in considering the struggle between the President and the courts in the following chapter.

In view of the appeal made by Mr. Roosevelt on behalf of political democracy, social justice, and a more attractive future, and the endorsement of him by such a large majority, why was it that so many of the thoughtful, the educated, and the experienced in public affairs were opposed to him? Why were opposition candidates able in elections to poll such large protest votes? Why did the opposition in proportion as well as in numbers grow as the years went on?

These are not questions to be answered by simply saying that opposition naturally grows in a free country, or that "selfish interests" found that progressive programs lamed their financial returns, or that organized opposition was a habit deeply embedded in American history and constantly practiced by politicians who had their way to make.

Even the "selfish interests" in American society, it might be argued, would have brought Mr. Roosevelt support in time, because of the changes in his own program.

It is necessary to search more deeply for the cause of a poignantly felt and widespread opposition to Mr. Roosevelt in 1936. It may be helpful, in so doing, to question certain basic assumptions made by those who supported him.

Was the interpretation, given his election of 1932, that it was a triumph of the people, sound in the perspective of the years? Had the country asked a thorough overhauling of its economic system by its selection of Democratic leaders in 1932? Did the legislation of the critical year 1933 produce lasting confidence and provide a basis for satisfactory solutions? Was the conduct of the President in his dealings with the Congress or with the press that of a leader of superior stature? Was Mr. Roosevelt's conduct of foreign affairs as soundly based and as concisely stated as to make possible the formulation of a policy that would insure national security?

Mr. Roosevelt's conception of the Presidency, as he saw it in 1936, and the way he had functioned in the light of that conception during the first administration should be used as one basis for judging his influence upon the American system and his success in office.

Out of office and in an opposition party, his type of leadership would not have been at its best. In view of his record, it is difficult to think of him as a minority leader year by year urging a forlorn hope. His participation as Vice-Presidential candidate in the campaign of 1920 is a case in point.

Nor is it possible to envisage him providing patient and enduring leadership in a long campaign to present a particular program to an uninterested and unresponsive voting population.

As a leader of the Congressional opposition, he would have been at a disadvantage, lacking knowledge of economics and the technicalities of legislation, and being unwilling or unable to co-operate with men of equal responsibility.

But from the outset, the Presidency afforded him an opportunity to govern and to lead, in his own way. His concept and use of this office is clearly indicated by the kind of followers that composed his immediate group of advisers. Perhaps more revealing still was the kind of opposition he incurred at each stage of his Presidency—never more clearly than in the campaign of 1936.

Against a background of a generation of political history (1900-1936), the American people returned to office a President who under the slogan of "New Deal" and speaking for "The Forgotten Man," had provided a government in the pattern well recognized by radicals and progressives. This was a fact. No previous leader had done it—not even Woodrow Wilson in the first year and a half of his administration.

Why had it been possible for Franklin Roosevelt to win confirmation in 1936? Were the people convinced that they could turn back on the road that led to national growth? Did they realize that Roosevelt's road meant, by contrast, another way of life? Or had they re-elected Roosevelt because they had been saved by him and were still frightened into believing his charges against the conservatives?

It is highly doubtful that, in the perspective of years, it will appear that the American people had in 1936 decided upon so positive a change. In the first place, a great minority—vocal, powerful, and long experienced—said "No!" This minority had been unable to make a clear cut campaign on the basic issues— as they could have done had they dared to nominate Herbert Hoover.[14]

On the other hand, the radicals were not convinced of the soundness of Franklin Roosevelt's program, even though they praised it.[15] They knew it for what it was—the result of the planning of a combination of discordant elements that were bound to the party machines of the North as well as to the ultra-conservatives of the South.[16]

But, although opposed by the financial interests of the country, by the *conservatives* of the South, and by the radicals of real conviction, Franklin Roosevelt and his heavy majorities in all parts of the nation were returned to complete control of the national government.[17]

A comparison of the election results in 1936 with the out-

---

[14] On November 10, 1936, Miss LeHand, the President's secretary, wrote to Raymond Moley asking him about a memorandum on White House stationery, dated June 3, 1935, in which the President had written, "How many dollars will you give me against one dollar that Hoover will not be the Republican nominee in 1936? I will give you twelve to one on all the money you can get." Moley in reply to Miss LeHand wrote, November 13, 1936, "I did make the bet with the President and won. So he owes me a dollar." The President paid, November 16, 1936, enclosed in a letter of Miss LeHand to Moley. (President's Personal File 743, Roosevelt Library). In commenting upon President Roosevelt's attitude toward Mr. Hoover, Moley wrote (*Twenty-Seven Masters of Politics*, p. 26), "Roosevelt entertained a view that only Hoover among the notables in the Republican party possessed the massive convictions and intelligence to provide an alternative to the New Deal."

[15] President Roosevelt, in accepting the support of the American Labor party in New York State, wrote to them on September 16, 1936: "It gives me much pleasure to become your candidate. . . . Opposed to us are all of the forces of reaction and special privilege." (*Public Papers, 1936*, p. 357.)

[16] A week prior to the election, nation-wide straw votes, including the widely quoted *Literary Digest* poll, gave Landon a victory.

[17] This election was to be the high water mark for the candidate of the Democratic party in the nation. This is seen in the following membership elected to the Senate and House, 1932-1944.

Election Year	Senate Dem.	Rep.	Others	Vacant	House of Representatives Dem.	Rep.	Others	Vacant
1932	60	35	1	0	310	117	5	3
1934	69	25	2	0	322	102	10	1
1936	75	16	4	1	333	88	13	1
1938	69	23	4	0	261	169	4	1
1940	66	28	2	0	268	162	5	0
1942	57	38	1	0	222	208	4	1
1944	56	38	1	1	242	190	2	1

come in 1932 is productive of real understanding of the meaning of this election. For the majority in 1932 had been made up in large part of rebels, insurgents, and those hitherto deprived of political power. In 1936 the majority were endorsing what their leaders with their support had been able to do. Yet no decision had been made in acceptance of any program except one—"Do not thwart the will of the People"—as expressed by President Roosevelt.[18]

It followed that every issue was now to be fought anew—in the Congress and in the country. Turmoil, confusion, and incoherence were to characterize practically every discussion and prevent clear cut decision on the most important issues. The country was to know no political peace.

---

[18] At the first Cabinet meeting following the election, the attitude and personnel of the Supreme Court were discussed. "I think that the President is getting ready to move in on that issue . . ." wrote Secretary Ickes (*Secret Diary* (1933-1936), p. 705).

Chapter X

POLITICAL EXPERIMENTATION

THE OVERWHELMING popular victory of 1936 placed the President before a Congress controlled by a huge Democratic majority. Under these circumstances, the President's party in both houses might be thought of as willing to follow his leadership because any program he offered would obviously be assured of widespread support by the people.

There was to be far more than a two-thirds majority in each body of the Seventy-fifth Congress. The President was prepared to use this power.

The mood that prevailed in President Roosevelt's thinking at this time is revealed in his second inaugural address, January 20, 1937:

> . . . . In this nation I see tens of millions of its citizens—a substantial part of its whole population—who at this very moment are denied the greater part of what the very lowest standards of today call the necessities of life.
>
> I see millions of families trying to live on incomes so meager that the pall of family disaster hangs over them day by day.
>
> I see millions whose daily lives in city and on farm continue under conditions labeled indecent by a so-called polite society half a century ago.

I see millions denied education, recreation, and the opportunity to better their lot and the lot of their children.

I see millions lacking the means to buy the products of farm and factory and by their poverty denying work and productiveness to many other millions.

I see one-third of a nation ill-housed, ill-clad, ill-nourished.[1]

This message, broadcast by radio, was received with enthusiasm and led to an emotional outburst of personal devotion by millions of citizens.

Yet as the accepted leader of a great popular movement favoring generally a new social order, and specifically a wide variety of reform measures, the President as executive was in an awkward position. He had worked himself into it, particularly by his campaign speeches of 1936.

There existed no sure means of accomplishing the task he had set for himself. Sectional divisions of his own party were manifest among the Democrats in the Congress, where the divergent purposes of his farm, labor, and industrial supporters were more than ever apparent. Many of his administrative agencies had been set up in a period calling for swift action. They were hopelessly entangled in detail and in quarrels as to jurisdiction. The Supreme Court had stood across the path of much legislation already passed.

National unity was as urgently needed in 1937 as in 1933— perhaps more—and a national leader was essential. But now the masses need not be won. They already were won. How could the President, under the circumstances, perform the task before him? What method could he use to persuade Court and Congress?

Instead of pushing at once for the measures discussed in the recent campaign, the President, maintaining that administrative ineptitude and judicial disapproval had been deterrents to the development of his earlier programs, proceeded to recommend a reorganization of administrative functions in the Execu-

---

[1] *Public Papers, 1937,* pp. 4-5. Samuel I. Rosenman, *op. cit.,* p. 142, says, "I recently re-examined the original drafts of this speech, which are now in the Roosevelt Library; they show probably more work, corrections, inserts, substitutions and deletions by the President than any of the other speeches."

tive Department, and drastic changes in the Court organization. These proposals came as a surprise to the American public. Such fundamental changes in the government had not been discussed openly in the campaign.

Each of these proposals would, if successful, greatly enhance the powers of the Executive Branch. Opponents at once said that this would change the system of values that had hitherto been attributed to the separation of powers. The more aggressive supporters of the President asserted, however, that this was the only way to save fundamental American democracy.

The Court did not respond to popular demand, as did the President. Indeed, it could not, because of the mode of appointment and life tenure of its members. The Congress, selected by various segments of the electorate, did not respond to a *national* demand as did the President, subject to the suffrage of all.

The plan for reorganization of the Executive Department called for concentration of the powers of more than one hundred administrative commissions and boards, increasing their direct relationship to the President and to administrative assistants acting for him. In terms of efficiency, much could be said for this proposal. But for at least a decade vigorous criticism had been directed at the rising power of administrative agencies.

The Supreme Court had furnished the President with an obvious target. Under the American system, it could not have been otherwise. In fact, this target was suited to the weapon he had used from the outset—opposition to those who would thwart the public will.

This was in accordance with the pattern of conflict long used by leaders of progressive programs in each of the parties. The "financial interests" had afforded an easy target in 1933, and revelations of corrupt practices seemed to justify the course of the President. Strong-willed Presidents had many times used "banks" and "courts" as devils, and there was certainty of popular response to the device.

The Court that had passed judgment upon the far-reaching program of the New Deal consisted of nine justices—"nine old men," as they were termed by advocates of change. Their average age was sixty-eight years. Willis Van Devanter had been appointed in 1910; Charles E. Hughes had been appointed first in 1910, resigned in 1916, and was reappointed in 1930; James McReynolds was appointed in 1914 and Louis Brandeis in 1916. George Sutherland and Pierce Butler joined the Court in 1922. Harlan Stone was appointed in 1925, Benjamin Cardozo in 1932, and Owen Roberts in 1930. Seven justices were appointees of Republican Presidents, while McReynolds and Brandeis had been appointed by President Wilson.

As a matter of fact, of course, the justices of the Supreme Court had not been a unit at any time in their thinking, even when decisions were unanimous.[2] Four only—Van Devanter, McReynolds, Sutherland, and Butler—were definitely conservative. Brandeis, Stone, and Cardozo were classed as liberal. Hughes and Roberts fell somewhere between the two groups in their general attitude, and this had been reflected in their decisions.

That the President interpreted the overwhelming vote of 1936 as a mandate of the people had been shown clearly in his address to the Congress on January 6, 1937. He said at that time:

> The Judicial branch also is asked by the people to do its part in making democracy successful. We do not ask the Courts to call non-existent powers into being, but we have a right to expect that conceded powers or those legitimately implied shall be made effective instruments for the common good.
>
> The process of our democracy must not be imperiled by the denial of essential powers of free government.[3]

The impulses of aggressive leadership which increasingly had come to dominate the President led him to this fully developed attack upon the branch of government that obstructed the path of his program. This should have surprised no one who had followed with care his statement of objectives, his methods, and the developments of his first term in the Presidency. By general testimony of friend and adversary alike, his prevailing

---

[2] Of a dozen decisions of the Court involved in the discussion, four had been unanimous, and two had been rendered with one dissenting vote. Only three cases recorded 5-4 decisions.

[3] *Public Papers, 1936*, pp. 641-642.

mood after the election of 1936 was one of elation in his great personal triumph, which seemed to imply approval of his programs as he had stated them.

Just when the decision was made to urge changes in the composition of the Supreme Court is still subject to conjecture. There are numerous "inside" views. How many were a party to the program as finally proposed will remain in doubt for some time to come. But we know from unquestioned sources that the matter engaged the President's attention as early as the spring of 1935.

The Court had announced three decisions (all unanimous) on May 27, 1935. One of these was the invalidation of the National Industrial Recovery Act by unanimous vote of all nine justices. This Act had been of particular interest to the President. In his press conference four days later, he denounced the action of the Court, comparing the decision in significance to that in the Dred Scott case. This was the famous "horse and buggy" statement.[4]

Henry Stimson wrote to the President deploring the "horse and buggy" statement, and saying that the proposal of Constitutional amendment dismayed him. "Stimson thought that the President was being unfair to the court in not recognizing the degree to which it had been slowly but carefully developing the law so that the federal government would be able to handle the economic problems engendered by the industrial revolution." But to this the President replied: "Anybody who can work the thing out a little faster than the five to ten years I mention will receive a gold medal at the hands of the President!"[5]

George Creel, who knew the President well, later wrote:

> I first became aware of his deep and even bitter feeling in August, 1935, when we were preparing the article entitled "Looking Ahead with Roosevelt." In June the Supreme Court had wiped out all of the codes set up under the NRA, and the President made no effort to hide his anger as he spoke of the decision. While admitting that there had been extremes and absurdities, he insisted that the fundamentals of the act were

---

[4] *Public Papers, 1935*, pp. 205-221. The President said, "We have been relegated to the horse-and-buggy definition of inter-state commerce."

[5] *Personal Letters, 1928-1945*, I, 485.

sound and vital, and that the Court had gone out of its way to place a stone in the way of progress. After considering NRA accomplishments in some detail, he set his jaw and dictated the following as his idea of how the article should start off:

"It is the deep conviction of Franklin D. Roosevelt that the Constitution of the United States was never meant to be a 'dead hand,' chilling human aspiration and blocking human-ity's advance, but that the founding fathers conceived it as a living force for the expression of the national will with respect to national needs. . . . The thing that has come to be called the New Deal is Franklin Roosevelt's conscientious, deliberated effort to continue the Constitution as a truth and a hope, not as a mere collection of obsolete phrases.[6]

The situation as it later appeared to the President reveals a clear and definite line of thinking. The President had consid-ered various proposals, including suggested Constitutional amendments, and dismissed them all as inadequate to meet the need. Most important in his mind in rejecting this course was the matter of time. It would take too long, and the cumber-some method called for would give unusual opportunity for special interests to defeat the will of the majority.

But also, an amendment would not meet the need, in that the Constitution itself was adequate, and indeed the Court within its proper function was adequate. "The only trouble," wrote the President, "was with some of the human beings then on the Court." Merely adding justices would not cure the evil. What was needed was "new blood, new vigor, new experience, and new outlook."[7]

Soon after the election in November of 1936, the President had asked the Attorney General and the Solicitor General to formulate plans for legislation enabling the Executive to alter the existing personnel of the Court.[8] Mr. Roosevelt consulted with few and had not discussed the matter with leaders in the Congress. The issue, as he was to state it, was not therefore as yet before the people, although on December 26, 1936, an article by George Creel presenting the President's views was

---

[6] Creel, *op. cit.*, pp. 290-291.
[7] *Public Papers, 1937*, lxiii-lxiv.
[8] *Selected Papers of Homer Cummings*, p. 146.

published in *Collier's,* as a result of consultation with Mr. Roosevelt as described above.[9]

To a press conference on February 5, 1937, the President expressed belief in his solution of the problems of "judicial tyranny," saying:

> As you know, for a long time the subject of constitutionality of laws has been discussed; and for a good many months now I have been working with a small group in going into what I have thought of as the fundamentals of the subject rather than those particular details which make the headlines.
>
> In this review of the Federal Judiciary we have come to the very definite conclusion that there is required the same kind of reorganization of the Judiciary as has been recommended to this Congress for the Executive branch of the Government.[10]

Later in the same day, in a message to the Congress, the President presented his proposals, including a draft of a proposed bill. Much that was included in the bill related to a reorganization of the federal courts as a whole, as well as to measures to prevent undue congestion of calendars and delay in decisions.

The proposal of vital importance, as is well known, was that the number of Supreme Court Justices be increased from nine to fifteen. Included was a plan of retirement for justices already in service. The President would be empowered by this bill to appoint one new justice for every one on the Court over seventy (who might or might not retire, as he saw fit). The underlying argument, as the President stated it to the Congress, was that:

> Modern complexities call also for a constant infusion of new blood in the courts, just as it is needed in executive functions of the Government and in private business. A lowered mental or physical vigor leads men to avoid an examination of complicated and changed conditions. . . . Life tenure of judges, assured by the Constitution, was designed to place the courts beyond temptations or influences which might impair their judgments: it was not intended to create a static judiciary.[11]

---

[9] Creel, *op. cit.,* p. 294.
[10] *Public Papers, 1937,* p. 35.
[11] *Ibid.,* p. 55.

The intensity of the President's feeling was revealed in full measure, when, four years later, he wrote:

> The reactionary members of the Court had apparently determined to remain on the bench as long as life continued—for the sole purpose of blocking any program of reform. Although it had become, on the average, the most aged Court in our history, although six justices had passed the age of seventy, not a single vacancy had occurred during my first term in office. The bench had been created almost entirely by appointments by conservative Presidents; and it was now continually passing economic and political judgments, almost month by month, on a liberal program of recovery and reform.[12]

Viewing the matter more directly, the President at the same time wrote:

> By the time of the election of 1936, however, it had become clear that this new concept of government [New Deal program] and of its relation to economic and social problems was in danger of complete frustration. . . . For a dead hand was being laid upon this whole program of progress—to stay it all. It was the hand of the Supreme Court of the United States. . . .[13]

The President noted that in the three years beginning in October, 1933, the Court had set aside twelve statutes, five within a single year. The same course had been pursued by the Court in 1936. In February, in a decision dealing with water power, the Court so limited the power of the government in the Tennessee Valley Authority as to leave doubt as to the possible public use of the great power projects under construction in other parts of the country. In May, the Court set aside a statute enacted to deal with problems in the bituminous coal industry. What the President termed "the climax to this course of destruction" came in the June decision nullifying the statute setting up a minimum fair wage system for women in industry.[14]

By this time, it was the President's opinion, "the Congressional program, which had pulled the nation out of despair,

[12] *Ibid.*, lxi-lxii.
[13] *Ibid.*, l-lii.
[14] *Ibid.*, lii-lvii.

had been fairly completely undermined." [15] In all the summaries made by Mr. Roosevelt in the course of the struggle that ensued, and in his review presented four years later, were no revisions of his earlier reasoning, nor additions to his statement of objectives and promises of the use of possible victory.

The President maintained all along that the social and economic program of the administration was good, and had been endorsed by popular mandate. The courts had stood across the path of the popular will. They should be made to conform. All matters of detail were unimportant compared with the assertion of need in government of executive power backed by the will of the people.

The essential simplicity of the political thinking of the President was hereby revealed in the naïve manner in which he presented the issue to the Congress. It is true that in campaigning he had repeatedly used the argument of liberal-conservative alignment. Even in explaining his conduct in later years he adhered to this. But the alignment on the issue in debate was not what he said it was, and the alignment of persons was not that of liberal versus conservative.

The reaction—in the Congress and in the country at large—to the President's proposals for Court reform at once moved the debate, if not into the realm of higher politics, at least into the arena of convinced antagonism. Perhaps the average voter did not fully comprehend what was meant when it was pointed out that in its decisions the Court had not just said no, but had given reasons. But the voter could not but see that opposed to the proposals for changing the Court were a considerable number of well-recognized liberals, many of them in the President's own party.

Much has been said by conservatives of the fact that the Republicans left the opposition leadership to Democrats. That was good partisan politics. More important, it gave full recognition that such outstanding independents as Senator Burton K. Wheeler, Hiram Johnson, William E. Borah, and Joseph C. O'Mahoney were opposed. It was noticeable that early adherents of the New Deal, such as Raymond Moley and William Hard, were openly opposed.

---

[15] *Ibid.*, lviii.

The attention of all the people was given this struggle. At the outset, reaction against the President's plan was violent. The opposition grew as it became evident that all previous alignments on the New Deal program and legislation were broken. Interviews of well-known leaders indicated not only that party lines were broken, but divisions in groups of labor and farm interests had appeared. The opposition of the lawyers was almost unanimous. Industrial and financial interests were of course opposed. The press of the country was overwhelmingly opposed.

The assertion of the President as to a congested Supreme Court Calendar gave an opening for opponents of the Judiciary Bill to take testimony of the Court as to facts. This led to a personal appeal to Chief Justice Hughes. He prepared a statement which he gave to Senator Wheeler, who presented it to the Senate. Subsequently it was agreed by the closest adherents of the President that the testimony of the Chief Justice more than anything else brought victory to the opponents of the bill.[16]

In reporting (June 14, 1937) adversely on the proposed legislation, the members of the Senate Committee on the Judiciary unanimously agreed:

It would subjugate the courts to the will of Congress and the President and thereby destroy the independence of the judiciary, the only certain shield of individual rights. . . . It points the way to the evasion of the Constitution. . . . Its ultimate operation would be to make this Government one of men rather than one of law. . . .

And in language that reflected the depth of the antagonism that was felt toward the President and his supporters, it was declared:

It is a measure which should be so emphatically rejected that

---

[16] According to Merlo J. Pusey (*The Supreme Court Crisis,* II, 756), the letter stated that "The Supreme Court is fully abreast of its work. When we rose on March 15 (for the present recess) we had heard argument in cases in which certiorari had been granted only 4 weeks before—February 15. . . . There is no congestion of cases upon our calendar. This gratifying condition has obtained for several years."

its parallel will never again be presented to the free representatives of the free people of America.[17]

In mid-June the hearings of the Judiciary Committee had been concluded, and by vote of 10 (7 of them Democrats) to 8 the majority termed the bill a "needless, futile, and utterly dangerous abandonment of constitutional principle." [18]

Nevertheless, the debate in the Senate continued for many weeks. The alignment was at times slightly altered. Despite pressure brought to bear by the administration and its supporters, the opposition was sufficient in the final tests to defeat the bill. Proposed reforms in lower court procedure were provided by appropriate legislation.

After eight months of struggle in this Seventy-fifth Congress, it was pointed out by informed commentators that no affirmative result had been achieved. Significantly, in this period of vital national necessity, no bills of importance had been passed. The proposed reforms in reorganization of executive departments were denied, in part at least due to increasing distrust of the President.

For the first time since 1933 a national debate had taken place. This debate had been concerned with the basic philosophy underlying the government provided by the leadership of Franklin Roosevelt. Not even in the Presidential campaign of 1936 had there been such a debate. The only nationally known voice insisting repeatedly upon debate had been that of Herbert Hoover, beginning with the appearance of his book, *The Challenge to Liberty*, in 1934.

Mr. Hoover viewed the new developments in the United States in the light of experiences of executive usurpation abroad. He found the analogies alarming.

The depth of feeling aroused in this debate lifted it into the realm of high politics, where for a time thought was finally given to the ultimate results of such experimentation as the President had proposed.[19]

---

[17] *Senate Report No. 711, 75th Congress, First Session*, p. 23.
[18] *Ibid.*
[19] Writing in July, 1937, Mr. Hoover presented a full statement of the issue as seen in its political aspects. ("The Crisis and the Political Parties," in the *Atlantic Monthly*, 160, (September, 1937), 257-268.)

In a letter to the *New York Times,* an old friend of Mr. Roosevelt wrote:

If the court as guardian and umpire is to be destroyed, let us not pretend that we are doing anything else. Let us frankly abolish the Constitution and adopt a system of parliamentary absolutism or its alternative, a dictatorship. For one who knows the President it is impossible to believe that he is aiming at a future dictatorship; but it is also impossible not to recognize the packing of the Supreme Court as exactly what a dictator would adopt as his first step. The President may not know where he is going, but he is on his way.[20]

To this public letter, the President made personal reply to the effect that:

There are some of us who believe, however, that unless this nation continues as a nation—with three branches of government pulling together to keep it going—you might find yourself unable to write to the papers a quarter of a century hence. You see that I am seeking to save your freedom of expression! [21]

In the course of the debate in Congress, much attention and time were given details of change, disagreements as to meaning of the bill as presented and amended, and measures to bring about a compromise, or at least a limited decision. In the final outcome, outright defeat met all proposals attempting to alter the Supreme Court. Yet the action of the Court in the meantime, and the interpretation given it by the President at the time, blurred the issue again and again, and left a residue of deep dissatisfaction.

The President stated in the autumn of 1937, enlarging upon this interpretation in his later review, that the Court had in fact been *forced* into line.[22] Indeed, Mr. Roosevelt insisted that the change in the viewpoint of the Court came soon after his message in February of 1937. He drew again upon the argument that courts were an ever-present menace to popular will.

---

[20] *Personal Letters, 1928-1945,* I, 669-670.
[21] *Ibid.,* p. 669.
[22] In a memorandum prepared at the White House in May or June, 1937, the President had enumerated the decisions of the Court that apparently bore out his view. *Ibid.,* pp. 685-686.

Pointing out that the Court had reversed itself in the Minimum Wage case in March, he wrote:

> This remarkable about-face came because one justice decided to change his vote of nine months earlier. Here was one man —not elected by the people—who by a nod of the head could apparently nullify or uphold the will of the overwhelming majority of a nation of 130,000,000 people.[23]

The President did not consider the technical changes that had been made, meanwhile, in the original law or in texts of subsequent legislation approved by the Court. He was content to write:

> It would be a little naïve to refuse to recognize some connection between those 1937 decisions and the Supreme Court fight. . . . The blunt fact, therefore, is that by this time the Supreme Court fight had actually been won, so far as its immediate objectives were concerned.[24]

Late in March of 1937 the Supreme Court had rendered three decisions upholding the Railway Labor Act, the Farm Mortgage Act, and the rewritten Minimum Wage Law. Soon after, on April 12, the Court upheld the Wagner Labor Act. The President felt that the Court had now come to approve the reform measures of the New Deal. He said:

> There has been a reaffirmation of the ancient principle that the power to legislate resides in the Congress and not in the Court; and that the Court has no power or right to impose its own ideas of legislative policy, or its own social and economic views, upon the law of the land.[25]

Surely no broader assertion of the people's power could be made. The President felt not only that the American system had been able to function effectively, but also that the spirit of the apparent change in the Court had been within the American practice of self-government.

Obviously, in the light of such assertion by the President, who had led in proposals for drastic change, it was of little avail in controversy to argue the merits of the basic Constitu-

[23] *Public Papers, 1937,* lxvii.
[24] *Ibid.,* lxix-lxx.
[25] *Ibid.,* lxxi.

tional position of the Court, or to consider the changes in the legislation passed by the Congress that had led the Court to its reasoned conclusions.

But it should be pointed out that in the case of three of the laws declared Constitutional, careful rewriting in revision of original statutes had protected states' rights, and altogether, much clarification in the meaning of the Congress had aided the Court in its decisions upon the basic issues. The Court had not taken a stand against the New Deal. Such a blatant misrepresentation could not be maintained. The majority—and in the four leading decisions all jurists—had asked for Constitutional legislation.

The President had brought the Court into the maelstrom of politics, and gloried in his accomplishment. In asserting not only that he had won, but also that the Court had altered its opinion due to pressure, the President gave additional reasons for a growing belief in the opportunism by then so prevalent in administration politics. Black was white and white was black, depending upon the point of view.

Given less consideration was the far more important fact that the Court, by maintaining its essential structure, owing to the refusal of the Congress to follow the President's proposals, was in a position to assert its powers in years to come—not in politics but in law.

It is not within the scope of the present inquiry to present the case against the President's proposals nor to analyze the arguments of his opponents. The fact that the leadership in the Senate struggle was in the hands of members of the President's own party should make clear that their arguments had great influence with the undecided portion of the electorate. So good a cause, as it seemed to the President's supporters, brought out in friend and foe alike superior accomplishment. No one was apt to doubt that it was a great cause, and the decision one of deep significance.

It must be said, however, that in the longer view it is not the case for the Court, or the arguments of scholars in Constitutional law that are most significant for the student of the history of the year 1937. As "politics" had dictated the purpose, method, and explanation of defeat made by the President, so it was "politics" that had successfully defended the Court in the Senate. Consequently the issue—in the eyes of the people—had not been settled. This was the basis for an increase in their distrust of government—executive, legislative, and judicial.

In passing a judgment upon the action of Franklin Roosevelt with reference to the Court, the explanations elaborated by his immediate advisers and by himself in later years must be included. Truly, great was the provocation in the eyes of the crusader for the New Deal. And basic had been the struggle between "the law and the people" in the history of the previous half-century.

Nevertheless, in 1937 the people of the United States were not immune to the worship of personal power which at that particular time had such appeal to a large part of mankind. Americans, too, could blunder into disaster. To substitute an insistent call for immediate revision of fundamental law for a careful, painstaking, and honest appreciation of disputed issues —which takes time, long debate, and an acceptable decision— was to forsake a fundamental of American life. Yet this was what Franklin Roosevelt did.

The Supreme Court fight is a complete example of the President's procedure in "politics." [26] The point of view he maintained appears to be that by his proposals, backed as he asserted by the people, he forced the Court against its will to approve of the measures associated with the New Deal. Said he:

> For that reason I regard the effort initiated by the message on the Federal Judiciary of February 5, 1937, and the immediate results of it, as among the most important domestic achievements of my first two terms in office.[27]

Had the bill drafted by the President's advisers and submitted to the Congress by the President on February 5, 1937, been enacted, the Court would have been transformed by the personnel of the President's appointments.

However, despite Congressional defeat, the President was able within a month, upon resignation of Justice Van Devan-

---

[26] It is amply revealed in Joseph Alsop and Turner Catledge, *The 168 Days.*
[27] *Public Papers, 1937,* p. xlvii.

ter at the age of seventy-eight, to make his first appointment to
the Court, that of Senator Hugo Black of Alabama.

Before the close of his second administration, the President
had appointed four other justices—Stanley Reed of Pennsylvania, former Solicitor General, Felix Frankfurter of Massachusetts, William O. Douglas of New York, and Frank Murphy
of Michigan.[28] These were followed by James F. Byrnes of
South Carolina in 1941 (replacing McReynolds); Robert Jackson of New York, former Attorney General, in 1941 (replacing
Hughes); and William Rutledge of Iowa (replacing Byrnes)
in 1943. By the time of the President's death in 1945, every
member of the Court except Justice Roberts and Justice Stone
were Roosevelt appointees.

Writing to William Allen White on October 13, 1938, the
President returned to his view of the reason for his own action
with reference to the Court:

> Here is a problem which I suggest to you in the utmost confi-
> dence—a problem not so much of politics but of principle. Two
> years ago I took the position, because I believed in it from the
> bottom of my heart, that the Supreme Court should be broadly
> representative of the Nation—i.e., every section of it . . . eight
> sitting Justices of the Supreme Court come from east of the
> Mississippi. . . . That means two-thirds of the acreage of the
> United States has no representation—and one-third of the popu-
> lation has no representation.[29]

Yet it is notable that, with the single exception of Justice Rutledge, the President did not, by his own appointments to the
Court, obtain "representation" west of the Mississippi.[30]

Chief Justice Hughes was aware of the importance of the
matter of age in all discussion of the Court. In a letter to
Arthur Krock of March 21, 1936, Mr. Hughes said:

> . . . in speaking of retirement at seventy-five, it is well to
> remember not only the example of Justice Holmes, but that

---

[28] They replaced Cardozo, who died in 1938 at the age of sixty-eight; Butler
who died in 1939 at the age of seventy-three; Sutherland who retired in 1938 at
the age of seventy-six; and Brandeis who retired in 1939 at the age of eighty-
three.

[29] *Personal Letters, 1925-1948*, II, 817-818.

[30] C. Herman Pritchett, *The Roosevelt Court*, p. 14, states: "The Court as
thus re-made by President Roosevelt has turned out to be perhaps the most
controversial in American History." This work contains a detailed examination
of the background and experience of the appointees.

of Justice Brandeis and Justice Van Devanter who are still going strong at seventy-nine and seventy-seven.[31]

In a series of six lectures delivered at Columbia University in 1927 (between his terms of service on the Court), Mr. Hughes had dealt with the question of retirement, voluntary and compulsory, and summarized the record of Court retirement in terms of age.

In the volume in which these lectures were published as *The Supreme Court of the United States,* he wrote: "The community has no more valuable asset than an experienced judge," [32] and "Doubtless there is a time when a judge reaches, on account of age, the limit of effective service, but it is very difficult to fix that time." [33]

In referring to this volume, in response to a query by Mr. Krock, the Chief Justice remarked in his letter of March 21, ". . . you are welcome to anything you can pick up in those observations—made at a time when I had no notion that my freedom of utterance was soon to be curtailed."

Although the President, on the recommendation of Justice Hughes upon his resignation for "considerations of health and age," appointed as Chief Justice in 1941 the same Justice Stone who had voted to upset NRA and against a half-dozen New Deal enactments,[34] it is clear that Franklin Roosevelt finally got the kind of Court that he wanted.[35] It is equally clear that he did not get it by the methods he advocated.

It is not without ironical significance that Mr. Roosevelt designated the volume of his *Public Papers* devoted to the year 1937, *The Constitution Prevails.* Yet the reasons he advanced are not those recognized by his opponents who would agree that the Constitution had indeed been maintained.

To President Roosevelt must be ascribed the decision to curb the powers of the Court, to change its composition, and in

---

[31] Charles E. Hughes Papers, General Correspondence, 1936-1939, Library of Congress.

[32] P. 74.

[33] *The Supreme Court of the United States,* p. 75. See also Samuel Hendel, *Charles Evans Hughes and the Supreme Court,* pp. 246-275.

[34] Merlo J. Pusey, *Charles Evans Hughes,* II, 788.

[35] In the spring of 1935 he had said to Secretary Perkins: "What the Court needs is some Roosevelt appointments. Then we might get a good decision out of them."

so doing, to change its place in the American Constitutional system. He clothed this decision and defined its action in arguments that were based upon the power of the temporary majority to have a government that does the work this majority demands. He accompanied his argument with passionate appeals to carry over the announced objectives of more social democracy for the people of the United States.

His approach to the problem of the Court as he saw it was in direct line with earlier attacks—if not always in method, certainly in declared objective—throughout his career in public life. He stood as a champion of the "people" against the action of entrenched "forces" which were opposing, thwarting, and killing democratic government. That the opposition in composition and in argument—within the Congress and among the people—did not justify his charges, was not admitted by the President at any time.

Had the President won endorsement of his plan, the results would have changed the structure of government in the United States. Mr. Roosevelt would have been master in such a fashion that the Congress in turn must have followed his will, until the will of the master *he* acknowledged—the people—altered its views and consequently its decisions in the elections that were to come.

But the President was defeated, and, despite his own vigorous contention—shared by others as well—that he had won his objectives, his intention had been denied. Roosevelt remained the declared champion of the people, but after this defeat the danger—in his leadership—to Constitutional government was lessened.

The struggle, however, had weakened all courts in the eyes of millions of citizens, and it weakened the President in all his subsequent relations with the Congress. It had, therefore, weakened the American practice of self-government.

In the perspective of years, it is of minor importance that by 1941 the Supreme Court comprised a new panel of justices except for two. That a President returned to office should in due time, by appointment, name a number of justices to the Court had always been American practice. This was American democracy in action.

One subsidiary aspect of the outcome of the Court struggle has been given little attention. Mr. Roosevelt's appointments brought into being a Court composed of men who were the product of active political experience. Justice Black, former Senator, as well as Justice Murphy, former Governor of Michigan, and Justice Byrnes, former Senator, had been elected to public office prior to their appointment to the Court. Frankfurter had been a very active member of the President's inner circle of advisers. Reed, Douglas, Jackson, and Rutledge had held high administrative office. This was the Court that was to be "in touch with the wishes of the people" in giving a flexible interpretation to the Constitution.

The most important conclusion to be drawn—in large measure drawn at the time of the President's final defeat on this score—was that the President's methods, as revealed, and his reasoning in defense of those methods were those of a would-be dictator. The fight had revealed as never before the dangers residing in the use of such power as Mr. Roosevelt had assumed in an overwhelming popular mandate.

Strong-willed Presidents had fought battles with the Congress and with the Court. But no previous President had used the methods of Mr. Roosevelt, and no other President had defended Presidential action as he was to do. Leadership it certainly was —self-confident and self-justifying leadership. The President, writing in 1941, said:

> I made one major mistake when I first presented the plan. I did not place enough emphasis upon the real mischief—the kind of decisions which, as a studied and continued policy, had been coming down from the Supreme Court.[36]

Many who flocked to the President's banners in this fight were fully conscious of the step they were taking. In fact, they gloried in it. They were favorable to this kind of revolution in the prevailing practices of government. The language of class warfare was used throughout by advocate and opponent alike.

In a world ripe for revolution—abroad if not at home—the appearance of a would-be dictator here did not seem out of the picture. The President himself, visualizing possible defeat, said

[36] *Public Papers, 1937*, lxv.

at the Democratic Victory Dinner on March 4, 1937: "If we do not have the courage to lead the American people where they want to go, someone else will." [37]

Millions of people, for the moment, lost sight of the basic issue in following the man to whom they had already given such great power. They heard him appeal to them (in a radio broadcast on March 9, 1937) in language that was dramatic, in argument that was plausible, and in ringing conclusions that could not but weaken the whole fabric of Constitutional law. For he finally said:

> The Court has been acting not as a judicial body, but as a policy-making body. . . . By bringing into the judicial system a steady and continuing stream of new and younger blood, I hope, first, to make the administration of all Federal justice speedier and, therefore, less costly; secondly, to bring to the decision of social and economic problems younger men who have had personal experience and contact with modern facts and circumstances under which average men have to live and work. This plan will save our national Constitution from hardening of the judicial arteries.[38]

In the perspective of history, it is possible that the outcome of the struggle over the proposals of the President will rank with other denials by the representatives of the people to programs urged by Presidents who insisted that they voiced the deepest desires of the people. But it is hard to appraise the ultimate importance of a denial. This much can be said with some assurance. Deep scars were left on the reputation of Franklin Roosevelt as a leader.

[37] *Ibid.*, p. 121.
[38] *Ibid.*, pp. 125-128.

Chapter XI

FUNDAMENTAL NATIONAL DIVISIONS

SHARP DIVISIONS now appeared in almost every political combination that had hitherto existed. The out and out radicals had prospered upon the diet of recent months, yet were apprehensive of a reaction that might engulf them. No conservative could face the future with equanimity. No liberal could anticipate an early return to orderly government. It was clear that the clash, turmoil, and inconclusiveness of the political struggle of 1937 had had catastrophic effect upon the public mind in the United States.

Was the President attacking Constitutional government, or was he, as he said, correcting abuses that had arisen? The issue was a sharp one. The President's fight over the Court had intensified the disagreement within the Democratic party.[1]

The methods used by the President had driven a considerable number of the members of the Congress to a position of personal antagonism which could never be forgotten. Efficient legislative action was now impeded. On every issue before the Congress there was uncertainty. The President had revealed

---

[1] *Personal Letters, 1928-1945,* I, 645.

himself as desiring to depend in large measure upon personal persuasiveness rather than upon accepted social and political principle. His influence in the Congress was therefore weakened, although with the people as a whole, who did not understand the issues involved, he was apparently still strong.

To meet this new situation, it was imperative that Mr. Roosevelt advance on two fronts: first, on behalf of yet more democracy, and second, to provide advanced measures for social justice. To accomplish this, despite the recent setback, the administration must move faster.

It was now clear how influential the young radicals had become in support of the President's call for a more powerful government, at the same time that he was actively opposed by an increasing number of members of the Democratic organization in and out of Congress. This was to be reflected in the Congressional elections of 1938.

The record of the Congress for the period November 1937 to June 1938 also reflected this situation. Pressure groups and sectional interests were more active—blocs formed and combinations reformed—within the Democratic majority. Ample evidence of Congressional ineptitude appeared as a bewildered Congress failed to agree on any constructive suggestion.

This situation provided opportunity for the advocates of strong executive action. The President—consciously or unconsciously—lent aid to their view by proposing a huge new spending program in order to counteract the business recession of 1937.

The steps by which this became the program of the President may be summarized. The collapse of the stock market in October, 1937, indicated the dangers threatened by lack of confidence of financiers in the policy pursued by the government. Assurance given them by Secretary Morgenthau and others that government would take active measures to balance the budget were met with hostile disbelief.

This had a part in the decision of the President early in January of 1938 to open the floodgates for an extensive spending program. Such a program would remove the threat of mounting unemployment, and the consequent weakening of New Deal candidates in the elections of the ensuing autumn. It was a conspicuous admission that "human needs" took precedence over budgetary economics.[2]

Announcement of this program meant, in fact, that the spenders—Hopkins, Henderson, Corcoran, and others—were in control. The President was accepting again the program of economists who were urging increased government expenditure as the basis for increasing the national income and consequently producing widespread well-being.[3]

Certainly the President was advocating in 1938 the importance of "economics" in politics, and predicting that a party that curtailed expenditures and practiced economies would, if elected to office, be speedily retired by the people. Again the assertion appeared, with emphasis upon "proofs," that Mr. Roosevelt had "saved capitalism." His program should, therefore, be accepted, for greater dangers lay ahead if it were not.

The Congress was urged again to delegate to the President power to redistribute and consolidate governmental agencies. Here again was assertion of the absolute need of a strong Executive. The President's view as expressed subsequently in 1941 was:

> Many of the great measures debated in 1937 and 1938—farm legislation, reorganization of government, minimum wages and maximum hours, increased public works, monopoly controls, judicial reforms, water power development, low-cost housing—have, by now, become more or less accepted as part of our economic life. It is a little difficult, therefore, to look back even across the short period to 1938 and remember how bitter and how difficult was the struggle—in the Congress and out of the Congress—which was necessary in order to have some of these laws adopted. The opposition to them—chiefly from the same sources which had opposed the whole program of reform since 1933—developed into "blitzkrieg" proportions. Misrepresentation as to motives, and falsehoods as to objectives and results, became common practice, especially in the columns of some of the large newspapers.[4]

---

[2] See Henry Morgenthau, "The Struggle for a Program," cited by Rosenau (ed.), *The Roosevelt Treasury*, p. 310.

[3] Referring to the position taken by some of his advisers (Henderson, Currie, and the Corcoran-Cohen group), the editors of the *Personal Letters* write: "Politically F.D.R. sympathized with their approach; economically, it is clear from these letters, he leaned toward his conservative advisers and wanted to balance the budget." *Ibid.*, I, 646.

[4] *Public Papers, 1938*, p. xxvii.

One aspect of the public feeling aroused by the defeat of the President on the Court issue was generally overlooked by commentators at the time. Widespread antagonism to Court denials of Congressional power had always existed, and this had markedly increased since the opening of the twentieth century. The growth of popular enthusiasm for popular rule—the product of the progressive movement and the mainstay of Roosevelt's strength in his first administration—produced an atmosphere in which such a program as the President had presented was sure to produce fighting against those who thwarted the popular will.

Now that a considerable number of members of the Congress, in defeating the Court Bill, had aligned themselves with the "reactionaries," it was clear that they must be retired from public life. So the stage was set for the President's attempt to purge his own party.

Naturally many members of the Congress were deeply concerned by the drift of affairs. Some were vocal in their denunciation of the leadership of the President, as he continued to appeal to labor and farmer support. Others were content to continue the positive opposition which they had shown in the struggle over the Supreme Court issue.

In this situation, two developments were inevitable. Increasingly, denunciation of personal power filled the press and was repeated in the Congress. The President—logically as well as emotionally following the road he had always envisaged but seldom trod—proposed now to eliminate from the Democratic party some Congressmen and Senators who had opposed him.

This action of the President in the Congressional elections of 1938 was a full recognition of the realignment of parties that had been emerging more and more clearly in the Congress. Not for a hundred years had it been so patent that the living alignment was to be found between the President's supporters and those who opposed him.[5]

The Republicans in the Senate increased by seven, and in the House, by ten. Within each of the parties were innumerable social, economic and sectional blocs.

---

[5] It recalled the alignment of 1829-1831, "Jackson men" versus "anti-Jackson" men.

The President's view remained the same when he wrote of it in 1941:

> In these primary campaign speeches, I made it clear that I was not trying to dictate to the people of any State as to how they should vote. What I was trying to do was to impress upon them the necessity of voting for liberal candidates—if they wanted a continuation of the liberal kind of government which they had since 1933.[6]

But by the beginning of the Congressional session in 1939 it was evident that the President was weaker in the Congress. Whether lack of a coherent program among his advisers—or failure to hold a majority of all members of the Congress—was the cause, cannot be determined. It appeared to most commentators that Presidential government by Democratic party acquiescence was over.

When Mr. Roosevelt explained in retrospect why he entered upon a purge in the campaign of 1938, he selected for the basis of his argument the proposition that the Democratic party was liberal and the Republican party, conservative. In this light he sought to interpret politics and the alignment of his administration. It was far too simple, and was very misleading.

It would be possible to write the history of the first fifty years of the twentieth century in those terms. It has been done. Yet such an approach explains little of the history of the United States in terms of building, of governing, or of growth. It presents an unreal contest in a world of contrived issues and obvious inconsistencies.

It would be more realistic to divide the electorate as a whole into radical, progressive, conservative, and reactionary elements. Both great parties have had members of each degree of political purpose in their ranks and even among their leaders. In truth, each party organization has been conservative and sometimes reactionary, and each party membership has contained elements that were radical as well as those that were progressive.

Seldom have minor parties been devoted for a long period to

---

[6] *Public Papers, 1938*, p. xxxii.

any single approach. Even the Socialist party cannot be termed completely radical. In its days in office in local areas, it has been progressive rather than radical.

No reactionary has dominated the nation except for brief intervals, although groups of reactionaries, again and again, have delayed action and given opportunities for a protest vote to express itself before a national audience.

On the whole, the legislation of the first half of the twentieth century has been brought about primarily by the work of progressives. On the whole, the administration has been the work of conservatives.

Yet the accepted alignments for political control in any Congress have been on Democratic-Republican lines. Mr. Roosevelt claimed for the Democratic party a lengthy program of reform. On the whole, this was the fact. But Republicans supported many of his measures, some of which were originated by Republicans.

An impressive record of Republican legislative accomplishment existed prior to 1933. Democrats were known to support many of these measures. Numerous Republican conservatives, on the other hand, despite the leadership of Republican progressives, had opposed the legislative program of their own party.

Thus, by the middle of the second term of Franklin Roosevelt, a fundamental shift in the bases of American politics had taken place. A variety of causes, most of them not clearly evident until ten years later, contributed to this change. Some causes, however, were obvious at the time.

The rise of organized labor to a place of determining power, particularly in the city vote, was first in importance. The decline of agriculture in an industrial nation had been, nevertheless, accompanied by an increase in the political power of organized farmers who as a minority played an important part in reshaping political lines, particularly at the time of elections. The rapid technological changes of a decade or more had produced a new and highly articulate middle class. These new political elements were changing the bases of the planning of political managers.

Of all groups in the American scene, none were so sure of their purpose and so fired by the prospect of victories for a New America as were those who espoused a new radicalism. This radicalism was new not only with respect to its volume—hitherto unknown in the United States—but in outlook and purpose as well. Radicalism has always been present in America. Indeed it has been almost synonymous with "Americanism."

The depression years had produced millions of discouraged, disillusioned, and defeated Americans. They flocked to many havens in the years between 1929 and 1939. Programs to alleviate distress by dispossessing property owners had been advanced by Long, Townsend, Coughlin, and others.

Violent protest was their watchword now; redistribution of wealth, the answer; taking over of the government, the method advocated. Never had the United States of America seen anything like this on a national scale, although the symbols had all been used before.

Only in the perspective of years does it become clear that, unknowingly, Americans were joining in the emotional reactions that had become the mainspring of revolution in western Europe. These radicals themselves would have been the first to deny any such identity of program, for they were Americans of the most highly developed isolationist sentiment.

But this was not true of the "intellectual radicals." They were by nature internationalists and disposed to make over America. This, because of the developing political situation, the "intellectuals" were presently able to do.

Under the leadership of Franklin Roosevelt, the Democratic party had absorbed many radicals—of both Fascist and Communist inclination—and had won the elective support of many more. Minor radical parties at this time were of little importance except as a destructive threat. They might be classed with the doctrinaire parties long present and always unsuccessful in America. Despite his frequent repudiation of the pronouncements of such parties, the final vote of their members at the polls was cast heavily in the President's favor.

The new radicals as a whole found cause for their existence in the maladjustments of economic life in industrial America. They now drew heavily upon European experience. The dominant group that emerged under the leadership of the intellectuals—under whatever party banner—were natural advocates of a revolution on an international front.

Approaching the problem of daily living through the media of books, ideas, and theories, these Americans naturally found that systems of thought were not bound by national boundaries, nor by previous pronouncements of experts in the field of experience. It was natural, as well, for them to find much that was wrong not only with American conditions, but with American methods. They saw little that was unique in American history. Quite apart from their program of economic change and of social planning, they were rebels against time, experience, and existing standards in general. ˙

The new approach of these radicals was reflected in the change which came over the nature of argument as to what constituted good citizenship. In the 1920's the case for more attention to the informing of the citizen could be summarized thus: If the American voter was to be an efficient member of society, this would necessitate his education in problems of citizenship. In particular should he be led to appreciate the methods by which experts in government arrived at their conclusions, and then urged to apply such careful methods in his own thinking. It should be impressed upon the citizen that governments engaged in extensive programs of regulation and control had to be supported by public funds.

In a word, government should be brought to the attention of the citizen as his agent for protecting himself and others. As his agent it must of course be supported by him as well as by other citizens. The good citizen would need also to see that widespread co-operation was the only way of insuring a continuance of basic freedom of speech and of press. Only as a citizen, at the center of American society, came to realize how interrelated were all questions of freedom and co-operation, regulation and cost, could he arrive at reasoned conclusions on public affairs.

All such approaches to good citizenship—which following World War I were influential in educational circles as well as in the realm of progressive political thought reflected in the journalistic world—were based on the assumption that general education of an increasing body of citizens would provide the essential intellectual background for a freely functioning society in the twentieth century. Good government could be provided only in a good society by a good citizen.

This emphasis upon the duty of the citizen and his ever continuing and increasing obligations tended to render less important his privileges and his rights. Incomprehensible though such an approach appears today, it was thought that the citizen aware of his duties would be more independent than others in his thinking and less dependent upon unforeseen developments.

It is true that such an approach to the fruitful functioning of self-government had to meet many critics. The critics doubted man's ability to carry effectively this self-imposed task. The citizen must depend upon new masters for his salvation.

The new masters were not to be chosen for political preferment or from those who controlled the different units of an economic society. They were to be men equipped by superior knowledge of government, economics, and the other social sciences, to tell the mass of men where the truth lay, and to guide them in reaching desirable goals. The role of men around the President, his unofficial advisors, took on transcendent importance.[7]

The new radicalism had little to say in favor of the previously accepted American approach to good citizenship. Its supporters saw in America an opportunity for a new radical party that would stand somewhere between the leadership of Franklin Roosevelt and the followers of the late Huey Long. The first plank in their program was economic democracy, which was all-important. In the second place, the government must not merely regulate but actually control great business. Third, the government would develop all public works. Fourth, fiscal policy should be such as to spend more and more money to raise the national purchasing power. There was no danger in public indebtedness, because the people would owe themselves.

Radicals had reached a point where they talked of economic democracy as they talked of political democracy. This was well

---

[7] See Harold Laski, *The American Presidency*, pp. 258-260.

shown in the educational program of some progressive educators.

As they presented the case, the schools were to produce not only a living democracy but a new society. "Opportunity" had been insufficient to provide the New America with a self-supporting and self-governing body of citizens. Equality and liberty for all meant that the new schools, by providing a new education, would provide such citizenry. The practice of democracy in the schools was a necessary prelude to the success of democracy in the government of the nation.

Precedents, leadership, and previous standards were under attack. The subject matter and the method of the new education were in process of formulation. Everything was in flux, and as teacher, student, and citizen discussed the problems, methods and objectives, a program would emerge that would necessarily give first place to the free citizen.

But throughout this program of progressive education ran the basic argument to the effect that economic democracy had disappeared and that the schools must show the way to restore it.

The soil in which this new product grew was well adapted to it. Education had always been the hope of democracy in America. But now the educators were providing the meaning of this democracy and asking that it be accepted in the gospel of the new Americanism. It was natural that progressive educators found arrayed against them elements who believed in America as it had previously existed. This school system—as all else in American public life—was now to become the football of politics.

It was only natural that eventually the argument should shift to a discussion of the freedom of the teacher to teach. How free was he? Free to teach his subject—yes—within the areas of competence judged by his fellows in that field. In the social sciences, however, he was teaching subject matter that was the subject of debate in politics—on which the supporter of schools had opinions.

The basic argument of the progressive educators was that the expert not only knew the truth, but should be protected in his right to teach it. But in claiming too much as a propagandist for his new gospel, namely, that he was the builder of democracy henceforth, the progressive educator was opposed, and those who opposed him, he termed "reactionaries."

The most important weapon in the arsenal of the progressive educators was their plea for tolerance of new ideas. Freedom of speech, according to this reasoning, meant freedom of education—and this meant freedom for the teacher. Carrying the theory a step further meant freedom to teach without bias—and insistence that the pupil and parent of the pupil listen without bias.

This of course created an unreal situation. There was no such teacher, no such pupil, and no such parent. But there was the progressive educator—who said it was so—and who under cloak of tolerance presented the cause of *freedom* as sufficient to solve the problems of society as well as of education.[8]

So, too, the work of radicals in politics was to establish the belief that economic democracy had disappeared in the United States and that a revision of political democracy was a means of restoring it.[9]

It appeared to mean, as forthright radicals claimed, that in addition to making the government responsive to the people, the government must now go into business. Certainly that had been the outcome of the program of Franklin Roosevelt as a result of the legislation passed under his leadership. It should

[8] Albert Lynd, in *Quackery in the Public Schools*, pp. 250-252, in referring to William H. Kilpatrick as the leader of a group of colleagues at Teachers College, Columbia University, including George S. Counts and Harold O. Rugg, who advocated a "planned society" the blueprint of which would be created by teachers, says: "I do not believe that he [Kilpatrick] can be accused of anything more subversive than gullibility, of a kind that was widely fashionable during the 'twenties and 'thirties, the heyday of academic leftism."

[9] A group of economists, viewing the situation, summarized it thus:
"For the danger exists that businessmen, obsessed with a devil theory of government, will attempt to use their economic power to suppress democracy and place in its stead a dictatorship supposedly dedicated to the fulfillment of their desires. . . . Such a dictatorship would revive economic activity, but it would be activity devoted increasingly to producing weapons of death and destruction which must sooner or later be used to plunge the country into a holocaust of slaughter and bloodshed." *An Economic Program for Democracy*, by Seven Harvard and Tufts Economists: Richard V. Gilbert, George H. Hildebrand, Jr., Arthur W. Stuart, Maxine Yaple Sweezy, Paul M. Sweezy, Lorie Tarshis, and John D. Wilson (Vanguard Press, 1938), p. 90. This book was recommended by the President in a telegram to his son, James, on February 2, 1939 (*Personal Letters, 1928-1945*, II, 857). In a note following, the editors wrote, "This little book, which reflected the Keynesian approach to full employment, was a bible of the New Dealers." (*Ibid.*, p. 858).

be noted that Woodrow Wilson and Theodore Roosevelt had argued for strong government to protect business and to provide competition.[10] But now, change in previous practice was advocated against the rise of possible dictatorship in the United States. Americans were to choose Franklin Roosevelt or another in his image, or fall into the hands of the "economic royalists" who were ever ready to take over—never more so than in 1938.

It is difficult for Americans who did not experience the shift of public opinion in the years 1937-39 to realize the vital changes that came over American feeling in those years. At the outset there was a genuine belief in the efficacy of American democracy to meet the problems of the new day. True, there were deep cut divisions as to the way this was being done. But somehow, although the American people had disagreed, it was thought that they had adhered on the whole to old patterns of disagreement.

Americans felt with positiveness that neither communism nor fascism had anything to offer them, and said so. But then, instead of continuing to develop the instrumentalities of democracy, a considerable number of people assumed the point of view that the future of America rested in an agreement with communism, in order to defeat fascism. Some said that communism was a natural outgrowth of democracy.

This point of view appealed to those who had international sympathies or at least believed that many problems were common to the nations of the world. The tendency, heretofore prevalent in America, to develop the existing genius for self-government in this nation of pioneers, receded in favor of emphasis on the programs of other peoples.

This led, in education, to an attempt to develop world-mindedness in place of what was thought of as self-interested provincialism. World history, for example, was stressed at the expense of national history including our own. This was intended to promote tolerance, as it did. Americans had much indeed to learn from others, and from earlier experiences. Yet in the attempt at generalization, Americans lost a sense of their own derivation, their own past, and their own convictions. The

---

[10] In this connection, note the summary by Herbert Hoover of "The Constructive Character of the Republican Party," *New York Times*, October 18, 1952.

result was a dangerous mood of acquiescence in a world of revolution.

Into this intellectual atmosphere surged the advocates of greater social democracy. Basing their arguments on fundamental belief in the people, the new radicals convinced many who listened that Americans had yet to create a real democracy in the United States. Here was a fertile field for those who had less regard for precedent than for innovation—who saw in the new distribution of power, opportunity for the assertion of natural right over proved accomplishment. To these the blueprints of communism had a natural appeal.

Naturally many of those who conceived of a new Utopia whereby Americans might once more attain equality, saw possible allies in advocates of communism—and in national terms this meant Russia. The likenesses were striking—an all-powerful state; economic well-being of the citizen; the declaration that the people were given natural political recognition.

The radicals saw that arrayed against this program would be the natural enemies of the new American democracy. The enemies abroad were the totalitarian states. The enemies at home were the "imperialists" who had exploited the masses both at home and abroad.

From the diplomatic recognition of Soviet Russia in 1933 until the pact between Hitler and Stalin in 1939, this was the gospel easily acceptable to radicals in the United States. Then for a brief period, as will be seen, the majority of American radicals rejected this affinity with Russia. But when Hitler repudiated his alliance and attacked Russia, American radicals were happy to find that the United States could be engulfed in the war upon "imperialism" in which Communist Russia was now our ally.

The extent to which the upholders of this pattern of thought influenced the American political scene was emphasized by the support given the movement for the nomination of Henry Wallace for the Vice-Presidency in 1940. On the whole, there was agreement that in a possible third election of Mr. Roosevelt, the American people would have a leader who could be counted on to carry this battle at home and abroad.

The President often spoke directly to youth, ascribing to

them attributes of enthusiasm, patriotism, and hope. He repeatedly asked young people not to expect too much of their elders, and yet not to approve of what they had done. A notable example of his approach was that of a radio address on October 5, 1937. It was a clever attack upon thought and the wisdom that flows from considered experience. After decrying the work of universities and of newspaper editors, he said:

> It is unfortunately true that in respect to public affairs and national problems, the excellently educated man and woman form the less worthwhile opinions, for the simple reason that they have enough education to make them think that they know it all, whereas actually their point of view is based on associations with others who, in their geographical outlook, are about one inch wide.[11]

From such a viewpoint, how inadequate and how inconsequential in the actual solution of problems seemed the effort through all the years of patriotic and experienced public men to find solutions for the problems that beset the nation. The whole elaborate, scientific approach to the study of public problems was of less importance than for everyone to be interested because he was ill informed, and to be certain and eloquent because he had yet so much to learn!

So bleak is the picture here painted of the insidious way in which radicals, especially young radicals, were taken in by this opportunistic philosophy, that one is led to raise this question: Was it possible that the currents of revolution were too strong for anyone in office in the United States, even Franklin Roosevelt, to resist? How could even he control such elements? [12]

The chief argument of those who were feeling, if they were not actually thinking, outright revolution, was that everyone was insecure. Surely a new way to the future must be found. This made approval of some of the doctrines of communism easier. Soviet Russia had in 1935 decided upon a shift in policy, which was followed by the appearance in western Europe and the United States of what came to be accepted as the "popular

---

[11] *Public Papers, 1937*, pp. 412-413.
[12] In 1939 Joseph Alsop and Robert Kintner, in their book, *Men Around the President*, recounted in detail episodes of the period 1933-1939 which clearly show the work and the results obtained by the individuals that occupied the place of intimate advisers to the President. It was an ever-changing personnel.

front" approach. This made it possible for American radicals to say that they saw communism as a natural development of democracy.[13]

Socialism had been and was urged as a method of preserving democracy. But communism appeared to most students to solve the problems of economic democracy by destroying political democracy. It had been natural for American radicals to stand as they did against Nazism. They knew in their American experience what this meant. For, as they saw it, here was a combination of two old-time enemies—the financial promoter and the gang leader—plus in Germany, military trappings. Yet it was the same enemy of the free spirit.

But as against communism there was no such stand by radicals because, in the experience of American liberals, the causes and roots and objectives of communism seemed not only familiar but acceptable. Even the slogans appeared to have a familiar sound. And so it was that for a time many were misled. Furthermore, throughout his years in office men of Communist sympathy had access to the President—and he listened to them.

It is, therefore, not strange that a few of these who were Americans in positions of primary responsibility in the national government, were later charged with being the agents of a foreign power active in undermining the national interest of the United States.

By 1937 it was clear that the leadership of Franklin Roosevelt had altered beyond easy recognition all existing political parties, including his own. It may be argued that he was but the victim of forces far beyond the control of even so successful a politician as he had proved himself to be. But it was his view as a personal leader who stood upon popular support with intention to further popular programs, that had taken the meaning out of Republican protest, out of splinter party appeal, and in the end out of Democratic party doctrine. If the political

---

[13] The testimony of Earl Browder before the Senate Committee on April 27, 1950, must be given due weight. In his view as leader, then, of the Communist party recognized in most of the states as a political party in elections, it was not a conspiracy for the overthrow of the existing government of the United States. It was a party of protest, well recognized in American politics. In a letter to the *New York Times*, April 19, 1954, Mr. Browder wrote: "In politics, of course, the main weight of Communist influence was thrown behind Roosevelt and the Democratic party, for historical reasons. . . ."

parties that had existed could have been barred from further activity, the real nature of the change would have been seen.

Could the President have gone to the country—without party support and not opposed by parties as such—it is probable that a majority of the electorate would have endorsed him and whatever program he offered at the time.[14] The radicals saw this. It was a reflection not only of the mood elsewhere in the world, but in truth a reflection of many of the deeper currents of our own history that had been obscured by our natural aptitude for compromise rather than clear cut decision.

The progressive tradition in American political feeling had an important part in determining the state of mind in which upholders of the President often met the charge that they were really Communists. The retort often on their lips was, We are "simply trying to improve the social order and give the underdog a chance." [15]

Despite all that could be said—and was said repeatedly in press, on the radio, in pulpit, and in public forum—against the dangers of personal rule, a large section of the American public craved a dictator. The deepest wound that had been given the American practice of self-government had been given by its professed friends. Every argument, every program, every success on behalf of the American people made them less able to perform the functions of a self-supporting people. They asked security and were disposed to pay the price, whatever it was.[16]

As has been seen, the fundamental divisions in American

---

[14] By comparison with the situation twenty years earlier under Wilson, the issue is made clearer. See Matthew Josephson, *The President Makers*, p. vii.

[15] *The Secret Diary of Harold L. Ickes* (1933-1936), p. 653. But in *The United States, A Graphic History*, published in 1937, text by Louis M. Hacker, appear the concluding words: "Nevertheless the outlook for the real future was bright. . . . More and more American workers of hand and brain were uniting to defend their liberties. It was inevitable that they should use this mass power to free themselves from a system of production—the profit system—which was every day proving it had outlived its usefulness."

[16] Writing of the prevalence of cynicism in 1938, Nicholas Roosevelt, in *A New Birth of Freedom*, wrote (pp. 15-16): "Gone are the old ideals—gone, in fact, are any ideals, for the new creed of security is a coldly materialistic doctrine. It denies the teachings of religion and the values of things spiritual. . . . To those who hold these beliefs the Declaration of Independence is nothing but bombast and the soldiers who died at Valley Forge were fools." Louis Untermeyer, writing the following year in *From Another World*, in a "Foreword by Letter," addressed to his sons, (p. 7), said: "And there is the world in which we are now living, the world of undeclared wars and methodical violence, of political aggression and moral disintegration, a world of fear which has exchanged the forces of security for the security of force."

political feeling which had emerged during the first two terms of Franklin Roosevelt's Presidency were altered—for a time—by a new development in Europe. That the Nazi leader, Hitler, entered into a compact with the Communist leader, Stalin, could be easily comprehended by most Americans. Yet it shocked beyond measure the radicals in the United States, and led to a re-formation of political lines.[17]

Russia was now linked with Germany as an enemy of democracy. It became clear that disagreements among radicals in the United States had roots in a misunderstanding of what communism really was. On the whole, the revelation of the pact and its meaning to the free world strengthened the hand and argument of all conservatives. And, as will be seen, this enabled the President to win many conservatives to his standard for the war in which the United States was about to engage.

Yet facts were facts. In six years of experimentation the national debt had been doubled. In every one of the years the administration had been in the eyes of the accountant "insolvent." "Private business" was still the basic interest of Americans in every walk of life. "Capitalism" had been saved because, with all the experimentation, the national government stood back of all "costs." So it was at last clear that not "Big Business" nor "Big Labor," nor "Big Farmers" would save the United States, but "Big Government."

---

[17] For a summary of the effect of the change upon the position of parties and individuals, see Allan Nevins, *The New Deal and World Affairs*, pp. 192-193.

Chapter XII

AN AGGRESSIVE FOREIGN POLICY

IT WAS MANY TIMES evident throughout his administration that, in the conduct of foreign relations, President Roosevelt was not free to develop a program based solely upon his own view of the world situation. Nor was he free to act upon the reports and recommendations of his State Department, and of his personal representatives abroad. The President must first of all consider the views of the international situation held by his constituents. He must meet their proposals for action. He must meet their opposition to any steps he might take or any pronouncements he might make.

The assertion that Mr. Roosevelt early in his administration provided a "liberalization" of our foreign policies refers primarily to declarations favorable to friendly relations with Soviet Russia, with Latin American countries, and with all governments that would accept proposals for disarmament and would consider a lowering of tariff barriers. During his first term, President Roosevelt left Secretary Hull "in almost full charge of foreign affairs." [1]

---

[1] Hull, *op. cit.,* I, 194.

The President felt that his sharp and destructive ultimatum to the London Economic Conference in the summer of 1933 had been confirmed by the approving response of the American people. Thus, when in January of 1935 he was aware of widespread opposition to the proposal that the United States join the World Court, he did not push the matter. The resolution for adherence to the World Court with reservations had been favorably reported by the Senate Foreign Relations Committee. Yet the debate in the Senate had revealed not only the powerful emotional appeal of the isolationists, but also the opposition of many supporters of the New Deal. Once again the need of a successful domestic program led the President to abstain from working his will in an international program.

The debate on the World Court had not been confined to the Senate. The electorate was deeply concerned—not so much in the details of events abroad as in the question of American isolation from the effect of these events. The revelations of the Nye Committee investigations, which had begun in March of 1934, heartened the conviction of those who believed that active American involvement in foreign affairs in the earlier years of the century had been in every way detrimental to the national interest and security.

Moreover, the emphasis placed by the Nye Committee upon the assertion that "bankers, arms makers and profiteers" forced us into the World War in 1917, seemed to confirm the conception of many that the real conflict was between "selfish forces" and the people as a whole. This explanation was of course far too simple. Yet for this reason it made millions aware of the danger of militarism as symbolized by dictators in foreign lands.

The utterances of Secretary Hull and of the President during 1934 and 1935 alarmed those who would refrain from participation in world affairs. On May 2, 1935, Secretary Hull told the Chamber of Commerce of the United States that "It is the collapse of the world structure, the development of isolated economies, that has let loose the fear which now grips every nation, and which threatens the peace of the world." [2]

Several months earlier, in recommending to the Senate adherence to the World Court, the President had said, "At this period

---

[2] *Ibid.*, I, 391.

in international relationships, when every act is of moment to
the future of world peace, the United States has an opportunity
once more to throw its weight into the scale in favor of peace." [3]
Again the argument of the isolationists was a simple one.
Experience had shown that when the United States had asserted
its right in time of war to ship munitions, to lend money, and
to permit its citizens to travel in danger zones, in due time it
had become involved in armed conflict. Now the wise precau-
tion was to refrain from such action.

This was the setting for the passage by the Congress on
August 31, 1935, of a Joint Resolution, providing that in the
case of war between two or more foreign states, the President—
in proclaiming the fact—should add that it was illegal to export
arms, ammunition or implements of war from the United States
to any belligerent. The President was empowered as well to
forbid American citizens to travel on ships of a belligerent
nation. The President signed the bill "reluctantly."

A careful and informed observer subsequently wrote of this
action: "By this the United States professed to have no concern
about what happened to any other people anywhere. The neutrality act was the complete, if not the final expression of the
peace-at-any-price feeling. It was as impractical as it was immoral, a pathetic fallacy raised to the highest degree, but it was
thought the Congress believed the voters wanted it at the time
it was enacted." [4]

The President himself is reported to have said in 1935, "Despite what happens in continents overseas, the United States
shall and must remain unentangled." [5] His growing concern was
reflected in his annual message to the Congress on January 3,
1936, when he said:

The rest of the world—Ah! There is the rub.

Were I today to deliver an Inaugural Address to the people of
the United States, I could not limit my comments on world
affairs to one paragraph. With much regret I should be compelled to devote the greater part to world affairs. Since the
summer of that same year of 1933, a point has been reached

---

[3] *Public Papers, 1935*, p. 41.
[4] Chenery, *op. cit.*, p. 264.
[5] Moley, *After Seven Years*, p. 377.

where the people of the Americas must take cognizance of growing ill-will, of marked trends toward aggression, of increasing armaments, of shortening tempers—a situation which has in it many of the elements that lead to the tragedy of general war.[6]

Six months later, civil war broke out in Spain. As the conflict widened in its influences upon the policies of every European state—arraying the interests of Germany and Italy against those of France and England—the President recommended that a legal embargo be provided against both sides. This was accomplished by an Act of January 8, 1937, forbidding export of munitions to either of the opposing forces in Spain. The United States, under its President, was now more isolationist than ever.

But the events of the years 1933-1937 had made it abundantly clear that President Roosevelt could not carry on his work as molder of foreign policy in an isolationist vacuum. He was in a position where policy and policies had to be considered in the light of events beyond our borders and, on the whole, beyond our control. Yet always the purposes, desires, and knowledge of his constituents, the people of the United States, had to be considered.

Effective leadership consisted in relating world events and American public opinion—and doing so constantly. Aiding the President in constructing a policy—but very little in determining his timing and his decisions—were his "experts" on the scene and at home. For four years—until October of 1937—there was no definite indication of a fundamental change in policy, which was one of aloof but watchful waiting.

It is true that in the closing hours of the Presidential campaign of 1936, Franklin Roosevelt had warned the American people that in a world of war and rumors of war, the United States might not be able to maintain neutrality, non-involvement and at the same time, a proper defense of American interests.

A nation preponderantly isolationist in feeling was not greatly interested in such a declaration. Nor did the people take note beyond an awareness of distant danger in certain events in

---

[6] *Public Papers, 1936,* p. 9.

foreign lands which took such an increasingly alarming turn upon the outbreak of undeclared war between Japan and China in July, 1937.

The Spanish Civil War had by this time become the center of the attention of those who saw not only the "rebels" and the "loyalists," but observed that Germany and Italy and Russia were increasingly disposed to take sides. Informed Americans looked apprehensively toward Europe.

The Neutrality Act had been passed by the Congress by an overwhelming majority and had been signed by the President on May 1, 1937. It was widely believed that, in view of the record during the years 1933-1937, the administration would not attempt a program at variance with this expression of American feeling. The President did nothing and said nothing to indicate a change.

Consequently, however welcome to advocates of more vigorous action, the speech of the President at Chicago on October 5, 1937, was a definite surprise to the majority of the American people. It was a warning to the warring nations of the world that:

> There is a solidarity and interdependence about the modern world, both technically and morally, which makes it impossible for any nation completely to isolate itself from economic and political upheavals in the rest of the world, especially when such upheavals appear to be spreading and not declining.[7]

This Quarantine Speech was also a warning to the American people:

> . . . . The peace, the freedom and the security of ninety percent of the population of the world is being jeopardized by the remaining ten percent who are threatening a breakdown of all international order and law. Surely the ninety percent who want to live in peace under law and in accordance with moral standards that have received almost universal acceptance through the centuries, can and must find some way to make their will prevail.[8]

---

[7] *Public Papers, 1937*, p. 409.
[8] *Ibid.*, p. 410.

The "way" to enforce peace was then hinted by the President as he said:

> When an epidemic of physical disease starts to spread, the community approves and joins in a quarantine of the patients in order to protect the health of the community against the spread of the disease.[9]

With war raging in fact, if not in declarations, in Asia and Europe, this meant a suggestion—in terms of prescription as well as diagnosis—that the United States might help the freedom-loving peoples to save themselves from epidemics that beset whole populations under the close control of rulers who were engaged in enlarging and increasing the prevalence of war, pestilence, and disaster. A private citizen might express such a view and urge such a suggestion without consequence. For the President to do so, precipitated the United States into a discussion of the possibility of being caught in the maelstrom of war.

Yet no program was proposed by the President, and no implementation was provided the announced policy. In his press conference the day following the Quarantine Speech, the President was asked how he would reconcile the policy he had outlined with the policy of neutrality laid down by the Act of Congress. He replied: "Read the last line. . . . 'Therefore America actively engages in the search for peace.' " When pressed further, the President would add only: "I can't tell you what the methods will be. We are looking for some way to peace; and by no means is it necessary that the way be contrary to the exercise of neutrality." [10]

If the President could obtain the support of the American people in sufficient volume to control the action of Congress, he could—in this world of conflict—throw the weight of potential power against the aggressors. Possibly this warning would win a contest for peace by making it clear that—if not heeded by the dictators—the United States would forsake its neutral role. No other honest interpretation was possible.

---

[9] Hull states that he and Norman Davis proposed to the President in September that he make a speech on need of international co-operation—and do it in a city of heavy isolationist sentiment. The speech was prepared in the State Department, but altered by the President. "We did not have the celebrated 'quarantine' clause in our draft." (*Memoirs* I, 544-545.)

[10] *Public Papers, 1937*, pp. 422-423.

It might be argued that the threat would be sufficient to insure peace, but nevertheless it meant that in such peace or cold war the power of the United States was pledged at last to more than non-involvement. The nation would not, however, be engaged in what might be termed co-operation with one side in the struggle.

Nevertheless, the President said, "It is an attitude, and it does not outline a program; but it says we are looking for a program." [11] And he added later in the same press conference, "There are a lot of methods in the world that have never been tried yet." [12]

What was this in fact but active participation in world politics? The method was that of "quarantine" of the aggressor. That was far from isolation.

Now the President must fight the isolationists, as he had not hitherto done. For he could not hope to win them to his point of view, even though many of them had supported most of his domestic policies. They had been courted by the President in the campaign of 1936, and they had actively supported his re-election. So definitely radical was he in the eyes of conservatives, that even though some of the latter saw advantage in support of Great Britain and France, they could not be expected to tolerate preparation for war under his leadership.

Foreign governments and peoples might hitherto have been uncertain as to the extent of American participation in affairs beyond American borders. Now, however, they were no longer in doubt as to what the President would say and do, provided he could secure and hold the support of the American electorate in this new "attitude." It was clearly seen by those with perspective, moreover, that a large minority in the United States were prepared for the action of the President.

His was now a program of internationalism that appealed to those who had never forsaken their dream of the League of Nations. As a dynamic approach to the problem of world peace, the President's new position appealed to a vastly larger number who had grown increasingly restive under the stark realities of world politics since the failure of the London Con-

---

[11] *Ibid.*, p. 423.
[12] *Ibid.*, p. 424.

ference in 1933. This departure from previous policy was, they thought, a movement toward co-operative action which they defended as a necessity against the rule of the dictators. It was a clear choice for the United States—if it could be made clear to the dictators.

Yet in his four years in office, Franklin Roosevelt had refrained from participating in world politics except as leader of a nation with a national policy that was properly termed isolationist. He had won the support of the people while under partisan attack in the campaign of 1936, declaring that we would not enter upon war but would maintain neutrality.

For the President knew the elements in the United States that would be opposed to aggressive action. As the European conflict increased in intensity, he observed the gathering of strength in favor of refraining from any involvement. Such forces praised neutrality. So did he.

But the President was in a position of executive responsibility. His critics could ignore protective measures. He could not. Of course he did not. He instituted measures for the national defense. As will presently appear, Mr. Roosevelt's conception of measures necessary to protect the United States included the furnishing of aid to its friends in the struggle already shaping abroad.

Opposition to any aid abroad and to any form of intervention must now mean opposition to the President's policies. He must in turn, therefore, fight isolation because isolationists would destroy a policy developed to avoid war. The European war constantly forced his hand. So did the attitude of the America First organizations, of which there came to be several hundred.

The outbreak of a European war in 1914 had forced Wilson to formulate a foreign policy for his administration. His party had adopted it in 1916. His subsequent development of foreign policy—and his program for international organization—were fought within the Democratic party, as well as in the Republican party, and within the great American electorate as a whole.

Franklin Roosevelt was familiar with this story and had been a participant, particularly in the final plans of the campaign of 1920. By experience, he was acquainted with every basic issue in the debate upon the nature of American participation in

affairs beyond American borders. By inclination as well as by
experience—and by temperament as well as education—he was
disposed to play a leading role in an adjustment of world
affairs. But he knew that to do so, he must secure endorsement
from the American people.

The President's Quarantine Speech put him at the head of
those who believed something must be done to bring order
into the chaos of international relations. Could he lead the
American people on this issue? He was to try to do so.[13] But
during the years 1937 to 1940, as in the United States from
1914 to 1917, the majority of the American people were definitely and with conviction opposed to aggressive national
action.

The difficulty in which the President found himself was
never more clearly revealed than in his message to Congress on
January 4, 1939:

> We have learned that God-fearing democracies of the world
> which observe the sanctity of treaties and good faith in their
> dealings with other nations cannot safely be indifferent to inter-
> national lawlessness anywhere. They cannot forever let pass,
> without effective protest, acts of aggression against sister na-
> tions—acts which automatically undermine all of us. . . . There
> are many methods short of war, but stronger and more effec-
> tive than mere words, of bringing home to aggressor govern-
> ments the aggregate sentiments of our own people.[14]

Yet the policy of the administration must be one to convince
a majority of the American people that measures should be
taken to threaten aggressors by aiding those who opposed such
aggressors. This meant taking sides in the contest that was
raging. The President asked of the Congress a half-billion dollars for national defense, the bulk of which was to be used in
building aircraft.

The aggressors abroad now knew who their greatest potential

---

[13] Secretary Hull was to relate in retrospect (*op. cit.*, I, 546-547) that in the
autumn of 1937 the President responded enthusiastically to a peace plan
evolved by Under Secretary Welles which called for a spectacular White House
meeting of all the diplomatic representatives on Armistice Day. "The colorful
drama to be staged in the White House appealed to him. For several years he
had pondered the idea of inviting the heads of the nations of Europe to hold
a meeting with him at sea. Around a table aboard a battleship or cruiser he
would work out with them a lasting peace."
[14] *Public Papers, 1939*, pp. 1-3.

enemy was. However much the freedom-loving nations suffered, they always had hope that eventually America would win their cause for them.

For two years the debate was carried on in the United States and only the final, definite outbreak of war in September, 1939, made clear what was implied in the President's declaration of October, 1937, and his appeal to Congress and the people, as well as to the dictators. In the midst of this debate it was widely believed that the President had said in a secret conference with members of the Senate Committee on Military Affairs, "The American frontier is on the Rhine." [15]

More and more at this time the attention of the American people concentrated on the conflict for power in Europe. Organizations were formed to further programs that would aid the Allies—or programs to insure American isolation. As another Presidential election year approached, it was clear that each of the parties would be divided upon the issues of aid and isolation. But neither party would be for war—nor for aggressive action that would precipitate war. In such a situation, it was of primary importance to decide upon the leader to be placed in the position of supreme responsibility in the world—in peace or in war.

This was not an unusual situation for the American people. In the years 1914 to 1917 both parties had been divided. In 1916 the plea that President Wilson had kept the United States out of war was a forceful influence in deciding the election of that year. Then, as in 1939-1940, a few advocated war. And that fitted the American pattern of thought.

In 1940, as in 1920, the American party system did not lend itself to clear cut discussion of opinion on American participation in international affairs. Nor could isolation to the extent of refusal to co-operate with others who might favor peace and democratic government be made a reasonable political issue. In short, American public opinion had to find ways of meeting such issues and reaching a decision outside the customary arena of debate on the election of a President, or upon participation in war. The question now, as the American people saw it, was

---

[15] This was denied by Mr. Roosevelt in his press conference of February 3, 1939. (*Ibid.*, p. 115.)

the form and extent of their co-operation with other nations who might be going their way.

When the Russo-German non-aggression pact was announced on August 23, 1939, it appeared that all of the President's attempts to prevent outbreak of a major war had come to naught. The aggressive forces in Europe were obviously marshaling for war. This alliance also showed how impolitic it was for the people of the United States to believe that to the Russian Communists democracy meant what it meant to Americans. The Communists had allied themselves with the Fascists.

For six years and more prior to this pact, Russia had been looked upon with great favor by radicals in the United States. They believed that Russian communism was leading the way to a better world. Now—as so often before in the history of the United States—it became glaringly apparent that European politics meant something quite baffling to most Americans. This realization appeared to strengthen the contention of the isolationists that the United States should keep out of the European struggle.

With the German attack on Poland in September, 1939, and the entry of Great Britain and France into the war against Hitler, it appeared at once that American policy to preserve peace had failed. Although aid and sympathy had been promised those who had now for several years been threatened by force, it was thought by some that uncertainty as to the extent of American action had failed to deter Hitler. On May 10, Ambassador Bullitt in Paris cabled that the British Ambassador to France "had told him three times that his Government had one real fear. This was that German Foreign Minister Ribbentrop might succeed in persuading Hitler that Germany could fight England and France without risk because there was no possibility of their obtaining military supplies from the United States." [16]

Prior to the outbreak of war, President Roosevelt had attempted, by appealing directly to the ruler of Germany and to the master of Italy, to halt the march of aggression in Europe. He had failed. Speaking in Canada in August, 1938, the President had said:

---

[16] Hull, *op. cit.*, I, 646.

The Dominion of Canada is part of the sisterhood of the British Empire. I give to you assurance that the people of the United States will not stand idly by if domination of Canadian soil is threatened by any other Empire.[17]

To the Congress early in 1939 President Roosevelt had stated that war was not the only method of halting aggression.[18] His meaning was obscured by the fact that within a week he was asking of the Congress an additional half-billion for defense. The President renewed his efforts toward a solution in Europe, asking the two dictators in April to bind themselves not to make aggressive moves for ten years, and to enter a conference of European powers. Here, too, he failed. He was nevertheless unable to persuade the Congress to annul the Neutrality Act. The President afterwards said that this lack of action on the part of the Congress had much to do with the coming of the war when it did—two months later.

The world was now divided between the democracies and the totalitarian states. The conflict was irrepressible. Therefore, the United States must give aid to those who were fighting for democracy. The President urged that by giving aid and enabling the democracies to win, we would take a part that would make it unnecessary for us to go to war.

The logic of this position was impossible. It seemed to overlook completely the fact that the side that we wished would lose would not, in case it felt it was about to lose, refrain from attacking us.

With the outbreak of actual war in Europe, the whole situation in which the President must formulate his policies was changed. Everyone knew that the President was not neutral in his thought. Indeed, there was an overtone of admission of that fact in his radio address to the nation on September 3, when he said:

Let no man or woman thoughtlessly or falsely talk of America sending its armies to European fields. At this moment there is being prepared a proclamation of American neutrality. This would have been done even if there had been no neutrality

---

[17] Public Papers, 1938, p. 493.
[18] Public Papers, 1939, p. 3.

statute on the books, for this proclamation is in accordance with international law and in accordance with American policy. . . .

This nation will remain a neutral nation, but I cannot ask that every American remain neutral in thought as well. Even a neutral has a right to take account of facts. Even a neutral cannot be asked to close his mind or his conscience.[19]

The change in the administration policy rested in the fact that, whereas appeals for a peaceful solution could be made before the outbreak of war without seeming to actually take sides, appeals after the outbreak would be in terms of aid and comfort to the nations that had been attacked. These nations were on record as opposing the use of force except in retaliation in case of attack. "By the end of the fateful year 1939 . . . basic guarantees of peace for the United States had been written into the record by President Roosevelt and the supporters of his administration," wrote Charles A. Beard.[20]

But this summary ignores the fact that tremendous pressures had been at work to force more aggressive action.[21] It ignores as well clear evidence of the President's personal view. When Russia had attacked Poland in November of 1939 the President denounced the action, and called for an embargo against Russia.

The events of the European war in the spring and summer of 1940 emphasized again and again the difficulty of the President's position. He must make every move, if not every utterance, in terms of a world at war in which the United States was "neutral." Yet he must be seen as preparing his own nation for possible war. Preparation for defense was the only course of action that could be taken.

Mr. Roosevelt's denunciation of Mussolini at Charlottesville in June was in an address prepared in the Department of State. It was suggested to the President that he omit the sentence, "On this 10th day of June, 1940, the hand that held the dagger has struck it into the back of its neighbor," and he removed it

---

[19] *Ibid.*, pp. 462-463.
[20] *American Foreign Policy*, p. 263. For detailed treatment of this period see W. L. Langer and S. E. Gleason, *The Challenge to Isolation, 1937-1940*, especially pp. 45-51.
[21] For example, the letter of Henry L. Stimson to the *New York Times*, March 6, 1939, urging a direct military understanding between the United States, and Britain and France.

from his text, "but changed his mind en route to Charlottesville and reinserted it." [22]

The President's policy was well expressed in the conclusion of his address:

> In our American unity, we will pursue two obvious and simultaneous courses; we will extend to the opponents of force the material resources of this nation; and, at the same time, we will harness and speed up the use of those resources in order that we ourselves in the Americas may have equipment and training equal to the task of any emergency and every defense.[23]

More and more emphatically the President henceforth stated his objectives to the American people in terms of national defense. In his message to the Congress in explanation of the destroyer deal with Great Britain, he was to say:

> Preparation for defense is an inalienable prerogative of a sovereign state. . . . This is the most important action in the reinforcement of our national defense that has been taken since the Louisiana Purchase. Then, as now, considerations of safety from overseas attack were fundamental.[24]

From this point onward the primary objective of the President was to win from the Congress means to aid the Allies. It was no longer to provide a pacific American program. This was involvement in war—short of war. It made less and less appeal to potential allies of the United States, however much it served to make more palatable the draught of medicine that the American people and the Congress were forced to take. They were to keep out of war, but it was not isolation. They aided freedom-loving nations, but it was not internationalism. They were in a game of power politics. The President's "quarantine" pronouncement was but another indication of the President's predilection to play a lone hand, and his insistence upon pursuing in international affairs the role of the lone wolf. As in the case of the London Conference of 1933, he was maintaining that the nation would act—if it acted—alone, or at least on its own initiative.

The policies of the President throughout his first administra-

[22] Hull, *op. cit.*, I, 784-785.
[23] *Public Papers, 1940*, p. 264.
[24] *Ibid.*, p. 391.

tion should have prepared the alert and well informed to expect something of the kind, particularly as the events of the autumn of 1937 increased the danger of a violent outburst both in Europe and in the Far East. In fact, the people of the United States were prepared for no action of any kind, for they were really unaware of the dangers abroad.

If "quarantine" meant reopening the question of American participation in a world association of nations, then indeed public opinion would tear to shreds such a proposal. If it meant that in the situation created by the rise to power of the totalitarian leaders, the United States was to pursue a policy of active association with other so-called liberal powers, a new alignment would be required. In this development the isolationists would have the advantage. There was a chance, however, that "quarantine" meant neither of these. Was the President proposing at this time to strengthen the national interest by an aggressive nationalism?

In the game of power politics in which the President was slowly leading the people, he was to use all the means at his command: vital amendment of Neutrality Acts; cash and carry provisions; the destroyer deal by Executive Act; and finally a personal conference with the Prime Minister of Great Britain. The listing of the Four Freedoms was an effort to give the process of American participation a program of international promise.[25]

Meanwhile, the President was concerned with the national defense. Speaking to the American people in a Fireside Chat on May 26, 1940, when "over the once peaceful roads of Belgium and France millions are now moving, running from their homes to escape bombs and shells and fire and machine gunning," Mr. Roosevelt said:

[25] In estimating Mr. Roosevelt's responsibility, due weight must be given to the conclusion of Langer and Gleason, *op. cit.*, p. 776, "While conceding that it took courage to embark upon so grave a transaction [the destroyer deal] on the eve of a national election, one must recognize that Mr. Roosevelt's way had been carefully prepared by those organizations which not only plotted a safe course for him but also carried the burden of public education. The destroyer deal was at least as much the achievement of private effort as of official action and should be viewed as a truly popular national commitment to share in the conflict against Hitler to the extent required by American security."

There are some among us who were persuaded by minority groups that we could maintain our physical safety by retiring within our continental boundaries. . . . Obviously, a defense policy based on that is merely to invite future attack. . . . To those who would not admit the possibility of the approaching storm . . . the past two weeks have meant the shattering of many illusions . . .[26]

In addition to defense measures, the administration "was frantically trying to get together every available weapon for Britain," wrote Secretary Hull of the last days of May.[27] With the fall of the Low Countries on May 10, the President had said:

We have come . . . to the reluctant conclusion that a continuance of these processes of arms presents a definite challenge to the continuance of the type of civilization to which all of us in the three Americas have been accustomed for so many generations.[28]

Yet it seemed to the President that although "we should do better to keep the fighting away from our own back yard," as Hull wrote later, there was one point on which he "and I had not the slightest doubt; namely, that an Allied victory was essential to the security of the United States." [29]

The development—as was true of the outbreak—of the war in Europe had a profound effect upon American public opinion. Divisions up to that time had been based upon a deep-seated belief that in some way this terrible catastrophe would be avoided. All alignments in the years 1933-1939 had been predicated upon the possibility of a truce—or agreement—to which the United States could without war lend its help.

Isolated, strong, and prepared to help those who believed as they did, Americans could really refrain from participation in war—so millions of them had thought. But now they were not so sure. The United States might actually stay out of the war, rather than enter as it had in 1917. Yet the American people

---

[26] *Public Papers, 1940*, p. 231.
[27] Hull, *op. cit.*, I, 775.
[28] *Public Papers, 1940*, p. 184.
[29] Hull, *op. cit.*, I, 766.

must prepare for real defense in view of the fact that ultimately the United States might be attacked.

This change in the public view resulted in an altered opinion of the President. This was true of his supporters as well as of those who yet opposed him. Henceforth Franklin Roosevelt must act the role of a national leader in a national crisis. Gradually all questions, domestic as well as foreign, came to be seen in the light of Presidential act, utterance and plan. In war there is one leader. Although the United States was not at war, in the eyes of everyone it was a nation that must be ready to wage war.

So, too, the President entered into a new phase of his leadership. It was not that his public utterances changed in general content—except as they reflected the changing pitch in international relations. There was no evidence of change in the direction of the President's thought as to the need of national defense first of all. There was a lessening of emphasis upon the possibility of international co-operation. That was to reappear later.

In the new situation, America was in itself the hope of the future. America must be united and strong. The increase in Franklin Roosevelt's popularity as President was marked, and was to explain some of the events of the following months.

The policy of President Roosevelt has been shown to be aggressive, yet always subject to possible adjustment. A balancing of forces at home with forces abroad was accompanied by refusal to make clear what the United States might do. In this uncertainty, strength lay with one who remained in power. A definite clash at home, which might have easily led to defeat in 1940 was avoided. Involvement abroad was likewise avoided. In refusing to join the forces of the freedom-loving peoples, Mr. Roosevelt counted upon the totalitarian states' refraining from attack upon the United States.

The one unmistakable fact was that the President said the nation would stay out of war, and that was precisely what a majority of Americans wished to do.[30]

---

[30] A somewhat different view is stated by Charles and Mary Beard, writing in the winter of 1938-39: "Nevertheless, the central drive of the Roosevelt administration was in the direction of intervention, as official declarations and armament measures indicated." (*America in Mid-Passage*, I, 500.)

Chapter XIII

1940: A NEW ALIGNMENT AT HOME

A S THE YEAR 1940 opened, the interest of the American people was absorbed by the coming Presidential campaign and election. Deeply embedded in the habits of more than a century and a half, this manifestation of American democracy appeared to all who gave it thought to be as certain as the rising of the sun. Profoundly influenced as Americans now were by events beyond their borders, nevertheless they considered all public questions before them—and all personalities involved—in relation to this exhilarating practice of self-government.

In this election the administration was to defend a record of eight years in office. In the most recent instance of this kind in 1920, an administration had been overwhelmingly repudiated. On that occasion, a combination of opposing forces had successfully convinced the electorate of the need of a change.

Now there was again clear indication that opposing elements and leaders who were dissatisfied for various reasons were eager to join in a campaign to change the administration. This was a familiar phenomenon in American politics. Only ten Presidents had been elected a second time, and the latest of these, Woodrow Wilson, had won a second election by a narrow margin. Was Franklin Roosevelt to be returned to office a third time?

Mr. Roosevelt's administration had won popular support even in the crucial Congressional election of 1938. In eastern and some middle western states the margin of victory had been slight, but the Democratic party organization—despite losses—had maintained majority control of both House and Senate. It is true that these majorities were seriously divided on most of the issues before them, but they had a partisan control of the Congress and on occasion responded affirmatively to the leadership of the President.

Deep personal antagonisms arising out of disagreement on programs proposed by the President and his close personal supporters did not alter the fact that the ruling power in legislative matters was provided by the Democratic party organization in House and Senate. Even the efforts of the President to purge those Democrats who had opposed him, had not broken the united front of the Democratic party organization in face of partisan attack from Republicans. The Democratic party entered the campaign of 1940 as a formidable antagonist.

The Republicans, with 23 members in the Senate and 168 in the House, constituted the national opposition to all Democratic Congressional action. Long before this, the Republican party had lost to the Democratic side its more outstanding insurgents. The majority of the remaining Republicans in both Houses were united on domestic issues. On foreign affairs they were divided. But only a handful could be counted on to urge programs of affirmative action on foreign or domestic questions, for theirs had been a program of denial.

The Republicans had furthermore shown no indication of intention to support the policies associated with the leadership of the Republican President who had been defeated for re-election in 1932. That leadership—as expressed by Mr. Hoover during the second administration of Mr. Roosevelt—gave the Republicans a platform on which to debate the proposals of the administration. But they felt that millions of American voters viewed with bitterness the record associated with Mr. Hoover's administration.

The rebellious spirit so widespread among Americans in the 1930's had little representation in the Congress or in organized party protest. Four "independents" in the Senate were matched by an equal number in the House. There was little expectation, in the impending Presidential election, of a large vote for third party candidates. This vote had been three percent of the total vote cast in the election of 1936. Neither expectant Republicans nor apprehensive Democrats thought that a third party would play a determining role in the election of 1940. Thus was reflected American experience.

There were, in fact, deep-seated divisions within the membership of both major parties, for each had contained radicals. By 1940 almost all of these were actively working within the Democratic party. This was a factor of fateful significance.

The two-term limitation upon Presidents had long been a fetish of American politics. In early discussions of the approaching election year, Democratic party managers had been outwardly disposed to recognize this custom as barring the renomination of President Roosevelt.

The search for a nominee had brought forth a routine display of such party possibilities as James A. Farley, Cordell Hull, and Vice-President Garner. Others discussed by supporters and commentators included Paul McNutt, Henry Wallace, William O. Douglas, Harry Hopkins, and Robert Jackson.

It was thought that the designation of a successor by the President himself was an all-important matter. It was known that the nominee must run on the record of the administration. Thus it was early recognized that if the chosen nominee were to be elected, he would need support from the same elements that had supported the President.

As the campaign was envisaged by practical politicians, the Democratic nominee, to win, must be certain to hold the southern states. This meant 157 electoral votes. With these votes assured him in the Electoral College, he must add 109 votes from at least four of the larger states, probably New York, Pennsylvania, New Jersey, and Illinois or Massachusetts. This meant a candidate satisfactory to organized labor and to the city machines.

Moreover, the candidate had to be one who could be nominated in the Democratic National Convention. Nomination might be fraught with more uncertainty than the election itself. In the convention, all party factionalism would have its full opportunity. If no outstanding candidate could be found who could unite such dissimilar interests, it might be the part of wisdom to nominate a party regular. Such a candidate would of necessity count on the party regulars and could count on the mass appeal of Mr. Roosevelt to bring him sufficient votes to win—if not an impressive popular victory, at least a majority in the Electoral College. Such a man as Democratic National Committee Chairman James A. Farley fitted into this picture.

The situation in the autumn of 1940 called for leadership in foreign relations. Here no routine party nomination—no "holding operation"—would be certain of success. The administration to be chosen might become a war administration. This was a possibility but not a certainty.

The new administration must expect to provide national security by furthering American interest in terms of informal alliance with nations fighting for freedom against dictators. This course had already been chosen by the President, and in this choice the people had acquiesced. It was not possible, of course, for a Democratic nominee to call for anything approaching the stand of the isolationists. On the other hand, no reading of the national mind registered a call for war.

Even at the opening of the year 1940, the President's position on the question of his possible renomination was not clear to his closest advisers. It was said on good authority that at times he considered Hopkins and more often, Hull, as a possible successor.[1] Mrs. Roosevelt wrote later that she "had every evidence to believe that [her husband] did not want to run again."[2] But silence on his part precluded the development of effective campaigns for others who might aspire to the nomination.

For many months there had been much public discussion of the possibility of Mr. Roosevelt's renomination. As early as the autumn of 1939 the more reliable public opinion polls showed marked popular support. Throughout the period from October, 1939, to the convention in July, 1940, confirmed "New

---

[1] "From the end of 1938 until July, 1940, President Roosevelt expressed himself to me as definitely in favor of my being his successor in 1940," wrote Cordell Hull (Op. cit., I, 856. See remainder of chapter for additional discussion.)

[2] Eleanor Roosevelt, This I Remember, p. 212.

Dealers" were pushing Roosevelt's renomination. According to Secretary Hull, "The third term was an immediate consequence of Hitler's conquest of France and the specter of Britain alone standing between the conqueror and ourselves. Our dangerous position induced President Roosevelt to run for a third time." [3]

It was the testimony of Judge Rosenman, as well, that "By the beginning of the summer, 1940, I took it for granted that the President had decided it was his duty to accept the nomination." [4]

Prior to the certainty of the renomination of the President, Republican organization leaders professed to see in the dilemma of the Democrats an excellent opportunity for the opposition to win in a straight two-party contest. The possibility of the renomination of former President Hoover was little discussed. There were sporadic outbursts of "draft Hoover" sentiment, but this had no appreciable effect upon party managers or upon Republicans in office.

This in itself was indicative of the division of Republican conviction on foreign relations. Moreover, the Republicans were still victims of the chaos attributed to them in 1932. No critic of the administration had delivered such devastating blows at the policies of the President as had Mr. Hoover. Yet his utterances often fell on deaf ears of Americans who held no such convictions as to the results of socialism and communism as had become part and parcel of Mr. Hoover's thinking over many years during his residence and public service abroad.

In his address to the Republican Convention on June 25, 1940, Mr. Hoover undertook to bring the foreign background he had experienced into the thinking of his listeners. Before turning to the pressing questions of the war itself, he said:

Two years ago I was the invited guest of some twelve European countries. That gave me an unique opportunity to inquire into some things that might help the American people.

I wanted to know more of what ideas and pressures had plunged these nations into dictatorships.

---

[3] Hull, *op. cit.*, I, 855.
[4] Samuel I. Rosenman, *op. cit.*, p. 200.

There will flash into your minds that it was Communism, Fascism, or Nazi-ism. That is not what I refer to. They were the effect. I was seeking the cause. Liberty had been weakened long before the dictators rose under those banners. There was a long poignant drama before the last act in this gigantic tragedy of civilization.

There were many disintegrating forces. But also in every single case before the rise of dictatorships there had been a period dominated by economic planners. Each of these nations had an era under starry-eyed men who believed that they could plan and force the economic life of the people. They believed that was the way to correct abuse or to meet emergencies in systems of free enterprise. They exalted the state as the solvent of all economic problems.

These men thought they were liberals. But they also thought they could have economic dictatorship by bureaucracy and at the same time preserve free speech, orderly justice and free government. They can be called the totalitarian "liberals." They were the spiritual fathers of the New Deal.[5]

As for the situation in the United States, Mr. Hoover said:

This crisis in America is not to be obscured by any events abroad. We have witnessed a steady sapping of our system of liberty and the mismanagement of government for the last seven years. During all this time we have had 10 million chronically unemployed, 18 million of our fellow Americans have been continuously on relief. Agriculture has been held afloat by government subsidies. Unending deficits and huge increases in debt threaten the financial stability of the government. Our industry and business are hesitant and are afraid. In this decade, we have actually decreased in national income and national wealth for the first time in 150 years. America has gone backward. The human consequence is that one-third of our people are frozen to poverty.[6]

Yet even in the Republican Convention it was apparent that recent events in Europe overshadowed all discussions of national political issues. It was true that public opinion showed majority sentiment against entering the war. The people were nevertheless overwhelmingly for aid to the Allies.

---

[5] *Addresses Upon the American Road, 1940-1941*, p. 208.
[6] *Ibid.*, p. 206.

The abandonment of the two-term tradition in the renomination of President Roosevelt in 1940 re-emphasized the fact of his personal ascendancy. Protests against a third nomination, both in his party and by commentators outside, were mild indeed compared with what might have been said about the significance of such action. The most critical problem might prove to be—not the effect upon Mr. Roosevelt but the effect upon the electorate.

His nomination emphasized, of course, the disappearance of rival leadership on a national scale in the Democratic party. But primarily it made clear that a revolution had been accomplished in the nature of the appeal that the traditional Democratic party could make to the electorate. It was a Roosevelt party. And it had been abundantly clear since 1937 that the program was Roosevelt's as well. The national Democratic party, as such, had disappeared, although the forms and names remained.

Yet the inquiring student of American self-government will do well not to accept easy explanations of the renomination of President Roosevelt in 1940. It is oftenest said that developments in Europe made the renomination inevitable. This is a superficial observation, born of the conviction that the American people had lost their sense of national independence. Thousands, of course, felt that way, and they dominated the immediate explanations of the event.

Fear did grip the delegates at Chicago, but it was a fear born of confusion, uncertainty, and despair as to party success without Franklin Roosevelt. Yet this fear was not unmixed with doubt as to the best means of conquering despair. Party workers knew in their hearts that a tradition in politics was an awesome antagonist, and tradition said "no third term."

The Democrats knew, too, that long years in office had produced a tremendous opposition, not so much to the party or to its candidate as to the array of personal adherents of the President. He was a symbol of great personal success in the Presidency, but his party had not always derived benefit therefrom.

Yet it is never to be forgotten that throughout his career, Mr. Roosevelt was a Democrat in the party sense known to all. Without his identification with the historic party, his career cannot be understood. His success lay in complete recognition of the influence of party control in American life. Outside of the party, there would have been no career for such a leader as Franklin Roosevelt—in New York, in the nation, or in the world.

But to be a Democrat—in this sense—was worlds away from being a Socialist or a Communist. It was not a matter of doctrine, nor even of close party membership. It was the constant use of "party" in a sense understood only by Americans so immersed in party tradition as to give it no qualifying thought, that brought success to President Roosevelt.

The proceedings of the Democratic Convention at Chicago present a vivid picture of the sway of self-interest in the work of traditional party adherents. Repeatedly the convention was "out of hand" because the party organization leaders were so completely overshadowed by the power of the President's personal advisers, particularly Harry Hopkins and Frank Walker.

The part played by Hopkins in this convention revealed to thousands who had no real idea of the importance of the President's personal advisers, the inadequacy of the party organization to meet the needs of a powerful President already in office. Judge Rosenman later wrote: "In the last five years of the President's life—the most important years—Hopkins was unquestionably the most influential of those who worked with him." [7]

Party leaders like Farley, Garner, and Glass were pushed aside. Not by argument, nor by the conviction of convention delegates, but by the realization that the President's word was final, was this done. And his word proved to be final on the Vice-Presidency as well.

Eloquent was the testimony yielded by the grouping of interests that had been brought to the support of the ticket. Had the President's party become—as some said it was—a labor party, Roosevelt need not have been the only candidate to be considered. Had it been a party pledged to increased international co-operation, Roosevelt might have had rivals—at least at the outset. Had it been—as indeed it was in the Congress—a party of the South, a Southerner of conservative views, such as Rayburn or Byrnes, would have been a strong opponent. Had it been primarily a Democratic organization ticket, Farley

---

[7] Rosenman, *op. cit.*, p. 229.

would have been a natural nominee. But Roosevelt's party it was.

Most significantly, the President as candidate insisted that the convention choose for his running mate not a Southerner, not an organization man, not a labor leader, but Henry Wallace. Here was a representative not only of the progressives and of the farmers, but a Cabinet officer. It is true that Wallace was deeply distrusted by party leaders. He was, nevertheless, a Roosevelt idealist in both domestic and foreign affairs. Wallace's vision of the downfall of imperialism everywhere and the increase of well-being everywhere made him a natural choice of Roosevelt for the Vice-Presidency in 1940. In a word, Henry Wallace as a personal choice emphasized the personal nature of the President's appeal to the nation.

The nomination of Franklin Roosevelt for a third term was accompanied by drama that emphasized the appeal of the President to the elements that had made and were still to make for electoral success. He was called the one man to meet the crisis. And in accepting the call, he had emphasized his independence by insisting upon the nomination of Henry Wallace as well, in opposition to powerful elements in the Democratic party. By this act, more than by any alliance, the President emphasized his own embodiment of liberalism. He lost few internationalists by so doing.

The record of the administration, appealing though it might be to those who through organizations or otherwise would "aid the Allies," was adversely regarded by certain German and Italian groups and by the anti-British—including the Irish. Nor was there support of the President as candidate by those who frowned upon exchanging destroyers for bases and those who were to be shocked by conscription in time of peace.

Among the Democrats who did not support the President now were James A. Farley, who declined to continue either as Chairman of the Democratic National Committee or as Postmaster General. His place as chairman was taken by Ed Flynn, New York City political leader.

At the opening of the year, experienced Republican party leaders had recognized that only by a division of the Democratic vote could they win. Aiming at such division, they felt they could afford to organize their campaign upon a conservative basis and nominate a candidate satisfactory to the majority of normal Republican voters. This candidate, it was believed, with the assistance of dissenters from the Democratic party, could win.

Governor John W. Bricker of Ohio was thought to be such a candidate. The followers of Governor Thomas E. Dewey and Senator Arthur Vandenberg among the convention delegates were also within this pattern of conservative appeal. Yet a conservative candidate appeared less promising when it became certain that the President would be nominated in the Democratic Convention.

Thus, realization by the Republicans of the need to provide an alternative candidate with a definite program—and also a new outlook—gave decided impetus to the pre-convention campaign of Wendell Willkie. In the eyes of his supporters, he fitted this picture of party need. He represented, in his record as public utility executive and public speaker, the trenchant critics of the New Deal. Yet he was not associated with the Republican record in Congress on foreign relations. Willkie fired the imagination of those business men who somehow had developed a yearning for both liberalism and internationalism which they could not find in the Roosevelt candidacy, lamed as it was by a record of radicalism in domestic affairs.

Willkie was nominated through the work of "amateurs" and was grimly accepted by the regulars. For in fact the Republican party was a Peace Party. Its representation in Congress had been almost unanimous in opposing conscription and repeal of the arms embargo. And, despite Mr. Hoover's plea to the Republican Convention that war be avoided, Mr. Willkie was himself supporting the President on the means for national defense. Willkie would abstain from war, yet would recognize that the United States was part of a world in which alliances had best be made.

In the earlier phases of the campaign there appeared to be logic, that is, logic in politics, in the choice of Willkie as the President's opponent. Of course Willkie's nomination by the Republican Convention was made with one overwhelming purpose—to defeat Roosevelt. From Roosevelt what electoral support could be taken? Not the South; not the West; nor the East if labor could be held and youth could be attracted. Perhaps Willkie could outmaneuver Roosevelt in his appeal to labor and his appeal to youth.

For the first time on a national scale, Roosevelt was seriously challenged in terms of his own making. Willkie had been a Progressive and a one-time supporter of Roosevelt. Willkie called attention to the fact that a better job of co-ordination of government could be done than had been done. In accepting the changes in government—if not in detail, certainly in principle—that had followed the election of 1932, the Republican candidate said that he could carry on this new type of government better than could Mr. Roosevelt and his followers. Apparently the drive back of Willkie's candidacy combined the support of successful men who knew the modern world of government and of business.

The coalition government provided in the Roosevelt revolution had been accompanied by increasing uncertainty as to the relationships between business and government. This was in part due to unwieldiness inherent in the methods of the President. But also it was due to the fact that Mr. Roosevelt relied for political success upon three elements that were antagonistic and distrustful of one another—the political machines of the cities and of the South, the rival labor organizations, and the rival farm organizations. In this situation, Wendell Willkie asserted that he could do more than restore efficient government. He would relieve the government of political strain.

The central issue of the campaign—notwithstanding this absorbing domestic aspect—was the strength and purpose of the administration in foreign relations. Yet the Democratic party declaration made strange reading for those who were fully aware of the development of Mr. Roosevelt's foreign policy.

. . . . The American people are determined that war, raging in Europe, Asia and Africa, shall not come to America. We will not participate in foreign wars, and we will not send our army, naval or air forces to fight in foreign lands outside of the Americas, except in case of attack.[8]

---

[8] Democratic Party Platform, 1940.

When, on September 3, the President informed the Congress
of the negotiations with Great Britain whereby "this Government has acquired the right to lease naval and air bases in Newfoundland, and in the islands of Bermuda, the Bahamas,
Jamaica, St. Lucia, Trinidad, and Antigua, and in British
Guiana," he said:

> This is not inconsistent in any sense with our status of peace.
> Still less is it a threat against any nation. It is an epochal and
> far-reaching act of preparation for continental defense in the
> face of grave danger.[9]

Yet, as will be recalled, the President had deemed this the
most important action in national defense taken since the Louisiana Purchase. Clearly, the intent of the Democratic party
platform did not coincide with the intent of the President, who
saw the danger and had already repeatedly brought the re-
quirements of defense to the attention of the Congress.

The Democrats, in the eyes of the majority of the American
people, became a War Party for the period of this campaign.
The record of Franklin Roosevelt was such that in no campaign
for election could a candidate take from him the support of the
majority of the internationalists and of the liberals. He was
their kind of man. The memory of his "nationalism" in 1933,
and his hesitation in the period 1934 to 1937, could be easily
forgotten in contemplation of his challenging assertions and his
action in foreign affairs during the years 1937 to 1940.

The President placed national interest above campaign politics in his statement that he would keep at his task and would
not campaign. For the nation, under the President's leadership,
despite the peaceful declarations of the Democrats, was mobilizing for possible war. This situation fitted the President's
temper of mind. He was appealing to the people in a national
cause. Previous alignments upon domestic issues seemed of less
and less significance. It was now all-important to go forward
in efforts to preserve the nation—in the world of nations; to do
so by preparing for defense while avoiding war. But at all costs,
the nation was to be strong in face of possible enemies abroad.

Just before the meeting of the Republican National Convention, the President had called into his Cabinet two out-

---

[9] *Public Papers, 1940*, p. 391.

standing Republicans, Henry L. Stimson and Frank Knox. Stimson had been Secretary of State in the Cabinet of Herbert Hoover. Knox had been Vice-Presidential candidate of the Republicans in 1936.

The President toured the industrial plants engaged in production of war materials, and he spoke to audiences of the national needs in face of danger.

The President was pleading for peace and freedom through national unity. His aides in planning and writing his speeches —Sherwood, Hopkins, Rosenman and others—presented the central theme effectively. The President's speeches were masterpieces for a public man playing—as none before so daringly—a leading role on the world stage. At Boston on October 30, he said:

> I have said this before, but I shall say it again and again and again.
>
> Your boys are not going to be sent into any foreign wars.
>
> They are going into training to form a force so strong that, by its very existence, it will keep the threat of war far away from our shores.
>
> The purpose of our defense is defense.[10]

Yet three matters continued to seem of transcendent importance to routine partisans: the President's candidacy violated the "no-third-term" tradition; experienced leaders within his own party still opposed his candidacy; continued violent disagreement and uncertainty within the administration lamed efficient American government action in a world at war.

According to a number of the most experienced commentators, the election of 1940 was the bitterest in half a century. This was not surprising. Three objectives were stated and restated by the Democrats: defensive measures against aggression; measures to insure greater economic well-being; and measures for the social welfare of the people.

The Republican candidate, Wendell Willkie, presented a program different in detail rather than in principle. This was historically sound, for the Republican party, notwithstanding its recent record in the Congress and the pronouncements of

---

[10] *Ibid.,* p. 517.

many of its leaders, could rightly claim all three of the Democratic objectives in its own past history.

Too little attention has been given the changing moods of thousands of private citizens as the war engulfed one after the other of the countries of western Europe. A commentator said of June 21, 1940, "This is the longest day and darkest day" in the history of our own people. Why could this be said? The aggressive advance of Hitler, the catastrophic fall of France, the mounting siege of Britain—brought many in America to fear that the United States was now in grave danger. An important change in the attitude of business men was noted after May of 1940. Hating war and loath to be dragged into it, nevertheless many of them chose to support the President in the election of 1940.[11]

General use of the radio by 1940 was thought to change the entire problem of campaigning. A huge electorate spread over a continental area could be reached as never before. By voice on the air, Presidential candidates of the major parties could reach millions who might never see them. Yet it was obvious that personal presence was still important, particularly in the case of an individual appearing for the first time as a candidate for the Presidency. Wendell Willkie and his managers took this view.

After his nomination and prior to the formal opening of his campaign in mid-August, Willkie made numerous appearances in the Mountain West and Middle West. In September he began a tour that continued until the eve of the election, including 18,500 miles by train, 8,800 by plane, and 2,000 by automobile. With the exception of northern New England and the South, he appeared in every section of the country, speaking in thirty-two states. In New York, California, Wisconsin, Indiana, and Illinois, he appeared many times. He made more than five hundred addresses.

Much of the time Willkie seemed to stand by himself, except for self-appointed aides. His was therefore a weak position. Facing the test of meeting innumerable audiences, he needed the support of organization that dealt in masses, that is, experi-

---

[11] Roland N. Stromberg, "American Business and the Approach of War, 1935-1941," in *Journal of Economic History*, XIII (Winter, 1953), 58-78.

enced party workers who knew how to reach the voters. He impressed all by his frankness, but the audience was too vast to be won by personal approach.

Although, as has been said, in September and the first half of October the President's addresses were incidental to trips of official character, he nevertheless appeared to the crowds who heard him as the candidate of the Democratic party.

On October 23 Mr. Roosevelt began an intensive campaign confined to near-by points in Massachusetts, Connecticut, New York, New Jersey, Pennsylvania, and Ohio—all states with heavy industrial population. He made nine major addresses. His voice was harsh and strident in his fighting mood on foreign policy. He said he was placing the truthful record before the people. No one but the President could do this. *He* was the record!

Hard hitting and defiant, his appeals, composed by a battery of experts in public relations, were addressed by a master political salesman to small business men, to small investors, to farmers and laboring men, and to racial and religious minorities. Always the consummate actor in a great drama—and none was so packed with unbearable emotion as this one in 1940—Franklin Roosevelt was superbly successful in reaching those members of his huge audience who felt that here indeed was the most moving performance of all time.

Yet Sherwood wrote of this: "Of all the political battles in which he had been involved, this campaign of 1940 is, I believe, the one that Roosevelt liked least to remember."

Traditionalists, with a small sense of the world that had developed so rapidly since 1937, quite honestly continued to say that the election of Roosevelt was improbable because the sober sense of the American people would lead them to reject the third term. They would vote to "clean up the mess in Washington," and, most of all, they would defend America— but without war.

The decision of the voters in November returned Mr. Roosevelt to office. The outcome as recorded in the county vote in states where he had campaigned intensively, particularly in the city areas, revealed the probable effect of the two campaigns as planned by the contestants. The sharpness of the issue was re-flected in the small vote for minor party candidates, which reached the lowest point—except for 1928—since the opening of the century.

Yet to what extent the outcome of the election was a judg-ment upon the President's policies, it is impossible to say. His program of accomplishment had been challenged in detail, in method, and in cost; yet not—as Mr. Willkie saw it—in basic objective either in domestic policy or in foreign relations. To the majority of traditional Republicans, it seemed that Willkie lost because he did not appear to differ sufficiently from the President.

It may be said with considerable truth that as the "conserva-tives" had no candidate in this election, so too, the "radicals" had no candidate. On the whole, both candidates were near the middle-of-the-road on domestic matters: Roosevelt left of cen-ter and Willkie right of center. On foreign policy, as has been seen, there was by late autumn no clash between them.

In the election, Mr. Roosevelt polled more votes than in 1932 (even with the American Labor vote in New York, he had fewer than in 1936). He had 53.9 percent of the votes cast, by comparison with percentages of 60.2 in 1936 and 57.4 in 1932. It was, however, a national endorsement, for the President car-ried every section of the nation except one, and captured the electoral votes of thirty-eight states. He won heavy supporting majorities in both Houses of Congress.

A close student of his campaigns concluded: "The setbacks of his second Administration, the third-term issue, and the war scare had reduced his vote, but he kept together most of the divergent elements that had supported him in previous cam-paigns." [12]

Another commentator observed: "Emergencies by their very nature present abnormal political conditions. By way of illustra-tion, most observers believe that the emergency of 1940 was a more deciding factor in the re-election of Franklin D. Roose-velt for a third term than was any popular departure from the anti-third-term conviction." [13]

---

[12] Gosnell, *op. cit.*, p. 188.
[13] Ewing, *op. cit.*, p. 24.

History records the fact that 44.7 percent of the voters supported the Republican nominee. They comprised a motley array of interests, but their opposition to Franklin Roosevelt was the principal bond of union. They included pacifists and isolationists.

As in the two previous campaigns, a majority of the newspapers of large circulation were opposed to Mr. Roosevelt's candidacy. Unquestionably the largest proportion of the educated classes opposed his continuance in office. The upper-income groups were opposed. In the judgment of those opposing the President, his record in office was not such as to warrant their approval.

Many factors entered into this disapproval. Foremost among them were Mr. Roosevelt's Socialistic objectives, his slap-dash methods of administration, increasing manifestations of personal rule, and seeming disregard of the costs of government expansion. One judgment stands above all others. His opponents did not trust him.[14] But that the masses did trust him was overwhelmingly demonstrated.

Such a division of response requires more than passing mention. The arguments urged by responsible opponents of the President were based upon factual surveys of huge indebtedness, widespread unemployment, and appalling inefficiency in administration. However much these revelations aided in preparing a case, they were of little avail in reaching the majority of the electorate, who considered them of secondary importance.

Perhaps the outstanding result of Franklin Roosevelt's influence on American life had been in giving first place to what was termed the "human aspects" of politics. The President and his supporters had insisted that the call for American self-government simply meant "Let the people decide." This was accompanied by continuous attack upon those who would make

---

[14] Late in the campaign, Herbert Hoover, believing "that the whole future of the American people hangs upon the decision of this election," wrote Chief Justice Hughes, urging him to resign "with a declaration to the country of the complete necessity for a change in the Administration." (Pusey, *Hughes*, II, 785-786. Mr. Hughes made an oral reply—in the negative, according to a confidential source.)

government an efficient instrument in paying its way, in limiting its objectives, and in requiring definite results.

Commentators on the outcome of the election could not foretell the results of the people's decision, however much time and thought they gave to envisaging the future. Not only was the "atmosphere" of the campaign of 1940 unlike that of 1932 and of 1936, but the general attitude toward the President (both for and against) was of a different order. He had been President for eight years and most of the charges against him were so familiar as to have little influence except upon those who made them.

The new factor—not present in either previous campaign—was that created by the President's foreign policy. He was, most of all, the "representative" of the United States in the world. No one in reality could rival him in that capacity. His was a new role for an American President.

This much, however, was certain. Emphasis upon the New Deal was gone, despite the attempts of Mr. Roosevelt—at this time and later—to merge it in the larger issue at stake in the world. The leader chosen for the Presidential term 1941-1945 would be the leader in the role that the United States would play in the international affairs of that period. It was in his hands to determine the direction of events, insofar as they could be determined by action of the United States, because he had the endorsement of the American people and a *fixed term of office*. Mr. Roosevelt had already indicated that world affairs were America's business, and he intended to have a leading part in their settlement.

This conviction was expressed repeatedly in the weeks following the election. In his press conference of December 17, the President said:

. . . . In the present world situation of course there is absolutely no doubt in the mind of a very overwhelming number of Americans that the best immediate defense of the United States is the success of Great Britain in defending itself; and that, therefore, quite aside from our historic and current interest in the survival of democracy in the world as a whole, it is equally important from a selfish point of view of American defense,

that we should do everything to help the British Empire to defend itself.[15]

In the meantime, the peril to England was increasing. In his
Fireside Chat of December 29, 1940, the President said:

Never before since Jamestown and Plymouth Rock has our
American civilization been in such danger as now. . . .

I want to make it clear that it is the purpose of the nation to
build now with all possible speed every machine, every arsenal,
every factory that we need to manufacture our defense material. We have the men—the skill—the wealth—and above all,
the will. . . .

We must be the great arsenal of democracy. For us this is an
emergency as serious as war itself. We must apply ourselves to
our task with the same resolution, the same sense of urgency,
the same spirit of patriotism and sacrifice as we would show
were we at war.[16]

Securing nomination and election for a third term in 1940
was one of the most significant achievements of Franklin
Roosevelt's career. He was Commander-in-Chief of a nation
not yet in a war, but in fact at home and abroad using great
power to force its will upon the world in defeat of the dictators.
Thus the American people came to the end of the most fateful,
most tragic, and most terrible year thus far in the history of
modern man.

As the President said in his Christmas message, mature
people could not be merry. But millions did echo his thought
that they could be happy in that they were done with doubts;
they were now without fear. But to thoughtful men and women
who read of London in flames, the future seemed dark indeed.

---

[15] *Public Papers, 1940*, p. 604.
[16] *Ibid.*, pp. 634-643.

Chapter XIV

A NEW ALIGNMENT ABROAD

FOR THE PEOPLE of the United States, the final year of uneasy
peace opened with alignments abroad clearly marked. The
year would witness dramatic transformation of these alignments.
At the outset, nevertheless, Germany and her ally, Russia, were
threatening the existence of Britain, the last stronghold of
democracy on the European side of the Atlantic.

The answer to any public question that could be stated in
such a crisis for the West depended upon what the administration would be able to accomplish in the field of foreign relations. For diplomacy was still the only weapon in use by the
United States. The outcome of the election of 1940 had—in
truth—settled nothing except that the American people would
go on disagreeing as to their relationship to the world conflict
to such an extent and with such vigor as to forestall any conclusive united action.

Never was it so clearly apparent that the majority of the
American people hated the idea of engaging in war. Yet it was
also clear that they were deeply concerned emotionally as well
as economically in the fortunes of the war that was raging.
Americans knew they were in grave danger of attack. There
was, many thought, question only as to the time when the at-

tack would come. It was indeed the difference of opinion as to the time of an attack by a hostile nation—either Germany or Japan—that gave rise to disagreement as to the best means of defense.

In a world at war, the final determination of the place of the United States was the responsibility of one man, the American President. In the Constitution of the United States, the President is given great power in the conduct of foreign relations. Yet the framers were not providing an Executive who would participate in world politics, as President Roosevelt had been doing since the outbreak of war in Europe in 1939. Indeed, their primary intention had been a withdrawal from the "European system." The President was not free under the Constitution to proceed as a monarch with unlimited powers.

Yet the President must act and authorize or fail to authorize action by the diplomatic and military representatives of the United States. And however much the members of the Congress might temporize in response to the hesitation of their constituents, the President was responsible for the national security. That meant first of all national defense.

President Roosevelt in 1941 was far in advance of any such limited view. Pursuing a foreign policy that had made the United States a virtual participant in the war, he had severely condemned aggressive moves by the dictators. As has been seen, the President denounced Mussolini in unmeasured terms in June of 1940. Finally, the United States had indicated its basic lack of neutrality when the President announced the destroyers-for-bases agreement with Britain on September 3, 1940.

The President was prepared to pursue the same policy in his third administration. On January 6, 1941, in his annual message to the Congress, "at a moment unprecedented in the history of the Union," he said:

> . . . the United States as a nation has at all times maintained clear, definite opposition, to any attempt to lock us in behind an ancient Chinese wall while the procession of civilization went past. Today, thinking of our children and of their children, we oppose enforced isolation for ourselves or for any other part of the Americas. . . .

I find it, unhappily, necessary to report that the future and safety of our country and of our democracy are overwhelmingly involved in events far beyond our borders. . . .

I have recently pointed out how quickly the tempo of modern warfare could bring into our very midst the physical attack which we must eventually expect if the dictator nations win this war. . . .

As long as the aggressor nations maintain the offensive, they —not we—will choose the time and the place and the method of their attack. . . .

The need of the moment is that our actions and our policy should be devoted primarily—almost exclusively—to meeting this foreign peril. For all our domestic problems are now a part of the great emergency.[1]

The President termed this annual message "unique in our history," and called for a speeding-up of the process of changing "a whole nation from a basis of peacetime production of implements of peace to a basis of wartime production of implements of war." [2]

In this message came the clarion call for "four essential human freedoms." Following each declaration were the prophetic words "everywhere in the world." These four freedoms, according to Mr. Roosevelt, were "freedom of speech and expression . . . freedom of every person to worship God in his own way . . . freedom from want . . . freedom from fear." [3]

Few questioned the desirability of these freedoms, but many a realist saw at the time that the basic point at issue was raising a standard of living in order to give these freedoms to everybody—everywhere in the world.

The European belligerents and those in the Far East were well aware of the President's policy with reference to "wartime production of implements of war." So, too, were the opponents of the President in the United States. What Mr. Roosevelt would do or not do—or what he would say or not say—were of the utmost importance. He was prepared and eager to play

---

[1] *Public Papers, 1940,* pp. 663-666.
[2] *Ibid.,* pp. 666-668.
[3] *Ibid.,* p. 672.

the role for which he felt himself equipped by experience and conviction.[4]

The President, having long since taken the position that aid to the Allies was an important line of defense, suggested the arrangement that came to be known as Lend-Lease. By this arrangement, the President would be authorized "to sell, transfer title to, exchange, lease, lend or otherwise dispose of . . . any defense article to any nation whose defense he found vital to the security of the United States." This proposal of the President was passed by Congress with heavy majority backing, despite Republican opposition, and became law on March 11, 1941. Mr. Roosevelt had thought of it as lending arms as a neighbor would lend garden hose to put out a fire.[5] His apprehensions of the "fire" were that:

> If Great Britain goes down, the Axis powers will control the continents of Europe, Asia, Africa, Australasia, and the high seas—and they will be in a position to bring enormous military and naval resources against this hemisphere. It is no exaggeration to say that all of us, in all the Americas, would be living at the point of a gun—a gun loaded with explosive bullets, economic as well as military.[6]

This Lend-Lease arrangement was characterized by Prime Minister Churchill as the "third turning point in the war." [7] Admiral Leahy, who was United States Ambassador to Vichy France at the time, later wrote, "All my colleagues at Vichy felt that this action had virtually put our country into the war. It was a boost in morale for many of the sincerely pro-Allied officials in the various Vichy government departments." [8]

---

[4] In his third inaugural address on January 20, 1941, President Roosevelt spoke from the *seventh* draft of a proposed speech. Even so, in delivery he inserted the word "isolation" for his word "inaction" in a sentence that was to read, "If we do not, we risk the real peril of inaction." He wrote on the copy used "isolation and inaction. Signed Franklin D. Roosevelt." Copy examined in the Roosevelt Library. Rosenman in a note to this address (*Public Papers, 1941,* p. 7) writes, "After delivering the speech, the President underlined the word 'inaction' and wrote on his reading copy, 'I misread this word as "isolation," then added "and inaction." All of which improved it'!"

[5] *Public Papers, 1940,* p. 607.

[6] *Ibid.,* p. 635.

[7] Radio address from London, June 22, 1941, as reported in the *New York Times,* June 23. Mr. Hull described the Lend-Lease Act as "one of the most revolutionary legislative actions in American history." (*Op. cit.,* II, 925.)

[8] Leahy, *I Was There,* p. 22.

The United States, under the President's direction, had extended its patrol system for the safety of the Western Hemisphere and it was announced on April 10 that the United States would establish bases in Greenland.[9] In July, American troops were landed in Iceland to reinforce and relieve British troops guarding that republic, and American forces were likewise sent to Trinidad and British Guiana, where bases had been obtained from Britain in the destroyer-base agreement of the previous year. Ultimately, by arrangements with Queen Wilhelmina of the Netherlands, American forces were sent to Dutch Guiana to insure the continued availability of strategic bauxite used in the United States for the manufacture of aircraft aluminum.

The President on May 5 ordered the Secretary of War to arrange for the construction of "a fleet of heavy bombers to give the democracies command of the air."

All of this Mr. Roosevelt could do, as well as proclaim an unlimited national emergency on May 27, by virtue of the authority vested in him as President of the United States. In explaining the necessity of supplementing the action taken in September of 1939, following the outbreak of the European war, the President declared that "a succession of events makes plain that the objectives of the Axis belligerents in such war are not confined to those avowed at its commencement, but include overthrow throughout the world of existing democratic order, and a worldwide domination of peoples and economies through the destruction of all resistance on land and sea and in the air. . . ."[10]

On July 26, President Roosevelt, acting under authority vested in him by the Constitution of the Commonwealth of the Philippines as well as by that of the United States and "as Commander-in-Chief of the Army and Navy of the United States," ordered that the land and sea forces of the Philippines be placed under United States commands.

At the same time, Mr. Roosevelt appealed to the Congress to extend the one-year limit on service of men selected for the

---

[9] By agreement with the Danish Minister in Washington acting "on behalf of the King of Denmark, as Sovereign of Greenland. . . ." (*Public Papers, 1941*, pp. 96-98.)

[10] *Ibid.*, p. 194.

armed forces. The ensuing debate in the Congress was "sharp," and the Senate by a 45-30 vote and the House of Representatives by only one vote (203-202) authorized the President to extend to eighteen months the period of service under the Selective Training and Service Act of 1940.

On June 20, Mr. Roosevelt had said in a message to the Congress on the sinking of the *Robin Moor*, by a German submarine, "We are not yielding and we do not propose to yield." [11] On September 11 in a Fireside Chat to the nation, the President, reporting the sinking of the United States destroyer *Greer* by a German submarine, and referring to other German attacks on American ships, said:

> In the face of all this, we Americans are keeping our feet on the ground. Our type of democratic civilization has outgrown the thought of feeling compelled to fight some other Nation by reason of any single piratical attack on one of our ships. We are not becoming hysterical or losing our sense of proportion. . . .

> It would be unworthy of a great Nation to exaggerate an isolated incident . . . it would be inexcusable folly to minimize such incidents in the face of evidence which makes it clear that the incident is not isolated, but is part of a general plan. . . . It is the Nazi design to abolish the freedom of the seas, and to acquire absolute control and domination of these seas for themselves . . .

> . . . when you see a rattlesnake posed to strike, you do not wait until he has struck before you crush him.[12]

Yet it was not until October 9 that the President formally requested the Congress, by amending the Neutrality Act of 1939, to authorize the arming of merchant ships and the entry of American vessels and cargoes into the ports of "belligerents" in receipt of Lend-Lease from the United States. The legislation requested was finally passed by the House of Representatives in a vote of 212-194 and by the Senate, 50-37. Clearly the Congress was reluctant, as it had been in the matter of extending selective service, to meet the President's request. How

[11] *Ibid.*, p. 230.
[12] *Ibid.*, pp. 386-390.

could a powerful President be placed by the legislative branch of his government in such a paradoxical situation?

The actual situation in which Mr. Roosevelt found himself as he entered upon his third term may now be examined. Backed though he was by a popular endorsement in the election—and with a stated term of office of four more years—yet he was actually in a weakened position because of the enemies he had made. He could not win support for a program that was emphatically and solely his own. There were too many in his party, in the opposing party, in the ranks of the disillusioned —who would oppose the program and distrust the sponsor.

Yet with endorsement by the people and party support in the Congress, Franklin Roosevelt was bound to push his own purpose. Aid to the Allies came first. Then followed the struggle over preparations for defense. Both of these programs were contingent upon the success of the President's effort to defeat the isolationists in the Congress and in the nation. Domestic programs must wait upon the outcome of these struggles. The President said so. Postponement of the advance of domestic reforms was less dangerous than before the attention of the nation came to be concentrated upon foreign affairs, since the notable increase in war industries did much to alleviate the problem of unemployment that always led to restlessness.

Until December 7, a contest raged in the United States over the policy to be pursued by this nation at peace in a world at war. The antecedents of this major debate lay deep in the continuous discussion of American foreign policies since the end of World War I. All the idiocies, dishonesties, and futilities of armed conflict on a global scale had left the majority of the American people openly distrustful of European peoples and their governments.

In the period 1933-1937, Mr. Roosevelt had seemed to be moved by this feeling of the mass of Americans. From 1937 to 1940, however, his words, his acts, and his recommendations had given rise to uncertainty as to his real convictions. Many questioned the wisdom of his way of avoiding American participation in the war raging since September of 1939. There were more of such questioners than those the President referred to as "that small group of selfish men who would clip the wings of the American eagle in order to feather their own nests."[13] Millions of Americans did not see what the President saw in the threat of aggression running amuck in the world.

Mr. Roosevelt, as candidate in 1940, had insistently declared that Americans would not wage "foreign wars." This was not contrary to his position as President from 1933 to 1940. Yet now he felt it necessary to repeat this. He meant that the United States would not attack; it would not take an aggressive role in the field of battle. This was definitely the interest of the masses of American people. But the President knew—and his advisers knew—that every action of this government in any way affecting the nations locked in a global struggle was in fact a participation in that war. It could not be otherwise.

The American people—as a whole—were sympathetic to the movement to aid others fighting for what in general were their own objectives, without themselves participating in the war. It was not only that they wished to remain at home to pursue the familiar path of peaceful isolation. Deep in the national consciousness, as well, was profound disbelief in war as an instrument of sound national policy. Americans were interested, therefore, in other means—any means—of resolving the desperate situation in which the government of this nation was confronted by forces beyond its control.

Consequently, careful attention was given those who argued that avoidance of the conflict was possible. It is foolish to denounce the great movement for isolation at this time as the work of conspirators, pacifists, and traitors. Wrong the isolationists might be—and subsequent events seem to prove they were mistaken—but until the dictators actually attacked there was an American case for remaining aloof from the struggle. This case appealed to millions of the fellow citizens of the isolationists.

The basic reason for this lies in the conception of American history held by the majority of Americans. That history—as they have seen it—arose out of the initial struggle of Americans of the eighteenth century to free themselves from the European system, and continued in the struggle of nineteenth century

[13] *Public Papers, 1940*, p. 665.

Americans, usually successful, to stay clear of it. That the American people had been less successful in keeping to themselves in the twentieth century was a basic cause of grievance for many who thought only in terms of the American continent or of the Western Hemisphere at most.

The crux of their argument was this. Let peoples outside of the United States fight a war of extinction. When peace came, the United States would be in a position to deal with the victor advantageously without war. Or, if the victor were to insist upon war, the struggle would then be in defense of the homeland.

Those who were persuaded of this view found encouragement in Hitler's march against Soviet Russia on June 22, 1941. It might now be possible to withdraw from the world outside the Western Hemisphere. The cause of freedom might be served best if one great nation—the United States—preserved freedom for itself.

This was a defensible position if one accepted all its demands, and if there could be possibility that the United States might not be attacked. It was this approach to the American problem in a world at war that accounts for the deep-seated opposition to any warlike moves and the passage, by only a single vote, of the bill to extend the period of selective service training beyond the limits of a year. This outlook was reflected as well in the slight margin by which the Neutrality Act was amended to permit the arming of merchant ships.

On the details of their own foreign affairs, the American people as a whole were uninformed. This was true despite the attention given the subject by the press, by writers, and by public forums of all kinds. Of course segments of the population were designedly misinformed by the agents and advocates of particular nations or causes. This misinformation was in continuous need of refutation by the President.

It was necessary for the administration, as well as for its critics, to state the case in a fashion to arouse the electorate. Organizations that abounded to take care of the people in their thinking and to direct the course of events by the application of political pressures, operated in such a field of opportunity.

The immediate objectives of the leading pressure groups were clearly seen. To help the Allies win, to keep America out of war—were objectives urged by authoritative voices saying both could be achieved. The immediate objective of the President was to prepare the United States for war. It might be said —and was said—that this was the best way to avoid war. In any case, it was the best way to make sure the Allies would win.

Franklin Roosevelt's own actions and words were influenced to a considerable extent by the effect of the work of the America First Committee upon American public opinion. This organization, from its inception in September, 1940, in the midst of the President's campaign, until its disbanding following the attack on Pearl Harbor, expressed the view of a powerful and influential group of citizens. It aroused strong sentiment in opposition to participation in the European war. There were 450 chapters and a claim of 800,000 supporters in every section of the country.

No other group of opponents exercised such influence on a national scale, and none achieved such recognition by the administration. Those close to the President felt that this influence upon him was a very real deterrent, mobilizing sufficient public backing at times to check his policies.[14]

But with the realization of Hitler's perfidy toward his declared ally, Soviet Russia, all far-sighted Americans were driven to unite on one objective—to protect the United States in the deepening crisis. The desirability of defense measures was generally admitted.

The people nevertheless were still divided—as they had been in the campaign of 1940—on every issue that Franklin Roosevelt had presented to them in eight years of office. They were also divided on the *extent* of American participation in the war that had now engulfed the entire world outside the Western Hemisphere.

It became clearly evident that the United States was participating in the war—though still on its own terms. One ques-

---

[14] Wayne S. Cole, *America First: The Battle Against Intervention 1940-1941*, p. 198. See also, Walter Johnson, *The Battle Against Isolation*, on the Committee to Defend America by Aiding the Allies.

tion remained to be answered. When would Americans move to active participation with men as well as arms? Would it be in the Western Hemisphere, in the Pacific, or in Europe?

The task of the President continued to be threefold: he must deal through diplomatic channels with foreign powers and combinations of powers; he must hold his leadership of the political combination of divergent groups that supported his policies in the Congress; and he must continuously inform the electorate of what he was doing in such a way as to hold their support.

Yet the President must not reveal his purposes too completely to foreign nations or their sympathizers. Finally, he must at a time of admittedly great national danger maintain not only a prosperous economic structure, but also a military and naval strength that would make the nation truly invincible.

The President's political problems at home were closely related to his actions in the international sphere. To maintain the New Deal he must recognize the necessity of increasing his support by labor, for he was weakened by loss of the backing of a considerable number of progressives who as isolationists would no longer follow him.

Isolationists and reactionaries, aided by pacifists and incipient pacifists, were in agreement in checking the President. But, in addition to the support of convinced internationalists, he now held the support of those sympathetic with communism who had not always been identified with the extreme New Deal contingent.

Thus the conflict at home was widened as the natural alliance of reactionaries as opposed by liberals was seen to be world wide. This had long been the President's essential explanation of the alignment he was seeking to strengthen—the democracies against the dictatorships.

Portents of the future appeared with the German advance on Russia. At this time the President said that he did not know the answer to the question whether Lend-Lease would be available to the Russians. In realistic terms this meant that, if the United States government sent aid under Lend-Lease to Soviet Russia, it would be under the assumption that Russia's defense was necessary to the security of the United States! [15]

The President, despite his misgivings about the denial in particular of freedom of religious worship by the Soviet government, "foreseeing the great role which Russia was ultimately to play in the winning of the war, was anxious to expedite aid to Russia." [16] He was to find Prime Minister Churchill of like mind in their August meeting.

By those of critical view, the President was not seen as arousing the United States to aid the Allies in order to defend America, but as the leader of a movement fighting "imperialism" and "dictators" on behalf of communism abroad and on behalf of the New Deal at home.

The people as a whole, believing that the United States was supporting Britain, did not see that the new alignment with Soviet Russia abroad, and incidentally with the Communists at home, would eventually turn into an alignment *against* Britain, whose *empire* Prime Minister Churchill would refuse to liquidate.

However, for the time being the organization of the President's effort to defeat the isolationists brought to his support many persons who in their eagerness to aid the Allies—as the first defense of America—were quite willing to follow the President in his aggressive foreign policy. This was certain to lead to war unless the Axis powers should collapse.

It was former President Hoover who, looking into the past and evaluating the familiar assertion of the day that "Hitler was out to conquer the world," warned the American people of the future that was in store for them if they should ally themselves with communism. On June 29, 1941, in a radio broadcast from Chicago, reminding Americans of the recent fate at the hands of Russia of Finland, Poland, and of Estonia, Latvia and Lithuania, democracies whom we "nursed in their infancy" with hundreds of millions of dollars, Mr. Hoover said:

No doubt we will promise to aid Russia. But the war to bring the four freedoms in the world will die spiritually when we make that promise. . . .

[15] *Bulletin of the America First Committee* for July 7 and July 16, 1941, opposed extending Lend-Lease to Russia, pointing out that this would be aid to enemies of the "American way of life."

[16] *Public Papers, 1941*, p. 419.

Practical statesmanship leads in the same path as moral statesmanship. These two dictators—Stalin and Hitler—are in deadly
combat. One of these two hideous ideologists will disappear in
this fratricidal war. In any event both will be weakened. . . .

To align American ideals alongside Stalin will be as great a
violation of everything American as to align ourselves with
Hitler.

Can the American people debauch their sense of moral values
and the very essence of their freedom by even a tacit alliance
with Soviet Russia? Such an alliance will bring sad retributions
to our people. . . .

Again I say, if we join war and Stalin wins, we have aided him
to impose more communism on Europe and the world. . . .[17]

The interest of the people as a whole in the turn of events
abroad was momentary and subsided quickly. Never had it
been so clear that in affairs at a distance—in space as in time—
the majority of the people, adolescent and inclined to see persons and acts in elementary terms, regarded symbols and myths
as somehow endowed with reality.

The strident call of the day for all help to crush Hitler had
more meaning for the American people of 1941 than any logical
analysis of the inevitable character of Soviet communism.
Prophets who said that a victory for communism was as much
to be feared as a victory for fascism were indeed without honor
in their own country.

Nevertheless profound changes in American outlook upon
the world came to be realized in the late summer of 1941.
There was at this time a growing conviction that despite the
military might of the dictators, the forces of liberalism were
strong in all nations.

The inconclusiveness of dictatorship in meeting the basic
problems of subsistence in peace or war gave the United States
once more an opportunity to prove that it had a democratic
answer for world problems as well as for those of the American
people.

---

[17] As quoted from "A Cause to Win," *Five Speeches by Herbert Hoover on
American Foreign Policy in Relation to Soviet Russia*, pp. 9-10. This address
was first printed as a separate pamphlet entitled "A Call to American Reason."
Many letters of comment upon it favored the position of Hoover. (Hoover
Library files.)

Thus there appeared in the forum of public debate a broader issue. It is worthy of careful examination, even though the catastrophic changes that came at the end of the year made it seem impossible of clarification until after the winning of the war. The position might be stated as follows:

Isolationist and interventionist alike were living in an unreal world, reviving ghosts of days that were gone. Neither position had place in a world of war and revolution—and indeed of any peace that could be won and held in the world that came into being with the inventions of the twentieth century. Peace could be secured only by abandoning each position.

Only through the union of democratic peoples everywhere could there be conquest of the forces of revolution and reaction that existed in every land, including the United States.

It followed that while there was yet time, there must be a union of all those who believed in the basic soundness of democracy. Let them look beyond flags, and beyond constitutions and officials. Let there be a union of democratic peoples, and a federation of associated powers.

From this point of view, the cause of the British was the cause of all Americans who wished for an alliance of freedom-loving peoples. Since September, 1939, the President had carried on correspondence with the Prime Minister of Great Britain. It was apparent that in due time a meeting between the representatives of two great English-speaking peoples would result in an agreement as to the purpose of the war.

This meeting, which finally came in mid-August, 1941, was reported by the President to the Congress on August 21, and its results, in a joint declaration by him and Prime Minister Churchill termed the Atlantic Charter. This was described by the President as a "declaration of principles" which at this time "presents a goal which is worth while for our type of civilization to seek." [18] The eight "common principles" in the national policies of their respective countries on which he and Mr. Churchill based their hopes for a better future for the world were:

First, their countries seek no aggrandizement, territorial or other; Second, they desire to see no territorial changes that do

[18] *Public Papers, 1941*, p. 334.

not accord with the freely expressed wishes of the peoples concerned; Third, they respect the right of all peoples to choose the form of government under which they will live; and they wish to see sovereign rights and self-government restored to those who have been forcibly deprived of them; Fourth, they will endeavor . . . to further the enjoyment by all states . . . of access, on equal terms, to the trade and to the raw materials of the world . . . Fifth, they desire to bring about the fullest collaboration between all Nations in the economic field with the object of securing, for all, improved labor standards, economic advancement, and social security; Sixth, after the final destruction of the Nazi tyranny, they hope to see established a peace which will afford . . . safety . . . freedom from fear and want; Seventh, such a peace should enable all men to traverse the high seas and oceans without hindrance; Eighth, they believe that all of the nations of the world . . . must come to the abandonment of the use of force.[19]

This declaration of the joint aims of the English-speaking peoples was in no sense a treaty or even an agreement. However, when later twenty-six nations signed the United Nations Declaration on January 1, 1942, they pledged themselves to the "common program of purposes and principles" set forth in the Atlantic Charter. In the mind of the American President, the ideas symbolized by the Atlantic Charter were obviously related not only to the "four freedoms", which he had affirmed on behalf of all peoples, but also to the "Society of Nations" which he had had in mind for many years, and which later he espoused as the United Nations.[20]

As Prime Minister Churchill subsequently said, this "Charter" which was the product of a secret meeting of government and military leaders of the United States and Britain held off the shores of Newfoundland was a "star" of hope to the British. But, as was said later, "Churchill did not need the Charter to bolster war morale. Roosevelt needed it to create one." [21]

---

[19] *Ibid.*, pp. 314-315. There has always been a great deal of misunderstanding about the Atlantic Charter. The "original" of the Atlantic Charter is in the form of a draft of a press release. This press release draft was subscribed by Franklin D. Roosevelt for both himself and Winston Churchill. In other words, at the bottom of the document appear the names of Franklin D. Roosevelt and Winston Churchill, both written in Roosevelt's hand. (Director, Roosevelt Library.)

[20] *Ibid.*, pp. 316-317.

[21] Louis Fischer, *The Great Challenge*, p. 67.

This historic meeting, which was the first of a series of conferences between the President and the Prime Minister, also marked the climax of the union of interest with Britain which had prevailed in the United States since the outbreak of the European war in 1939.

British support of Russia might be a war measure. Mr. Churchill had said, "Any man or State who fights against nazism will have our aid." [22] The willingness of the American President to aid Russia might be a war measure. But in fact it introduced the alignment within the Big Three that was to spell disaster for the hopes of those who wished for a British-American alliance of the English-speaking peoples.

With the attack of Germany upon Russia on June 22, there had been a shift of interest in the United States. For here again, the President and his advisers could claim to see in the pretensions of Russian communism something more nearly akin to democracy than the colonial empire of Great Britain. Many American citizens saw more in the claims of communism than they did in the claims of the liberal British tradition. Even the isolationists could see that Russia was no longer allied with Germany and that such a foe as Hitler, who had turned against his ally, was formidable indeed.

It cannot be forgotten that President Roosevelt was responsible for the recognition of Soviet Russia in 1933. There was much in the conduct of the American administration from 1933 to 1941 that suggested radical advance along lines familiar in Communist propaganda. The atmosphere of the years of growing tension, 1937 to 1939, might seem to suggest American interest in Britain. This, however, was more anti-Fascist than pro-British in character. It was the period of the activity of the Popular Front that won many young Americans to what was represented to be the Soviet point of view.

President Roosevelt wrote to Ambassador Leahy in France on June 26, 1941: "Now comes this Russian diversion. If it is more than just that it will mean the liberation of Europe from Nazi domination—and at the same time I do not think we need worry about any possibility of Russian domination." [23]

---

[22] *New York Times*, June 23, 1941.
[23] Leahy, *op. cit.*, pp. 37-38.

At the same time that the President won liberal support for his policy of aid to Russia, it became evident that numbers of Americans were willing to underwrite British and French imperialism, but not Russian communism. However, in the autumn of 1941, the forces opposing fascism in general were suddenly united.

It was not, as some said, adroit politics on the part of the President that made American defense his first call. Any President would have stood first of all for American defense. All of the vitality of an aroused patriotism was available for defense of America. As the danger increased, nevertheless, it was the prestige of Presidential office that attracted supporters to the President's program, for it was an unaccustomed program for Americans.

So too, the arguments of the isolationists and of the America First group appealed less and less as the people saw that dictators lived in a world of continuous and spreading war. Abhorring war, fearing and detesting dictators, the majority of Americans wanted the free nations to win because they were —despite all that could be said of differences—going in the same direction.

But to some, known as isolationists and critics of the President, the realignment in Europe seemed to renew the opportunity of the United States to remain aloof from the war. Americans did not want to save communism, and then save Europe for communism—these persons asserted.

Yet, however much this point of view appealed to conservatives, it did not appeal to liberals who believed that out of this war might come the crushing not only of the Fascist dictators, but also that of imperialism. This would lead to the ultimate triumph of the two great "democracies," the U.S. and the U.S.S.R. On his trip to Russia in 1942, and after his talk with Stalin, Wendell Willkie was reported as saying that the future belonged to America and the Soviet Union. He outlined a plan for not "stirring up Russia" by opposing her.[24]

Of the President's Navy and "Total Defense" Day address on October 27, 1941, stating that "we Americans have cleared our decks and taken our battle stations," Admiral Leahy wrote

---

[24] *New York Times*, January 2, 1944.

later: "To me, this was as nearly an open declaration of 'undeclared' war as it would be possible to formulate. . . . The various legislative and executive actions that had followed in rapid
succession during the preceding six months caused me to wonder if the President really thought he was fooling anyone about
our not being at war." [25]

The President was eventually to win over his adversaries at
home because he was attacked by his adversaries abroad. But
American entrance into the war actively on the side of the
Allies—through attack by the Axis on the United States—had
not yet come about as the autumn of 1941 deepened.

Throughout the period just discussed, the eyes of the American people had been upon events in Europe. The signing by
Japan of a treaty of alliance with Germany and Italy on September 27, 1940, had, however, made them aware that it was
not only in Europe but in the Far East that American interests
were endangered.

It was recalled now that early in the second year of Mr.
Roosevelt's first term in office, the Japanese had warned that
American interest in the free development of China was unwel-
come. Three years later, when the conflict between Japan and
China burst forth in mid-summer of 1937, much evidence of
American public opinion in favor of China was revealed. The
administration had maintained a neutral position.

However, in December, 1937, had come an unprovoked attack by the Japanese upon Americans operating the gunboat
Panay on the Yangtze River. Although the American government had asked apology and received it with damages, there
remained a residue of deep suspicion of Japanese intentions.

This was justified, for in the next year other incidents occurred involving maltreatment, by the Japanese, of Americans
in China. The American government charged the Japanese
with violation of the "Open Door." The Japanese government
stated bluntly on November 3, 1938, that it was interested in
the development of reconstruction in East Asia along Japanese
lines. This "new order" for Asia, "linking China and Manchuria to the Japanese system," [26] was formally rejected by the

---

[25] Leahy, *op. cit.*, p. 52.
[26] Hull, *op. cit.*, I, 569.

American State Department. Japan now knew full well that the United States stood across its path in the Far East.

Had the American people known—as their leaders did—of the real character of the militaristic Japanese Cabinet that came to power in September of 1941, they would have realized that Japan was as actively their enemy in the Pacific as Germany with its striking submarines was in the Atlantic. The real conflict had now become global and the basic issue was the same everywhere.

For the time being, it was to the interest of the Axis to keep the United States out of active participation in the war. When either Germany or Japan felt that the interests of the United States should be challenged, Americans might well expect a direct attack.

Meanwhile, uncertainty prevailed as to the role of Russia in the Far East. It was well known that Russia feared Japan. President Roosevelt, in a message to Premier Konoye on July 6, attempted to induce Japan to refrain from attacking Russia from the east, now that Hitler had attacked from the west.[27]

Japan's opportunity in the Far East was not like that of Germany in Europe. Nor was it like that of Britain in the world. An American policy to save Russia could not be matched by one to save China. China's status as a world power was such as to make for an unusual partnership in diplomacy and in war as measured against partnerships with European powers. China was in this global war, but not of it.

Furthermore, the President discounted the Japanese fear of communism in China. He told Ambassador Nomura that "the people of China were constituted very differently from those of Russia and had a philosophy that stabilized and guided them along much broader lines. China," he said, "was not really communistic in the same sense as Russia, and Japan had an undue fear of Communism in China." [28]

Although the President referred to his "patience" in dealing with Japan, it would seem that by mid-summer of 1941 he had despaired of a peaceful settlement in the Pacific. He had, however, opposed a statement of British-American accord for the

---

[27] *Ibid.*, II, 977.
[28] *Ibid.*, II, 990.

Far East when it was proposed by the British at the Atlantic Conference in August. As the President related to the Congress on December 15, "In July of this year the Japanese Government connived with Hitler to force from the Vichy Government of France permission to place Japanese armed forces in southern Indo-China, and began sending her troops and equipment into that area." [29] The President had thought of this, which he said "caused us very great concern," as "parallel with the Hitler methods in Europe." [30]

Mr. Roosevelt on July 26 had frozen Japanese assets in the United States, at the same time placing an embargo on the shipment of aviation fuel, gasoline, and oil to Japan. Explaining to a press conference at the time that oil had gone hitherto to Japan "with the hope—and it has worked for two years—of keeping war out of the South Pacific," [31] the President made it clear that he was stiffening the position of the United States against Japan.

The rapid development of tension in relations with Japan during the autumn brought a virtual ultimatum on November 20, when the Japanese government "presented a new and narrow proposal, which called for supplying by the United States to Japan of as much oil as Japan might require; for suspension of 'freezing' measures; and for discontinuance by the United States of aid to China." [32] Thus, it was American support of China—based on a long tradition in American diplomacy—that finally forced a breakdown of negotiations with the Japanese.[33]

The administration favored increasing aid to the Allies. Yet there was certainty that the people of the United States would not voluntarily enter the war. The administration had adopted a policy in the Far East that stood across the path of Japanese advance. If the administration maintained that policy, Japan might choose to attack the United States. If the Japanese did

[29] *Public Papers, 1941*, p. 548.
[30] *Ibid.*, p. 501.
[31] *Ibid.*, p. 280.
[32] *Ibid.*, pp. 548-549. In a press conference on December 2, 1941 (Press Conferences, vol. 18, p. 336, Roosevelt Library), replying to a question as to negotiations with Japan, the President said: "We are at peace with Japan. We are asking a perfectly polite question." This followed the President's discussion of the Japanese advances in Indo-China.
[33] Current, *op. cit.*, p. 148, claims "The Stimson doctrine was at last in full effect."

so—in such a way as to arouse the American people—the purpose of the President would be served.

The question remains: Did President Roosevelt expect an attack on Pearl Harbor? Did Washington anticipate such an attack? The evidence now available suggests that, although both Washington and Hawaii should have anticipated the possibility of a surprise attack, there was no definite expectation of the precise attack that came suddenly on December 7, 1941.

The arguments of those who hold the President responsible for the "disaster" are that: The Administration did have evidence of the imminence of such an attack; they purposely refrained from transmitting this to the military and naval commanders on Hawaii in order to insure a Japanese attack; and that if Hawaii had been informed it is possible the Japanese would have refrained from attack there. The matter has had much discussion.[34]

"On the night before Pearl Harbor when Harry Hopkins suggested that the United States might strike first, Roosevelt . . . almost repeated Wilson's words when he said: 'No, we can't do that. We are a democracy of peaceful people. We have a good record. We must stand on it.' "[35]

The America First Committee on December 6 succinctly stated that "The Administration, and the Administration alone, will be completely responsible for any breakdown in relations with Japan. The Administration has taken it upon itself to demand actions from Japan that in no way concern the national interests of the United States. None of our territorial possessions are in any way involved."[36]

---

[34] See Admiral Robert A. Theobald, U.S.N. (retired), *The Final Secret of Pearl Harbor*, and Captain T. B. Kittredge, U.S.N.R. (retired), "The Muddle Before Pearl Harbor," in *U.S. News and World Report*, December 3, 1954.

[35] Jonathan Daniels in *The End of Innocence*, p. 209. Hanson W. Baldwin asked General Marshall and Admiral Stark two questions raised by Theobald's book on *The Final Secret of Pearl Harbor*: Did President Roosevelt use the fleet at Hawaii as a decoy to incite attack? Did the President ask you to withhold information from commanders in Hawaii? Both answered "No" to both questions. (*New York Times*, April 18, 1954.) Samuel Flagg Bemis, in reviewing Richard N. Current, *Secretary Stimson: A Study in Statecraft*, in the *New York Times Book Review*, April 18, 1954, answered the question: Did the Stimson doctrine cause the attack of Japan upon Pearl Harbor? "She went to war because, as captured Japanese archives show, the European conflict seemed to her warlords to present the opportunity of a nation's life-time to conquer an opulent empire in Greater Eastern Asia. . . ."

[36] *Bulletin of the America First Committee*, December 6, 1941, quoted by Wayne Cole, *op. cit.*, p. 193.

Nevertheless, it is clear that the President's policy by no means seemed to the American people to justify the attack on Pearl Harbor which came on December 7, less than twenty-four hours after Mr. Roosevelt had dispatched a personal appeal to Emperor Hirohito to avoid war in the Pacific. The United States Senate Committee investigating in 1945 the Pearl Harbor attack concluded that "The President, the Secretary of State, and high Government officials made every possible effort, without sacrificing our national honor and endangering our security, to avert war with Japan." [37]

At the same time that the nation as a whole rallied to defense, there continued under cover of this new apparent unanimity,[38] deep divisions on the war aims and the peace to follow.

Whereas the basic policies of Mr. Roosevelt had not *justified* the direct Japanese attack, the United States had stood across the path of Japan in the Far East, just as the United States had stood between the Axis and victory in Europe. Thus the President had led the nation into a position which would inevitably be challenged. The opponents of such action by the United States had at the center of their protest a simple program of non-participation in international affairs. They were logical in representing accurately a basic historic and enduring nationalism of deep influence upon the American people. It must be remembered that the President had not taken this position of opposition to the Japanese advance in the Pacific as rapidly and completely as many of his advisers, notably Secretary Stimson, would have done.

A profound and far-reaching result of American entrance into the war—however involuntary—was the alliance with the forces of communism. A war measure, in order to defeat the Axis, it was called in Britain and in America. A "win the war" atmosphere was conducive to startling results. It obliterated for the time being, for millions of people, their active antagonism to communism, as it strengthened the forces in the United

---

[37] *Report of the Joint Committee on the Investigation of the Pearl Harbor Attack, 79th Congress, 2d Session, Senate Document* No. 244, p. 251.

[38] William Allen White wrote, on the eve of Pearl Harbor, "I am one of those in the 75 per cent of Americans who, for a year, have been ringing up in the Gallup Poll as favoring the President's foreign policy. I am also of the 95 per cent who have been ringing up in the Gallup Poll for this same period as wishing to avoid war." *The Autobiography of William Allen White,* p. 642.

States favorable to communism. This seemed to prove to those who fought the President and all his policies that they had been right in distrusting him and his purposes. So even during the war, the basic struggle of opinion in the United States was deepened.

The President's foreign policy had carried the American people into a world from which they now could not retreat. Yet he looked upon the important decisions of the year, viewing them in perspective, as constituting a program for the defense of the United States. He said each move had been forced upon him by events outside the nation and beyond his control.

Now that he was directing a nation at war, he hoped the United States might give direction to a world willing ultimately to live at peace. So the stage was set in Washington for the drama that was to enter a new phase with the end of the year. The financial-industrial might of America would supply American armies and the people would supply the personnel of those armies. But the great instrument of the people's power in Washington—the administration—came to be manned by experts and advisers who were prepared, as they said many times, to build a new world. And for this they were to pay dearly.

Chapter XV

DESIGN FOR VICTORY

THE PRESIDENT was fully aware of the changed situation now that the United States was in the war of nations but not yet prepared for global war. "His terrible moral problem," as Frances Perkins said, "had been solved by the event" of Pearl Harbor.[1] Mr. Roosevelt laid the groundwork for every subsequent explanation of his conduct in his address to the American people, by radio, on December 9, 1941. "The sudden criminal attacks perpetrated by the Japanese in the Pacific provide the climax of a decade of international immorality," he said. "Powerful and resourceful gangsters have banded together to make war upon the whole human race. Their challenge has now been flung at the United States of America."[2]

By the Japanese attack upon its possessions in the Pacific and the declaration of hostilities by its enemies in western Europe, the United States was plunged into war. No longer was President Roosevelt preparing for defense, and giving aid to par-

---

[1] *The Roosevelt I Knew*, p. 380.
[2] *Public Papers, 1941*, p. 522. The President, in his address to the Congress "Asking That a State of War Be Declared Between the United States and Japan," had referred to Japanese attacks against Malaya, Hong Kong, Guam, Wake Island, and Midway Island, as well as the attacks on Hawaii and the Philippines. (*Ibid.*, pp. 514-515.)

ticipants in the war already raging. He was now in truth Commander-in-Chief of a nation at war.

Throughout the foregoing discussion of Mr. Roosevelt's foreign policy from 1937 to 1941, emphasis has been placed upon his public utterances. When it has been possible to discover exactly what he said in private conversation, this has been included. But on the whole, there is doubt—and presumably always will be—as to the President's innermost thoughts. Thus one may only surmise what must have taken place in many a conversation of which there is no record. The President, with all his interest in history, did not keep such records and at times advised others against so doing. The policy was intensified as the nation engaged in war.

American participation in World War II imposed upon the President a role of personal leadership for which his utterances had long prepared both his constituents and the leaders of nations with whom he had to deal. This leadership was expressed primarily in conferences, as will be seen. In these conferences and in preparation for them, the President depended upon his experts.

Prior to American participation in the war, the President had repeatedly called attention to violation of agreements, violation of boundaries, and wholesale disregard of long-accepted international practice. He had previously been able only to protest. Now he could do more. He could throw the influence of the United States in the balance on behalf of better order. He could furthermore use power to meet power. He must fight fire with fire. Being the man he was, he could do this with great moral indignation.

The President who, without asking the Congress for a declaration of war, had prepared the way to war by his vigorous attacks upon the dictators; who had provided aid to the Allies through the Lend-Lease arrangement; who had, further, encouraged practices that brought about attacks upon American ships and citizens—had also done more. In August of 1941, he had held an all-important conference with Prime Minister Churchill. He had authorized policies in the Far East in support of China. In all these ways he had expressed the view of convinced internationalists and had been applauded by them.

He had finally appealed, as well, to extreme nationalists. But he had been opposed by all isolationists.

Deeper than this political alignment, which was in fact a very unstable one, was a fundamental disagreement as to the President's purpose. How far could a President carry the nation into war by preparing for war, by the use of diplomatic pressures, by the supply of arms to favored belligerents, and by the practice of threatening language? President Roosevelt must bear all of the responsibility for the decisions that provided these measures. To defenders of the President, they were measures to avoid war. To opponents of the President, they were measures that led inevitably to war.

In the view of the masses of the President's fellow citizens, war had finally come by action of enemies that he had long warned were planning the destruction of the United States. Americans were now not disposed to question any longer the steps by which they were forced into a position of defending themselves. Overwhelming was the evidence in popular "polls" that the people thought the President had done everything possible to avoid the war.

The record seemed to be a confused one, however, and time was to show, by the gradual unfolding of factual evidence, that many mistakes had been made by the administration. Yet, in the months that followed Pearl Harbor, it was difficult to show that war could have been avoided except by the surrender of positions that few Americans were willing to surrender.

Had the United States been permitted to continue to wage the war by proxy Americans might have been left relatively unharmed and free to prepare for the inevitable conflict, if not in war, certainly in diplomacy, that would find them in basic opposition to the victorious Axis powers, or the victorious power of communism.

But the conflict had come to the United States. Americans had allies as well as enemies. The American people must win the war. On January 1, 1942, the United States, with China, Britain, and the Soviet Union, as well as twenty-two other nations, signed the Declaration of the United Nations.

The first year of the war for the United States was one of disaster, of mounting defeat, and definite uncertainty as to the

outcome. In 1917 there had been emotional uplift in defense
of American ideals on behalf of the freedom-loving peoples of
the world. In 1942, despite all the emphasis given by the President to the idealistic purposes of the United States, there was for
the most part only grim determination to carry through what
had to be done. In the naïve enthusiasm of World War I,
Americans might feel at least for a time that they were waging
a war to make the world safe for democracy. They could not
in World War II, however much was talked of peaceful arrangements following the war, believe that it was a war to reconstruct
the world in the image of American democracy. They knew
better.

Yet the American people must defeat their enemies. Then in
a world of nations they must try to construct a union within
which later struggles would have to be carried on. In this venture of the 1940's, Americans had come to think of themselves,
through the actions, if not the words of the President, as a
nation of great power. Ideals were not thought to have first
place in the conception of this struggle.

For three years prior to the entrance of the United States into
World War I, Woodrow Wilson had, by act and statement, led
the American people to accept the basic ideas that were at
Paris incorporated in the Covenant of the League of Nations.
In essence, this League was an expansion of the idea that was
basic to the making of the United States, which was a league
of sections. In President Wilson's conception of the League of
Nations, the *power* of the United States as a nation among nations was minimized.

From the outset, President Roosevelt was disposed to play the
role of the leader of the most powerful nation in the world of
nations. It had long been known that he wished to avoid the
mistakes of his illustrious predecessor, Woodrow Wilson. This
was thought to indicate that he meant to avoid minor mistakes
and political errors. The differences, however, lay deeper than
that.

As has been seen, Mr. Roosevelt had refrained from affirmative leadership in foreign affairs in the first four years of his
administration only to emerge in the second term with an aggressive foreign policy. Both attitudes were related to a basic

policy, that of a nation playing power politics. This nation, playing power politics, was presenting to the world not an American dream of internationalism, but an American practice of militant and successful nationalism. This was in time to bring to the President's support all the aggressive adventurousness of militant Americans.

The immediate results of this policy are seen in the pooling of economic and military resources with Great Britain and in the early and frequent conferences of the British Prime Minister and the American President.[3] The results are seen in active aid to Russia and alliance with Russia. They are seen likewise in the effort to make the Chinese Republic in the Far East a contributing ally to the British-Russian-American alliance.

How far the United States had traveled under Mr. Roosevelt's guidance in the previous ten years is seen in the genuine acceptance and eager interest that all Americans felt in the repeated conferences of the leaders of the great states—conferences held at first in Washington, but also in Quebec, then at Casablanca, at Cairo, at Teheran, and finally at Yalta.

In these conferences, not a representative speaking for the United States of America, but the American President himself with all of the powers residing in his office, participated for the United States in meetings to which came the national representative of each of the Allied powers. This was politics on a grand scale. As will be seen, Mr. Roosevelt did not always transfer his inimitable skill in domestic politics to the weaving of the larger pattern. Yet, by temperament, conviction, and success, Mr. Roosevelt was equipped to play a role in international conferences of a personal character. He had indicated how he felt in the first year of his administration by destroying the type of American participation exemplified in the London Economic Conference. His personal interest in the long-delayed formal recognition of Soviet Russia was another indication of his attitude. From the day of his Quarantine Speech in 1937, he had in correspondence, in instructions to personal envoys, and in

[3] Mr. Churchill was in Washington from December 22, 1941, to January 14, 1942. On January 1, the Declaration of the United Nations was signed in Washington.

addresses to the Congress and the people, taken a fundamental position from which he never moved.

This in essence was that, as the head of a great state, he was in a position to deal personally with rulers of other peoples—presumably directly—always for the benefit of his constituents. No one of the leaders who met with President Roosevelt in conference was left in doubt as to his conception of what he was doing. It was the cause of Churchill's ready response and later disillusionment. It was the explanation of Stalin's grudging acceptance and, later, of his truculent opposition. It explains as well the uncertainties and the final disillusionment of Chiang Kai-shek.

Hanson Baldwin's explanation is that "The Presidential ego unavoidably became stronger in Roosevelt's closing years. His great wartime power, the record of victory, the high esteem in which he was held by the world, and the weakness of the State Department all combined to reinforce the President's tendency to depend upon himself." [4]

The President's active participation as Commander-in-Chief in all war plans came as a matter of course. His immediate personal advisers were most often Harry Hopkins and Admiral William D. Leahy, recalled from his post as Ambassador to Vichy to serve as Mr. Roosevelt's personal military adviser. As the war developed, the President relied increasingly upon the advice of General George C. Marshall, his Chief of Staff, and upon that of Generals King and Arnold. No one was left in doubt as to Mr. Roosevelt's bold and imaginative grasp of the military and naval situation around the globe.[5]

Admiral King recalled that sometime previous to the conference at Pearl Harbor in the summer of 1944, it had been suggested to him by Admiral Leahy that the President liked the title "Commander-in-Chief," and wished that other designations that conflicted in any way might be altered.[6]

President Roosevelt's active interest in diplomatic arrangements was taken for granted. If, as has often been asserted, he thought of himself as his own Secretary of State, it can be said

[4] *Great Mistakes of the War*, p. 8.
[5] Leahy, *op. cit.*, p. 106.
[6] E. J. King and W. M. Whitehill, *Fleet Admiral King*, p. 567.

as well that he thought of himself as combining the powers that were usually associated with either monarch or dictator.[7]

The vast aggregation of individuals drawn to Washington to aid in winning the war and preparing for the peace held positions in many departments, a great number of them in the State Department. But in the end there was for them one master, one guiding hand, one determining force.

Because the early moves of the President had appeared to be in defense of the British Commonwealth of Nations, there continued until near the end of the war a general acceptance of the reality of a strong British-American alliance in all matters of diplomacy, as well as of military operations.[8] Russia and China were definitely and necessarily secondary. This dominant role of the British, as seen by the public, was personalized in the joint boards of control, and most of all in the six major conferences of the Prime Minister and the American President.

The full significance of this complete shift of supreme power to the American President would have been clearer to the millions who eagerly watched, had they not continued to rely upon the well-known fact that this President had to proceed in a way to maintain support in the Congress and to be certain of approval by the electorate. Though master of the situation he might be in the council of military advisers or in meetings of administrative department heads, yet in the Congress he must persuade and play politics. And to the people he must in the end make explanation that would appeal to them in choosing representatives. He was not in their eyes a monarch addressing his loyal subjects.

Thus in the year 1942 there was much activity in the Congress, and there was a record that must be examined. And late in the year there were to be Congressional elections.

The problems of party politics were increasingly complicated by the economic pressures of groups, blocs, and special inter-

[7] In view of the aggressive attitude of Secretary Stimson as fully revealed in subsequent years, it is important to note that, in the words of Current, "After Pearl Harbor he [Stimson] was included in few top-level conferences on strategy and seldom had access to the White House, except through such go-betweens as Harry Hopkins." (*Op. cit.*, 213.)

[8] Secretary Hull (*op. cit.*, II, 1472) wrote: "On the military side, the efforts of the two countries were integrated to a degree probably never previously reached by any two great allies in history."

ests. Ever present was the threat of inflation. Although the nation had since 1933 become accustomed to countless regulations affecting private business, private interests found increased reason—even in time of war—for opposing price ceilings, wage controls, and rationing provisions. The President could not rely only on reason or persuasion in such matters. At times, outright pressure must be used. Rosenman wrote in 1949: "The President's central strategy was to bring the various segments of the economy into balance. . . . By bringing both wages and farm prices into line, the President achieved the objectives of stabilization." [9]

In the New York State gubernatorial election appeared clear evidence that the President's hold on his party was weakened by his break with Farley. The Democratic candidate, John Bennett, was defeated by Republican Thomas E. Dewey.

As a result of the Congressional elections in November, 1942, the Democratic majority in the House was reduced. The new Congress stood 222-208 with four Independents. The Democrats lost ten seats in the Senate. The decline in total vote in the Congressional elections may have indicated indifference upon the part of the voters.[10]

As the activities of Franklin Roosevelt in the years of the war are considered, it may be well to state the point of view taken by the chief participant in his constant effort to look out upon the unfolding of events. It should be emphasized that no one in the world occupied a position comparable to that of the American President in the years 1941-1945. He was Commander-in-Chief of American armed forces. He exercised, in fact, the power of a dictator in determining American foreign policies. However, in mobilizing the industrial might of the United States, he had three tasks: first, to lead his supporting majorities in the Congress; second, to keep in touch with a public opinion that was supporting him; and third, to meet daily and hourly the mounting criticism of his work in all fields of activity. After all, in the end he would be responsible to his ultimate master, the American people.

The story of Franklin Roosevelt's life in these years, hitherto

[9] *Public Papers, 1942*, p. xiii.
[10] See Gosnell, *op. cit.*, pp. 193-194.

partially censored, is now being written, and will continue to be written for many years to come. The publications of the government, as well as the revelations of participants in diplomacy, in the armed forces, and in politics are daily adding to knowledge. But even now it is possible to narrate what happened as it appeared to the chief participant. For he explained his actions endlessly—in letter, speech, and order—and finally in summaries that, if not actually written by him, bore the stamp of his approval as "official."

From the point of view of this narrative, the most revealing evidence—if not at first glance the most important—was not what he "arranged" with other powers, or what he induced American industry to produce and American finance to support, or even what he led his military and naval commanders to do. It was how he won and held the support of the people. They, his clients—or masters—paid the bill in money, in bodies, and in the daily life they led then and in the years after the war. In the American conception of democracy, the President had to keep their support and approval.

As the President saw it in the early days of the war, events had justified his leadership from 1937 to 1942. To the Congress he had said on December 11, 1941, of Germany's declaration of war against the United States, "The long known and the long expected has thus taken place." [11] He had aided those who were now our allies. He had not "gone to war," but had led in efforts to prepare for the defense now so sorely needed. His opponents at home had stood against these measures.

Now that the United States was in the war, there was a continuous movement toward a unity of command, so that unity of purpose would be realized in a vision of freedom-loving peoples. The Declaration of the United Nations on January 1, 1942, was but the beginning of a grand plan for the future. If nothing succeeds like success, it is equally true that a far-seeing leader may claim support if his unfolding program seems to meet the needs of the hour.

Criticism of the President assumed a new phase as the nation entered the war. Critics viewing the conduct of war knew that it included all matters on the home front, as well as all diplomatic relations with friend and foe.

[11] *Public Papers, 1941,* p. 532.

The President could of course speak with authority as leader of his people. But his pattern of thought and his choice of language in face of criticism revealed little change. It was, as he saw it, a world struggle in which the forces of evil were ranged against the upholders of right and justice. Selfish and arrogant policies might easily deprive Americans of their friends and place winning the war in peril. A leader long shown to be, by act and word, a tribune of the people was a natural leader in such a crisis.

In the perspective of a dozen years, it is clear that deep in the American consciousness there existed even in 1942 an appreciation that the President was on firmer ground, historically speaking, than he had ever been. The President was now asking that the American people wage war in order to insure peace. Not to wage war had been a negative policy. But to prepare for peace —to lead others in organizing a peace-loving world—that was a policy that Americans could and did embrace affirmatively and with deep conviction.

If an attempt were made to state in summary form what Americans believed to be the objectives of American foreign policy at this time, there would probably be agreement that these included: unconditional surrender of all enemies; self-determination of liberated peoples; insistence upon sanctity of treaties under accepted international law; post-war rehabilitation, including access to trade and raw materials; provision in the economies of nations to insure freedom from fear and want; and the establishment of a system of security which would insure co-operation, disarmament, and peace.

In the perspective of time, such emphasis upon world order caused profound disagreement among the Allies. Any co-operation with a totalitarian state was dangerous. There was of course ample reason for confidence in the British. In the case of Russia there was realization, upon the part of informed and critical observers, that co-operation in war might not be followed by co-operation in peace. Why was this not clear to the President?

He and his advisers had participated in a domestic revolution in the United States, and many of the supporters of the New Deal openly admired the Communist advances in Russia. A "liberal" in the Roosevelt sense was conditioned to give Russia a favorable hearing. How basic was the President's position was to be seen in his declaration in favor of an Economic Bill of Rights in 1944.

It was not until the war was won and the agreements made in war were known, that the people of the United States were able to see, once more, that the basic divisions in the United States had not been changed by the unity for wartime needs. Forces favorable to the New Deal and to a democracy as envisaged by the liberals were predisposed to look with favor on Russia. Only as Russia was revealed as imperialistic, aggressive, and "totalitarian," did communism appear dangerous.

Too little critical attention has as yet been given the power of the President's personal advisers in this period. The war afforded the President opportunity to rule through advisers as never before. His conception of personal government was supported by the use he made of experts in particular fields, such as foreign relations.

His advisers, of whom Harry Hopkins had the most continuous responsibility, were as a rule far removed from currents of popular feeling, and, holding no elective offices, were not subject to popular disapproval. They functioned in the field of ideas. As most of them were not charged with the responsibility of executive action in either civil or military affairs, they were not subject to the restrictions that are implicit in popular support.

Yet the President's advisers represented—in a democracy—the attempt of the executive elected by the people to find a way of solving, through exact information and wide knowledge, problems that the people did not and could not comprehend. Everything depended upon such advisers, not only in formulating policy, but also in making decisions.[12]

---

[12] The dilemma caused by differences of opinion between the "public" and the "experts" was dealt with by Charles Malik (Ambassador to the United States from Lebanon) in a paper before the American Political Science Association in September, 1953. He called for "some permanent, high planning authority free of politics." The Operations Coordinating Board within the National Security Council set up by President Eisenhower in September of 1953 was an attempt to meet this need.

In 1943, the year of conferences, there were six major meetings, more than in any other year of the war. President Roosevelt was the major figure in five of them, and his representative, Secretary Hull, led in the action taken in the sixth conference. Each marked a milestone in the journey to the end that gave Allied victory in arms. Each provided a momentous decision affecting the interests of the people of the United States.

At Casablanca in January, when decision was made to invade Italy, came the Declaration for Unconditional Surrender. In May in Washington came the decision to increase the bombing of Germany. At Quebec in August came the decision to invade German-occupied France and to launch an Asiatic military expedition under joint control. In October, Secretary Hull journeyed to Moscow and there, with Foreign Secretary Eden of Great Britain and Foreign Commissar Vyacheslav Molotov of the U.S.S.R., made an agreement for the establishment of the United Nations, together with declarations favorable to setting up democratic regimes in Italy and Austria and a demand for trial and punishment of war criminals. At Cairo in November, President Roosevelt agreed with Chiang Kai-shek that the Republic of China should have control of Manchuria. Later in the month at Teheran, Roosevelt, Stalin, and Churchill agreed upon plans for the launching of the second front.

It was not until the end of 1943—nearly two years after the entrance of the United States into World War II—that Britain and the United States agreed upon and announced a policy regarding the objectives of the war in the Far East. At Cairo, November 22 to 26, Roosevelt and Churchill, meeting with Chiang Kai-shek, affirmed a war against Japan until her unconditional surrender. Territories taken from China were to be restored, and it was agreed by the three powers that in due course Korea was to be free and independent.

Thus the President of the United States was not only participating in world war as Commander-in-Chief of the armed forces of the nation, but he was participating in declarations as to the determination of sovereignty in foreign states of both Europe and Asia. He furthermore obtained agreement to his proposals for a United Nations Organization to be set up following the war.

How far the American President could go as Commander-in-Chief depended upon the advice of his military aides and the acquiescence of the military leaders of the Allied powers. But in stating that unconditional surrender should be a condition imposed upon the vanquished,[13] and in the agreement that there should be formal trial of war criminals, the President of the United States was exercising his undoubted influence as a personal leader in the realm of high politics. The American people as a whole applauded both declarations. Each decision was fraught with uncertainty, and neither had a solid grounding in past experience nor in international practice.

Fully at war, the American people were eager to get the grim task done with. On the whole, the military leaders—although not as a rule the military critics—were correctly reflecting the feelings of the mass of American citizens when they recommended, authorized, and carried forward programs of ruthless warfare in saturation bombing of populated areas, and finally, near the end of the war, in use of the atomic bomb.

Their Commander-in-Chief by temperament, point of view, and expressed conviction was a well-recognized leader in warfare. Although the actual use of the atomic bomb took place following his death, the fact remains that he was responsible for the development of the weapon itself.

Although much discussion of enslaved peoples and their ruthless masters took place before American participation in the war as well as afterwards, in the diplomacy of the war as conducted by President Roosevelt there was not any such conception of war as an instrument of national policy as actuated the statesmanship of Prime Minister Churchill.

Differences of opinion between Mr. Churchill and Mr. Roosevelt were frequently apparent in the conduct of the war.

---

[13] All reliable evidence places the responsibility for this upon Mr. Roosevelt, who upon his return from Casablanca said: "The only terms on which we shall deal with any Axis Government or any Axis factions are the terms proclaimed at Casablanca: 'unconditional surrender.' In our uncompromising policy we mean no harm to the common people of the Axis nations. But we do mean to impose punishment and retribution in full upon their guilty, barbaric leaders." The President "softened this somewhat a few months later," by a statement that "the people of the Axis need not fear unconditional surrender to the United Nations." Meanwhile, however, "the phrase itself spread more widely than the qualification." (Hull, *op. cit.*, II, 1570-1571). See also *Personal Letters, 1928-1945*, II, 1504.

Deeper yet were their differences in consideration of problems that must be at the heart of any settlement at the end.

Throughout the war, widespread in the United States was the demand for rapid action. It was expressed by large numbers of self-termed liberals who called for an early second front in Europe to relieve the pressure on Russia. Later the same elements asked for a rapid closing of the war in the Far East by forced union of conflicting factions in China. Likewise, the same elements called for an international organization at the end of the war that should include all nations.

None of these demands arose out of a clear-eyed recognition of the basic purposes of Soviet Russia, nor out of an understanding of the long history of the failure of balance of power agreements to bring enduring peace.

Yet the President and his immediate advisers must bear the responsibility for not bringing to the people a realization of the danger inherent in such involvement in the maelstrom of world affairs. Franklin Roosevelt had once said that it was the duty of the statesman to educate.[14] Here it was that he failed in that supreme duty, because he believed that he could "persuade" Stalin to accept a new code of international relations, and because it appeared that, under stress of war, the ancient "imperialism" of western Europe—which the President detested—might be liquidated.

The consideration of two "might-have-beens" may now be helpful. Had the United States entered the war as an independent belligerent, it would not, in all probability, have found it possible to endorse an attempt for a knock-out victory. It would not have allied itself with a nation so thoroughly at variance with American historical ideals as was Soviet Russia. And it would not have emerged as the leader in an attempt to build all nations into a world organization.

The second "might-have-been" is found in the explanation of the degree to which American assertiveness rested in truly overwhelming strength. Had the United States endured a long period of enervating warfare; had this country been invaded; had the nation faced the necessity of carefully planning not only

---

[14] See chapter III, p. 69.

the means of warfare but the agencies productive of peace—it is probable that an overwhelming sense of power would have been tempered by recognition of harsh reality. War at home would have clarified the national situation. War at a distance never did.

In the direction of American war effort, the President's task was one of co-operation. He must use all of the resources of the nation. This meant winning and holding the support of many Americans who had opposed him. For this portion of his task of co-operation, his record of performance and his habit of statement had ill prepared him for full success.

It was true that the attack at Pearl Harbor had united the people for pursuance of war. Leaders in all walks of life pledged allegiance to a full program of support for the administration. Yet soon it was clear that the President was not merely the official Commander-in-Chief of a nation at war. Nor did he merely offer full co-operation to those whose support he sought. He demanded agreement and submission to the ends he declared to be the objectives of the United States.

Co-operation with the nations opposed to the Axis was of course the immediate objective of the United States. This had been true for more than a year and a half before the United States was involved in the war. Co-operation with the British had been personified in the relations existing between the President and the British Prime Minister.

Upon the entrance of the United States into the war, as has been seen, Mr. Churchill came to Washington at once on the first of his frequent visits. This visit symbolized the transfer of the center of the free nations to Washington. Now it was clear that in the world struggle the English-speaking peoples in Europe, America, and Australasia were the backbone of the opposition to the combination of Germany, Italy, Japan, and their satellites.

The new alignment of power, after Hitler's betrayal of his ally, necessitated an increase of co-operation with Russia. Here the task of the President was of a different order. Persistently, Mr. Roosevelt believed that his eagerness to co-operate on personal terms with the heads of states would bring the desired results in the case of Marshal Stalin. The President had felt that personal co-operation was essential in 1933 at the time he took initiative in recognition of Russia.[15] And he continued to feel that way almost to the end of this struggle, certainly during what he believed to be his success in the conference at Yalta in 1945. The basic decision in 1933 had perhaps been the fatal error.

The year 1943 was one of relative calm in American politics at home. Preparations were under way for the electoral tests of 1944, but for the time being the President seemed in the eyes of the public, as well as his own, the Commander-in-Chief of all the people.

The year at war was one of continuous advance against the enemies everywhere. In May the Allies were in control in North Africa and preparing for the attack upon Italy. In early July, Sicily was invaded and the advance upon the mainland of southern France began. Two months later Italy surrendered.

Meanwhile, the Battle of the Atlantic had been won. Likewise, the spring and summer of 1943 witnessed the advance of American forces in the islands of the Pacific. This was accompanied by such destruction of Japanese ships and planes as to insure early exhaustion of Japanese naval and air power.

Each of the series of conferences of Allied leaders emphasized through repeated and wide publicity that therein was seen the effectiveness of co-operation in winning a conflict of world proportions. As has been pointed out, Mr. Roosevelt attended five of these conferences in the course of the year. Of these, Mr. Rosenman wrote: ". . . it was he who made the final decisions; and it was his leadership which dominated the major decisions which involved international diplomacy or politics." [16]

It was not until a year after American entrance into the war that the Axis was clearly on the road to defeat. This did not mean that the Allies had won—although by November, 1942, in Africa, Europe, and Asia the tide had turned. It meant rather that the Allied successes in North Africa, the holding of Stalingrad against the Germans, and the nature of the distribution of naval and military power in the Pacific made it clear that noth-

---

[15] See F.D.R.'s letter to Stalin in 1943, p. 361 of this book.
[16] *Public Papers, 1943*, Introduction, p. vi.

ing would ultimately stand against the might of America in alliance with Britain and Russia.

China could not be ignored, although efforts to use this potential power against Japan were on the whole unavailing. China was not equal to the task in Asia—as was Russia in Europe—of defeating the Axis. A Communist China at the time might have done a more effective job, thought a number of Americans.

Throughout the year there was public discussion of the objectives of the war in terms of world organization. This was in line with the secondary arguments of the President in the formulation of his foreign policies ever since 1937. He was interested in the conditions that were to exist in the United States in the years that followed the end of the war. He was also conerned with what were termed the blueprints for peace. Both of these interests were essential if he maintained his point of view and continued to have the support of his New Deal adherents as he now led those who were primarily interested in international organization for peace.

A United Nations Organization was much in Mr. Roosevelt's mind at this time, according to the most reliable witnesses of his daily thought. This meant, as an objective, world-wide co-operation in matters of food supply, of stabilized currencies, of international banking, and of course in reconstruction and rehabilitation.

In promoting in 1943 the idea that war veterans should be given careful protection and support, and the idea that the United States would be able to aid nations and peoples abroad who were in need, the President was appealing to two deep-seated convictions of the American mind.

As supporters of the President well knew, however, there were deep divisions in American thinking about foreign nations and about co-operation with them once the war was won. Administration followers found that the isolationists—who were so easily denounced because events had seemed to prove them mistaken—did in fact represent a widespread feeling of the American people even in time of war.

The majority of these Americans had gone through World War I and its ugly, painful, and mystifying aftermath. Now, even though again in war, they were astonished at the news of revolutions abroad. They were bewildered by the reactions of foreigners. Finally, they were fearful in their thought that a peace might be made in terms unfavorable to the United States. Frequently these "conservatives" were startled by the President's declaration of aims.

What Americans clearly saw was that America had been attacked. They saw as clearly that the Allies would win the war. But few of them found it easy to think in global terms. Fewer still could think of promising continued co-operation with other peoples.

It must be emphasized that armed attack upon the United States, not logical argument about world politics, had brought the American people to accept war. Could there be a "Pearl Harbor" that would force them to accept such a United Nations as the President envisaged? Could the people be brought to see that in the end, power backed by ruthless purpose might destroy their world? Unless this could be done, the chances were excellent that they would slip into the familiar grooves; that they would feel safe and happy upon a familiar road that had brought them so much satisfaction before rude highwaymen had borne down upon them.

A portion of the President's argument could be easily accepted, namely, that America was open to attack. The American people, only 140,000,000 in a world of billions, were engaged in total war. Yet when the President took the position that the favored situation of the United States due to isolation and other considerations in the past could not be regained, and that the present active participation in world politics must be maintained—a great mass of his fellow citizens refused to be convinced. They were not interested in world revolution, nor in the abandonment of national sovereignty. Nor were they much interested in the spread of an easy and quick democracy for other nations. They were not international minded. The war did not change this.

An affirmative program for peace on American terms would have had a better chance of endorsement. But declarations in favor of the good things of the past did not insure political success for those who, throughout the past ten years, had deplored so much that the United States had done. When "colonialism" was discussed as a cause for war, it was not easy to make this convincing to Americans who felt that the United States had been a successful colonizing nation. When eulogy was given the "four freedoms," it was frequently remarked that these freedoms and others had already had their fullest realization in the United States. When order and efficiency were emphasized as essential for the winning of the war, it was perhaps natural for many Americans to remember how much these qualities had meant to America at peace.

When President Roosevelt talked of a peaceful world achieved by arrangements dictated by successful nations, his people knew full well that his leadership in the United States had been marked by experimentation and reform—not by peace. He had never at any time given adequate emphasis to the success of the American experience. He had not built upon the faith of America that stood first in the hearts of his fellow countrymen.

Mankind—as well as its leader—must choose its road. The American people knew from experience that men and nations have lived in a world of continuous strife. They knew that varying stages of political development among peoples create deep divisions in belief. They knew that American democracy was not doctrine but daily conduct. They distrusted all assertions that ran counter to these realities.

Early in his first administration, the most devastating critic of the President had admitted that he was a master in stating objectives; that—for a time—he had the advantage of those who saw obstacles and possible failure unless the ways and means available to a democratic people could be used effectively. Again, the President was stating objectives, and at the same time placing burdens in blood, prestige, and resources upon the American people that they must carry far into the future. Only an atmosphere of war would have led them to consider assuming such a burden.

But, as always, the President was using arguments that had wide appeal for the masses of men. At the same time that masterly moves in preparation for peace were made in organization for food distribution and in monetary agreements, moves were made to appeal to liberals in Puerto Rico and the Philippines.

The President was talking of an expanded economy that would buy in the United States more security, more employment, more education, health, and recreation. He was providing the groundwork for an Economic Bill of Rights that was pronounced in the next Presidential campaign.

Much, if not all, of the President's policy that came to be identified as American foreign policy during the war, was based upon the belief that a United Nations Organization would take the place of the principle of "balance of power" as the great determining force in the international relations of the future. Only as there was implicit belief in this agency, could one understand how during the war American policies came to include much advice to the British, the French, and the Dutch that they prepare to abandon their colonial empires.

Furthermore, the military decisions to destroy the centers of industrial power in Germany and Japan were made possible by the failure of Mr. Roosevelt and at least some of his advisers to realize that in so doing they would give to Russia, by removal of German power in Europe and Japanese power in the Far East, the opportunity to expand as never before. To the Chinese Communists appeared at the same time the opportunity of dominating the Far East if they could overwhelm the Nationalists under Chiang Kai-shek.

Unless ideological agreements united the great powers, there was no hope in a United Nations as a deterrent to nationalism.[17] The earlier recognition that Stalin was dictator and not a "democrat," and that China, in its undeveloped political state, was a menace to a world of orderly procedures were certainly often in the President's mind. Throughout the period of the winning of war in Europe, there were attempts again and again to hold Stalin to working agreements and to bring the Chinese leaders into a co-operative movement for peace.

In this situation, success for Stalin and failure for the United States in China were predestined. It is not necessary to stress

---

[17] ". . . Rooseveltian tendency toward international altruism, too often unmoderated by practical politics, seems a strange manifestation in one who domestically was 'a pragmatic and consummate politician. But it must be remembered that the vision of a 'brave new world' was strong in Roosevelt's mind, and his optimistic nature and the great inner wellspring of his faith in man sometimes affected his judgment." (Baldwin, op. cit., p. 7.)

the existence of Communist infiltration and Communist spies in the American government. More important, however, in the perspective of years—and vastly more important in influencing the masses of Americans—was the stark fact that the administration did look with favor upon the objectives of Russia as far as they were then understood. This was logical and inevitable, as has been seen in tracing the record of the administration since 1933.

Had Mr. Roosevelt and his advisers, particularly Harry Hopkins, not been basically favorable to the "democratic" objectives of communism, they could not have so administered the government as to bring convinced fellow travelers into positions of great power and sometimes of determining influence. Only because the President had such a tolerant view of the Russian government, could he have believed that he could, with all his persuasive powers, win Stalin to such programs as that of the United Nations and full participation in a plan for world economic control. Roosevelt believed that Stalin, though a leader of great ruthlessness, could, by maneuver and influence, be brought into a union of democratic nations. This folly was realized only with the ending of the war.

Chapter XVI

PLANNING A NEW WORLD

THE YEAR 1944 vividly revealed the pattern of the immediate future, at home and abroad. The war against Germany and Japan was not won, but the certainty of the winning was clear. Plans for the organization of world peace were advanced, and the alignments revealed were later to be all-important. In the United States, decision was made to maintain the President in office. Thus the disposition of political forces in the nation was fixed for the next four years.

Near the end of the critical year 1943, at the conference at Teheran (November 28-December 1), a meeting of primary military importance to the United States, Russia, and Britain, renewed emphasis had been given post-war objectives of the Allied powers. In reporting upon this—as well as upon an earlier conference at Cairo (November 22-26) with Chiang Kai-shek—President Roosevelt in a radio address on December 24, 1943, brought home to the American people, as never before, the actual participation of the United States in World War II. He said:

> On this Christmas Eve there are over 10,000,000 men in the armed forces of the United States alone. One year ago 1,700,000 were serving overseas. Today this figure has been more than

doubled to 3,800,000 on duty overseas. By next July 1 that number overseas will rise to over 5,000,000 men and women.[1]

With the development of this vast military state, mobilization had brought about, in addition to the drafting of men for military service, a national registration of all males in the advanced age group forty-five to sixty-four. War production had brought about control of strategic materials. Labor controls included the fixing of hours in industry and strikebreaking by the United States Army in Michigan and Pennsylvania. More than a dozen national agencies were established to control civilian life and push the war effort.

In describing the meetings at Cairo and at Teheran with the leaders of other states, the President stressed that "We came to the Conferences with faith in each other. But we needed the personal contact." Prime Minister Churchill, the President said, "has become known and beloved by many millions of Americans."[2]

As early as March of 1942, the President in writing Churchill had said: "I tell you that I think I can handle Stalin personally better than either your Foreign Office or my State Department."[3] At Teheran, President Roosevelt had met Marshal Stalin for the first time. Of him, Mr. Roosevelt reported: "He is a man who combines a tremendous, relentless determination with a stalwart good humor. I believe he is truly representative of the heart and soul of Russia; and I believe that we are going to get along very well with him and the Russian people—very well indeed."[4]

In the Generalissimo (Chiang Kai-shek), the President said he had met "a man of great vision, great courage, and a remarkably keen understanding of the problems of today and tomorrow."[5]

---

[1] *Public Papers, 1943*, p. 553. In the same address, the President said: "There have always been cheerful idiots in this country who believed that there would be no more war for us if everybody in America would only return into their home and lock their front doors behind them." *Ibid.*, p. 560.

[2] *Ibid.*, p. 555.

[3] Quoted by Chester Wilmot, *The Struggle for Europe*, p. 138. But General Deane wrote of Teheran: "Stalin appeared to know what he wanted at the Conference. This was also true of Churchill, but not so of Roosevelt." (John R. Deane, *The Strange Alliance*, p. 43.)

[4] *Public Papers, 1943*, p. 558.

[5] *Ibid.*, p. 556.

Of the future, the President said in this address:

Britain, Russia, China, and the United States and their allies represent more than three-quarters of the total population of the earth. As long as these four Nations with great military power stick together in determination to keep the peace there will be no possibility of an aggressor Nation arising to start another world war.[6]

Referring to "well-intentioned but ill-fated experiments of former years" that had failed to keep the peace, Franklin Roosevelt pledged himself as "President and Commander-in-Chief to see to it that these tragic mistakes shall not be made again."[7]

Further international relationship was to be safeguarded, the President told the people, but only "big, broad objectives, rather than details" had been discussed with the world leaders, although they had agreed "that if force is necessary to keep international peace, international force will be applied—for as long as it may be necessary."[8] To those "fighting for peace" at the time, this seemed good logic.

As an indication of the means thought of at the time by the President, he said: "Essential to all peace and security in the Pacific and in the rest of the world is the permanent elimination of the Empire of Japan as a potential force of aggression."[9] And "Germany must be stripped of her military might and be given no opportunity within the foreseeable future to regain that might."[10]

But a clearer indication of hard thinking that underlay all plans for the future was seen in the establishment in November, 1943, of the United Nations Relief and Rehabilitation Administration, an agreement by forty-four nations to aid liberated peoples in Europe and in the Far East. Subsequent agreements were made in 1944 and 1945. The flow of aid showed in two years a contribution of three-fourths of the necessary funds by the United States government.

The declaration issued at Teheran in December, 1943, had

[6] *Ibid.*, p. 558.
[7] *Ibid.*, p. 559.
[8] *Ibid.*, p. 558.
[9] *Ibid.*, p. 556.
[10] *Ibid.*, p. 557.

been specific regarding post-war aims, for it had urged the getting of the active participation of all nations, large and small, to eliminate tyranny and slavery, and to achieve a day "when all peoples of the world may live free lives untouched by tyranny according to their varying desires and their own consciences." [11]

The movements thus foreshadowed had important developments as the year advanced. At Bretton Woods in July, 1944, representatives of forty-four nations agreed upon a plan for an International Monetary Fund, and for the establishment of an International Bank of Reconstruction and Development.

The following month (August 21) at Dumbarton Oaks in Washington, D.C., the representatives of the United States, Britain, Russia, and China met. Before they disbanded on October 7, they had agreed upon a charter for a permanent international organization for maintaining world peace and security.

This preliminary draft included provision for an international police force. It is noteworthy that in this tentative draft, decision as to voting power in the proposed Council was postponed. Neither Russia nor the United States was willing at this time to forego a possible veto power in actions involving the interests of either.[12]

In this preliminary work of representatives of the Treasury Department, as well as of the State Department, members of the staff of young men and women had a part. As has been shown, the leadership of President Roosevelt in both domestic and foreign affairs had emphasized the liberalism and progressive aspects of all American effort. In the period of United States participation in war, as well as in the earlier period of "preparation," a large number of persons in the service of the American government looked upon developments in Russia—under Communist leadership—with interest and often enthusiasm. Naturally, in the circumstances of the time, it could not have been otherwise. Imperialism and reaction were at the time common enemies.

It was later to be remembered that some of these Americans entrusted with responsibility were traitors to their government,

---

[11] *Ibid.*, p. 533.
[12] The President, by personal appeal to Stalin in correspondence, attempted to reach a compromise. (Hull, *op. cit.*, II, 1700.)

in that they were secret agents of a foreign power. But beyond doubt, as a whole, these highly informed and effective administrators and advisors were loyal Americans. They naturally read into the pronouncements of the powers at war the wishes that were dominant in their own minds. In this, they represented a very great section of the American people.

President Roosevelt, despite all the work of his own government in preparation for peace, continued to be primarily interested in his activities as Commander-in-Chief. His public statements were evidence of this and they had widespread influence upon the currents of public opinion in the year of the Presidential election.

The President's activities, which were now circumscribed, included personal visits to the centers of military production. A people's war was one in which the work of military men and of industrial leaders had high rating in the public mind as compared with the continuous work of those preparing blueprints for peace.[13]

In June, 1944, attention was concentrated upon the cross-Channel landing in the actual invasion of German-occupied Normandy and the subsequent advance into other territory occupied by Hitler's armies. By the end of August, most of France was occupied by Allied forces, and Belgium and Luxembourg as well. But the year ended with the Germans still holding most points of their own frontier.

The advance of the Allies had been costly in men, and supplies had not kept pace with advancing troops. Ground forces had defeated the Germans, however, and victory was now only a matter of time.[14]

The American public gave less attention to the advances of the Russian armies from the east. Churchill repeatedly disagreed with Roosevelt on the conduct of the war on the continent. As a result of Roosevelt's domination of the military argument, the Russian armies were unimpeded in their sweep

---

[13] See Hull, *op. cit.*, II, especially chapters 93 and 122. Hull held two interviews with Charles E. Hughes in Washington, D. C. on April 23 and May 7, 1944. (Notes in Hughes Papers, Library of Congress.)

[14] General Eisenhower in his Report of the Supreme Commander dated July 13, 1945, said "The war was won before the Rhine was crossed." (P. 121.)

westward into East Germany, and by the end of the year were about to enter Rumania and Hungary.

It should be added, however, that on April 7, 1945, in a cable to General Marshall, General Eisenhower said: "I am the first to admit that war is waged in pursuance of political aims, and if the combined Chiefs of Staff should decide that the Allied effort to take Berlin outweighs purely military considerations in this theater, I would cheerfully readjust my plans and my thinking so as to carry out such operation.[15]

In mid-September, President Roosevelt met with Prime Minister Churchill in Quebec, where a year before they had agreed upon the invasion of France and a joint program in Asia. Now in 1944 they tentatively approved the "Morgenthau Plan" sponsored by Secretary of the Treasury Morgenthau and prepared by his staff as the pattern of the peace to be provided in Germany.[16] Hull and Stimson had opposed this. The President later disapproved the plan. In October he gave instruction that specific planning for post-war Germany should cease.

The essence of this plan, the announcement of which caused much bitterness and argument among the American people, then and later, was that Germany's industry would be dismantled and reduced to that of a country primarily agricultural in character. The plan proposed to so strip and weaken all industrial power that no industrial nation would re-emerge. Equipment in factory and mine not already destroyed by enemy action was to be removed or destroyed.

The Pacific campaign had given Americans cause to become acquainted, as never before, with the islands of the Pacific and the immense distances of that ocean. The summer successes of 1944 were followed by re-entrance of American forces into the Philippines in October. But the costs in blood had appalled the American people, and when the year 1945 opened, it was clear that the invasion of the islands of Japan was soon to come. In fact, in February the Japanese brought forward an informal offer of surrender, approaching the Russian Ambassador in Tokyo as intermediary, but the Russians "set their price of

---

[15] Quoted by Wilmot, *op. cit.*, p. 693.
[16] Hull, *op. cit.*, II, chapter 115, especially pp. 1604-1605; 1621-1622.

mediation so high that the Japanese temporarily dropped the matter." [17] The war was to be waged eight months longer before the Japanese surrender in August.

Although the President was Commander-in-Chief with respect to all military operations—and gloried in this—he constantly interested himself in American preparation for the international organization to be set up at the end of the war. He had not wished such words as "international organization" to be used at the time of announcement of the Atlantic Charter, but there was no doubt then as to the general intent of his leadership.

At the time of the Quebec Conference in September, 1944, the President prepared a memorandum recalling his thinking as expressed in the plan he prepared in 1923.[18] He quoted from the summary of this: "It takes over all that is best in the existing League, including the great humanitarian and economic enterprises of the League. . . . Many changes, however, are made both in the machinery of the League of Nations, and in the obligations of the individual member nations." [19]

Then he continued, as of September 15, 1944: "The Plan sets up an Assembly as does the plan discussed at Dumbarton Oaks. It sets up an Executive Committee instead of a Council in continuing session. This Executive Committee would have been composed of eleven members—five so-called great powers and six small nations." [20]

A careful line of distinction should be drawn between the contribution of the President and that of the State Department in considering the emerging plan for the United Nations Organization. There is, as well, a line to be drawn between the agreement of nations· to outlaw war and the actual establishment of an international league of power. The President's policy from 1937 to 1939 had strongly urged the first; after 1941, it had become definitely the second.

Yet in the repeated action of the President—both before and after the outbreak of the European war—there was definite

---

[17] See Baldwin, *op. cit.*, p. 96.
[18] See p. 44 of present volume.
[19] *Personal Letters, 1928-1945*, II, 1540.
[20] *Ibid.*, pp. 1540-1541.

unreality in this distinction. His continuous participation in joint conferences with Britain and Russia was an acceptance of the familiar method of diplomacy of great powers. It need have nothing to do with an international organization of many nations. Indeed, the success of this method of conference among great powers might spell the defeat of any vital world organization.

However, from the outbreak of the European war in 1939 until the meeting of the United Nations Conference in San Francisco in 1945, there was continuous activity in the State Department, as suggested and supported by the President, toward the drawing up of a plan for the United Nations Organization. There was also within the State Department continuous development of a program dealing with post-war foreign policy which had world organization as its goal.[21] Furthermore, as early as January, 1942, Mr. Roosevelt had brought a declaration of twenty-two nations into being.

The President repeatedly gave support to the work of the agencies of the State Department, using their prepared materials in conferences held at Teheran, Cairo, and Yalta.[22]

But the fact that the President merged his own foreign policy negotiations with the plans being made for world organization, is seen in his address to the Congress after his return from Yalta when he said: "This time we are not making the mistake of waiting until the end of the war to set up the machinery of peace." [23]

And then came full acceptance of world organization as the goal—in words that were an ultimatum to the American people: "There can be no middle ground here. We shall have to take the responsibility for world collaboration, or we shall have to bear the responsibility for another world conflict." [24]

[21] The wide extent of this planning may be seen in its entirety in *Postwar Foreign Policy Preparation 1939-1945*, Department of State Publication 3580.

[22] Cordell Hull wrote in 1948 (*op. cit.*, I, p. 195): "The President, with rare exceptions, could scarcely have been more considerate toward me as Secretary of State throughout my twelve years in that office. . . . With the exception of his conferences with Mr. Churchill and Marshal Stalin, which he regarded as being primarily military, he virtually always sought my advice or concurrence before taking an important step in foreign relations."

[23] *Public Papers, 1944-1945*, p. 578.

[24] *Ibid.*, p. 585.

That the President saw no "middle ground" is to be judged against the background of his conception of the "politics" of internationalism. He had eagerly co-operated with Britain. There the Laborites were soon to be in power. He had led in an aggressive pro-Russian attitude in the period of the war. With such "liberal" allies, the United States could hope to lead in the United Nations.

Looking forward with the President, one might see the bare outlines of a Marshall Plan and of a Point Four Program. More important than the fact that, later, Americans were to find themselves opposed to the Russian Soviet imperialism, is the fact that the international policy of the United States was based upon the assumption that economic democracy, which thrives on economic prosperity, can be counted on to provide the basis for political democracy. Billions of dollars spent for foreign aid can easily be seen as a natural outgrowth of a situation in which millions of dollars were spent to underwrite democracy at home.

It is not strange that in 1942 the interest of many prominent American leaders was concentrated on the problems of the peace to which they yearned to return.[25] By 1944 it had become the obsession of all, including Franklin Roosevelt.

Inevitably division of opinion arose as to the extent to which national power—be it sovereignty or military strength—might be lessened. Except for those who clung to nationalism as the one hope, all agreed that there must be a strengthening of some international organization. Yet on this, the gulf between the position of Mr. Roosevelt and that of his critics was to be deep indeed.

Throughout the final years of the war, apprehension grew among the American people as to "the arrangements to be made at the end." The ultimate choice of means would be made by the people. There was continuous discussion in forum, on radio, in journal, and in the press.

The explanations of policy by experts, especially those in or

---

[25] See in particular *Prefaces to Peace*, including Wendell L. Willkie, *One World;* Herbert Hoover and Hugh Gibson, *The Problems of Lasting Peace;* Henry A. Wallace, *The Price of Free World Victory;* Sumner Welles, *Blueprints for Peace.* (Cooperatively published by Simon and Schuster, Doubleday, Doran, Reynal and Hitchcock, Columbia University Press, 1943.)

of the government, or by those who had served officially or unofficially beyond the seas, were given careful attention by interested citizens. This included a large number of Americans always interested in "hearing" and in "talking" about public affairs. It led one State Department official to remark that "those who really know, do not talk; those who talk, do not know." [26] Herein lay one of the principal dangers, to be revealed only at a later time when the chasm between experts and the public came to be of pronounced political importance.

To meet a need of explanation to interested persons, Committees on Foreign Relations sponsored by the State Department were organized in various cities of the country. The dominant note in the discussions was not one to excite the enthusiasm of the average citizen or his immediate political representatives. For emphasis was placed upon the need of a greater "internationalism" among the American people, and constant criticism was offered of past performances of the United States in foreign affairs.

If emphasis on internationalism had been urged as a measure of self-defense, it would have been more easily understood. Some leaders presented it in that light, but on the whole, "internationalism" remained to millions of people a thought—hard to take—not an experience to be welcomed.

Despite their regard for the Presidency, the American people had always been Congressional minded, in that they placed faith in their elected representatives in Senate and House. Had Mr. Roosevelt—or his chief advisers—adopted a policy of continuous discussion, the people would have felt more assured. Attempts were made to do this, it is true, but partisan forces were too powerful to permit it.

In *Fortune* magazine for August, 1943, appeared a proposal whereby the President and Secretary of State would inform the Congress and the people on foreign policy and encourage public discussion that would provide a basis for American public opinion and develop a sense of international experience on the part of the people.[27]

---

[26] Confidential source.

[27] It proposed, in brief, that: (1) The Secretary of State appear once each month before Congress for debate and question on foreign policy; (2) that the Chairmen and members of Committees meet with the President and Secretary of State in private discussion to decide what to withhold from public debate;

But by the time this approach was used—with intelligence and courage—in the meeting of the United Nations at San Francisco in the spring of 1945, the chance of preparing the public mind for peace had been lost.

The year 1944 ended with promise of eventual victory for the Allies in the next few months. There was absolutely no possibility by that time of a German or a Japanese victory. But what form would defeat take for Germany, or for Japan?

There were questions which transcended the problems of winning the war—to which Mr. Roosevelt had given so much attention—ever since December, 1941. Upon these so-called political problems wide differences of opinion existed among the people of the United States as well as among the leaders of the Grand Alliance. Brought forward for immediate discussion —and eventually, for definite decision—were such thorny issues as "colonialism," "imperialism," and "spheres of influence."

In judging the action of Mr. Roosevelt upon these questions, careful attention must be given his relations with Winston Churchill. At the outset it is clear that both men visualized their relationship as that of colleagues in a single great enterprise: the determination of the future of freedom-loving peoples. Of these, the United States and Britain were the most important, if for no other reason than that they were the most experienced and had the best promise of democratic government in the future.

Both men thought in terms of history, and visualized themselves as actors in a developing drama. No such personal relationship had hitherto existed in the history of the two peoples. It is difficult to see how any other two men could have co-operated as they did. Their co-operation is a salient fact in modern history.

It will be recalled that in September, 1939, at the outbreak of World War II, President Roosevelt communicated with Winston Churchill, who had been made First Lord of the Ad-

(3) that the Secretary of State make full written semi-annual reports to the Congress; (4) that the Secretary of State provide the Congress with full analytical and interpretative material on foreign problems as they arose; (5) that the President, in public addresses to Congress and the nation, elaborate the problem and explore the programs in order to inform the people, reassure foreigners, and make the people international-minded not by edict but by experience.

miralty.[28] From that time forward, they carried on a continuous correspondence summarized by Mr. Churchill in 1945 as "seventeen hundred messages," in addition to "one hundred and twenty days of close personal contact," commencing at Argentia in August, 1941.

The actions of Mr. Roosevelt, and his explanation of them at the time and subsequently in his summary of events as he saw them, must then be seen in this unofficial setting of co-operation by two men, each charged with tremendous political power, but each fully conscious that he was subject to the disapproval at any time of his own constituency. Neither was a king nor a dictator. Was this relationship between two powers foreshadowing a plan for the future?

The American people, as far as they realized this particular development in foreign relations, accepted it as a matter of course. Indeed, had there not been a general background feeling of common purpose, it would not have been possible. No other peoples could so act together as did the British and the Americans at this time.

It is in this frame of reference that attention must be given the agreements and the disagreements that appear in the narrative of these years. Differences as to policy and purpose were ever present. Outright disagreement as to war measures was frequent. This was to be expected, even if the basic unity in common military purpose had persisted to the end of the war.

As long as Churchill was his constant colleague and supporter, the President was able, within the coalition, to work his will as Commander-in-Chief. Prior to the attack upon the United States by the Japanese, and the declaration of war by Germany, Mr. Roosevelt had made it his primary purpose to bring aid to the British, that is, to the work of Mr. Churchill. With American entrance into the war, the center of strategy was transferred from London to Washington, where the Prime Minister and the President met several times, in addition to their meetings elsewhere.

How far were the actions of Mr. Roosevelt from 1941 to 1945

---

[28] Franklin Roosevelt had met Winston Churchill while Assistant Secretary of the Navy. (*Public Papers, 1941,* p. 315). See Bruce Hutchison, *The Incredible Canadian: A Candid Portrait of Mackenzie King,* for an appraisal of the influence of the Canadian Prime Minister upon the association between Roosevelt and Churchill.

determined by his unusual relationship with Mr. Churchill? How much attention did Mr. Roosevelt give, in his thought as well as in his action, to the developing frictions with the British? Some of the answers to these important questions are available.

At Quebec on August 19, 1943, Roosevelt and Churchill had entered into a secret agreement as to use of the atomic bomb, then in process of development in both countries but further advanced in the United States. The two who shared the secret pledged each other "not to use the atomic bomb against each other, and not to use it against any other country unless both Britain and the United States agreed." It was further agreed to share information on atomic development between the United States and Britain.[29]

This agreement was in the minds of Churchill and Roosevelt as they approached the end of the war—with Stalin as a third party excluded from knowledge of the agreement and, it was hoped, from knowledge of the project. Churchill recalled after the war that even at the Potsdam Conference with President Truman, Stalin did not appear to have had previous knowledge of the success of the experiment on the New Mexico desert.[30]

The President was able to hold the support of the American people because he appeared to dominate the Allies in the conduct of the war. Yet Mr. Roosevelt became aware, particularly after 1943, that the British had other claims than those that appeared of paramount importance to him and were known to the American people.

The President, while in no way relinquishing his grasp upon the conduct of a successful war, was planning the means by which a United Nations Organization would emerge at the end or before the end of the war. Mr. Roosevelt was moving, consciously or unconsciously, to favor the Russian view of the strategy of the European war as opposed to the view of

---

[29] *The Private Papers of Senator Vandenberg* (edited by Arthur H. Vandenberg, Jr.), pp. 359-361, "The secret wartime atomic arrangements on which President Roosevelt and Prime Minister Churchill had agreed, at Quebec and Hyde Park meetings, were not entirely clear in the official records, and it was not until 1947 that some high officials acquired detailed knowledge of the agreements. . . . Vandenberg declared that he thought the Hyde Park and Quebec arrangements were 'astounding' and 'unthinkable' . . ."

[30] *Triumph and Tragedy*, pp. 637, 640, 670.

Churchill and the British. Both of these developments, as they became clear in the actions of the President, raised questions that brought him into less cordial relations with Churchill.

As it can be said with certainty that Churchill never forgot that he did not intend to permit a liquidation of the British Empire, it can be said with equal certainty that the President never forgot that he had repeatedly pledged the American people a unity of the nations of the world that would in itself spell the doom of imperialism, including colonialism, as well as of dictators.

In a word, the close relationship of Churchill and Roosevelt endured to the point of saving the world from Hitler. It was not to continue when urgently needed to save the world from Stalin.

In truth, beyond winning the war, the objectives of the two leaders had never been the same. Nor were the purposes of the peoples they represented the same. One leader spoke for Britain out of a long experience of the vicissitudes of the politics of Europe. The other spoke for America out of an experience not so lengthy, but very vivid, of freedom from the problems of the balance of power, and a belief that unity of all nations was possible if certain basic purposes were agreed upon.

Furthermore, Britain had waged war for its very life and would continue to live in its citadel with only a moat to separate it from a dangerous Europe. Americans had waged war, from a continental fortress surrounded by vast oceans, to insure that wars would not be waged again.

Near the end of the year 1943, President Roosevelt expressed in fullest terms the basic approach that he took to the entire problem of world maladjustment caused by war. Addressing representatives of forty-four nations (comprising the United Nations Relief and Rehabilitation Administration) [31] at Washington on November 9, he said:

> When victory comes there can certainly be no secure peace until there is a return of law and order in the oppressed countries, until the peoples of these countries have been restored to a normal, healthy, and self-sustaining existence. This means

---

[31] Not to be confused with the later United Nations Organization.

that the more quickly and effectually we apply measures of relief and rehabilitation, the more quickly will our own boys overseas be able to come home.

We have acted together with the other United Nations in harnessing our raw materials, our production, and our other resources to defeat the common enemy. We have worked together with the United Nations in full agreement and action in the fighting on land, and on the sea and in the air. We are now about to take an additional step in the combined actions that are necessary to win the war and to build the foundation for a secure peace.

The sufferings of the little men and women who have been ground under the Axis heel can be relieved only if we utilize the production of *all* the world to balance the want of *all* the world. In U.N.R.R.A. we have devised a mechanism based on the processes of true democracy . . . that can go far toward accomplishment of such an objective in the days and months of desperate emergency that will follow the overthrow of the Axis.

As in most of the difficult and complex things in life, Nations will learn to work together only by actually working together. Why not? We Nations have common objectives. It is, therefore, with a lift of hope, that we look on the signing of this agreement by all of the United Nations as a means of joining them together still more firmly.[32]

Such an appeal arose directly out of the fundamental belief of millions of Americans, regardless of party or of national origin.

But as President Roosevelt approached the end of the road he had traveled between internationalists and isolationists—a road that he had first termed aid-in-order-to-avoid-war—he found himself facing two antagonists. Having abandoned continentalism and having embraced what has been termed collective internationalism, he was faced with the certainty that each of his potent allies had entered upon the building of a new world order with quite other ideas.

Britain was of course pledged to an imperialistic internationalism, however tempered by self-government in its dominions.

---

[32] *Public Papers, 1943*, pp. 503-504.

Russia was devoted to international communism—despite all gestures to the contrary.[33] To arrange for the exploitation of these conflicting ideas in a world forum was to insure deadly and continuous conflict, even if the United States had not found both inimical to its own purposes.

To the people of the United States it was to be expected that this alignment would seem confusing. It did. But in due time, clearer lines of division appeared. When the war ended, the old continentalism reappeared in the United States. But the parties to the most vigorous debate were those who favored a United Nations Organization devoted to democracy and those who would accept the United Nations as a means to enlarge the areas open to communism. Democracy faced communism—at home and abroad.

---

[33] For example, on May 22, 1943, Moscow announced the dissolution, on May 15, of the Third International (Comintern).

Chapter XVII

1944: TRIUMPH AT HOME

UNDER A PARLIAMENTARY FORM of government there would have been no general election in the United States in 1944. The war policies of the President were not in general dispute, as had been his foreign policy programs four years earlier. Although approaching a climax, the war had not been won. As yet the President's plans for the peace, well advanced by the Committee on Post War Planning in the State Department, were not in general public discussion. His party had strong majorities in both Houses of Congress.

The Democratic party leaders were dismayed that in an election year they had to consider—and vote upon—an increased tax bill as proposed by the President. They prepared a bill of their own which the President vetoed. This was followed by a violent outburst of intra-party quarreling in the Senate, as well as in the House. At the climax, Senator Alben W. Barkley resigned as party Leader, denouncing the President's program. Subsequently the Senate Democrats re-elected Barkley and passed their own bill over the President's veto. The President acquiesced.

On the issues that were first in the minds of voters, a powerful minority opposition had not developed. There was of course plenty of criticism, most of it familiar throughout the preceding twelve years. Yet no opposing national leader commanded the support of a minority that could have demanded a vote of no-confidence on any major issue.

Had there been in the government of the United States a provision that ex-Presidents have seats in the Senate, unquestionably Mr. Hoover would have presented there an indictment of the policies of the administration. Throughout the twelve years of Roosevelt rule, the former President had been, in speech, article, and book, a critic of the Roosevelt policies, domestic and foreign. Mr. Hoover had, as well, presented alternative programs. He held a large following and exercised great influence.

But in the United States as it was, a Presidential election came, and the issue was the President himself. Should he continue to lead? The Presidential campaign of 1944 gave Mr. Roosevelt opportunity to state once more his objectives: to win the war for the United States; to establish a United Nations Organization; and also to provide safeguards for the economic structure that was to be the United States in a world recovering from war.

The President did not need to elaborate upon his political objectives within the United States, for those were written into the history of twelve years in office. As he was to say in July, "the very simple issue is the record of the administration." Objectives could, however, be restated for the benefit of the new voters, for the encouragement of the vast governmental staff, and for the guidance of the electorate as a whole.

For such a task, the President was well prepared in his own thought and by the personal advisers who were to give him continuous aid in this test of strength. But there was for a time fairly general agreement—even among those who were most devoted to personal rule as a necessity—that the state of the President's health in 1944 might dictate retirement. The strain of the war years had been terrific, and the President had been twelve years in office.[1]

---

[1] A. Merriman Smith, who saw the President daily, wrote of the press conferences, "We saw Franklin D. Roosevelt die over a period of about a year." (*Thank You, Mr. President*, p. 1). See Herman E. Bateman, *The Election of 1944 and Foreign Policy* (Doctoral Dissertation, Stanford University, 1953), pp. 308-335, "The Issue of the President's Health."

Personal rule in war had brought its natural result. There was no one but the President to assume the guidance of Congress, the direction of military operations, and the leadership of the people. All this could not be done by a designated successor. Yet the President, expressing his own feeling in the matter, in a letter of March 13, 1944, to Benjamin V. Cohen said, "I am feeling plaintive." [2]

How far the people of the United States found themselves the prisoners of their own action is seen in the fact that there was very wide agreement that President Roosevelt—if he were able to do so—should perform the supremely important task of leading them.

Millions of Americans were not in a mood—in 1944—to consider the possibility that they had made a mistake in becoming involved in the war, or in waging the war as they did. They were disposed to remember that many of those now seeking to take power from the administration and the Democratic party had opposed measures for security, for defense and for aid in the years 1939 to 1941. They were not yet much moved by charges that inept diplomacy had brought Japan into war with the United States and had given its people the humiliation of Pearl Harbor. Nor as yet did a considerable majority feel that Russia was an enemy of the United States.

To many a student of the Presidential campaigns of Franklin Roosevelt, the campaign of 1944 has seemed to be an anticlimax. As a campaigner, Mr. Roosevelt was known more widely and more thoroughly than any of his predecessors, or any of those who had campaigned for the Presidency. What now could be said by advocate—or opponent—that had not been said?

As early as January, the President approved of a plan to have a report prepared and issued by the Democratic National Committee, showing in agriculture, labor, banking and housing the national situation in 1933 and comparing it with that in 1944.[3]

The war that absorbed general interest throughout the year 1944, as it had the three years preceding, revealed the President

---

[2] *Personal Letters, 1928-1945,* II, 1501. Cohen had suggested that Mr. Roosevelt not run for a fourth term, but become chief executive officer of the postwar United Nations Organization.

[3] Roosevelt to Lowell Mellett, *Personal Letters, 1928-1945,* II, 1487.

as primarily Commander-in-Chief. In this role he had displayed qualities of leadership well known to everyone. His opponents now in the campaign felt reasonably free to point out his familiar weaknesses and his usual mistakes. Even had the President not been the center of discussion in 1936 and 1940, he would have been in 1944. Personal leadership was definitely the issue.[4]

The President's announcement of candidacy was made on July 11. To meet the charge of too long continuance in power, his reply was that he was drafted in the emergency. On the whole, that assertion was accepted as an accurate statement. Closely akin to this acceptance was a widespread feeling that at such a critical juncture in waging war and preparing for peace, it would be unwise to change leaders.

Pushed to the limit, the claim of need for a change meant pressing the charges on the way Americans were waging war and the way they were preparing for peace. For the President had been the guiding and often the determining force in both fields. It was hard to establish the point that those basic issues ought to be debated in 1944.

A point of attack within the Democratic party would have been to name a candidate other than the President. Under some forms of government, it would have been possible to shift leaders and move to first place one of the President's close supporters. In American party practice, however, a Presidential candidate (whether in office or newly presented) had to be nominated in a national convention and then elected by popular vote. President Roosevelt could accept a draft, but he could not plan to step down and let Vice-President Wallace take power in January of 1945. Indeed, Mr. Roosevelt failed to secure the renomination of Mr. Wallace to the Vice-Presidential candidacy in July.[5]

---

[4] "My objectives as I see them call for finesse, a skillful statecraft that cannot be exposed to view," said Mr. Roosevelt, according to an article by Forrest Davis, published in the *Saturday Evening Post*, in May of 1944. This article had been submitted to Stephen Early, the President's secretary. It is not known whether the President saw the article in manuscript, which was returned to Mr. Davis on April 1. The President wrote Davis on June 14: ". . . your two articles, while containing, of course, a number of minor mistakes which do not affect the sense of the articles, are exceedingly good and exceedingly fair." (Letter of Director of Roosevelt Library, December 10, 1953, to author.)

[5] Wehle, *op. cit.*, p. 223, states that in conversation with the President in which Wehle termed Wallace "as superficial and impulsive," on March 15,

The failure to renominate Vice-President Henry Wallace has been given too little critical examination. His personal weaknesses—as a candidate—have been emphasized. This was in itself an admission of lack of a majority favoring the New Deal.

The President's part in the substitution of Truman for Wallace has been given extensive treatment by all who have written of the 1944 Convention. The facts seem to be, as far as the President was concerned, as follows:

He was aware of the distrust of Wallace expressed by various elements in the Roosevelt following. Mr. Roosevelt himself discussed substitutes with many persons. He expressed lack of conviction that many of those suggested would meet the need. Finally on July 14, he wrote to Senator Jackson, who was to be permanent chairman of the convention, stating that if "I were a delegate, I would personally vote for his [Henry Wallace's] renomination."

But on July 19 the President wrote to Democratic National Committee Chairman Hannegan, "You have written me about Harry Truman and Bill Douglas. I should, of course, be very glad to run with either of them." Hannegan used this statement with great effectiveness, but actually the decision was not made by Roosevelt. The convention was under the control of a combination of political forces that made sure that the "joint ticket" would poll the full vote of the Democrats.

The elimination of Wallace and the nomination of Truman by the Democratic National Convention is seen in perspective as revealing again, as so often in the twelve years of Roosevelt's rule, the true nature of the party basis for his success.

It was said at the Chicago Convention that no one except Roosevelt could unite the nation on the administration policies —in war and in peace. That was true. Yet more important was the fact that no one in sight would be certain to hold together the factions of the party that had brought success at the polls. No one knew this better than Mr. Roosevelt.

Had the President held a national following above and beyond party lines in 1944, he need not have depended as he did at Chicago upon a political convention. This party gathering,

1944, Franklin Roosevelt asked him, "What do you think of Truman?" but gave no indication of his intention.

in spite of every evidence of disunity, emerged with a ticket that would be backed at the November election by labor leaders and many of their followers (heavily Democratic), by the Political Action Committee (Democratic), the Solid South (Democratic), and by the Democratic city, state, and national machine organizations.

There were some who said that the election of 1944 was a fine demonstration to the world that Americans could pause and consider during war whether the President or someone else should be returned to Presidential office. Of course the United States had held a wartime election in 1864. But such commentators had little real comprehension of the place that party organization had come to occupy in American politics.

There was great vitality in the Republican opposition—greater than at any time in the previous twelve years. Basically this was due to facts that have been overlooked in emphasis on the small Republican membership in Senate and House and the long absence of Republicans from participation in the administration of government.

Republicans knew that the longer the lease of power to the Democrats, the more decided would be popular unrest and desire for change. As experience had repeatedly shown, twelve years was about the limit of endurance of one political party in power. Moreover, the war had brought back into national consciousness the high importance of the superior qualities in business, finance, and industry long associated with Republican leadership. Furthermore, the war had tended to heal pre-war breaches among the Republicans on questions of preparedness, defense, and national security.

To contest the re-election of Mr. Roosevelt, a national political party did not need to be organized. It was already in existence. However, the Republican party as a whole was still badly divided, as it had been throughout the Roosevelt years, upon issues and upon choice of national leadership. But more important than these divisions, which had left scars and had given some aspirants repudiation the public could not forget, was the fact that in thirty-eight of the states existed a powerful Republican party organization. In more than half of the states this organization had a majority support of the voters within the areas of its control.

This national party organization—built upon state organizations and relying for its lifeblood in money, personnel, and effort upon party organizations within county, district, and precinct—was to place a candidate for the Presidency in the contest. It was to formulate a campaign of real distinction; it was to encourage and support Congressional and senatorial candidates. It was a gigantic organization. Irrespective of surface manifestations of lack of popular interest in its activity, it intended to provide a real—and, as was hoped, a successful—political campaign. It was to spend seventeen million dollars.

Thus, the Commander-in-Chief of a nation in the throes of global war was to be subjected to a national movement to recall him from office and place in his stead an opponent who, if elected, would take over the burdens of war-making and the plans for peace-making. The Commander-in-Chief, who was at the time in the midst of negotiations with the Allies, was to find it necessary to defend himself and his record in the critical months from July to November. Neither Stalin nor Churchill faced repudiation by his own people in 1944.[6] Roosevelt did.

The Republicans did not choose to offer their leader of 1940, Wendell Willkie, who had in that campaign challenged the President so effectively and won wide acknowledgment as a statesman of world vision. Neither did the Republicans choose as their candidate their former President who for twelve years had challenged the views of Mr. Roosevelt on every major issue.

Mr. Hoover, appearing before the convention, attacked "personal diplomacy." In a telling and prophetic utterance, he said: "And the Teheran Conference raises another question. Under our form of government the President cannot speak for the Congress or the conclusions of American public opinion. . . . These do not come by secret diplomacy." [7]

The Republicans chose to lead them and to formulate the campaign of repudiation, a candidate of neither great national nor international reputation who two years earlier had been elected governor of the President's own state. In choosing

---

[6] Later Churchill anticipated a general election "after Hitler's defeat."
[7] *Addresses Upon the American Road, 1941-1945*, p. 253.

Thomas E. Dewey, the Republicans took a familiar American road, and the Republican campaign proved to be familiar in plan and in development. It was highly dangerous to the Democrats because of its lack of coherence. It matched the character of the opposition. Incoherence had won Presidential campaigns before.

Appealing to the American people, who were absorbed in the winning of the war, the Republicans naturally asked that the record of twelve years be considered as a basis for judging the future. They asserted that the record was a black one. They had said that before. But the emphasis they now gave it was sinister. And this emphasis was remembered even after the campaign was lost.

The Republicans asserted that the costs of government were assuring national bankruptcy. They pointed out that, quite apart from the questionable desirability of objectives that cost so much, were two glaring weaknesses they could correct: the chaos in Washington caused by makeshift bureaucracy; and the waste due to faulty and sometimes dishonest administration. These were serious and important indictments. Inevitably a campaign of such factually based argument brought censure upon the President himself.

In a sense this was unfair, and the people thought so. The costs, the waste, the inefficiency were inherent in the American political system as operated by the party in power. Administration heads, Congressional committees, wartime agencies, most of all the Democratic National Committee and its close associates—were not directly blamed. They were not running for the Presidency. Yet the only way to change the situation was to defeat the President and thereby change the political personnel of the rulers in Washington.

All of the charges against Mr. Roosevelt that had been made in previous campaigns were repeated. Accusation ranged from gossip as to petty peccadilloes—so dear to the masses of men and women—to condemnation of a determined, selfish, and utterly amoral dictatorship. It is doubtful whether any of these charges, large or small, had much effect upon anyone who did not already believe them.

But one fact of importance in the President's personal leadership did warrant careful consideration by a careful voter. Here

too, the basic question was overridden with so much supposition, innuendo, and falsehood that it is difficult, even after the
event, to discern the real facts. The campaign ended with no
absolute certainty upon this question on which the facts seemed
so much at variance. The question was this. Had the President
the physical ability to continue to carry on the duties of his
office?

To meet the charges, mostly unpublished, of severe illness
and possibly impending death, the President's method was to
show himself to the people as he did in the closing days of the
campaign. Yet this demonstration of endurance proved nothing. It persuaded many, it is true. But the very effort of the
President demonstrated how important was the real issue upon
which real evidence was lacking.

One episode of the campaign casts light upon the methods of
Mr. Roosevelt. On July 13 he wrote from the White House to
Wendell Willkie in New York.

> What I want to tell you is that I want to see you when I come
> back, but not on anything in relationship to the present cam-
> paign. I want to talk with you about the future, even the some-
> what distant future, and in regard to the foreign relations
> problems of the immediate future.

> When you see in the papers that I am back, will you get in
> touch with General Watson? We can arrange a meeting either
> here in Washington or, if you prefer, at Hyde Park—wholly off
> the record or otherwise, just as you think best.[8]

Four days later from the "Presidential Special" train passing
through Nebraska, Mr. Roosevelt wrote former Senator George
W. Norris, who had written the President protesting against
the possible nomination of Willkie as Vice-Presidential candidate on the Roosevelt ticket, "I don't think there is any possible
danger of Willkie, though feelers were put out about a week
ago." [9]

After the President's return, the *New York Times* carried an
account of the President's letter to Willkie of July 13. Asked
to comment, Mr. Willkie said: "It is true that Mr. Roosevelt

---

[8] *Personal Letters, 1928-1945*, II, 1520.
[9] *Ibid.*, 1522-1523.

has written me asking that I confer with him. I would much
prefer that no such conference occur until after the election,
but if the President of the United States wishes to see me
sooner, I shall of course comply." [10]

At a subsequent press conference (August 21), the President
in answer to a question said that he had not invited Willkie to
Washington.[11] Reminded by his secretary that he had, the
President then wrote again to Willkie, saying that he had forgotten the letter of July 13 and adding:

> The interesting thing is how word of my note to you got to
> the Press. I have been trying to find out where the leak was
> down here, as I regarded it as a purely personal note between
> you and me. As far as I can remember I said nothing about it
> to anybody, though it is possible that I told Leo Crowley that
> I was going to ask you if we could talk the subject over. I am
> awfully sorry that there was any leak on a silly thing like this
> —but I still hope that at your convenience—there is no im-
> mediate hurry—you will stop in and see me if you are in Wash-
> ington or run up to Hyde Park if you prefer.[12]

The editors of the *Personal Letters* in a note state, "There is
little doubt that F.D.R. genuinely was looking forward to
working with Willkie on the peace settlements. F.D.R. knew
Hull wanted to retire and he was already casting about for
someone to become the executive of the nascent United Nations. But before the matter could be worked out one way or
another, Willkie died, on October 8th." [13]

Having accepted the nomination, Mr. Roosevelt intended to
be re-elected. As he saw it, everything that he had declared to
be a prime objective would be in jeopardy if he were not re-
elected. He had sacrificed Henry Wallace, to be sure, that the

[10] *Ibid.*, 1532.
[11] On this day Willkie met John Foster Dulles, adviser to Governor Dewey,
at the Dulles residence in New York. They issued a statement to the effect that
their conference had to do with international organization to follow the end of
the war. Willkie's biographer states that both agreed upon the need of an
international police force. Only by act of Congress could American participation
in such a plan be brought about. . . . But Willkie felt that Congressional
control should end there. Willkie felt that use of force must be left to the
discretion of the President. "Dulles was loath to leave the President free from
continuous legislative supervision." (M. E. Dillon, *Wendell Willkie*, p. 352.)
[12] *Personal Letters, 1928-1945*, II, 1532.
[13] *Ibid.*, pp. 1532-1533.

uncertainty of his own re-election might not be too great. He said that he would not wage a campaign. This was nonsense. Everything he did or said was a contribution to a campaign on his own behalf. Visiting the army and navy leaders in the Pacific, reporting to the people from Bremerton, Washington, on the progress of the Pacific War, visiting innumerable war plants, even remaining in seclusion for recurrent periods—explained as a part of wartime security—all emphasized that President Roosevelt was the candidate and that he was the issue.

The final plunge into the campaign, as understood in the game of politics, came in September in the President's address to the Teamsters' Union. Only a people blinded by twelve years of propaganda and absorbed in the winning of a war of survival could overlook the blatancy of the appeal in that address. The response of the audience present and on the air was clear proof that a large portion of the voters would follow through and support their champion.[14]

Early in October the President asserted that he had not sought and would not have the support of Communists. Nevertheless, had the Democratic candidate not attracted in New York State the support of the American Labor party (496,405 votes) and the American Liberal party [15] (329,235 votes), the first of these parties known to have heavy Communist membership—the President would have lost his own state to the Republican candidate.[16]

The closing ten days of the campaign included major addresses in Philadelphia, Chicago, and Boston, as well as much publicized appearances in New York. The fifty-mile drive in an open car, part of the time in a driving rain at a freezing temperature, symbolized, in its emphasis upon the vigor, stamina, and resolution of the candidate, how important it seemed that this leader be continued in power. It was final proof—if proof be necessary—that as far as Mr. Roosevelt was concerned, ballots in the United States of America were won through the compre-

---

[14] Perhaps the clearest view of the President's inner resolve at the time appears in the words of Rosenman, writing his highly eulogistic Introduction to the *Public Papers, 1944-1945*, p. vii, when Rosenman says, "The speech [before the Teamsters' Union] had just the results the President intended."

[15] Wallace and Truman addressed a Liberal party meeting in Madison Square Garden on October 31, 1944.

[16] Robinson, *They Voted for Roosevelt*, p. 199.

hension and emotion of the masses. The manifold issues raised by the opposition need not be discussed except in the most general terms. The important point was to continue in the government those who worked continuously on behalf of the people.

The American people in their history had had much experience with such assertions by prominent leaders. Sometimes they had followed these leaders for a time. Oftener the people had repudiated them after a while. What predecessor of Franklin Roosevelt would have taken the course he did in the campaign of 1944?

But nothing succeeds like success, and Mr. Roosevelt had succeeded in politics. He was to add another victory at the polls. All of the "ifs" and "buts" and "might-have-beens" were as nothing in the eyes of those who saw swift results and listened eagerly to be told hourly what all of this popular support of the popular leader meant.

In reality, the election was not easily won, and the victory was not overwhelming, as earlier victories had seemed to be. The total vote was less by two million, though including 2,691,160 ballots of men in the armed services. The President had in the Democratic vote a smaller percentage (51.7%) of the total vote than in any of the previous elections.[17]

Yet to the man in the street here was the one leader who had pushed aside all other leaders within his own Democratic party. He was, furthermore, the man who had defeated Hoover, Landon, Willkie—and now Dewey, who had polled a huge vote in 45.9 percent of the total.[18] Roosevelt was a man who had found it necessary on occasion to retreat before the demands of the Congress or of the Court, but who was always supported by the people. So the image of the champion campaigner appeared to all.

But a test of Democratic national appeal in 1944 is to be found in a comparison with the vote of 1936, when Roosevelt had 60 percent of the total vote. Outside of the South, the Democrats had a lead of 6,000,000 in 1936; in 1944 it was less than 800,000.[19]

---

[17] Ibid., p. 41.
[18] Ibid., p. 41.
[19] Ibid., pp. 32-40, including maps of the vote by counties.

Of this gigantic game of politics—played incessantly during the stresses and strains of a global war—there was little comprehension and less interest on the part of the people as a whole. It was necessarily of first concern to the President and his advisers.

However much the President stressed united objectives in explanation of the war in which the American people were engaged, the war's existence rather than its effect dominated public discussion. This hard fact emphasized the dangers that lay in any interruption of the program by a change of administration and caused the outcome of the election to seem inevitable to many who had not voted for the Democratic candidate.

Mr. Roosevelt had appeared in the closing days of this campaign much as he appeared in earlier campaigns. This in itself made a deep impression on his audiences. He emphasized five points. He reviewed the events of the war and made it clear that the United States under his leadership was succeeding. He reviewed, particularly in his address at Chicago, the record on behalf of the masses of people and promised in a new Economic Bill of Rights a continuance of prosperity for all.[20] In ending his campaign at Boston, he reiterated that "we" had been attacked and therefore "we" were at war. He repudiated communism, but did not associate himself with those who were suspicious of "our" ally, Russia. In his final appeal, made in New York, he emphasized over and over again the basic idealism of the concept of the United Nations.

Between the nomination in July and the intensive weeks closing the Presidential campaign, the President had conferred with the naval and military chiefs in the Pacific, Admiral Nimitz and General MacArthur. The decision to retake the Philippines was made. Following this, attempts were made by the President to unify the Allied effort in China. Vice-President Wallace had gone to China in the spring on such a mission, and during the summer and early fall, two additional missions had been sent by the President, one headed by Donald Nelson and

---

[20] Public Papers, 1944-1945, p. 371.

a second by Patrick Hurley.[21] The primary purpose of each was to bring about such concentration of Allied efforts as to make China a real barrier to future Japanese advance. The failures of the missions were due to the division of the Chinese between the followers of Chiang Kai-shek and the Communists.

Writing to Joseph Stalin just before leaving from San Diego on this trip, Mr. Roosevelt acknowledged "the very delightful framed photograph of you," and said: "The speed of the advance of your armies is amazing and I wish much that I could visit you to see how you are able to maintain your communications and supplies to the advancing troops." [22]

At Quebec in September there was agreement between Prime Minister Churchill and the President that British effort would be increased in the Pacific once the European war approached an end.

Meanwhile, the conferences at Bretton Woods and Dumbarton Oaks were preparing the way in post-war planning, not only in terms of international organization, but specifically in terms of international monetary policy.

Whereas the enemies in 1944 were Germany and Japan, as everyone knew, and the great ally was the British Commonwealth of Nations, the uncertain element, as was not so generally recognized at the moment but came to be as plans for the future unfolded, was the intention of followers of communism symbolized in Europe by Soviet Russia and in the Far East by the Chinese Communists.

The President's own view of the campaign was expressed in general terms on the eve of the election and in public comment upon the outcome. But in private correspondence he was less restrained. Just before Christmas in writing to a friend, he summarized his feeling then by saying that he felt black and blue "after going through the dirtiest campaign in all history." [23]

In thanking Sidney Hillman for his aid, the President said after the election:

[21] The President sent to Chiang Kai-shek a letter dated August 19, 1944, introducing Hurley as former Secretary of War and Nelson as head of the War Production Board. ". . . they are both literally my personal representatives," the President added. (*Personal Letters, 1928-1945*, II, 1530-1531.)

[22] *Ibid.*, II, 1526.

[23] *Ibid.*, II, 1563.

I was glad to hear that the CIO in Chicago authorized the continuation of the PAC. I can think of nothing more important in the years to come than the continuing political education and political energy of the people, who do the jobs of this land, in determination that the American nation shall do the great job it can do for all.[24]

To Henry Wallace, the President wrote on November 27th: "I do not think there is any man in America who understands the meaning of the campaign we won this year better than you. . . . You and I know that we won only because we have stood and must stand for those things closest to the hearts of the people. They voted, I think, for a faith in the confidence that we would carry that faith forward to full victory for freedom on this earth and to the use of our full powers for plenty here at home." [25]

In a letter to his son James on November 13, the President said of his opponent, Thomas E. Dewey, "The little man made me pretty mad." [26]

In acknowledging a letter of October 28 from Hamilton Holt, the President wrote him on November 20:

I hate the fourth term as much as you do—and the third term as well—but I do not worry about it so much as a matter of principle. It would be a mistake, of course, to establish it as a tradition but I think I can well plead extenuating circumstances! The real meat of the question is not the length of term but the continued opportunity of the voters of the country freely to express themselves every four years. And there is the further question of the personality of the individual. You and I know plenty of people who love power of a certain type and who, with perfectly good intentions, would hate to give it up. I am not one of this type, as you know. For as far as individual

---

[24] *Ibid.*, p. 1557. Hillman and Philip Murray had issued a statement on October 7 calling upon labor to get out the vote for Roosevelt. The Political Action Committee claimed after the election that their support had elected 17 to the Senate and 120 to the House.

[25] *Ibid.*, 1557-1558. In August Roosevelt had told Wallace he could have any office in the administration except the State Department. Early in 1945 the President asked Jones to retire from the Commerce Department and Wallace was finally confirmed for the secretaryship of that department.

[26] *Ibid.*, p. 1553. Rosenman states in *Public Papers, 1944-1945*, p. viii, "There were several reasons for his campaign enthusiasm. The first was his personal dislike for his opponent."

preference goes I would, quite honestly, have retired to Hyde Park with infinite pleasure in 1941.[27]

In response to a telegram of congratulations from Norman Thomas, the President said:

Many thanks for that mighty nice note of yours. We certainly have lots of work ahead. I was amused during the campaign to think that now I am very far to the left of you. Do come to see me one of these days.[28]

To his press conference on December 9, 1944, the President said: "I am going down the whole line a little left of center."

To British Socialist Harold J. Laski, on January 16, 1945, the President wrote:

Our goal is, as you say, identical for the long range objectives but there are so many new problems arising that I still must remember that the war is yet to be won. I am inclined to think that at the meeting with Marshal Stalin and the Prime Minister I can put things on a somewhat higher level than they have been for the past two or three months.[29]

---

[27] Copy in Roosevelt Library. Quoted by Herman Blum, *One Star Final*, pp. 250-251.

[28] Roosevelt to Thomas, Nov. 21, 1944, in President's Personal File, 4840, Roosevelt Library.

[29] President's Personal File 3014, Roosevelt Library.

Chapter XVIII

THE SHAPE OF THE FUTURE

THE FOURTH INAUGURATION of Franklin Roosevelt was held on January 20, 1945, at the White House rather than at the Capitol. This had been the President's wish: he stressed simplicity and economy. At a press conference in November, in discussing plans for the inauguration, he had been asked whether there would be a parade and he had answered, "No. Who is there here to parade?"

The nation was at war on every front, but there was an overwhelming desire to finish and to resume the ways of peace. The President, in a radio address to the nation on January 6, had said, "We and our Allies will go on fighting together to ultimate victory." And in his inaugural address two weeks later, he stressed the fruits of victory:

> We have learned that we cannot live alone, at peace; that our own well-being is dependent on the well-being of other Nations, far away. . . . We have learned to be citizens of the world, members of the human community.[1]

---

[1] *Public Papers, 1944-1945*, p. 524. This address passed through several stages of preparation. In "Some Thoughts for Inaugural Speech," the President had written, January 6, 1945, "This country had to fear fear itself." This did not appear in the inaugural address. (Fourth Inaugural File, Roosevelt Library.)

In this expression of belief, President Roosevelt called for action.

As he entered upon his fourth term, he was burdened with greater tasks and faced with more intricate problems than ever before. The war raging in Europe and the Far East must be brought to a successful conclusion. This task had filled the days —and the nights—for more than three years. There must be such conclusion of that war as to insure a sound and expanding economy for the nation. This involved the adjustment of the nation to the economy of peace, as well as the distribution of diplomatic forces in such fashion as to insure a profitable relationship of the American economy to that of an exhausted and disrupted world.

As no part of the world had been free of the war, so no nation in the world lacked a role to play in whatever plans were instituted by the United States for a world economy. The President had led in stating objectives. The agencies of the American government had led in providing "blueprints" for the peace. Now the test of accomplishment involved tasks of leadership greater than any man had ever undertaken. In his message to the Congress, Mr. Roosevelt made it clear that days of stress and strain lay ahead.

The recent Presidential campaign had made the President fully aware of the multiplicity of interests and demands among the American people. He and his military advisers could move with certainty in the waging of war. He and his diplomatic aides could plan with care and caution the charters for international action. Yet in the task of political leadership within the United States, the President and his party associates must face the opposition and criticism of a growing minority—close to a majority of the voters of the country. All matters of budget, of expenditure, and of taxation must be handled in such fashion as to bring satisfaction to farmers, laborers, and white collar workers, at the same time that the financial structure was made to withstand the possibility of national bankruptcy.

Throughout the remaining months of his administration, the President's plea on all occasions was for unity of purpose and unity of action within the nation. As he emphasized the unity of the Allied powers in bringing the war to a conclusion, he asked of them that they form a more perfect union to carry forward the work for peace. At home, attacking the forces of opposition that on the whole had approved unity of action in war—but were preparing to oppose unity in time of peace—his dominant message was a call to the people to support the administration against this opposition. As always, he identified the program proposed in domestic and foreign affairs with the best interests of the masses of people in all lands.

It was a powerful appeal, deeply appreciated by all who believed in the President's objectives and still believed in the basic soundness of his program. But it had the weakness inherent in any such approach to problems that are not simple, upon which violent disagreement is assured, and wherein opposition —when it does appear—senses reason for resisting the very unity called for. Unity—as an objective—was in itself a denial of the basic soundness of democratic government. Unity had been needful in crisis, and as the events of the preceding twelve years had repeatedly shown, had accomplished "miracles." Yet in itself unity did not solve problems, and was always accompanied by compromises and arrangements that only deferred the day of reckoning.

No period of the President's direction of the foreign policy of the United States was so packed with events of transcendent importance for the future as the days between the middle of January, 1945, and his death in mid-April. The assault upon Germany from east and west entered what was to be its final phase. It was clear to Prime Minister Churchill, if not to President Roosevelt, that, while Hitler was to lose his battle against the Allies, Stalin was to emerge in the most powerful position in all central Europe.

At the same time, this impending crisis in Europe called for a declaration upon the part of Stalin as to the time that the Russians would enter the war of the Allies against the remaining member of the totalitarian group, Japan. That Stalin should bind himself to the entrance of Russia into the projected union of powers that was to emerge before the end of the war seemed all-important to President Roosevelt.

That the President had taken the initiative in seeking a conference with Churchill and Stalin, after the outcome of the election of 1944, was known. He felt—and this feeling was expressed by those about him—that the successful outcome of the war in Europe would raise at once questions of the disposition of Germany, as well as of the adjustment of boundaries in eastern Europe. Roosevelt knew that Churchill was deeply concerned as to the fate of Poland. The President was uncertain of Russian participation in the war upon Japan. He realized that all of the plans for a development of the powers of the United Nations Organization—foreshadowed in 1942—depended upon unity of action of Russia, Britain, and the United States.

To a considerable degree, the apprehensions of the President were well founded. Although a strong minority of the American people had "matured" in their thought of international relations since the United Nations Declaration of January, 1942, it was also evident that the more vocal elements in both political parties were now thinking in nationalist terms. On the surface, this meant an acceptance of plans for international security, but primarily, it was an acceptance of the great power of the United States as a nation among nations.

Republican leader Senator Arthur Vandenberg of Michigan, in January of 1945, was thought to be forsaking isolationism. He was; yet a careful reading of his plea for a permanent alliance of great powers leads to the conclusion that he was moved by the possibility that the United States—through its Executive —might act quickly and effectively in the international alliance to prevent outbreak of war in the future.

The President, in selecting his advisers for the forthcoming conference at Yalta in the Crimea, stressed the military purpose of the conference. It was just that—a military conference—to Stalin. But, as the record shows, military conferences during the war included in their purpose the entire range of diplomatic maneuver and of great power politics.

The major difference between the conferences of Yalta and Teheran was, of course, that by the beginning of 1945 the Axis was on the defensive on all fronts, and the problems of the post-war world took equal place on the agenda with military matters. Political discussions consumed most of the time at Yalta, whereas at Teheran military affairs had dominated the discussions.

A complete understanding of the Yalta agreements is to be

found not only in their purpose as conceived by Mr. Roosevelt, but also in their accomplishment of Russian ends. Stalin was to win acknowledgment at Yalta of what he had been moving to gain throughout the period of the war. He placed no reliance upon international pacts or organizations. He had used every means at his command to thwart British purposes on the continent, and he had so developed his military and diplomatic policy that in the end—that is, at Yalta—just before the collapse of Germany, it was Soviet Russia that was left in a dominant position in every part of eastern Europe, and that was prepared to make a stand for control of Berlin.

"It was inconceivable to me that Stalin would submit to the re-establishment of effective sovereignty in Poland, Latvia, Lithuania, and Estonia," wrote Admiral Leahy afterwards. "It also appeared probable that the Soviet Government, with its superior military power and its possibility of making a separate compromise peace with Germany, could force acceptance of Soviet desires in this matter upon America and Great Britain." [2]

Stalin's lack of interest in world organization could easily be explained in view of his dominant intent that Russia should be protected from its enemies. This meant that communism was to be protected within Russia by its extension outside of Russia.

Yet Mr. Roosevelt had said just before the conference at Teheran, "I just have a hunch that Stalin . . . doesn't want anything but security for his country, and I think that if I give him everything I possibly can and ask nothing from him in return, *noblesse oblige,* he won't try to annex anything and will work with me for a world of democracy and peace." [3]

The President, accompanied by Admiral Leahy on the cruiser *Quincy,* had arrived at Malta on February 2, 1945. Here he was met by General Marshall and Admiral King. Both Marshall and King felt that the President, despite his ten-day vacation on the journey, was "a very sick man." [4] Prime Minister Churchill

[2] Leahy, *op. cit.,* p. 185.
[3] William C. Bullitt, "How We Won the War and Lost the Peace," in *Life,* August 30, 1948.
[4] King and Whitehill, *op. cit.,* pp. 585-586. See W. G. Eliasberg, "How Long Was Roosevelt Ill Before His Death?" in *Diseases of the Nervous System,* XIV (November, 1953), 323-328, especially p. 327: ". . . there occur in Roosevelt's hand-writing an increasing number of signs of depressions, known from the hand-writing of circulatory depressives. . . . Roosevelt had an unusual ability

met Roosevelt at Malta, and they conferred on the reports of the military staff and on the agenda of the forthcoming conference. From here, "seven hundred persons, forming the British and American delegations," [5] went by air to the Crimea.

The American party included Secretary of State Stettinius, W. Averell Harriman, Ambassador to Russia, James F. Byrnes, who had been Director of War Mobilization, Chief of Staff Marshall, Admiral King, and a large party of State Department officials.

The conference began on February 4 and on February 11, 1945, the Yalta agreement was signed by Churchill, Roosevelt, and Stalin. Admiral Leahy was entrusted with the copy of the agreement, which he kept in his secret files at the White House.[6]

Of course it was to be expected that the military agreements were to be kept secret, particularly the time of Russia's entrance into the war against Japan. Yet Mr. Rosenman states that he does not understand the President's mistake in keeping secret the tentative agreement as to votes in the Assembly of the United Nations.

"Roosevelt apparently was prepared to make some concessions in order to get the machinery of the United Nations started. Therefore he had made no objections to the two extra Soviet votes.[7] Churchill, of course, did not object because he already had extra votes in the British Dominions," explained Admiral Leahy later. "I think the President realized the possibilities of adverse reaction back in Washington—because I learned later that he did secure from both Churchill and Stalin definite commitments that Britain and Russia would support the United States' request for two additional Assembly votes if such were proposed." [8]

Rosenman points out that shortly after the Yalta Conference,

---

to pull himself together and cover his depressions, along the lines of the 'keep smiling code' of our culture." The author concludes that these signs of increasing danger as early as 1940 were accentuated after 1944, and that Stalin and Churchill must have been aware of this at Yalta. He summarizes his view of "the tragic teachings of Roosevelt's decline."

[5] Churchill, *op. cit.*, p. 344.

[6] Leahy, *op. cit.*, p. 318.

[7] As late as the 998th—and last—press conference, April 5, 1945 (vol. 25, pp. 119-121, Roosevelt Library), the President held this view.

[8] Leahy, *op. cit.*, p. 310.

it became evident that a spirit of co-operation with the Soviet Union was not to continue. Mr. Roosevelt was shocked to learn that Stalin was not sending Molotov as head of the Russian delegation to the San Francisco Conference and protested to Stalin in a letter of March 24, 1945.[9]

Roosevelt "clearly was puzzled by what was happening. He was not yet ready to believe that Stalin had practiced pure deceit at Yalta," wrote Rosenman later. "He was under the impression that Stalin had been meeting stiff resistance from the Politburo since his return from the conference, and that he was yielding to it. The gradual breaking down of the close co-operation that had developed at Yalta had a depressing effect on the President. I am sure it hastened his death." [10]

Evidence of Roosevelt's recognition of the change in Russian attitude is seen in his cable of April 1 to Stalin [11] and a message to Churchill on April 12,[12] the day of the President's death. In these communications he maintained his position, in the view of Mr. Rosenman, that the agreements made at Yalta were not being kept by the Russian government and that the struggle as to the boundaries and spheres of influence in Europe and the Far East must go on.

Rosenman concludes his discussion of the Yalta Conference with a quotation from Secretary of State Stettinius: ". . . he had no illusions about the dangers and difficulties of dealing with the Soviet Union. President Roosevelt emphasized many times that we must keep trying with patience and determination to get the Russians to realize that it was in their own selfish interest to win the confidence of the other countries of the world." [13]

Yet to the end, as shown in his messages to Churchill and to

---

[9] *Personal Letters, 1928-1945*, II, 1577-1578. See Churchill, *op. cit.*, Book Two, chapter 7, "Soviet Suspicions," especially pp. 440-445.

[10] *Op. cit.*, p. 539. Sumner Welles (*Seven Decisions That Shaped History*. p. 165) wrote later: "When President Roosevelt returned from Yalta, he said that Stalin's position of supremacy seemed to have changed materially since the conference at Tehran. At Tehran Stalin had appeared to make decisions without hesitation, and with no indication that he needed to consult with any other Russian authorities. At Yalta, President Roosevelt felt that this was no longer the case. He had the feeling that the leaders of the Red Army had become far more influential. It is certainly true that from that time on there were many signs that Stalin's policy was designed to curry favor with the regenerated and transformed Red Army."

[11] *Public Papers, 1944-1945*, p. 546.

[12] *Ibid.*, pp. 546-547.

[13] *Ibid.*, p. 547.

Harriman in Moscow on the day of his death, the President maintained his tolerance and his faith that peace could be secured by the necessary unity of the great powers, including the Soviet Union. To Churchill he said, "We must be firm, however, and our course thus far has been correct." [14]

What did take place at Yalta? Despite the flood of statements already available, this question will be debated for years. Here is an outstanding example of the weakness of the President's view, so often expressed, of the wisdom of not keeping a record of conversations. Yet he had asked Admiral Leahy to attend "all these political meetings in order that we may have someone in whom I have full confidence who will remember everything that we have done." Leahy wrote later that he was "somewhat surprised at Roosevelt's request that I attend all the political meetings because he possessed what was practically a photographic memory. After his sudden death it occurred to me that perhaps at Yalta he may have had a premonition that he might not be present at the end of the war to call upon his memory for details in post-war discussions." [15]

Admiral Leahy noted that when the Yalta Conference was ended, "The American delegation, including Roosevelt and most of his staff, was weary but in a high mood. They felt the foundations of world peace had been laid in the eight days of almost continuous meetings at this former resort beside the Black Sea." [16]

---

[14] *Ibid.*, p. 547.

[15] Leahy, *op. cit.*, pp. 297-298. In addition to Leahy's account of the Yalta Conference, is the account by Secretary Edward R. Stettinius who took notes and later published the volume, *Roosevelt and the Russians; The Yalta Conference.* James F. Byrnes took shorthand notes in discussions he attended, and some of these appear in *Speaking Frankly.* Harry Hopkins took notes, some of which Sherwood provided in *Roosevelt and Hopkins,* but as Admiral Leahy noted, "at the time of the Crimean Conference the latter's [Hopkins'] prospects of survival were not promising." A State Department publication is forthcoming. The account of Prime Minister Churchill is given in Book Two, chapters 1-4 of *Triumph and Tragedy.* On July 13, 1951, former Ambassador to the Soviet Union W. Averell Harriman made a sworn statement on "Our Wartime Relations with the Soviet Union, Particularly as They Concern the Agreements Reached at Yalta," addressed to the Committees on Armed Services and Foreign Relations of the Senate in connection with the *Hearings on the Military Situation in the Far East,* printed as Part 5, Appendix of the Report, pp. 3328-3342, which was published August 17, 1951. See also *Hearings before the Committee on Foreign Relations, United States Senate, 83rd Congress, 1st Session, March 2-18, 1953.*

[16] Leahy, *op. cit.*, p. 291.

But Leahy noted that "There was another compelling factor that kept me from sharing in the feeling of great hope, almost exultation, that prevailed in our American delegation as we left Yalta, as to the practicability of maintaining world peace through the United Nations Organization. The essential agreement to destroy German militarism accepted at the conference would make Russia the dominant power in Europe. That in itself, in my opinion, carried a certainty of future international disagreements." [17]

Being, as he said, "of the firm opinion [about February 1, 1945] that our war against Japan had progressed to the point where her defeat was only a matter of time and attrition," Leahy wrote: "Therefore, we did not need Stalin's help to defeat our enemy in the Pacific. The Army did not agree with me, and Roosevelt was prepared to bargain with Stalin with the twofold objective of securing Russia's military assistance in the Japanese war and political support of the Soviet for the United Nations." [18]

The President was, according to Leahy, disappointed by Stalin's apparent unfamiliarity with the details of the United Nations Organization project, of which he had been apprised the preceding December.[19] "Churchill," reported Leahy, "in spite of an earlier coolness toward the United Nations idea, made a long talk apparently for the record, agreeing with the President's proposal. Stalin said he believed the greatest danger to the organization was differences among the three great powers and he wished to insure that in the future the Big Three would maintain a united front." It was Leahy's feeling at the time that "The Russian Chief of State . . . was definitely not in favor of organizing the United Nations." [20]

Against this background of attitude on the part of the three leaders, it is perhaps possible to draw a pattern of the struggle at Yalta.

---

[17] *Ibid.*, p. 323.

[18] *Ibid.*, p. 293.

[19] At Teheran, "Stalin did not seem to be favorably impressed by the President's proposal to give the smaller nations of the world an equal position in the preservation of world peace. Stalin stated his own ideas quite simply: If Russia, Great Britain, and the United States wanted to keep the world at peace, they had the military and economic power to do so and did not need the help of anybody else to police the globe." Leahy, *op. cit.*, pp. 209-210.

[20] *Ibid.*, p. 304.

Heretofore, Roosevelt had, as Churchill well knew, favored the strategy of the war that was advantageous to the Russians—although for reasons advantageous to American interest, partly in the saving of man power.[21] There was every reason for Stalin to feel that, in the triangle represented by Britain, the Soviet Union, and the United States, he could afford to humor President Roosevelt's wish with respect to the joint establishment of the United Nations.

It was agreed that reparations from Germany were to be paid in natural wealth, current production, and in forced labor. It was agreed that half of pre-war Poland was to go to Russia. The first was a violation of the Geneva Convention, and the second violated the purpose of the Atlantic Charter and the previously declared purposes of both Britain and the United States.

Two members of the triumvirate at Yalta, Roosevelt and Churchill, knew that the future—perhaps the very near future—held news of the existence of the most terrible weapon yet known in warfare. For more than two years prior to the final meeting of Roosevelt with Churchill and Stalin, the experiments in atomic bomb production had gone forward. General Graves on June 25, 1951, stated that he and Secretary Stimson had informed the President just before he left for Yalta that the atomic bomb was "a 99% certainty, and [would be] ready in August." [22]

Prime Minister Churchill later, at Potsdam, upon learning of the first successful atomic explosion "in the New Mexican desert," was to reflect that "Stalin's bargaining power, which he had used with such effect upon the Americans at Yalta, was therefore gone." [23]

---

[21] *Ibid.* Insisting that the Far Eastern agreements were made to reward the Soviet Union for entering the war against Japan at the earnest insistence of American military leaders and were, therefore, "not an item of foreign policy," but "war measures executed in time of emergency" to save human lives, Mr. Rosenman asks: ". . . what American mother or father whose boy was in the armed forces would have criticized the President in February, 1945, for making the military deal he did at the earnest solicitation of his military leaders?" *Public Papers, 1944-1945*, p. 543.

[22] *U.S. Senate Hearings on Military Situation in the Far East*, p. 3119. But Rosenman writes, in *Working with Roosevelt*, p. 535, "Neither the President nor anybody else at Yalta, in February, 1945, knew that the atomic bomb project was going to be successful."

[23] *Op. cit.*, p. 640.

Although the Far East had no part in formal discussion at Yalta, Ambassador Harriman informed Admiral Leahy that, at the private conference between Roosevelt and Stalin regarding Soviet participation in the war against Japan, it was agreed there were no decisions that could not be adjusted to the satisfaction of both nations. As reported by Harriman, Stalin made the following requests:

The Soviet wanted to obtain Port Arthur under a long-term lease.

Dairen was to be a free port.

The existing autonomy of Outer Mongolia would be preserved.

All of Sakhalin and the Kuril Islands would be returned to the Soviet Government.

The Soviet Government would be granted a lease of the Chinese railroads in Manchuria such as they had prior to the present war.

The fate of Indo-China would be open to discussion.

Siam was eventually to become an independent state.

American material would be provided for the Soviet war effort against Japan.

Lines of supply from the United States would be kept open.

American airplanes might be used from bases in Kamchatka and Eastern Siberia.[24]

The evidence from participants in the Yalta Conference thus far revealed is conflicting. But, as far as is now known, it was not the advice of his State Department, nor that of the President's military advisers that produced the final form of the agreements. As is now well known, Roosevelt and Stalin agreed substantially upon the items requested by Stalin on condition that the Russians enter the war against Japan.[25] It was understood that China should retain full sovereignty in Manchuria,

[24] Leahy, *op. cit.*, p. 310.
[25] Ambassador Harriman stated (*U. S. Senate Hearings on Military Situation in the Far East*, p. 3333): "President Roosevelt personally carried on with Stalin the negotiations leading up to the understanding on the Far East. I was present at the meetings when these matters were discussed and, under President Roosevelt's direction, I took up certain details with Stalin and with Molotov. Neither

and that the agreement concerning Outer Mongolia and the ports and railroads referred to would require the concurrence of Chiang Kai-Shek.

According to Sherwood, it was "quite clear that Roosevelt had been prepared even before the Teheran Conference in 1943 to agree to the legitimacy of most if not all of the Soviet claims in the Far East, for they involved the restoration of possessions and privileges taken by the Japanese from the Russians in the war of 1904. It is also clear that the failure to notify the Chinese immediately of the Yalta discussions was due to fear of the security of secrets in Chungking." [26]

But Stalin insisted that these agreements be put in writing in unmistakable terms and "This, in my opinion," wrote Sherwood, "was the most assailable point in the entire Yalta record, and the most surprising in that it involved Roosevelt in the kind of firm commitment that usually he managed to avoid. It denied him the postwar 'freedom of action' which he valued so highly. . . ." Sherwood added that it was his belief "that Roosevelt would not have agreed to that final firm commitment had it not been that the Yalta Conference was almost at an end and he was tired and anxious to avoid further argument. I believe that he was hopeful that, when the time came to notify the Chinese, he would be able to straighten the whole thing out with Chiang Kai-shek—but that hope, of course, was not realized." [27]

The concessions in Manchuria were in reality a violation of the agreement of Roosevelt with Chiang Kai-shek at Cairo in 1943. Yet, "The China question was on Roosevelt's mind constantly during the month preceding our departure for the Yalta meetings because of the growing seriousness of opposition to the National Government of Chiang Kai-shek," reported Leahy. "The Chief Executive was unwavering in his determination to support his wartime Far Eastern ally who had fought so bravely for so long against great odds." [28]

Secretary of State Stettinius nor any of his advisers, except for Charles E. Bohlen who acted as the President's Interpreter, had anything to do with these negotiations. Any suggestion to the contrary is utterly without foundation in fact."

[26] Sherwod, *op. cit.,* p. 866.
[27] *Ibid.,* p. 867.
[28] Leahy, *op. cit.,* p. 287.

Leahy states furthermore, on the basis of conferences with the President in January, 1945, that when General Hurley was sent to China by the President, "Hurley understood that his directive was to support the National Government and sustain the leadership of Chiang." But presently Hurley became aware of a plan among some American Army officers to "by-pass the Generalissimo," and make direct overtures of military aid to the Communists. The significance of this procedure was revealed when General Wedemeyer "was asked to secure passage to Washington for Mao Tse-tung and Chou En-lai, the top Chinese Communist leaders, for conferences with the President." [29] Although the plan was thwarted by Wedemeyer and Hurley, it was symptomatic of the impending struggle of the Communists to overthrow the Nationalist government of China, not without the aid of American military and governmental personnel acting upon unauthorized personal initiative.

As for the initial United Nations Conference, it was now proposed that it should convene in April, and Russia was won to the President's dream. There was discussion of the membership—and of the "veto power," in the proposed alliance. The Dumbarton Oaks preliminary conference had failed to produce agreement as to voting in the Security Council. It was now the President's proposal that each member of the Council should have one vote, and that on all matters of substance the vote of the permanent members must be unanimous.

Thus, although as events were to show again and again that it was Russia that was to obstruct by the veto power the early development of a world organization, it was not Russia but the United States that proposed the means for so doing. Mr. Roosevelt must bear this responsibility. In a real sense it was a carry-over from his nationalist compromise with internationalism in order to hold support of the majority in the United States.

As there is ample evidence that naval and army advisers were not in agreement as to the need of bringing in Russian aid in disposing of Japan, within the State Department as well there were disagreements as to "Russia." Adolph Berle testified before the House Un-American Activities Committee on August

---

[29] *Ibid.*, p. 289.

30, 1948, "As I think many people know, in the fall of 1944 there was a difference of opinion in the State Department. I felt that the Russians were not going to be sympathetic and cooperative. Victory was then assured, though not complete, and the intelligence reports which were in my charge, among other things, indicated a very aggressive policy not at all in line with the kind of cooperation everyone was hoping for, and I was pressing for a pretty clean-cut showdown then when our position was strongest." [30]

William C. Bullitt, according to Admiral Leahy said that America in 1943 had "sufficient power to force upon the Allies a policy to govern postwar international relations in Europe similar to the power possessed by Woodrow Wilson prior to the armistice that ended the last war in 1918." And, added Leahy, "He was convinced that immediately upon the collapse of Germany this power would pass from America to Soviet Russia, which latter nation would impose the peace terms and the geographical distribution of territory. This would inevitably result in Soviet ascendancy throughout Europe." [31]

At his press conference on board the *Quincy* on the return voyage, the President had admitted his disagreements with Churchill as to colonialism, concluding by saying that the latter was mid-Victorian. "Dear old Winston will never learn on that point." [32] In answering a question arising out of Churchill's statement as to the Atlantic Charter, the President was reported as saying: "The Atlantic Charter is a beautiful idea. When it was drawn up, the situation was that England was about to lose the war. They needed hope, and it gave it to them." [33]

That the President had "hoped it could be arranged to return the great Chinese port of Hong Kong to the sovereignty of the Chinese Government," [34] was matched by his view that "Indo-

---

[30] *Hearings Before the Committee on Un-American Activities, House of Representatives, 80th Congress, 2d Session,* p. 1296.

[31] Leahy, *op. cit.,* pp. 148-149.

[32] *Public Papers, 1944-1945,* p. 564. See also memoranda for Cordell Hull, *Personal Letters, 1928-1945,* II, 1489, 1493.

[33] *Public Papers, 1944-1945,* p. 564. Churchill, in responding to the President's reference to the Atlantic Charter in a conversation with Stalin at Yalta, said, "I replied that the Atlantic Charter was not a law, but a star," and later Churchill wrote, "and which will, I trust, long remain a guide for both our peoples and for other peoples of the world." (*Op. cit.,* pp. 393, 477.)

[34] Leahy, *op. cit.,* pp. 313-314.

China should not go back to France but that it should be administered by an international trusteeship." [35]

Of the discussions at Yalta, as reported by the President in his address to the Congress on March 1, 1945, the statement as to the United Nations interested the citizens of the United States most of all. Mr. Roosevelt said:

> The Crimea Conference . . . ought to spell the end of the system of unilateral action, the exclusive alliances, the spheres of influence, the balances of power, and all the other expedients that have been tried for centuries—and have always failed.[36]

The President had described the conference to the Congress as

> . . . a turning point—I hope in our history and therefore in the history of the world. There will soon be presented to the Senate of the United States and to the American people a great decision that will determine the fate of the United States —and of the world—for generations to come.[37]

Ever since the United Nations Declaration of January, 1942, the ultimate objective of the war for an increasing number of Americans was seen in this light. The ringing words meant much to American idealists, who saw in an alliance against enemies of "life, liberty, independence and religious freedom" and for "human rights and justice" the kind of crusade that had interested millions of Americans since 1917. The President's utterances throughout the war kept well to the fore these objectives of Americans as cause for taking up arms. Real progress in acceptance had been made as success crowned the efforts of the Allied powers.

Realists were at once aware that, whereas President Roosevelt was straining every effort to attain a unity of nations, Marshal

---

[35] *Personal Letters, 1928-1945*, II, 1489. "When the matter of making Dairen a free port came up," wrote Leahy, "I leaned over to Roosevelt and said, 'Mr. President, you are going to lose out on Hong Kong if you agree to give the Russians half of Dairen . . .' He shook his head in resignation and said, 'Well, Bill, I can't help it.' " (*Op. cit.*, p. 314.)

[36] *Public Papers, 1944-1945*, p. 586.

[37] *Ibid.*, p. 585.

Stalin was thinking of the United Nations Organization as an arena in which national rivalries would go on, as of course they would.[38] That Churchill loyally supported the idea of the concert of powers represented by the United Nations was natural, for it was in the British tradition of a means to provide balance of power.

It is to be emphasized that all who met at Yalta, whatever their exhilaration at impending victory, were tired and sick of the travail of war. The entire question of the extent of the mental exhaustion of the negotiators needs extensive examination. Rosenman, meeting Roosevelt on his way home from Yalta, was disheartened by his physical appearance. "I had never seen him look so tired . . . he was listless and apparently uninterested in conversation—he was all burnt out." [39]

It was Rosenman's conclusion that "the Yalta Conference produced the United Nations organization; committed the Soviet firmly to the war in the Pacific at an early date; and agreed to apply sound principles to the solution of many of the problems facing the Allies after the war." [40]

Writing in 1949, Rosenman gives full treatment, in summary, of the point of view of the President toward the conference at Yalta, its agreements, and its "success." [41] The point of view from which he writes may be seen in the words: "Ardent Roosevelt-haters, perpetual isolationists, and many well-meaning people . . . have sought to draw a picture of President Roosevelt at Yalta as . . . incapable of protecting the interests of the United States." [42]

"Had the Soviet Union carried out these agreements and adhered to the principles enunciated at Yalta," wrote Mr. Rosenman in 1949, "the world would be far along on the road to peace. The peace of the world is now in danger—not because

---

[38] Churchill, *op. cit.*, p. 355.

[39] *Op. cit.*, p. 522. Jonathan Daniels, in *The End of Innocence*, p. 18, wrote, ". . . as one of Franklin Roosevelt's secretaries . . . I remember . . . his august agility and audacity at the last, even when it was my job to screen all the grisly pictures of him which had been flown back from Yalta and to release only those which seemed least marked by what afterward we understood was his dying."

[40] *Public Papers, 1944-1945*, p. 544.

[41] *Ibid.*, pp. 537-548.

[42] *Ibid.*, pp. 537-538.

of Yalta, but because the Soviet Union has flouted the specific agreements which were reached at Yalta." [43]

Yet it is clear that the mystery of what "happened" at Yalta—and afterwards—will never be solved until and if the Russian view of this conference is at some future time made available.[44] Churchill recalled that at one point in the proceedings, Stalin had said, "My colleagues in Moscow cannot forget what happened in December, 1939, during the Russo-Finnish War, when the British and the French used the League of Nations against us and succeeded in isolating and expelling the Soviet Union from the League, and when they later mobilised against us and talked of a crusade against Russia." [45]

Americans were shocked when they later learned of the concessions to Russia in the Far East, not merely because of violation of previous agreements with Chiang Kai-shek, but because of their growing apprehension concerning the Far East. They had fought a war of agony in the Pacific—as they had been attacked from the Pacific.

The death toll in the Pacific war had been brought home to the American people in vivid terms because advance by island capture, and the union of ground forces, naval units, and air power in a joint enterprise could be visualized more easily than less dramatic forms of warfare.

An Asiatic settlement had become as vital to the American people, in their thought of it, as a settlement of the war in Europe. They were not looking for territorial advantage for themselves—a fact understood by the British but by few others.

Yet Americans were desirous of security, and as the war ended, it became increasingly clear that the vast Pacific Ocean was no longer of itself a protection to the western shores of the United States. The people of the United States were to realize the full meaning of this new insecurity when China fell to the Communists.

---

[43] *Ibid.*, Introduction, xi.

[44] Mr. Harriman reported (*U. S. Senate Hearings on Military Situation in the Far East*, p. 3341): "I believe that the Kremlin had two approaches to their post-war policies, and in my many talks with Stalin I felt that he himself was of two minds. One approach emphasized reconstruction and development of Russia, and the other external expansion."

[45] Churchill, *op. cit.*, p. 356.

Churchill's view of the deterioration of the Allied relations that immediately followed upon the Yalta meetings raises still another unsolved question. If President Roosevelt had survived, would the political results have been different? Mr. Churchill noted, "As a war waged by a coalition draws to its end political aspects have a mounting importance. In Washington especially longer and wider views should have prevailed. It is true that American thought is at least disinterested in matters which seem to relate to territorial acquisitions, but when wolves are about the shepherd must guard his flock, even if he does not himself care for mutton." [46]

Vigorous criticism of the President's actions at Yalta are at the heart of all discussion of the final outcome of the war. If Mr. Roosevelt, looking beyond the immediate problem at Yalta, had visualized the ensuing struggle in the world between the forces of communism and those of democracy, it is difficult to see what he could have done that he did not do. He must not take action that would lose Russian support in Europe, as well as in the Far East, for both wars had yet to be won. [47]

It must be repeated that in the early months of 1945 the American people were of the opinion that Russian aid was necessary to a military victory over Japan at an early date. Mr. Roosevelt's army advisers advocated Russian aid to save American lives. It is admitted that retaining Russian adherence to the waging of war cost promises as to the fruits of war in Europe and in the Far East. Yet, this accomplished, was Russia to be inside or outside the world organization? The decision of Franklin Roosevelt had to be, in view of his commitments to

---

[46] *Ibid.*, p. 455.

[47] Admiral Leahy summarized the President's case thus: "Russia was our ally, and up to June, 1944, took the full force of the mighty German Army. Fears expressed by many, some in high places, that Russia would make a separate peace with Germany, particularly when we were unable to mount a second front in 1943, had proved unfounded. Russia had kept every military agreement made before that time. As for political agreements, we had reached at Yalta the first major understandings regarding the post-war world. Stalin had shown a conciliatory attitude on the United Nations, on giving France a voice in the Control Council of Germany, and in agreeing to reorganization of the Polish and Yugoslav Governments. In fact, on almost every political problem, after a forceful statement of their views, the Russians had made sufficient concessions for an agreement to be reached, on paper at least. It is true that the ink was hardly dry on the Yalta protocol before serious difficulties in interpretation arose." (*Op. cit.*, pp. 317-318.)

the American people, that Russia would be included. This brought the struggle of communism versus democracy into the world organization at the outset.

Moreover, it is abundantly shown that the conception that Mr. Roosevelt had of the status of British imperialism in the post-war world was a factor in all his dealings with Mr. Churchill. This constantly played to the advantage of the Russians in negotiations and made for division of ultimate objectives between the British and the Americans.

Prime Minister Churchill was aware of this harsh reality. He not only faced the Russian designs in Poland and Greece and elsewhere, but he was also to face opposition to his leadership at home. And this opposition in Britain was to win, at least in part, in terms that suggested that Mr. Churchill's opponents, and not the war government, were truly representative of the purposes of the British people.

The conclusion must be that at Yalta the President, faced by the growing power of Stalin and by the progressive weakness of Churchill, made concessions that gave Russia unlimited strength in Asia as well as in Europe. This Mr. Roosevelt did, not only to bring Russia into the war in the Pacific,[48] but most of all to insure the objective that was his first concern, the establishment of the United Nations Organization with Soviet Russia as a member.

Surely the conferences of 1943-1945 had foreshadowed this. Mr. Churchill had made it all too evident how clearly he saw the impending struggle. This was not to establish the United Nations; it was not to bring the Soviet into war with Japan. It was, as Churchill saw it, a struggle to hold the Soviet in check. Surely the evidence of the long struggle for domination should have made this aspect of communism clear enough. A conservative, Churchill could see this; a liberal, Roosevelt could not.

To win the final battle for a United Nations that would provide for an equality of peoples and for an organization in which conflicts could be confined, Mr. Roosevelt had participated for

---

[48] In a press conference on the *Quincy*, February 23, 1945 (vol. 25, p. 064, Roosevelt Library), the question was asked: "Have the Russians been brought into the Combined Chiefs of Staff?" The President replied: "Yes and No. Russia will be in any discussions affecting her troops, but not in anything against Japan. They will have nothing to do with anything in the Pacific. It is an obvious fact that Russia has been neutral, and we will respect that neutrality."

ten years in the game of world politics; in the end he was to lose.

On the other hand, there is some evidence that "sometime in 1944, perhaps in July, the Kremlin reached a major decision: the Soviet Union would, as the war closed, act unilaterally, and not as a cooperative member of the Allied group. It was the real beginning of the cold war." [49]

Those who give adverse comment upon the President's agreements at Yalta might well broaden the basis for their criticism. Once the President entered the conference he was certain to be faced with the necessity inherent in a conference of power; he must negotiate, he must agree, he must make concessions. For no good can come from a view that this was only a conference of unity for war—although it was that—because it was as well the arena of the diplomatic struggle of great powers.

The President's acceptance of personal conference as a method to be used in war was in itself acceptance of a task that did not easily conform to the conception of the Presidency held by the people or supported by provision of the Constitution. Roosevelt had written to Stalin on May 5, 1943:

> I am sending this personal note to you by the hand of my old friend, Joseph E. Davies. . . . I want to get away from the difficulties of large staff conferences or the red tape of diplomatic conversations. Therefore, the simplest and most practical method that I can think of would be an informal and completely simple visit for a few days between you and me. . . .

After suggesting a meeting place "on your side or my side of Bering Straits," the President continued:

> I would be accompanied by Harry Hopkins, an interpreter and a stenographer . . . you and I would talk very informally and get what we call a "meeting of the minds." . . . You and I would, of course, talk over the military and naval situation, but I think we can both do that without Staffs being present.[50]

---

[49] A. A. Berle, in a review of Herbert Feis, *The China Tangle,* in the *New York Times,* October 4, 1953.

[50] *Personal Letters, 1928-1945,* II, 1422-1423. The President was asked in press conference, December 17, 1943 (after his return from Teheran), "What type would you call him [Stalin]? Is he dour?" Mr. Roosevelt replied, "I would call him something like me—he is a realist." (*Public Papers, 1943,* p. 550.) Admiral Leahy's comment was: "The talk among ourselves as the meeting broke up was about Stalin. Most of us, before we met him, thought he was a bandit

As Commander-in-Chief, Mr. Roosevelt's powers were great.[51] But, as representative of the United States in diplomatic arrangements and agreement, and particularly as the spokesman for the United States in proposing and urging a permanent union of nations that in itself was a surrender of national power, he was subject to the actions of his constituents. He knew that—and his rivals at Yalta knew that. He must win Stalin and hold Churchill—without losing the support of the people of the United States.

It follows that much of what he did—the agreements made and the method used—must be kept not only from the public but also from the President's colleagues in the government. These included his own appointees, such as Secretary of the Navy Forrestal, as well as supporters of his foreign policies in the Senate, such as Vandenberg.

Consequently, more important than criticism of his surrender—is the criticism that he should not have been at Yalta at all. The conference method, which had its dramatic beginning in 1941 in the meeting with Churchill, was pursued assiduously by Roosevelt throughout the war. Churchill could do this with impunity. He was only head of a government. Stalin could do it, of course, as dictator. But President Roosevelt as head of a State was, from the outset, always in an exposed position in the conferences because this was a method quite outside the usual practice of the American system of government.

It must be said that Americans as a whole came to accept this conference method as a necessity of war. In fact, it is certain that they gloried in the apparent success of such conferences. And the President—unlike Stalin and Churchill—was putting his faith in the United Nations as a new agency, not an old device.

---

leader who had pushed himself up to the top of his government. That impression was wrong. We knew at once that we were dealing with a highly intelligent man who spoke well and was determined to get what he wanted for Russia. No professional soldier or sailor could find fault with that. The Marshal's approach to our mutual problems was direct, agreeable, and considerate of the viewpoints of his two colleagues—until one of them advanced some point that Stalin thought was detrimental to Soviet interests. Then he could be brutally blunt to the point of rudeness." (*Op. cit.*, p. 205.)

[51] In a letter of December 3, 1943, to Stalin (President's Personal File 8587, Roosevelt Library), the President, in thanking him for courtesies at Teheran, had written: "I am just starting home and will visit my troops in Italy on the way."

But in perspective it is easy to see the dangers involved and the terrific costs that were paid in prestige and in men and matèriel by such personal agreements. It has been said that the practice led the President to by-pass his State Department and to commit the Congress beyond possibility of "undoing." Of course it did. And the President's dependence upon his military advisers was not matched by his reliance upon his civilian advisers.[52]

His personal confidence, his tendency to play hunches, his reliance upon the accomplished fact "in crisis"—all made for temporary success, but in the end fully revealed the method by which the United States entered into power politics in Europe and in Asia.[53] Speed of decision was thereby attained, and this was needed in war. The concentration of power of the enemy was thereby matched, but the game was played according to the enemy's rules.

Of course it was urged that if the great objective could be attained, then the rules would be changed. Conferences of the Big Three or Four or Five would be displaced by the emergence of the United Nations. Out of an iniquitous practice would come a reformed practice! In crisis there would be sacrifice—to obtain objectives. And of course if the great objective were attained, the colonialism of Britain and of France would be modified, and the imperialism of all nations, including Russia, would be checked. For, as has been observed, "Roosevelt's vision of peace included not only the ending of the colonial system, but the abandonment of what he regarded as its essential concomitants, spheres of influence and regional balances of power.[54]

A final judgment suggests itself to the effect that the alternatives to the President's policy must have produced even greater

[52] "His deep-rooted prejudice against . . . the permanent officials of the Department of State," and "At Yalta also such advice was lacking," are words of critical summary in Sumner Welles, *Seven Decisions That Shaped History*, p. 216.
[53] The effect of such assertion of power upon Americans of outstanding conviction is seen in the reactions of Arthur Vandenberg not made public at the time. See *The Private Papers of Senator Vandenberg*, in particular, pp. 150, 154, 360-361.
[54] Wilmot, *op. cit.*, p. 635. Sumner Welles, *Seven Decisions*, p. 150, illuminates the President's approach in an account of a talk with Mr. Roosevelt at Hyde Park in September, 1943. "He dealt for a while with one of his favorite projects, the severance of Indo-China from French control, and the establishment there of a United Nations trusteeship in which the Philippines should play a prominent part."

uncertainty in precisely the fields in which his policies seemed to fail, that is, in combating aggressive nationalism and in creating an effective world organization. For had the United States not joined the war; had the United Nations Organization not been founded—the situation in the world and at home must have been precarious indeed.

And it is said further by those who defend the record, that to belittle and traduce the advocates of international good-will reveals little comprehension of the nobility of those who seek a better world. Tragedy always attends warm-hearted and high-minded persons in a world of practical men.

Yet there had been another road, no less idealistic, and well within the choice of the American people. On June 29, 1941, Mr. Hoover had said, just after Hitler had invaded Russia: "If we go further and join the war and we win, then we have won for Stalin the grip of communism on Russia, and more opportunity for it to extend over the world." [55]

This prophecy was confirmed when Stalin said at Yalta, "I only want to have returned to Russia what the Japanese have taken from my country," and Roosevelt had said, "That seems like a very reasonable suggestion from our ally—they only want to get back that which has been taken from them." [56]

Surely a bias in favor of supposed Russian good-will could go no further. Repeatedly the President had been warned by those who knew Russia. To General Marshall, General Deane had written: "They [the Russians] simply cannot understand giving without taking, and as a result even our giving is viewed with suspicion." [57]

The spirit in which the President formulated his final agreements with the Russians may perhaps be judged in the light of advice given him by his close confidante, Harry Hopkins, who at the final session at Yalta wrote a note to Roosevelt in which he said, "The Russians have given in so much at this conference that I don't think we should let them down." [58]

Yalta—in perspective—becomes a symbol of the unending conflict between East and West. The historic roots lay deep in

---

[55] *New York Times,* June 30, 1941.
[56] Leahy, *op. cit.,* p. 318.
[57] Deane, *op. cit.,* pp. 84-85.
[58] Sherwood, *op. cit.,* p. 860. Russia declared war on Japan on August 8, barely a week before the Japanese surrendered.

Russian policy, past and present. There was no Western policy —at Yalta—except to counteract; no positive policy to guide the West. Thus, at Yalta a new map of Asia was foreshadowed as a new map of Europe was outlined. The determining power was Soviet Russia. Ignorant of—or resolved to ignore—historic background, Mr. Roosevelt and his advisers lost for the West.

Chapter XIX

INTO THE NEW AMERICA

UPON HIS RETURN from Yalta, the President addressed the Congress on March 1, 1945. His opening sentence was long remembered by those who were present, for he said, "I hope that you will pardon me for this unusual posture of sitting down during the presentation of what I want to say, but I know that you will realize that it makes it a lot easier for me not to have to carry about ten pounds of steel around on the bottom of my legs. . . ." This was the first time on a public occasion of this kind that the President had referred to his crippled condition. He also said that he had returned from his fourteen thousand mile trip "refreshed and inspired." [1]

Every point in the address had been anticipated by an eager press, and those who heard the President speak learned anew that—as far as he was willing to report upon it—the conference at Yalta had dealt with Europe and not with the Far East; that political arrangements for Europe were not settled; and that in the proposed union of nations, voting procedures had been

---

[1] *Public Papers, 1944-1945*, p. 570. At the press conference on the *Quincy*, February 19, 1945, en route from Algiers to Newport News, Virginia (vol. 25, p. 053, Roosevelt Library), the President said: "When I get back I am thinking of going up to Congress, to the well of the House, sit at a table in the well and have the broadcast [radio] from there. That would save time. I wouldn't have to do it again in the evening."

agreed upon but could not yet be announced. The President's tone of admonition and expression of hope gave reality to his vision of the America that was to emerge from the war.

Six weeks later—the day before Franklin Roosevelt's death—in preparing a draft of an address for Jefferson Day (April 13), the President's mood was one of recollection:

I remember saying, once upon a time in the long, long ago when I was a freshman, that the only thing our people had to fear was fear itself. We were in fear then of economic collapse. We struck back boldly against that fear, and we overcame it.

The last two lines of the address were written in longhand, the paragraph commencing:

The only limit to our realization of tomorrow will be our doubts of today. Let us move forward with strong and active faith.[2]

Into this New America Franklin Roosevelt was not to lead his people. He died of a massive cerebral hemorrhage on April 12, 1945.[3]

"It was a triumphant time for a great man to die," wrote Jonathan Daniels. "And his death gave a day upon which Americans could not only measure the growing dimensions and meaning of their victory, but also the world's debt and devotion to the man. . . . He stood already as the symbol of American destiny in his time. Better than any other man he understood that destiny." [4]

Franklin Roosevelt's leadership had seemed superb in action, in explanation, and in the response given it by the American people. Millions of men and women—not only in the United States, among the Allies, and in the nations to be conquered, but also in outlying parts of the world not at the time directly

---

[2] *Ibid.*, opposite p. 616.

[3] Mr. Churchill records (*op. cit.*, p. 477): ". . . at Yalta I noticed that the President was ailing. His captivating smile, his gay and charming manner, had not deserted him, but his face had a transparency, an air of purification, and often there was a far-away look in his eyes. When I took my leave of him in Alexandria harbour I must confess that I had an indefinable sense of fear that his health and his strength were on the ebb."

[4] "The Presidency," in *While You Were Gone*, edited by Jack Goodman, p. 117. "It was one of those rare and deeply moving and almost mystic moments when life suddenly turns to history, not before our eyes, but in our hearts," wrote Roger Butterfield in the *Saturday Review of Literature*, April 21, 1945, p. 13.

involved in the clash of powers—were affected by the President's death. His task was unfinished.

Winston Churchill later wrote: "Indeed, it may be said that Roosevelt died at the supreme climax of the war, and at the moment when his authority was most needed to guide the policy of the United States." [5]

The chief actor in a long drama packed with suspense and tragedy had been removed from the scene abruptly and without clear indication of the aftermath. The responses to the shock of his death are to be understood in the light of that fact.

The people of the United States, bereft of the leader but recently chosen by them to end the war and make the peace, found that the conditions of ending the war and of launching the peace had been laid down by the words and acts of that leader. In terms of Constitutional government, party victories, national security, individual well-being, and social health, the United States of 1945 was for the most part what Franklin Roosevelt had made it, and what he had led the people to think and feel that it was.

They had been deeply divided on the matter of Presidential leadership only six months before. Over 22,000,000 had voted against him. The people were more deeply divided on the major questions that now pressed for solution. Yet no minority leader, even the recent Republican nominee, stood forth with program or personality or promise for the future.

The one man who had challenged the President's leadership, his methods, and his accomplishments at home and abroad—and many of whose criticisms had repeatedly, by the after-event, been proved sound—had been twelve years out of office. During this period former President Hoover had had no part in the direction of the policies of the government, and was at the time of Roosevelt's death seventy years of age.

For those who had been close to President Roosevelt in his active leadership, the adaptation was hardest. To win the war was the task of his military advisers. To win the peace, preparations by the State Department were well advanced. To con-

---

[5] *Op cit.*, p. 471. Mr. Churchill added: "My relations with this shining personality had played so large a part in the long, terrible years we had worked together . . . I was overpowered by a sense of deep and irreparable loss."

tinue in the United States the programs of legislation and administration associated with the New Deal was to be the task of party leaders who were experienced and who had long been in the habit of following Franklin Roosevelt.

But no leader called to the Presidency could have been adequately prepared for such a situation. Certainly no leader could follow the path of one who had led so continuously and so long by methods that defied careful analysis.

Mr. Roosevelt's successor in the Presidency had not been an intimate, nor in any way had he been closely associated with the conduct of the war or in planning for the peace, or with the domestic program of the previous twelve years.[6]

The one man most clearly associated with plans for peace was the recently resigned Secretary of State. Yet even Cordell Hull had not been wholly sympathetic with the results of the President's methods of achieving the peace for which Hull had laid careful plans.

In view of the record of the previous twelve years no party leader in 1945 could be a real successor in directing the Democratic party. Of the President's intimate associates no one could step into the place that he had occupied as leader of the party and President of the nation.

Yet the official powers of the President passed without question or important incident to his designated successor, Harry Truman. Like earlier Vice-Presidents succeeding to office, Mr. Truman stated that he would carry forward the policies of the leader he had succeeded. No abrupt changes in party government were expected, and no violent outbursts of protest occurred as might have been the case, had Henry Wallace succeeded President Roosevelt.

---

[6] An editorial in the *New York Times* of January 16, 1953, reminded Americans that "In passing any sort of judgment on Mr. Truman's Administration one should begin by remembering that he was not trained for the awe-inspiring job that came his way. He had held an executive post in a county government in Missouri. He had been chairman of a Senate investigating committee that went intelligently into the conduct of war production. As Vice President for a few weeks he had had one or two Presidential errands to perform, but that was all. He saw Mr. Roosevelt privately only twice after he became Vice President. He was not in any way made acquainted with the Presidential problems, responsibilities and secrets. He had to learn the task—in some ways the heaviest in the world—from the ground up. His early appointments, notably in the Cabinet, seemed wise and not too political. He took up President Roosevelt's foreign policy where it had been left off."

Political parties appeared, on the surface, familiar. All commentators looked forward to the first party test in 1946 in the Congressional elections, and particularly to the Presidential election of 1948. There was no expression of doubt that Americans would continue their normal political practices.[7]

Although politics in the United States appeared to be carried on by the same major parties and a number of lesser and insignificant parties, nevertheless "blocs" in the Congress exercised more power than ever. Throughout the land was a federal payroll of tremendous size. The national government in Washington exercised its vast powers in a considerable measure due to the Roosevelt leadership, yet state and local governments had enlarged as well.

Indeed, heavy dependence upon government, a full result of President Roosevelt's administration, was now an accepted fact. Perhaps the most momentous change was the size and influence of military establishment—army, navy, air—with all of the supporting agencies.

The national security, based upon phenomenal industrial might and triumphant armies, seemed satisfactory to the people as a whole. Indeed, this security was given much praise as opening the way for greater national development. Widespread well-being of the masses of the people as a whole—although depending upon a still existent war economy—was not threatened by the anticipated return of early peace.

To meet the needs of the people of the United States in a chaotic world, the leadership of Mr. Roosevelt had been based upon the assumption that the *people* were the government. The people had repeatedly endorsed this view. Consequently, they obtained more of the government, and the government demanded more of them in money, in service, and if need be, in life itself.

On the surface, the people had greater power, exercised wider influence, and had more help from the government. Out-

---

[7] The Democratic party organization had been in control of the Congress— both House and Senate—for sixteen years, a longer uninterrupted period than any other party had enjoyed since the birth of Republican power in 1856. But whereas this period had been one of Presidential ascendancy, it was noted by political experts that as a national party, the Republicans had had in 1897-1911 and 1921-1931 twenty-four years of complete control of government, whereas the Democrats had had in 1913-1919 and 1933-1947 only twenty years.

wardly, too, they went about their daily lives in business, in
family, in church, in school and college much as they had before the problems of the contemporary world had absorbed the
attention of their government. In fact, the divisions of the
people were—as before—deepest in terms of economic interest.
Here the struggle was unceasing. But the government protected workers in the right to fight, as well as to work and to
play.

Democracy seemed to have an endorsement in every department of life. The fact that so many questions were obviously
unsettled caused little general concern because of the fact that,
as yet, no dead-end had been experienced in the road followed
in the previous twelve years.

Writing in July, 1945, the Chairman of the Advisory Committee on Social Security said: "At the end of its first decade,
the program established under the Social Security Act provides
a bulwark such as American families never before have had in
face of impending economic changes." [8]

Public expenditures for social security and related purposes
amounted to $4.6 billion in the fiscal year 1944-45. Of this, $2.4
billion was provided from federal funds, and $2.2 billion from
state and local funds. About half of the total amount supported
social insurance and related programs; one-fourth, health and
medical services; and slightly less than one-fourth supported
public aid.

As state legislatures had begun their sessions in January,
1945, forty-two governors recommended changes in state unemployment insurance, public assistance, and health programs.
Almost half of the messages recommended extension of cover-
age of unemployment insurance to employees of small firms,
reduction of the waiting period, and liberalization of benefits
in both amount and duration. About half recommended increases in public assistance payments, and slightly fewer urged
various types of measures to protect health, in addition to
regular public health activities.

Between V-Day and the end of the year, nine million persons lost their jobs in war industries and five million service-

---

[8] *Social Security Yearbook, 1944*, p. ii.

men were demobilized. Yet according to Census reports, only about two million persons were unemployed at the end of December.

As has been said, because he had been in a position of supreme power for a dozen years, President Roosevelt prepared the way for the America that was to emerge from the war. There is no need to weigh the extreme claims associated with the worship of his memory by devotees of a legend. For the facts are quite enough to show that the utterances and actions of the President were all-important in preparing the way.

In this New America arose questions of national banking; of executive usurpation; of national defense in a world still in the grip of war, starvation, and totalitarian rule. Upon each of these, followers of the late President were to be challenged by foes of earlier years who called for a reduction in taxation, a relief of private enterprise from restriction, a defense of American interests in the United Nations, and return to a government of separation of powers.

If, as was asserted, the New Deal and the New Internationalism had come to stay, it would not be for lack of continued opposition. Both political parties nevertheless suffered paralysis as these two programs were considered in formulating new legislative and administrative proposals.

But the New America was to have one aspect that none could deny. It was to be a military state. It must protect itself; protect the fruits of the war; police the world; and defend any commitments, international or colonial, that the United States was forced to underwrite.

Expanding power—symbolized in the possibilities of atomic energy for war and for peace—merely emphasized the deeper issue that cut to the depths of American society: the wish of many Americans to return to the ways of America prior to 1933 as opposed to those who would follow the path of Mr. Roosevelt.

In the New America the supreme expression of Presidential leadership was realized in the control of nuclear power. It was symbolic, perhaps, of the great power of decision and of final determination resting in the office of President. Both President

Truman and President Eisenhower were forced to accept possession of this transcendent power as a fact of daily existence.

Vigorous critics pointed out that the domestic problems of the United States, as it emerged from the war in 1945, were in essence the problems that had existed in 1933. Many asserted that the full result of the basic approach of Mr. Roosevelt was seen in all its inadequacy. This view arose out of the fact that he had conceived of the underlying problem of American politics as that of dealing with the action of selfish men. "Turn the rascals out," had been a familiar device in American politics, but no one had used "Expose the rascals" so effectively as had President Roosevelt.

So chaotic had American politics become in the years 1933 to 1945 that it was difficult to see just what real alignments would emerge in the political battle that would follow the death of the President. Of course the protagonists would be the Democrats and the Republicans. Each would have a program that would profess to solve the basic questions in American relations with other nations. But membership in the United Nations meant that most of the problems were to be dealt with later. As for the basic problem of American independence in the world—this was more important than ever.

The President who succeeded Mr. Roosevelt and who was to be re-elected in 1948, was the leader of the party that had won the war in collaboration with the British and the Russians. Both Britain and Russia were now in the hands of those who professed the same collectivist objectives as did the Democratic party. Consequently, in the alignment which gradually emerged, the Republicans in the United States were sharply critical of both domestic and foreign policies of the Democrats —and most emphatically critical of Communist influence in the American government.

The conservatives attacked Communist influence on the nation during the war and in the years immediately following the war. Those Republicans who seized upon this issue were assured of the initial backing of all Americans who were distrustful of radicalism, all who had been deeply convinced of the virtues of isolationism, and a great body of voters who felt that the charges of corruption within the administration were well founded. Corruption and communism seemed to them proper charges against the Roosevelt leadership.

The New America had not a tolerant atmosphere in which differences of opinion could be accepted as a matter of course. No post-war era has been tolerant. Not only must the passions of war have a long period in which to cool, but readjustments from war to peace economy provide conflict of unusual intensity. The American people had experienced this before.

Americans should have expected that the extremists would use the fundamental conservatism of the Republican party to aid them. The Democratic party had had and still had its extremists, but it was the Republican party that after the war harbored them in the most extreme form, because the Republicans alone held out hope for a change.

In truth, the office of President had been altered beyond recognition as Mr. Roosevelt exercised the powers of a dictator. The Constitution had been given deep wounds by his procedures. The courts had been brought from a position of wide acceptance to the necessity for self-defense. Party responsibility had been all but destroyed by the personal power exercised frequently to accomplish quick results. National security had been bought at tremendous sacrifice, not only of men and money, but also of prestige and character. Nor was this national security a reality.

The individual citizen had been raised in his own estimation, and particularly in his own physical welfare. But the basis of individual effort had been weakened at a time when adaptability to the world of change made it imperative that individual will power be retained and exercised as never before. Contemporary democracy was adrift in a sea of uncertainty, because for a dozen years the issues had been blurred and the basis for definite and positive judgment weakened.

A practice of habitual compromise had reaped its natural harvest of disillusion. Manipulation of standards of currency, experimentation in public works, a "practical" approach to social legislation, military preparation, secret foreign policy—had seemed to suggest that Mr. Roosevelt was following a middle course "a little left of center," as had been said, because he chose to do so.

Some admitted that this adherence to a middle way was more a necessity forced upon the President by the pressures of his time than his deliberate choice. Despite all of the indications that some of those supporting his regime would have gone much further than he did in remaking the United States, Mr. Roosevelt chose repeatedly—because of the solidarity of those forces in the United States calling for a conservative view—a compromise or a readjustment.

No matter how strong had been his own language in declaring, in review, that he had won his battle, this middle way pleased the mass of the people of the United States. That was precisely where they felt themselves to be, no matter what political ticket was supported.

By pursuing the "middle way," the President had forced both radicals and reactionaries to become more pronounced in their utterance. He raided the camp of each for phrases to use in either an aggressive or soothing manner. At times he even accepted a measure that one or the other group supported and made it his own. But always he would place an item of this derivation in a program that was well balanced, that is, in the "middle."

Mr. Roosevelt had frequently maintained that he was helping the people resume a familiar direction and reassert their traditional attitude. He assured them that he was doing what they, as conservators of old ways, and not radicals of a new dispensation, wished to do.

But in time it became clear that he had in fact, changed not only the direction but the fabric of American society and had done much to alter the American spirit of self-reliance and faith. Millions of Americans did not like the results. They found themselves committed to attributes of a collectivist state, and certainly to the central point of view of a Socialist philosophy. However much this continued to appeal to the radicals, of whom there were many, it did not satisfy those who had for the most part dominated in American society and government and who had done much to make the democracy identified with the "American way."

At the end of the war, it became more clearly evident than before that forces outside the United States had really won in their battle to make the United States a part of a world struggle between age-old antagonists, that is, entrenched economic, social and political power, versus the power of the mass of workers. In short, the United States had been brought to abandon the point of view that had given Americans their unusual opportunity in the eighteenth and nineteenth centuries. It was asserted that this opportunity no longer existed, and consequently the real struggle within the United States resembled the European struggle. The American people as a whole did not relish the prospect before them.

Whether after the close of the war, Franklin Roosevelt could have continued to lead the American people down the middle road that, as the shadows lengthened, more and more appealed to his imagination, will never be known. Whereas on the surface his political leadership seemed effective in 1944, yet in fact his acts in the last six months of his life indicated that the forces to the right and the left would be too great to overcome once the crisis had passed.

In view of the record of Mr. Roosevelt in this larger frame of reference—in what condition did he leave the people of the United States?

He had initiated an economic program that within the forms of government and previous practices of the governors, actually changed the economic life of every man, woman, and child in the United States. This program restored national morale and imposed a tax burden that could never be lifted. It provided social security as never before, and public works beyond the dreams of the most imaginative men of the nineteenth century.

President Roosevelt had asserted an aggressive nationalism, in a world of rampant nationalism, that led inevitably to attack upon the United States. At the end of the war the nation, within the United Nations Organization, found itself even more exposed to the developed dangers of nationalism.

Within the nation in these twelve years was developed a distrust of the basic democracy of the republic, as well as a social philosophy that included within its practices, if not in its pronouncements, many of the primary leveling objectives of communism. A whole generation of youth was cut off from the past by an eloquent proponent of revolutionary change.

Throughout the entire period of the Roosevelt Presidency,

the atmosphere of emergency had given first place to the man of action rather than to the man of thought.

With the close of the war, there were some who saw at last an opportunity to resume a faith that had been forsaken twelve years before. They welcomed an opportunity to reassert the basic alignments that had disappeared in the period 1939-1945. It was another eight years before this was attempted.

Underlying the President's foreign policies as he had explained them to the people were two basic principles: Americans were a peaceful people who desired only to keep less peaceful people from endangering the peace of the world; secondly, they were pledged to rules in foreign relations that only those of evil and sinister and selfish purpose would deny. The self-righteous attitude summarized in these two principles had a general appeal to the American people. When the administration insisted upon the observance of rules, it was for a high purpose. It was to correct others in their conduct. When Americans went to war, they did so reluctantly and for peaceful objectives. When they arranged peace at the end of war, it was to codify these high purposes and to insure a control of opposing forces.

The people had been told as a cause for fighting and as a reason for dying, that the world must provide an organization to insure peace and at least a measure of the discussion, adjustment, and agreement that were part and parcel of American belief in self-government. This organization was set up just after the close of the European struggle and before the final defeat of Japan. Its promise was a cause of great rejoicing.

Within this organization were to be the representatives of sixty nations, speaking many languages and living under widely different governments as well as divergent traditions. In this organization, the United States of America took the lead. The Charter of the United Nations represented much that America had contributed out of its own history. But several nations were notably powerful within the organization, and the basic questions that had caused the war were still posed for discussion and solution.

The leadership of Mr. Roosevelt had been such as to demand of the United States that it lead now in a world in which imperialisms and colonialisms must disappear. All the forces of radicalism could rally to that standard. All the forces of conservatism would question not only the possibility but the desirability of such immediate changes in the post-war world.

If well-recognized conservative governments in Britain and America and France had sent representatives to the San Francisco Conference, the issue would have been clearer than it came to be. For no liberal government was prepared to stand against the demands of the Communists who wished to use this opportunity to remove from control in the world the forces of colonialism and so-called imperialism which were obviously opposed to the best interests of the masses of men. In such a sea of uncertainty, the representatives of the communism of Russia were in an advantageous position. They were by their own profession the builders of a new world.

The American people were unwilling, even in the days of buoyant enthusiasm as to the future of the United Nations, to accept the Russian claims. Indeed, they were denied at once in word and in action. The American representatives fought the battle to such good effect that at the close it was clear that the leadership of free peoples and of people not yet free was to be in the hands of Americans.

However, this outcome was not satisfactory to a great number of radicals in the United States. They continued to favor Russia, openly or secretly. Many of them were still serving the American government. They were loath to believe that in the aftermath of war the fruits of radical programs would be lost.[9]

Yet as the struggle ensued between communism and democracy in Europe and particularly in China and the Far East, the

---

[9] "A dangerous number among the policy-making officials in the Administration were actual members of the Communist Party who were active traitors to the United States. A further group of loving fellow travelers followed the Moscow line. A much larger number were those groups bound by a common hatred of what they called 'capitalists' and 'reactionaries.' There were among them many intellectuals who advocated some sort of totalitarian economic system, in which personal liberty and constitutional government would be preserved. Many of them insisted Communism would evolve also into this form. In this they were halfway to Communism and it easily enlisted their sympathies. The actions of these groups, therefore, when not traitorous, directed their energies to help the Russians. By their penetration into high and low places in the government, and the natural sympathies of Roosevelt with so-called 'liberal' ideas, they were responsible for great actions—the character of which will unfold in Eastern Europe and China." (MSS of Herbert Hoover's *Memoirs on Foreign Affairs.*)

forces of the United States, often lamed by indecision and sometimes by treason, fought the battle for well-accepted American practice, notably in aids to economic recovery as a fundamental basis for the enlargement of areas of political liberty.

The six months that ensued after the death of President Roosevelt witnessed five events that had been foreshadowed and determined in a large measure by his leadership in World War II: Germany surrendered on terms that grew out of his initial suggestions; the atomic bomb was used as developed by experiments he had authorized; Japan surrendered, but not until after Russia had carried out its promise to enter the war in the Far East; the United Nations was launched with the adherence of fifty-eight nations as long planned by Mr. Roosevelt; and the Potsdam Conference confirmed Russia in its continuing control in eastern Europe, as agreements at Yalta had foreshadowed.

Each of these events attracted the eager attention of the American people. Each contributed to the general picture of the end of war and a resumption of peace. But no one or all of these together provided peace at home or abroad.

Emerging from the war with a military and industrial power unequaled, and unlike all others in the conflict as a nation untouched by the ravages of invasion or bombing, or both, yet the United States in impending economic confusion, political chaos, and social strain, was profoundly unhappy, and if not disillusioned, certainly in no mood to enjoy the fruits of peace.

There was a basic reason for this that bore no direct relation to any pressing question. It did not rest in the succession of Vice-President Truman. It rested in the fundamental uncertainty of the political alignment abroad and at home.

At the time of the death of President Roosevelt, the great unsettled question over the nations of the earth was the degree to which the masses of people should administer their affairs—social, economic and political—in a word, the kind of government that they would choose or at least accept in the years to come. The years of the war and the slogans of the war had raised everywhere this fundamental question.

There was a widespread feeling that despite wars and revolutions the basic problem of daily life had not been settled by victory in war nor by success in revolution. Outcome of war and shift of power could but prepare the way for patterns of government. The problems were, as before, the problems of self-determination.

For the time being, armed conflict, at least on a world scale, was to cease. Even to the simplest, it appeared that the world was to enter upon an uneasy armistice as the nations viewed the ruins of a gigantic catastrophe that had all but overwhelmed mankind.

As each nation, victorious or vanquished, emerged from the war, it was apparent that parties to the struggle now to ensue were present in every land. For the moment "left" and "right" would describe the alignment without too close examination into the composition of the parties. Older terms applied to these divisions such as conservative and radical, would presently reappear.

But everywhere these political alignments were obscured by the division between the defeated and the victorious. Even though this division was patently false, in general discussion there was as yet too little thought that within the former Axis powers were elements that should be seriously considered by the builders of the new order. It was thought that Communist and democrat must agree on the new government of Germany, however impossible it later appeared.

The United Nations Organization was to take as its province the entire world. The great nations were to lead, but others were to follow their lead. Not only would this organization provide a means of maintaining peace; as foreshadowed by agreements made at Bretton Woods and Dumbarton Oaks, it would also provide means of insuring an international economic structure and an international political opinion upon the rights of the individual and upon the powers of the national states.

Of course it was realized that in this body, as within each of the nations participating, disagreements would develop, divisions of opinion would appear, and indeed the whole matter of the purpose and scope and soundness of government would be in debate.

So each nation took on new life for the period of recon-

struction. Within each nation the battle for control of government became the interest of political parties. Some were
sympathetic to constitutionalism, some to democracy, some to
communism. A few had still the vestiges of fascism.

In this situation, if each nation could live unto itself or with
its freely chosen friends, all would provide a full measure of
self-government to the peoples involved. But the war had
shown that all nations must deal with all other nations, even
though within an international community.

The political alignment whose international implication was
now dimly seen was well known in American politics. It was,
as it had always been, an alignment of radicals versus conservatives. Radicalism, although tempered by adroit experimentation, had been in control of the government of the United
States for twelve years. This radicalism had brought into being
a powerful movement that now proposed to carry forward its
programs not only at home but abroad. It was opposed, as it
had been throughout the Roosevelt years, by a conservatism
that called for a return to the basic principles of Constitutional government.

Two important aspects were not seen by a great number of
persons. The first of these was the fact that the actual alignment was not identical with the two great parties in the United
States. Each contained in its membership radicals and conservatives. Second, and most significant, was the fact that American radicals had a natural interest in radical movements in
other lands. These movements had grown with the events of
the previous decade. More slowly, conservatives came to realize
that they too had a natural alliance with conservative forces
abroad.

The acceptance of a forum in the United Nations made it
essential that there be recognition of the possibility—if not the
inevitability—of the development of international political parties. A radical in the United States must of necessity sympathize
with a radical of another nation—Britain, Russia, China. A
conservative must find his natural counterpart in conservative
movements in other lands.

Deeper than convictions among conservatives and radicals as
to the nature of economic progress or social reform—or even

political platforms—were the convictions born of a basic position on problems of self-government. It was an incident of party politics that at this important moment a Laborite government was in power in Britain and a Soviet government in control of Russia. At such a time the government of the United States was radical in the sense that it had been for a dozen years. In no one of the "Big Three" were the "conservatives" in power. Yet the conservatives had had an important part in the industrial and financial efforts that had won the war.

In the projected forum of the international community, the forces of conservatism and radicalism appeared without immediate reference to national loyalties. Those of democratic persuasion took the lead from the United States; those of Communist belief took the leadership of the U.S.S.R. All would be well within the dreams of the founders of the United Nations if all parties confined themselves to peaceful means. But the U.S.S.R. was committed to spreading international communism, and the U.S.A. was destined by all its declarations to be the leader of liberty-loving peoples.

If economic independence had been possible to each of the nations asserting political independence, economic aid to the less prosperous by the more powerful would not have been necessary. But the world economically, socially, and politically was not at one economic stage or in one degree of political development. Nations ranged economically from the "haves" to the "have-nots." So the basic assumption of equality of treatment, or right, and of the power within the United Nations was false.

In this falsity lay a great strength of communism as represented by Soviet Russia, and a great weakness of the United States. The United States—because of its beliefs, its development, its success in self-government—could easily lead nations capable of a mature course of action. Russia, because of its later development, its protestations of representing the interests of the common man—but its practice of totalitarianism in control —might lead the nations of the world capable only, as yet, of limited self-government.

Everywhere within the nations then existing were groups holding divergent views. It was true of the United States, as its leaders were soon to find out, facing basic problems of self-government at home and abroad.

Under the leadership of Franklin Roosevelt, the American government had given billions of dollars to American citizens and to needy nations throughout the world. The object in each case was to provide relief and thereby to create a body of citizens or a group of nations capable of meeting the demands of livelihood and existence in the world in which they chose to live. The basic assumption in each case was that if succor were not provided there would be not only starvation but acceptance of totalitarian rule.

An economic future was the means by which self-government could be accepted and made successful. This was a product of American experience. Economic democracy had made possible political democracy. As a nation, Americans had prospered because of a wealth of resources and freedom to participate in their use. The United States had built the strongest economic unit in all the world. To continue doing so was essential.

Taking such a course of action, the Roosevelt leadership had won to its allegiance liberals not only in the United States but in other nations as well. This appeared to answer the need of those who viewed with alarm the concentration of political and economic power in the hands of a few men. It avoided the danger implicit in all mass movements cut off from economic resources. It disposed of the radicals and the would-be dictators at home, as well as the all-powerful dictators abroad. It was the basic gospel of American democracy. It attracted many who did not know its limitations.

The Roosevelt years had enabled the United States to escape the malady of dictatorship that had beset western Europe. During those years, however, the American tolerance of opposing viewpoints had permitted another enemy, communism, to elaborate its doctrines within the American household and, as events were to show, within the government itself.

It was natural for Russian Communists and their allies in the United States and elsewhere to continue to present the idea that the basic struggle was between communism and imperialism, and that the United States in its conservatism was really imperialistic.

Now had the divisions in the United Nations been merely

between radicals and conservatives, the United Nations would have been the forum of international political parties freely accepted by all nations and for all nationals. But the perpetuation in this international body of the purpose of revolution for Communist objectives made all of this a mockery.

So in self-defense American conservatives, joined by many American liberals, developed a violent opposition to communism, which in the United Nations was quite properly identified with Russia. If one favored Russia and communism, he was of necessity opposed to the interests of the United States. He might, if he carried his adherence to communism far enough, become a traitor to his nation, the United States.

Not long after Roosevelt's death Churchill had been moved to reopen the questions presumably settled at Yalta. On April 29, 1945, Mr. Churchill sent Marshal Stalin a personal letter in which he said, "There is not much comfort in looking into a future where you and the countries you dominate, plus the Communist parties in many other states are drawn up on one side, and those who rally to the English-speaking nations and their associates or Dominions are on the other. It is quite obvious that their quarrel would tear the world to pieces and all of us leading men on either side who had anything to do with that would be shamed before history. Even embarking on a long period of suspicions, of abuse and counterabuse, and of opposing policies would be a disaster hampering the great developments of world prosperity for the masses which are attainable only by our trinity." [10]

Mr. Churchill was returning to a view that had grown upon him for many months. He felt that the issues of the closing days of the war, "unnoticed by and unkown to the public," were not apparent to the American Chiefs of Staff, although, "as will not now be disputed, they played a dominating part in the destiny of Europe." In the period "between the fading of President Roosevelt's strength and the growth of President Truman's grip of the vast world problem," wrote Mr. Churchill later, "the United States stood on the scene of victory, master of world fortunes, but without a true and coherent sign. Brit-

---

[10] Churchill, *op. cit.*, p. 497.

ain, though still very powerful, could not act decisively alone. . . . The destruction of German military power had brought with it a fundamental change in the relations between Communist Russia and the Western democracies. They had lost their common enemy, which was almost their sole bond of union." [11]

The United States as a nation entered the post-war world with foreign commitments that were to influence the whole process of American domestic politics. Americans were not to withdraw from Europe. They were to aid other peoples to resist aggression. They were to adopt a Marshall Plan; they were to wage war in Korea. These were natural developments of pledges given by the President in the course of World War II —pledges that were to be made good by the Congress and the people *after* the pledge had been given.

In due time it was to become evident that quite apart from the partisan struggles that are always a part of the American story, the American people wished to consider and reconsider what they had—under the leadership of President Roosevelt— promised to do. Revelation—in time—of secret agreements made by the President shocked Americans. In particular was this true of the agreements made with Stalin at Yalta.[12]

The Communists, as a political party, had small place in American politics. General subversion of any great body of Americans was not accomplished during the Roosevelt years. The Communist approach to the problem of political control was utterly foreign to American practice, and for a time to American understanding. This philosophy and technique did not fit the American pattern of politics. Communists made progress, however, because Americans, starting from an inadequate understanding of Communist method, became the victims of misinformation and of their own idealism.

---

[11] *Ibid.*, pp. 455-456.

[12] Rosenman (*op. cit.*, p. 533) later said: "Present-day failure in this area is not due to anything that happened at Yalta. The principles and formula reached there were unassailable. What has happened is a result of the Soviet's refusal to carry out the agreement it made; the present Soviet position is a square repudiation of Yalta. And the Soviet was emboldened to take this stand by the speed with which our armed strength was scuttled as soon as victory had been won—a speed which American mothers and fathers loudly demanded of their Congress and of their Executive."

So, in the New America, the battle for freedom was to be the great theme of American development. Obscured by partisan politics and highly personal charges, great masses of Americans seemed to have forgotten that the real builders of the New America were not the frightened ones, who would hold power by pointing the finger of accusation at those in office, but the leader who day by day was using every means at hand to build an economic and social and political structure within which liberty could survive.

It was, however, only to be expected that the people—so long nurtured on attack upon those who were said to be disloyal to the people's interests—should have become accustomed to extreme language and personal attack. That this would continue to be the case in the Democratic party was assured by the presence of leaders who had been closely associated with Franklin Roosevelt.

That personal attack should appear in a most virulent form in the opposing party was inevitable because this method seemed necessary to outdo the political beneficiaries of Mr. Roosevelt. Even a cursory knowledge of politics and psychology —without knowledge of American history—should have prepared a nation for the demand that the State Department be "investigated," and for the activities of Congressional committees of investigation.

Repeatedly Mr. Roosevelt had insisted that the foreign policies of the United States were not those of an imperialist nation. This he could urge with conviction and with such proof in utterance and action as to mark out American purposes from those of other nations.

President Roosevelt and the people naturally opposed the military despotisms that dictators had forced upon their peoples. But they also distrusted existing "imperialism" of long standing among the British, French and Dutch. It was not clear to the President—nor to the American people—until the "issue of war had become the issue of peace" that underneath the pretensions of Russia as to interest in the common man was a totally different view of "democracy" than Americans had come to take for granted.

Had the widespread education in public affairs which characterized the first twenty years of this century continued in the ensuing thirty years, it is not conceivable that in the government in Washington or elsewhere, the adolescent view of domestic and foreign affairs that characterized many of the popular leaders in both political parties at mid-century would have been tolerated. They would have been laughed out of court.

Furthermore, the atrophy of the public mind on questions of economic livelihood and the rigidity of public opinion on loyalty and treason occasioned a simplicity of attitude toward subversion which suggests that the revolt of the masses had by this time reached the United States.

The changes in general education, brought on in large part by some of the progressive educators had altered the meaning of government to the citizen. This served to weaken his independence of thought and imagination. This in turn was repeatedly revealed by the growing importance of "practical men" in the arena of politics—the "primitives" of limited intelligence.

In the New America, it was inevitable that the "primitives," long nourished on war, should seek to prolong the sense of battle, first, by visualizing an enemy beyond our gates bent on our destruction; second, by finding in absence of actual war the need of fighting here at home.

The atmosphere of continuous conflict associated with the previous twelve years—and lack of opportunity in the war years for a real debate—added to the inevitability of this development. Moreover, the basic charges of the primitives were true; there was an alien enemy—Russian communism—and there were sympathizers with communism in America.

Closely akin to leaders of the common man who had deluged the world in blood and were leading millions to destroy the existing creative powers of civilization, the "primitives" were bringing into the new American environment an evil as old as history. This inquisition had as its object the detection of sympathy with the alien enemy, communism. The hunt for political heresy was as antipathetic to the genius of Americans as anything that the American people had ever experienced.

This harsh leadership need not have developed had not the "primitives" seemed to represent the basic interests of an immense and important section of the American public. These patriotic Americans, believing themselves high-minded and devoted to American ideals, nevertheless succumbed to the outlook of the times and saw the end as justifying the means, welcoming the activities of the "primitives" because they were opposing communism.

Did the nation emerge in 1945 with powers sufficient to protect its people in the decade to follow? The answer must be that, despite military and naval might, alliances with freedom-loving peoples, and carefully constructed organization for the elimination of world tensions—the American people were weaker than before and less prepared to meet the attacks of would-be rulers of the world.[13]

Did the nation emerge from twelve years of Roosevelt leadership economically sound? A national debt approaching three hundred billion dollars must raise a serious question. Two-thirds of this had been incurred for the war and its associated costs. But one-third of it was a debt incurred in carrying forward policies of relief and reform that placed reliance for the security of the nation in the individual security of the masses of men. Huge government expenditures had saved millions of people, and had won a war, but at a cost of grave concern to all citizens. Could this road lead eventually to anything but national bankruptcy?

Of less importance to national security and national economic well-being were other questions which pressed for answers. Was the Constitutional system unimpaired? Was the party system productive of real results in self-government? Was the individual citizen enjoying the civil freedoms that he had prior to 1933?

---

[13] A great American editor wrote in 1943: "After unconditional surrender . . . we are in for a ten-year struggle in which we must put our American energies, our American production, and the full strength of American credit— not into a grand do-good adventure, not into making the world beautiful and utopian, but into a cold-blooded, hardboiled attempt to put world civilization back on its feet. The capitalist system must not break down. Unless capitalism is willing to organize, to sacrifice, to envision its own self-interests in the re-newal and revival of civilization, war will be a failure. . . . And a weary, disheartened world will turn to some totalitarian tyranny and we shall regiment mankind in inevitable economic slavery." (William Allen White, *op. cit.*, p. 647.)

If an answer to each of these could be in the affirmative, there yet remained a question of grave importance. Was the individual citizen living in an atmosphere in which honesty, integrity, and generally accepted moral standards had any real claim amid the competitions of the modern world?

Mr. Roosevelt had urged optimism upon the American people on innumerable occasions, an optimism that was based in an expression of will power. He denounced dishonesty and lack of integrity, and he praised moral standards as basic for all action. He did so in a nation that in the 1920's had become doubtful of these verities of American life.

It is clear that the identification of the leader with the people had reaped its natural harvest. The level of national responsibility, of national life in general—was that of a majority of the American people.

In this New America the ideals of the Old America often seemed strangely out of place. In nothing was this revealed more clearly than in a wide acceptance of the view that "the end justified the means."

This "practical view" was shown during the war in gradual acceptance of destruction to the uttermost by every means known for the extermination of human life. This it was that prepared the way for general acquiescence, after the event, in the use of the atomic bomb at Hiroshima and Nagasaki.

Viewed in a longer perspective:

> The increasingly heavy international burdens which the American people have accepted since the war (involving the New World yet more closely in the fortunes of the Old) have devolved upon them largely as a result of the political and military mistakes of their wartime leaders, and especially Roosevelt, Marshall and Eisenhower, but these mistakes had to be made. The Americans had to find out for themselves that to strive for victory alone is not enough and that the balance of power must be the basis of peace. They had to learn from their own experience the difficulty of dealing with the Russians. . . . In the years following the war Truman's policy of firmness and preparedness—and of generous economic and military aid to Europe—would hardly have commanded such wide public support in the United States, if Roosevelt had not so diligently and sincerely sought to win the trust and co-

operation of Stalin and the Soviet Union. This was an essential
stage in the emergence of the United States to her present
world position, for during the decade between 1940 and 1950
. . . they [Americans] discovered once again the truth of the
words of Tom Paine. . . . 'Tyranny, like Hell, is not easily
conquered.' " [14]

In the New America, the people of the United States could
not feel that their assumption of a moral position in the world
was accepted. Whatever means were now taken to go back—to
reassert a former idealism—were met by taunts at home and
abroad that in the Old America things had not been what they
seemed, and that at last Americans had grown up to the stature
of maturity and what they must do now was to survive.

---

[14] Wilmot, *op. cit.*, p. 717.

Chapter XX

THE TRAGEDY OF LEADERSHIP

THE PRESIDENT PASSED from the scene he had dominated so long at a moment of high crescendo for all mankind. It was not a quiet passing. It was a dramatic event with every emphasis upon the greatness of the hero fallen. He had escaped martyrdom on the eve of inauguration. Twelve years later, carried away on the tide of victory for his design for the future, he appeared to suffer an inevitable martyrdom. This led a careful observer to conclude at the time that the figure of President Roosevelt will be "one of unexampled splendor" [1] in the view of succeeding generations. That he was identified with the masses of men makes this seem the more probable.

Yet, despite winning the war and maintaining the support of the American people, Franklin Roosevelt underwent the supreme tragedy of effective leadership. This tragedy lay not in the fact that death robbed him of triumph. The inexorable forces of his time engulfed the world, revealing the basic weakness and long-enduring follies that existed among the American people he had served so long.[2] The basic problems that the

---

[1] Alvin Johnson, *The Clock of History*, p. 242.
[2] *Newsweek*, April 23, 1945.

President had faced and for which he had offered solutions were still the problems of the American people.

In dealing with these problems in the decade following Mr. Roosevelt's death, American leaders of all shades of opinion and many degrees of understanding found that they had to contend with the continuing influence of the President upon the people. The majority of the electorate had voted for Roosevelt repeatedly, and a great many would go on voting the Roosevelt program for many years.

Such an assignment as was given him by the American people had been given no other. Seeking power and more power as a mode of self-expression—the dominant drive throughout his life—Franklin Roosevelt had taken to himself more power than any American had ever exercised.

From the outset he played the role in the grand manner. His physical handicap was in itself an aid. He was at the center of the stage. Most traveled of all rulers, wherever his plane or ship or car stopped, he became the focus of men's thoughts and emotions and actions. He was a mighty symbol of the United States of America.

If there were a throne in the modern world, here it was in all its grandeur. By personal inclination and by painstaking preparation, Franklin Roosevelt seemed to embody the powers of a man who had all the future for his own. However much the world outside the United States might recognize such a figure as familiar, nothing in the history of the United States —since the time when George Washington refused to have the attributes of a monarch or the title of King—had prepared the American people for this.

There is no escape from a fact repeatedly stated, yet often overlooked because of its utter familiarity: the ultimate authority, the American electorate, was responsible for Roosevelt's opportunity. His had been no arbitrary seizure of power, nor had duress been used in his elections. It was no contrived result that could later be proved false. Nor had illegal means been used in retaining his power. The people had said repeatedly: "Go forward as our representative in accordance with the programs and policies and objectives outlined."

Of course the tremendous reach of this Presidential rule had been possible because of the industrial and scientific might of the United States. This Mr. Roosevelt marshaled on behalf of the masses seeking to escape from the despotism of dictators. It was this mighty tribune of the people who authorized the experimentation and construction through which emerged the most destructive weapon in all history.

So far, indeed, had personal power asserted itself that President Roosevelt had within his grasp—as he neared the end—not only the creation of a structure for world peace, but the creation of a physical power that could destroy the world or build it in the image of an entirely new scientific perspective.

Buoyant, hopeful, zestful, eager, experimental, he had reflected the emotions that all youth felt and all who had passed youth remembered with either regret or misgiving—but usually with understanding. He dealt with the mass of mankind the world around, as he dealt with groups of his fellow countrymen, and as he was wont to deal with individuals who crowded about him.

Franklin Roosevelt saw himself in the role of a "happy warrior" even during the crises of his days of supremacy. And the American people—who in their lighter moments crave a hero in sport, on the stage, or in combat—saw in their President one who had triumphed over adversity, risen to great heights of personal achievement, and was mastering the forces of evil.

As politics for the majority of Americans had always been the favorite of all games, here, more nearly than ever before in their history, was a hero to match their dreams. He could "walk with Kings—nor lose the common touch," and had, in truth, "forced heart and nerve and sinew to serve his turn long after they [were] gone."

To the end, Franklin Roosevelt never left his class. He remained aloof in his feeling, his manner, his attitude. However much camaraderie existed, it was that of the leader relaxing with those who served him. His attitude in press conferences, his predilection for personal consultation with rulers of foreign nations, his superb confidence in dealing with political rivals —revealed that here was a man born to rule.

Dramatic were his repeated overtures to Hitler, to Mussolini, and later to Stalin. And these, in addition to his correspondence with other heads of states, were evidence of his use of the power of place to determine public policy, quite apart from the usual formal approaches through diplomatic representatives.

Franklin Roosevelt had a lively sense of his place in history. It could hardly have been otherwise. This had an important part in his ceaseless gathering of the materials bearing on his actions in public office. He expressed a view that must often have been in his mind when, in a tribute to Justice Oliver Wendell Holmes on the one hundredth anniversary of the birth of the Justice, he wrote: "It is the quality of great men that they continue to live long after they are gone." [3]

What a man says himself is of great value, but it must be measured always by his comprehension, his outlook, and his purpose. It is here, perhaps, that we are on the surest ground in judging how great a leader Roosevelt was. Of his conception of the majesty and power of the Presidency, there is no question. It is written large in his utterances and in his attitude, certainty, and finality in action.

Of his deep comprehension of the basic problems of statecraft there is grave question. His simplicity in explanation of what seemed to him the fundamentals of economics and politics, of philosophy and of science, is the best evidence of his limitations. He was thoughtful and deeply aspiring, but singularly naïve, particularly about himself. Consequently his record as prepared and his explanations of events for "the future historian" are often superficial and must be judged as such in any analysis and judgment of his contributions.

Specialists trained in the law and in economics find it more difficult to explain Mr. Roosevelt's methods than specialists trained in politics. The reason is apparent in his own primary interest. But specialists in psychology and history find much that is enlightening in his procedures and in his declared objectives. Nearest, perhaps, to a full understanding of his method of action and his use of language are those whose primary interest is in biography. The abiding interest that held Mr. Roosevelt throughout the years was in human beings, and most

---

[3] *Public Papers, 1941*, p. 47.

of all in the human being whose life he knew best and whose life he wished biographers to understand in all the years to come.

The historian of these fateful years in the life of the American people must face the problem of evaluating the mind of Mr. Roosevelt. He must not be deterred from a conclusion by realization that he is formulating a concept for his own use that has not the certainty of scientific analysis or the finality of a judgment of God.

There is much evidence. Contemporaries supply it in abundance, and it must be added, without fundamental agreement. There is easy escape in the oft-asserted conclusion that the mind of the President was complex, baffling, and beyond comprehension. But this will not suffice.

Of all the evidence available to the historian, none ranks in importance with three sources: first, *F.D.R.: His Personal Letters,* particularly to friends; second, his speeches, especially those that are known to be his own; and third, his extemporaneous remarks which have been recorded. Of these, the extemporaneous remarks, particularly in press conferences, are most revealing of the mind that, in its power of decision and opportunity of evasion, governed the United States for more than a decade and determined in great measure the lives of all peoples in the world for a half-dozen years.

On the basis of an examination of these sources, it is a conclusion here stated that the mind was one of vivid imagination, amazing grasp of detail, but also of unusual confusion, of inconsistency, often given to downright evasion. Explanation of his evasions and inconsistencies owing to the immensity of his task and the importance of keeping controls at all cost—does not change the fundamental conclusion.

A contemporary who watched as a close observer of the President throughout these years concluded that there was "absolutely no one who knew the President's mind." It was, he said, "Indolent, superficial, gay, deeply interested in the trivial —yet forced to deal with subjects and problems beyond its comprehension." [4]

_____
[4] Related to the author in confidence.

Perhaps as clear a reflection of the perplexity that Mr. Roosevelt caused even his most devoted supporters is to be found in *The Secret Diary of Harold L. Ickes.* It was "impossible to come to grips with him," wrote Mr. Ickes.

That the President's trait of seeming preoccupation with non-essentials—for whatever reason, deliberate or otherwise—intruded at important moments is admitted by Mr. Rosenman in his notes descriptive of the conference at Teheran, where Roosevelt was the moderator, arbitrator and final authority. "His contributions to the conversations," reports Rosenman, "were infrequent and sometimes annoyingly irrelevant, but it appears time and again—at Teheran and at Yalta—that it was he who spoke the last word." [5]

Testimony upon Mr. Roosevelt as administrator is practically unanimous to the effect that he was not efficient or effective. A lesser man or one burdened with lesser tasks could have made exact, direct, meticulous, and neat decisions. But in his performance of his function as administrator, he had to delegate great powers of administration, and he should have delegated more.

His task, as he conceived of it, was one that compelled confusion, inconsistency and inconclusiveness—and this for an ever-present reason. To keep in working order personal advisers, Cabinet officers, Congressional leaders and the press, he had to be all things to all men. And he alone could be judge of the timing, the emergency, and the outcome. The task called for a consummate artist in the field of guessing.

The problem of responsibility lends itself to endless debate. The explanation of policy and of action must wait upon further knowledge and upon clinical studies with respect to the personality of the President. The immediate responsibility for any decision is also open to serious question, for many men operated in this field. The words and acts of the President must be, in the annals of history, his own responsibility. Only the President in the august majesty of an office of great power can be brought to the bar of history.

It follows that much of the criticism of Mr. Roosevelt in the

---

[5] *Public Papers, 1943,* p. 536.

course of campaigns and throughout his terms of office is in-
admissible to the extent that it did not envisage him as ruler.
This clears the ground for a testing of Mr. Roosevelt as ruler,
and in the perspective of history that is a test that will stand
when all discussion of him as partisan leader will seem relatively unimportant.

That his knowledge often lacked depth—and that his imagination was always vivid—fitted well the role he sought to play.
That he did not have an unswerving body of principles and
that he was adept at accommodation, compromise and, on occasion, sharp trading, was the conviction of many of the people
who supported him.

Political leadership is not necessarily synonymous with personal leadership. The reputation of Franklin Roosevelt as a
political leader rests upon his use of the Democratic party, his
control of Congress, and his victory at the polls. In the sphere
of formulating programs and obtaining legislation, his claim as
a political leader is much less than his claim as a personal
leader.

In using political means for achieving political results, it
was usually his personal leadership that was the deciding factor.
This personal leadership was pragmatic—an individual playing
by ear. It was experimental—an individual using successive opportunities. It was intuitive—an individual sensing the popular
desires. It followed naturally that he kept power in his own
hands; that even his closest advisers felt that his moves were
unpredictable.

Perhaps the most complete revelation of the man who considered himself a ruler reporting to his people, and who was
asking to lead them by superior knowledge and experience—
above all, by wisdom and conscience—is found in his addresses
at the height of his campaigning. If ever there was evidence
that it is possible in the United States to develop the ruler of
a great people, it is found in the attitude, posture, and presumption of Franklin Roosevelt. Campaigning in the grand
manner, except for the first Presidential campaign he had no
dangerous opponent. He had adversaries, and he had to overcome obstacles. But he alone stood before the people armed
with "the truth," for he alone was "in a position to know it."
The very fact that it was put in persuasive terms, often lacked

aggressive emphasis, and rarely manifested the bombast of lesser men—made it the more effective.

The pronouncements of the President which served to present his point of view of the destiny of the United States and of the part he played in its achievement were couched in such terms that all could easily understand. The constant theme was individual aspiration; the ever-recurring call was for self-confidence; and the insistent and dominating assertion was that of belief in the power of men and women to govern because they *were* in fact governing themselves. No problem could not be solved.

In interpreting Mr. Roosevelt's utterances, it has been shown repeatedly in the foregoing pages that there is need to determine not only the sources of the ideas expressed, but also the process by which the speech came to be "his own."

So, too, in the analysis of the great acts of his administration, it is obvious that there were innumerable cases, as has been shown, where the decision was definitely his own. But countless—and in some cases major—decisions were products of other men's determination and power. An understanding of Mr. Roosevelt's action must therefore be based upon knowledge of the work of his chosen advisers.

The innumerable advisers who had so large a part in the years of Franklin Roosevelt's administration were not "practical men." They were, in a very real sense, dreamers. Of course the dreamers carried with them many practical men. But the remedies and the plans for a "new world" were the work of men who did not always count the cost in money, men, or morale. As zealots—dedicated to great causes—they struck a responsive chord in the hearts of many of their fellow citizens.

An unusual combination of political forces brought to the dreamers great opportunities that were continued through the years, until they could dream not only for America, but for all mankind. This had much to do with bringing Americans into World War II and into the United Nations Organization.

What is to be included in the composite picture of Franklin Roosevelt that is presented to a reader who did not know him, probably never saw him, and who must depend upon those who did, and upon the records that he kept and left for posterity? Into the composite picture must go first of all Roosevelt as he saw himself. It is written large in his explanations, written as he said for the guidance of later historians. Then there are the explanations and descriptions of his intimates, his associates, and the members of his family.

These must be constantly used, but attention must also be given to the work of discerning critics, both favorable and adverse, who observed and presented their criticisms in his lifetime. Most important of these are the specialists in a hundred lines of activity who watched what he did and said with far greater knowledge, larger perspective, and very different objective than he possessed.

One thing is clear. No picture of the President can be accepted as fully truthful that does not include these views. Fulsome eulogy or devastating denunciation are for other purposes than that which actuates those who wish to present an historic figure in the perspective of time.

It may well be that the final judgment that will endure when the Roosevelt era is surveyed, as is the Jackson era or that of Lincoln or of Wilson—as a period remote and somewhat less important—will be that made upon Mr. Roosevelt's "great decisions." It is a habit of men to regard their heroes in light of their deeds.[6]

Franklin D. Roosevelt shaped the history of his country—and of the world—because he always appeared to be affirmative. He proclaimed the affirmative attitude to be all-important. To the American people in despondency after a period of disillusionment he had said we can and will succeed! To a world sunk in the despondency of long suffering, he had said we can build a better world! And the magic rested in the fact that speaking with such assurance of objectives and not of obstacles, he reflected precisely what his hearers wished to hear.

For the years 1933 to 1945, it is clear that the leadership of the masses of men was the great theme to which history will give first place. Among the leaders, on the basis of determining

---

[6] As an example even in our own time, see the perceptive and eloquent summary of W. L. Chenery in his *So It Seemed*, chapter XXIII, and particularly p. 256.

influence in these years, first place must be given Mr. Roosevelt.

In arousing the public conscience of Americans to maladjustments which had been observed for generations but which had never moved any group in power to a comprehensive program of change, Roosevelt was able to formulate some of the needed changes and see them written into law. That in doing this, he aroused such intense antagonism on the part of many of the more thoughtful members of society was a direct result of the methods that he used. In declaring repeatedly that the championship of a program on behalf of the people was in itself an indication of its virtue and that all who opposed it were to be termed evil, he took a position which was unacceptable to those who found justification for public policy in sound programs and honest administration.

Roosevelt's leadership resulted in fundamental changes in the government itself: in tremendous concentration of power in the Executive; in building up a vast system of bureaucratic control of private business; and by adding direct economic support of the citizen to the careful adjustment of conflicting economic interests in a free enterprise system.

The revolution consisted in the complete shift of the American view of the role of government. *Government* under Roosevelt, and particularly the Executive, was to be all-powerful. The defense of this—if there was a defense—was that the people freely and frequently could pass judgment upon it. As long as there were free elections at stated times, there could not be overpowering objection to such a government. In protection of the people—that is, in this case the minority—against the possible action of such a government, the strong weapon in American practice was free speech and the free press. Any suppression of absolute freedom would tend to limit the field of criticism.

Franklin Roosevelt was credited by millions with being their savior. Yet, on the whole, this leadership—in method and result —was injurious to the slow working of democracy as Americans know it, and have thought of it in terms of the leadership of Jefferson or Lincoln or Wilson.

Dependence upon continuous consultation with unofficial advisers, upon acceptable compromise, and finally an arbitrary and personal decision—are characteristic of a tribal chieftain's

THE TRAGEDY OF LEADERSHIP

point of view. But it was limited in value in a world of developed science and knowledge. It was "Politics." [7]

The President who would deal with "kings" and who was surrounded by the men "of his court," and who could advise and counsel with many, must also gather from many sources the intellectual content of his pronouncements. As this practice grew, the habit of dependence upon conferences tended to dictate Mr. Roosevelt's direction of the policies of the United States.

Even before actual war came upon the United States, there was outstanding example of a determination of the actual direction of the American people, without their consent, in his proclamation of the Atlantic Charter.[8]

On the deck of a warship surrounded not by the chosen representatives of the people, but by his personal advisers and selected representatives of the army and the navy, he proclaimed the principles—as he saw them—that would cause the United States to enter upon a course that eventually led to involvement in war. As a platform for a group glorifying in the might of America for the righteous cause of all humanity, it was superb.

Military conquerors have high place in the annals of the race, and military leaders have been given high place even by the people of the United States. A basic reason rests in the acceptance of conflict as the primary condition of all mankind. Political leaders make it their chief concern to channel these conflicts into peaceful discussions and acceptable decisions.

Statesmen are those who, because of mental superiority, moral conviction, and energetic activity, provide peaceful victories. But no statesman, and certainly no political leader, has for the mass of mankind the hold upon the imagination that

---

[7] "The struggle [the President's] was a political one; it was neither clean nor pretty. . . . But all his experience taught him that scruples had to be compromised in politics. Fire had to be fought with fire." "The Compromising Roosevelt," by R. G. Tugwell in *The Western Political Quarterly*, VI (June, 1953), 320-340.

[8] The President said in a press conference on January 2, 1942 (vol. 19, p. 004, Roosevelt Library), "The Atlantic Charter didn't refer only to the Atlantic. It referred to the whole world. It happened to be on the Atlantic Ocean. That is why it was called the Atlantic Charter."

is accorded the conqueror. It is so easy to see what the conqueror does, so hard to judge what the statesman accomplishes.

Franklin Roosevelt presented himself to his people as a leader in conflicts in which they had deep interest. This was accompanied by praise of their accomplishments as they saw them. He fought the selfish "interests" that had engulfed the nation in ruin; he fought the political forces that stood across the path of the popular will; he fought the totalitarian rulers that would dominate the world. As Commander-in-Chief he came to his full powers.

Mistakes in military leadership may be traced directly to Mr. Roosevelt as Commander-in-Chief. Careful distinctions must, however, be made. The United States was plunged into World War II by a military defeat of first magnitude. Ever since the Japanese attack on Pearl Harbor, the American people in accepting the challenge to united effort, nevertheless questioned the seeming inevitability of that defeat. Some said that a political leader of great acumen, by means of legitimate diplomacy, had forced the enemy to attack first and by so doing, united the American people in support of Presidential policies. Others insisted, without the support of adequate evidence, that the defeat at Pearl Harbor came about through default by President Roosevelt and his military leaders.

The declaration for "unconditional surrender," however circumscribed by American military commanders, even though in part repudiated by the President near the close of the war, was a blunder of first magnitude. It stiffened every resistance and gave tremendous power to the extremists in Germany.

The initial approval of the Morgenthau plan was again a blunder that brought consequences of tremendous cost. It not only gave the German government additional reason for calling for continued resistance; it indicated a blindness to the facts in the case on the part of the American Commander-in-Chief. Such a plan, if adopted, even in part, would strengthen the power of Russia in central Europe and make certain future triumphs for communism.

The crowning mistake in the leadership of Franklin Roosevelt was neither insistence upon unconditional surrender, nor the intended devastation of Germany. A profound misconception of the international situation and an overwhelming belief in the efficacy of a new idealism to change the deep currents of world history led to a persistent attempt to make war serve a definite military result. This was defeat of the enemy without heed to the direct and immediate political result. Mr. Roosevelt shared a common delusion of his time that Russia, and others, would forsake revolution and concentrate upon progress within the nation, and that the Soviet Union could be controlled within the United Nations Organization.

On the other hand, had President Roosevelt as Commander-in-Chief fought the war in terms of collective internationalism, using corresponding methods, he would have been able to establish a union of peoples with great strength. But nationalism was stressed throughout the conduct of the war. This dilemma in time became manifest.

To win the objectives of the war, as he stated them to the American people, the President must in the end construct a means of international agreement, long an American dream but never an American practice. The dream faded, even though the form of belief was provided in the United Nations, for no dominant internationalism appeared. Nationalism emerged stronger than ever, because it had won the war.

Had the President comprehended the international situation as visualized in his own State Department, he might have listened to Churchill even at Yalta. "From some points of view," wrote an official of the State Department charged with responsibility in negotiations preliminary to the San Francisco Conference of United Nations, "the worst feature about this war is that it leaves one or two [nations] face to face with almost no pivot state between. . . . The fateful choice we have taken is to turn aside from what seemed the inevitable pyramidic structure of peoples finally under one power through conquest— which was for long, it seemed, the inevitable outcome of the military age we have lived in to date—to a combination of powers, acting on the principle of agreed forms of restraint and working with other states, in an international organization. This course has been chosen deliberately by the great powers concerned as the alternative to another war in which it would be almost if not actually impossible for one to contend successfully with the other without ruining itself and failing to gain a victory even so." [9]

Everyone has agreed that Mr. Roosevelt must be measured first of all as a world leader. He many times made it clear that he thought so. His era was a time of world tensions—and no amount of preoccupation with national concerns could make it otherwise.

An underlying weakness of his leadership lay in his acceptance of the pragmatic approach to the solution of both domestic and foreign problems. In essence, it was a refusal to take the stand for a distinctively American approach to the basic problems of capitalism. No political program that emerged in the Roosevelt administration was distinctly the expression of the American tradition. In the course of twelve years, at home and abroad, the President stood with the radicals, using the political party parlance of the "middle way" in both instances.

He would extend into the organization of the proposed United Nations the same alignments which he had done so much to strengthen in the United States. Naturally, therefore, he and his immediate advisers would favor the weakening and eventual downfall of all colonialism, of all so-called imperialism, and of the forces of capitalism that in Britain as well as America had built the modern world.

The persuasive ability that Mr. Roosevelt had so constantly used in domestic and in foreign affairs was based upon a willingness to consult and to compromise in the hope of preserving democracy. Having, in truth, no fundamental conviction of the importance of adhering absolutely to Constitutional government as Americans had known it, he likewise saw no necessity of constantly opposing the Communist as well as the Fascist enemies of that philosophy of society. Lack of conviction made it possible for him to assure himself and his followers that he had, in the pragmatic approach, the key to the future.

The recurrent theme of the period 1933-1945 is one of deepest tragedy among the people of the world—a long series of mournful events accompanied by loss of millions of human

---

[9] Confidential letter of March 17, 1945, addressed to the author.

lives by human violence. The villains in this tragedy were clearly marked. Yet, as clearly, there emerged a hero, a man of good intention who would battle the forces of evil and win. Again and again Franklin Roosevelt won the battle, but in the end he seemed to lose the war. Losing, he was still a hero, but his effort emphasized the tragedy.

Frustration is the result of an attempt to understand this tragedy. Talent he possessed—genius, let it be admitted—in sensing the needs and results of leadership. But did Roosevelt have a real grasp of leadership in ideas, in probing the unknown for answers in the social, economic and political fields? Again and again it would seem that only one immune to real learning and utterly unconscious of the intricacies and complexities of long-sustained argument could blithely assert as Mr. Roosevelt so often did that a solution had been found or was to be found.

By all tests he was a successful politician, the most successful of his day, if what is meant thereby is the manipulation of men, organizations, and programs to the end that the politician and his followers may remain in power. This was all-important if the politician was to take office away from the conservative and keep it out of the hands of the radical. Such a politician, in the course of his ceaseless activity, does accomplish much good, arouse much enthusiasm, and bring to his support millions.

But in terms of the ultimate solution of problems, or of placing such problems in the general stream of American development, he does incalculable harm. The American people accepted the pattern which was gradually woven by Roosevelt's leadership, and on the face of things millions profited from his action. But as the years passed, it became evident that the balance had to be paid.

Questions concerning the health and well-being of this powerful leader have been given much attention and will be given more as additional evidence is revealed. Most of the attention so far has been directed to the last two years of the President's life. Controversy has arisen over the reports of his illness and the failure of either his physicians or his intimates to permit "the truth to be known." This is important, because the tasks assumed by the President and those forced upon him by circumstances were such as to demand a chief in full vigor. Brushing aside all the evidence as to the extent of his deterioration, the basic fact admitted by countless witnesses is that for at least a year before his death he was not able to exercise his full powers.

The final picture of the President must be seen against the background of reality. He had been a cripple for twenty-four years. This fact had not seemed apparent to the people he had led for so long. Yet, despite the dramatic gestures of the campaign of 1944, it became increasingly clear to discerning observers that, in addition to being crippled, he was so borne down by the burdens of office that he could appear only occasionally to the general public.[10]

Always wilful—never more so than when thwarted in his desires and intentions, he dimly saw the defeat that was inevitable. Yet the evidence of the concluding years shows the struggle of a giant—at work upon a giant task—and aided in every possible way by those about him to do just this unceasingly to the very end. It was tragedy in a world setting.

During the years of his all-powerful leadership, Franklin Roosevelt made great decisions [11] that tower above all others in their influence upon the events of his time. Each of these decisions at the time either expressed the view of the majority of the American people, or appealed to them as desirable when the decision became known.

Certainly the majority of Americans wanted no co-operation with the defeated Hoover in the period of the interregnum. Yet the results were disastrous at the time and in the years that followed.

The public lauded the independence of the President in deciding not to co-operate in an attempt at world economic recovery by joint action of the free nations. By taking an American isolationist course in the world economic struggle at the time of the London Conference in 1933, Mr. Roosevelt broke up the conference, affording initial opportunity to the dictators to develop their destructive program.

The majority of Americans looked with no serious misgiving

---

[10] Yet a detailed examination of his responses in his last nine press conferences has convinced the author that the President was, at the time, in full possession of his capacity for thought and decision.

[11] See Sumner Welles, *Seven Decisions That Shaped History*, a brilliant exposition of foreign policy, published in 1950.

upon recognition of a Communist government in Russia in 1933. This opened the way to the long train of mistaken moves that finally brought the United States face to face with communism in Europe and in Asia.

That the majority hailed with enthusiasm the expenditure of public funds for relief, public works, and the vast plan of public utilities has been self-evident. Thus the nation was embarked on a long program of deficit spending resulting in inflation and the constant threat of national bankruptcy.

So, too, the people as a whole applauded President Roosevelt's attempt to curb the Supreme Court and thus to do away with the testing of the "New Deal" under the Constitution of the United States.

The people looked with suspicion on European dictators and acquiesced in the President's efforts to check them—by methods that led the nation to war. The basic decision was made by the President, and not by the Congress.

Public opinion supported the President's suspicion of Japanese expansion in the Far East and his decision to stand across the path of Japan. The steps in the diplomatic process were shrouded in darkness, but at the time of the attack on Pearl Harbor, the people gave evidence of their belief in the leadership of the President.

The people favored harshness toward enemies in World War II (Unconditional Surrender) and for a time looked with distinct favor upon severe limitation of the economic recovery of enemy peoples.

Furthermore, the people supported ruthlessness and ultimately approved the preparation of the atomic bomb to crush the Japanese. Thus was launched a new method of destruction which has brought the nations into a continuous struggle for survival.

The American people would join with other free nations in an effort to build an international organization—provided it protected American independence. Thus they facilitated a defense of nationalism and its principles within an organization whose chief international interest has proved to be the struggle against communism.

The most fateful of all Roosevelt's decisions was embodied in the secret agreements with Stalin made at Yalta in February,

1945. As has been pointed out in detail, these agreements were not known to the public at the time, and only in subsequent years have revelations come—not only in official statements but in the accounts given by other participants in that conference. The basic decision made by the President was to co-operate with the Russians in concluding the war and in the establishment of spheres of interest in the Far East. This meant that, in time, communism would threaten the entire continent of Asia.

Franklin Delano Roosevelt appeared in a great role on a vast stage, a hero not only to millions of his fellow countrymen, but also to millions of his contemporaries throughout the world. The role was tragic in a fateful drama—a man of fundamentally good intention overwhelmed by the forces of his time in a gigantic struggle to solve the pressing problems of his nation and of the world. President Roosevelt was a leader in a revolution at home and abroad. The revolution at home was a rearrangement of social and economic forces and a change of the function of government in American life. The revolution abroad was an attempt to substitute for the forces expressed in balance of power among nations the concept of international union to insure peace. The means he used, at home and abroad, to implement his ideas appear in terms of their development under his skillful and adroit direction. The struggle in the final analysis seems to be primarily one of intellectual grasp and moral discrimination. Roosevelt's failure lay in his unsuccessful attempt to justify the means or establish the ends he had in view. This was his personal tragedy. Inasmuch as on major decisions he had a majority support, it was also the tragedy of the American people.

PART TWO

1. *The Legendary Roosevelt*

During the decade following the death of Franklin Roosevelt, faithful followers of the late President have nurtured the legend that was powerful in the days of his active service. Myths that contributed to the legend were in the making even in the years of Mr. Roosevelt's preparation for the Presidency. That has been true of all who have occupied the Presidency. Every President has had a cult of worshippers.

In the case of Franklin Roosevelt it was inevitable for reasons that have been pointed out in the previous pages of this book. Roosevelt was President for twelve years and Commander-in-Chief for four years. These are known as the Roosevelt Years. Nothing can change that record.

The legend has grown as the years have passed, and there is every reason to believe that it will continue to grow and flourish long after this generation has gone. This legend includes: all opinion about Franklin Roosevelt of those who knew him or thought they knew him; all stories that have Roosevelt as the central figure and reason for being; and a vast array of impressions that linger after the event, the experience, and the story are forgotten. These impressions are reinforced by constant presentation of figure and voice in countless pictures and in recordings of spoken words which give the illusion—to all who see and hear—of being present and therefore participating either as actor or observer in the event that contributed to the legend.

Such a dream world of faith—and emotional uplift—bears remote relation to the world of fact that is available in the record of the years 1933 to 1945. It is this record that must be examined if Franklin Roosevelt's contemporaries are to judge him and his leadership in terms of the hard realities of the daily life of the man who exercised such immense power and had such transcendent influence.

But is it possible at this early date to express a considered judgment upon the action of Roosevelt in those years? As has been said in the Preface, it is possible—and it is necessary if we are to survive as a thoughtful and self-determining people. Easy assertion that the historian ought to wait until all contemporaries are dead, until all documents are collected—until all passions have cooled—is false in outlook and destructive in practice. It must be done *now*—as best it can be done—because something that passes for history is always in public discussion, and it is added to daily by those who are not interested in history, but in myths, legend, and propaganda. It is the duty of the historian to consider the false and the true, and to strive to present an authentic figure.

The reader of the printed material on Franklin Roosevelt that has flowed from the presses ever since he became President must have been impressed by the fact that each writer considered the United States and the administration of Roosevelt from his own point of view. Consequently, the level of discussion was determined by the writer's conception of the United States, of the Presidency, and of Mr. Roosevelt.

Some of this discussion has been on a very low plane indeed in all three respects. The picture of the United States and of its people has not always been truthful. The nation envisaged by President Roosevelt himself—as he looked out upon the world—and the people of whom he wrote and for whom he acted constituted a "great theme."

Only as the reader approaches this subject with the President's outlook does he realize what Mr. Roosevelt did and did not do— against a background of national and international fact. Consequently, we must dismiss, as of little importance, masses of gossip and speculation, innuendo, and denunciation. Neither Mr. Roosevelt nor the American people whom he represented were motivated by selfishness, small outlook, greed, and brutal purpose. Such individuals did exist. Mr. Roosevelt had to deal with that fact. But he never lost sight of the great, dominant purpose, the idealistic outlook, and the deep faith of the men and women who had built America.

In the effort to separate legend and fact—and to approach the reality of the present moment—attention has been given the following: the record as prepared by Mr. Roosevelt; the words of the President in print and in manuscript; the official record; the contemporary record as seen by commentators in the press and on the radio; the interpretations at the time and after the event; the memoirs of contemporaries; and the biographies of the President. The following pages provide the reader with that information to the extent possible in this particular book.

The materials are arranged within groups in *order of publication,* because it was in this way that facts were revealed and legends were created, and it is, above all, important to see *the process* of revelation in actual operation.

As a final indication of the belief of the writer that only as this process is ever present is there hope of real understanding, a final section is termed The Continuing Stream—presenting books and articles that have most recently appeared.

2. *Roosevelt as Historian*

As President of the United States, Franklin Roosevelt knew that a judgment upon his administration would be based ultimately on a full record. He did his best to furnish such a record as he saw it. This record was collected and preserved by the President and placed in the Franklin D. Roosevelt Library at Hyde Park, New York.[1]

No one of President Roosevelt's predecessors, not even President Hoover, made such a sustained effort throughout his administration to "prepare the way for the historians." This was a phrase used frequently by Mr. Roosevelt, and it was repeated by Mrs. Roosevelt and others.

Of course the record was partisan to the extent that it was written from the President's point of view. This is a very important fact, often ignored by commentators and critics. Naturally, the Presidency of Franklin Roosevelt must be viewed first of all from the point of view of Mr. Roosevelt himself. Yet it is essential that the circumstances of the keeping of his record be known.

On December 10, 1938, President Roosevelt announced his intention to house his personal and public manuscripts in a library building to be constructed on his Hyde Park family estate. Administration of the collection would be in the hands of the Archivist of the United States. The building was completed in 1940 and dedicated on June 30, 1941. Some materials were opened for use on May 1, 1946, but most of the collection had to await sifting by

---

[1] Beginning with the *First Annual Report of the Archivist of the United States as to the Franklin D. Roosevelt Library 1939-1940,* ten such reports were issued by the Archivist. Subsequent reports of the Archivist covering the Library have been incorporated in the *Annual Report of the Administrator of the General Services Administration.* The report for the year ending June 30, 1952, contains important material as to acquisition of additional materials of the President and of a number of his contemporaries. In a paper on Research Materials at the Franklin D. Roosevelt Library, read before a meeting of the American Historical Association in Chicago on December 29, 1953, Herman Kahn, the Director of the Library, gives the most exact summary available. Published in *American Archivist,* XVII (April, 1954), 149-162.

the President's personal secretary, Grace Tully, and his friend, the compiler of the *Public Papers,* Samuel I. Rosenman.

On March 17, 1950, it was announced that about 85 percent of the total volume of Roosevelt papers (1910-1945) were open for research purposes. The Administrator of General Services Administration wrote:

> It was unprecedented in American history for a President to leave his papers to the Nation. It was equally unprecedented for papers of a President to be made available 5 years after the close of his term of office.[2]

The papers that were not opened at this time were to be examined periodically by the staff, and it is believed that few papers will be restricted for a period longer than twenty-five years after President Roosevelt's death.

At the end of the year 1953, the total volume of the Roosevelt Papers was placed at about 6,644 cubic feet. Presidential letters cited by searchers are usually carbon copies or other copies of originals, which despite the possibility of handwritten additions or changes by Mr. Roosevelt on the originals, nevertheless remain the best source now available on important matters.

A press release of the General Services Administration in 1950 asserted that it was "rarely possible" to determine from Library materials "what transpired during President Roosevelt's conferences with a particular person at a particular time." For:

> It was *not* White House policy to make a stenographic transcript of President Roosevelt's conferences or discussions with his advisors or visitors, and there is usually no record of what took place at such conferences and discussions. This was a matter of conscious policy with President Roosevelt, who believed that the presence of any kind of a stenographer or any kind of a recording device during oral discussions or conferences served as a strong deterrent to the frank and honest exchange of opinions on delicate matters.[3]

This lack of first-hand source material was noted by the authors of a recent volume on United States foreign policy: ". . . since the late President left little in the way of notes, diaries, or memoirs, and since his closest associates concede their ignorance of his inmost thoughts, reliable and detailed information on the motivation of his foreign policy will in all probability remain forever lacking."[4]

---

[2] *Report of Administrator of General Services* (June 30, 1950), p. 69.

[3] *Ibid.* Director Kahn adds. ". . . very rarely is it possible to find in his papers a verbatim record of a conversation or even any general indication of the nature of the conversation." (*Op. cit.,* p. 5.)

[4] Langer and Gleason, *The Challenge to Isolation,* p. 3.

Among the categories of papers restricted by agreement among the Roosevelt heirs, Mr. Rosenman, and Miss Tully, together with others consulted, are reports of investigations of individuals and their applications and recommendations for governmental posts; any documents which are thought to contain "derogatory remarks concerning the character, loyalty, integrity, or ability of individuals" or information on their personal or family affairs, especially any that might harass them or their heirs; "documents containing information the release of which would be prejudicial to national security . . . [or] would be prejudicial to the maintenance of friendly relations with foreign nations"; and any communications addressed to the President in confidence. The White House Map Room Papers, deposited in 1951 by direction of President Truman, are not open for general research purposes.

President Roosevelt objected strongly to the use of the word "memorial" in connection with the designation of the Roosevelt Library, insisting that it was to be a research center. Had his papers gone to a special division of the National Archives in Washington, or to the Library of Congress Manuscript Division,[5] there would have been no question on the point. As it is, however, the visitor to the Roosevelt Library is conscious of a memorial atmosphere. The Library is adjacent to the Roosevelt family home and the Roosevelt grave. Thousands of the curious or reverent every month pour through the museum in the foyer of the Library where are on exhibit the gifts sent to the American President and his wife from every part of the world.

Quite apart from the Roosevelt collection, but housed with it, are the diaries, letters, and personal materials of a number of Mr. Roosevelt's associates, most of whom served in public life as aides to the President during the period 1933-1945. In the *Tenth Annual Report of the Archivist of the United States on the Franklin D. Roosevelt Library* appear the words:

Mr. Morgenthau's generous gift (Papers of Henry Morgenthau, Jr., 1934-1945) represents the bringing to fruition of a decision he made long ago to carry out the expressed desire of President Roosevelt that all of his associates record their activities, to the end that scholars might have at hand the information necessary to describe and evaluate the era that began in 1933.[6]

---

[5] In the Library of Congress, also, are to be found manuscript materials not only of Franklin Roosevelt, but of a number of public men who served in the period of his Presidency. In the Hoover Library at Stanford University are the public papers of Herbert Hoover, who throughout the period of Roosevelt's Presidency was the most vigorous critic of the policies of the administration.
[6] P. 3. "The so-called 'Diaries' of Mr. Henry Morgenthau, Jr., comprising some 900 bound volumes covering the period 1933-1945, are not diaries in any

Other major collections are the papers of Harry Hopkins and of John G. Winant. The papers of Charles W. Taussig, Herbert C. Pell, and the late Senator Elbert D. Thomas are also of importance, particularly for the war period.

If President Roosevelt visualized his contemporaries who survived him making use of this great Library he must have realized how restricted would be their research for many years to come. For, although the bulk of the material is available, that which is restricted for security reasons is perhaps of most importance to the contemporary. For example, as Mr. Kahn states, "the Map Room papers contain most of President Roosevelt's communications with the heads of other States concerning war matters during the period 1942-1945, as well as with the special emissaries he sent abroad on war missions." [7]

Only the gradual release of restricted material, through security "declassification" or otherwise, will make it possible to tell the whole story which Franklin Roosevelt intended to reveal.[8]

3. The Words of Franklin D. Roosevelt

Editions of miscellaneous writings by Mr. Roosevelt began to appear before his death in 1945. This was as he wished it, for the largest of the collections appeared under his own sponsorship, and with extensive editorial treatment by his intimate friend and assistant, Samuel I. Rosenman, an attorney and a Roosevelt-appointed New York State jurist, who had worked with him since the 1928 campaign.

The Public Papers and Addresses of Franklin D. Roosevelt appeared in thirteen volumes at the hands of three publishers. Random House issued in 1938 five volumes, entitled: *1928-1932: The Genesis of the New Deal; 1933: The Year of Crisis; 1934: The Advance of Recovery and Reform; 1935: The Court Disapproves;* and *1936: The People Approve.* On each title page were the words, "With a Special Introduction and Explanatory Notes by President

<hr>

real sense. They are, rather, a detailed record of his conferences, of his telephone conversations, and copies of important documents that went across his desk." (Kahn, *op. cit.*, p. 8.)

[7] *Op. cit.*, p. 8.

[8] At the President's press conference on April 24, 1942, the Director of the Roosevelt Library was present, and the President in introducing him to the correspondents said, "He sees that the record is adequately kept for future generations." (Press Conferences, vol. 19, p. 297, Roosevelt Library.)

Roosevelt." Each carried the statement: "The material in these volumes has been compiled and collated by Samuel I. Rosenman, Counsel to the Governor during the administration of Franklin D. Roosevelt as Governor of the State of New York 1929-1932."

The President explained in a brief General Introduction to the first volume that his "old friend" had the "complete and clear understanding both of national problems and of details of government" necessary to the "work of compilation and arrangement of the material" for the volume. Cabinet members, agency heads, and others assisted in gathering the material.[1]

In a Foreword to Volume I, Mr. Rosenman explained in general what had been included and what had been omitted. The volume covering the gubernatorial period was a special case, of course, in view of the prior appearance of the 1929, 1930, and 1931 volumes of the *Public Papers of [Governor] Franklin D. Roosevelt* (J. B. Lyon, Albany, 1930, 1931, 1937), New York State documents. The 1932 volume was published in 1939.

Mr. Rosenman chose to include in the Presidential volumes: Presidential messages to the Congress but not "formal messages" transmitting reports of agencies or those veto messages on private and local bills which he considered without national importance or significance. It is known that there were in all 372 message vetoes and 263 pocket vetoes during Roosevelt's Presidency.[2]

The compiler chose to include "practically all" of the formal, prepared addresses, while excluding "numerous" extemporaneous speeches and informal speeches, particularly those delivered by the campaigning President from rear platforms of trains or elsewhere during trips. Some of those speeches were referred to by place and date. It will be noted that, in general, because of this choice, nearly all words spoken by Franklin Roosevelt to public audiences (other than the press) without the prior aid of one of his teams of speechwriters were excluded from the volumes of his authorized *Public Papers*. This is a fact of the utmost importance.

Some press conferences, 220 in all from the total of 998, were printed in whole or in part in the thirteen volumes. The grand total of 998, which can be computed from the Foreword to the 1941 volume, must be viewed in the light of the word "regular" used twice by the compiler to describe press conferences included in the total. When an entire conference was not given, "important

[1] Correspondence, Roosevelt and Rosenman, on Compilation of Public Papers, Roosevelt Library.

[2] George C. Robinson, "The Veto Record of Franklin D. Roosevelt," in *American Political Science Review*, XXXVI (February, 1942), 75-78; also letter of G.C.R. to E.E.R. March 17, 1953.

excerpts" were presented, but not verbatim from the stenographic record. Instead, there was "minor editing," as Mr. Rosenman put it on three different occasions.[3] No explanation of what this means appears, but the specialist will note the very frequent use of ". . ." in the midst of remarks by the President.

The press conferences are, on the whole, the most revealing of all the documents published. The transcripts of these conferences are available to historians in the Roosevelt Library.[4] It is to be hoped that they may be made available in print or on microfilm.

Executive Orders of the President from 1933 to 1936, inclusive, were printed separately in numbered and unnumbered series and may be found in government document depository libraries; since 1936 they have been printed in the volumes of the *Federal Register*. The *Public Papers* set gives practically none of them.

Presidential Proclamations appear in the volumes of the *United States Statutes-at-Large* and, since 1935, in the *Federal Register* as well. As in the case of the Orders, the Rosenman set presents only those which were considered to be of "national and international significance." Not only would such a criterion be of necessity a subjective judgment, but it will be noted that biographers and other searchers interested in Roosevelt the President and the man would have an additional and quite different standard. It may be noted that possibly helpful lists of Orders and Proclamations appear in the close of the 1935 and 1937 volumes.

The following classes of materials were almost wholly excluded from the *Public Papers:* Presidential Appointments to Office; memoranda accompanying Acts of Executive Clemency; and White House Statements and Press Releases. Each of these groups of documents, even the Statements (which are not presumed to be written by the President), has special value for historians and biographers.

Some open, or published letters, and some message-letters of greeting appear in the set; the great bulk, of course, do not.

A few departmental statements and an assortment of letters addressed to the President appear from time to time in order to round out certain other documents, usually, it will be noted, in further justification of some controversial step taken by Roosevelt. Thus the *Public Papers* take on at times the aspect of a lawyer's brief.

The worker in these volumes is impressed by the statement of the

---

[3] *Public Papers, 1928-32*, xvii; *1937*, xi; *1941*, x.
[4] The transcripts of the conferences from November, 1944, to April, 1945, are particularly revealing of the President's state of mind.

President that he was preparing the record for the "future historian." But doubtless the scholar using this record should bear in
mind that it was prepared to convince readers, rather than to
present the record as it stood.

How exact and precise are the texts of the speeches, messages,
and other documents given in this thirteen volume set? When the
four volumes comprising The Macmillan Company portion of the
series appeared in 1941, they bore challenging titles: *1937: The
Constitution Prevails; 1938: The Continuing Struggle for Liberalism; 1939: War—and Neutrality;* and *1940: War—and Aid to Democracies.*

In 1950, under the imprint of Harper and Brothers, there appeared five years after Franklin Roosevelt's death the final four
volumes: *1941: The Call to Battle Stations; 1942: Humanity on the
Defensive; 1943: The Tide Turns;* and *1944-45: Victory and the
Threshold of Peace.*

It was in his Foreword to the *1941* volume, published after the
passing of the President, that Mr. Rosenman, possibly in response
to critics, discussed for the first time the nature of certain editorial
liberties which apparently had been taken with the texts of documents from the beginning. "President Roosevelt and I thoroughly
discussed the question of how his addresses should be printed in the
first nine volumes of this series," he wrote, "and the same general
principles have been followed in all thirteen volumes." [5] What were
those principles?

> The texts of the addresses printed in these volumes sometimes differ
> from the word-for-word stenographic record [in other words, what was
> actually said]. Therefore, persons listening to recordings of the Presi-
> dent's addresses, or who check with contemporary newspaper accounts,
> may occasionally find some discrepancies. . . . In all these volumes,
> in accordance with the instructions of President Roosevelt with re-
> spect to the first nine volumes, I have taken both the prepared, ad-
> vance text and the stenographic record of the speech as delivered and
> have tried to combine them.[!] As far as possible, the words of Presi-
> dent Roosevelt have been preserved as he delivered them. In many
> cases, however, I have edited the text to revise portions of the "ad
> libbing," or extemporaneous speaking. For example, during campaign
> speeches, the President would occasionally make extemporaneous

---

[5] In the spring and summer of 1941 the correspondence between Roosevelt
and Rosenman reveals the process of gathering material for these volumes. On
June 5, 1941, Rosenman wrote Miss LeHand, "The President promised to do
the two volumes of notes I left [*sic*] with him. . . . Macmillan are pushing me."
Later in an undated letter to Miss Tully he wrote of further delay. "Otherwise
the publication in the fall and publication in the magazine will be impossible."
(See note 11, p. 422.)

references to the local scene—in keeping with political custom—and these have been deleted where their meaning would not be clear, and where such remarks are entirely foreign to the speech itself.

In the case of the many unprepared and extemporaneous speeches delivered by the President, I have not slavishly followed the stenographic text. In this, too, I have followed the custom of President Roosevelt. The President himself would often re-edit the typed stenographic record of his extemporaneous remarks before an official text was mimeographed and released to the press. I have taken the same liberties with his extemporaneous remarks in these four volumes, as I did at his suggestion in the preceding nine.

Apparently the special duties of Mr. Rosenman have been more extensive than generally realized, including drafting and redrafting both *before* and *after* the delivery of addresses.

An important feature of the *Public Papers* is the inclusion of extensive comments or "Notes." Referring to the first five volumes, Mr. Rosenman stated that these were "written by President Roosevelt." [6] When the next four volumes appeared, he added that the Notes were prepared "not only for the present, but for readers in the years to come, who may wish to study the policies and actions of the President in the light of his own comments about them." [7]

And in his Foreword to the final four volumes after the President's death, he asserted, "in the first nine volumes . . . the introductions and explanatory notes were those of Franklin D. Roosevelt. In these four volumes [the final four], that material, perforce, had to be mine." [8]

The explanation seems clear enough at first glance, especially since in the first nine volumes the word "I," referring to Mr. Roosevelt, appears constantly (but not always; see *1933* volume, 245-246) while disappearing in the final four. Yet it will be noted that "were those of" is not quite the same as "were written by."

Moreover, in his Foreword to the *1941* volume, Mr. Rosenman went so far as to thank Kenneth W. Hechler, not only for assisting him in preparing the explanatory notes for the final four volumes, but in addition, because "he performed this same service for the 1937-1940 volumes." If Hechler "assisted" Mr. Rosenman on *those* volumes, what does the latter mean when he writes in the same essay that the "explanatory notes are those of Franklin D. Roosevelt"?

Mr. Rosenman has given detailed attention to the varied authorship of the Roosevelt speeches in his memoir, *Working with Roose-*

---

[6] *1928-32*, xviii.
[7] *1937*, xiv.
[8] *1941*, vii.

velt. Yet the comments by the President and by Mr. Rosenman in the *Public Papers* seldom if ever leave room for any thought that the documents printed there might not have come into being directly from the Roosevelt pen.

The "Note" to the final undelivered speech of the President, written by Mr. Rosenman on page 616 of the *1944-45* volume (published in 1949) reads as follows:

> This is the latest draft of the President's proposed speech. The last sentence was written into the typed draft in his own hand. The draft was not the final one; the preparation of the final draft was prevented by death. The President died at 4:35 p.m. Eastern Standard Time, April 12, 1945, at Warm Springs, Georgia. [The last sentence was, "Let us move forward with strong and active faith."]

In 1952 Mr. Rosenman chose to conclude his memoir with this last sentence in italics and in so doing he gave a somewhat more explicit version of the authorship of this proposed Jefferson Day address:

> A draft of the speech was prepared by someone on the staff of the Democratic National Committee. A copy of that draft was given to Jonathan Daniels, then acting as press secretary, who sent it to Bob [presumably Sherwood]. I was still in Europe and Harry was in the Mayo Clinic. Bob prepared a new draft in New York and sent it on to Warm Springs. The President, alone, had started intensive work on the speech, using Bob's new draft as a basis.
>
> The Jefferson Day speech was never fully finished, and of course was never delivered; it still required final polishing and correcting.[9]

In spite of this, Mr. Rosenman proceeded to say that the last two *paragraphs* of the speech should have been included in the prayers at the Roosevelt grave-side burial service, for "They were the President's last message to America and to the world—a message that was uppermost in his mind as he died." This, even though Mr. Rosenman went on to note that "The last sentence of these two paragraphs . . . [only?] was his own addition to the draft in his own handwriting."

Indeed, in the light of the astonishing authorship admissions in the Rosenman memoir, the student of history cannot but wonder whether the Presidential contribution to the Notes in the *Public Papers* amounted to any more than the wielding of an editorial pen over Rosenman drafts. Even if *that* was, in fact, the case, the Notes to the first nine volumes have special interest because of the presumption that every one of them had a close reading by Franklin

---

[9] *Working with Roosevelt,* p. 551.

Roosevelt previous to publication, and especially because of the time of their appearance.

Referring to Sherwood's statement on the "continuity and style of the President's speeches" (before Sherwood joined the staff) Rosenman writes:

> It bore out two things; first, that those of us who had worked with the President on speeches had learned to imitate his natural style in the drafts we had submitted to him; and second, that Roosevelt worked so hard and consistently on the speeches himself, made so many corrections, and inserted so many paragraphs of his own, that by the time the speech was delivered, it was thoroughly impregnated with his own style and personality. There was something about working with the President on speeches, something about listening to him deliver them, something about listening to him dictate paragraphs time and again, that seemed unconsciously to color our style and manner of writing.[10]

Each of the first nine volumes, moreover, carries an initial Introduction, dated, printed over a facsimile of the Roosevelt signature. The special pleading nature of these essays is evident throughout, and it is well to note that the Introductions to the Macmillan volumes ran serially (with some minor changes, omissions, and the addition of some material from the notes) in *Collier's* during the autumn of 1941. As its editor at the time, William L. Chenery, has written, "This was one of the very few times in history when a President in office has written for publication in a magazine." The articles which were the Introductions to the volumes were offered the magazine by a literary agent of Mrs. Roosevelt, with the resolve of the President to take no less for them than it had paid President Coolidge. "We had paid Mr. Coolidge a fat sum. Consequently haggling went on before we made a bargain." [11]

In June of 1953, Mr. Chenery suggested in retrospect, that the article-Introductions to the *1937, 1938, 1939* and *1940* volumes may have been prepared by Mr. Rosenman, not Mr. Roosevelt, and biographers of the President, as well as historians of the era, will want to weigh this judgment carefully. Again, the presumption of a thorough reading and final Presidential approval must go with the sentiments expressed in the essays.

Thus the *Public Papers and Addresses of Franklin D. Roosevelt* in thirteen volumes are a mixed blessing. They pose serious questions for the student, yet they are and will, of course, remain indispensable. The texts of many, perhaps most documents are

---

[10] *Ibid.*, pp. 232-233.
[11] *So It Seemed,* pp. 265, 268.

adequate, and the chronological arrangement is a convenience. Yet, because of the omission of documents, a misleading picture of Presidential activities is given. The Indices to each volume, and especially the Cumulative Topical Table in the *1944-45* volume, the work of Mr. Hechler, are essential keys to the Roosevelt era.

When this has been said, however, the eagerness of both the President and Mr. Rosenman to be of service to the "future historian," [12] "students of history," [13] the "future historian" and "readers in the years to come," [14] must be viewed with caution. It is evident that Franklin Roosevelt saw in these volumes a justification of himself as a fighter for liberalism and a defense of the Democratic party as an instrument of public service. Of the loyalty of Mr. Rosenman to his chief there can be no doubt.

The President expressed his "special thanks" to Miss Marguerite A. LeHand, Miss Grace G. Tully, and Mrs. Dorothy J. Brady for their "untiring help." Mr. Hechler and Mr. Rosenman's law partner, Mr. Richard S. Salant, both of whom aided so materially on the last four volumes in particular, were credited by Mr. Rosenman with "understanding appreciation of the principles of Franklin D. Roosevelt and . . . deep sympathy with his objectives and methods. . . ." [15] In summary, therefore, the *Public Papers* must be considered partisan in both intention and detailed execution, with all the significant liabilities and assets adhering to such publications.

As an example of the difficulty of obtaining the correct version of what was *actually said* by Franklin Roosevelt on certain occasions, the case of the campaign address before the Republicans-for-Roosevelt League in New York City, November 3, 1932, is instructive. The *New York Times* for November 4, 1932 (p. 14), gives what it calls "the text" of the address. Texts have been printed in two important collections—the Rosenman-edited *Public Papers, 1928-32* (pp. 856-860), and the New York State gubernatorial *Public Papers, 1932* (pp. 662-665).

Of forty-eight paragraphs given in the *Times,* the Rosenman text eliminates with the usual four dots paragraphs 2 through 33. The State document, without any dots or other indication whatsoever, dropped paragraphs 42 through 48. The State draft deleted Roosevelt's reference to that part of his earlier Topeka speech in which he said he had outlined a complete national plan "to restore its [agriculture's] buying power." It also deleted that part of his refer-

---

[12] *1941,* ix.
[13] *1928-32,* xiv.
[14] *1937,* xiv.
[15] *1941,* xii.

ence to his earlier Pittsburgh address [the economy speech] in which he had referred to an honest national budget system and proposed "the balancing thereof."

It was in reference to the Pittsburgh address, it will be recalled, that Mr. Rosenman, asked by the campaigning President in 1936 to prepare a new Pittsburgh speech explaining it away, replied after some hours of futile effort, "Mr. President, the only thing you can say about that 1932 speech is to deny categorically that you ever made it." [16]

Soon, he explains further, "the President gave up trying to 'explain' his 1932 Pittsburgh speech in 1936." [17] The Note to the speech in the *Public Papers,* however, is an effort at such an explanation, written probably in 1937 by one of the two men.[18] Various minor changes, deletions, and additions in wording between the three printed versions of the Republicans-for-Roosevelt address arouse interest, but need not be discussed here. It would appear that the text as given in the *New York Times* was the speech as prepared for delivery.[19]

Certainly the historian will do well to examine "the facts" and the setting for "the facts" in the Introductions and the Notes in the *Public Papers.* At some time every student of the President's addresses must make up his mind as to how much of that which is attributed to the President is his own. Occasionally the evidence is definite and unmistakable. But on the whole the only safe conclusion on the matter is this: The President uttered these words, and the responsibility, then, is his.[20]

Attention should be called to a *Calendar of the Speeches and Other Published Statements of Franklin D. Roosevelt, 1910-1920,* compiled by Robert L. Jacoby for the Franklin D. Roosevelt Library as its first publication (multilith), "that is in the nature of an aid to the use of papers in the Library." The Foreword by the Archivist of the United States, Wayne C. Grover, states that "As

---

[16] Rosenman, *op. cit.,* p. 87.

[17] *Ibid.,* p. 113.

[18] *1928-32,* pp. 811-812.

[19] In discussing the texts of the President's speeches, including mimeographed copies given to the press in advance, Sherwood, in *Roosevelt and Hopkins,* p. 943, wrote: "I believe the New York *Times* was the only newspaper which invariably transcribed the Roosevelt speeches and printed them in full exactly as delivered."

[20] "If on the basis of letters and speeches, a scholar should try to analyze Franklin Roosevelt's mind, he would emerge with a figure made up of Roosevelt and the fragments of Roosevelt's ghosts—Rosenman, Sherwood, Michelson, Grace Tully, Missy Le Hand, even the sprightly apparition of Harold Ickes." (Ernest R. May, "Ghost Writing and History," in *American Scholar,* Autumn, 1953, p. 460.)

a combined list, abstract and index to a hitherto scattered and virtually inaccessible group of papers, the calendar makes available for the first time to all scholars working in the field of American history for the period 1910-1920, as well as to those working on the career of Franklin D. Roosevelt, an important historical source." [21]

Scholars desiring to check against other versions the texts of the public addresses given in the *Public Papers* will find innumerable listings under the name "Roosevelt" in the *New York Times Index* and the *Readers' Guide to Periodical Literature*. The *Commercial and Financial Chronicle* carried many texts of important Presidential speeches. Reading copies, not fully reliable because of the "ad libbing" tendencies of Franklin Roosevelt, and early drafts of important speeches are in most cases available at the Roosevelt Library.[22]

Franklin D. Roosevelt conducted a massive personal correspondence. The file folders of outgoing and incoming letters now preserved at the Roosevelt Library doubtless outrank in sheer bulk such other voluminous collections as the Gifford Pinchot Papers and Woodrow Wilson Papers in the Library of Congress, and are far more extensive than the personal correspondence of Thomas Jefferson—whose papers are being printed exhaustively in fifty volumes.

One may safely say that no complete or "definitive" edition of Roosevelt letters will ever see print. Not only is the bulk overwhelming, but a very large proportion of the whole, despite the signature of Franklin D. Roosevelt on the individual items, clearly were not written by him. In many cases, indeed, it is difficult if not impossible to determine whether he wrote the letter or not. Doubtless there are instances of letters which he signed but did not even read; some form letters, it is asserted, were signed by employees who imitated his signature.[23]

Elliott Roosevelt, son of the President, with the help of various assistants, other members of the family, and the co-operation of

---

[21] "Although we hope some day to complete a calendar of speeches and other statements by Franklin D. Roosevelt for the period 1920-1928," the Director of the Library noted on November 9, 1953, "it now exists only in rough draft and is incomplete."

[22] An article of some interest is E. Brandenburg and W. W. Braden, "Franklin D. Roosevelt's Voice and Pronunciation," *Quarterly Journal of Speech*, 38 (February, 1952), 23-30; see also Lowery L. Cowperthwaite, "A Criticism of the Speaking of Franklin D. Roosevelt in the Presidential Campaign of 1932." Unpublished Dissertation in Speech, University of Iowa, 1951.

[23] Lela Stiles, *The Man Behind Roosevelt, the Story of Louis McHenry Howe*, pp. 122-123.

many intimates of his father, has produced a work with the comprehensive title, *F. D. R.: His Personal Letters* (Duell, Sloan, and Pearce. The four volumes bear the titles, *F. D. R.: His Personal Letters. Early Years* (1947), *F. D. R.: His Personal Letters. 1905 to 1928* (1948), and *F. D. R.: His Personal Letters. 1928-1945* (2 vols., 1950).

In the Foreword to the volumes for the years 1928-1945, Eleanor Roosevelt expressed the hope that "for future historians these will be a help in illuminating the reasons why my husband did certain things in certain ways." The editing, she felt, "was a heavy responsibility and one which only Franklin D. Roosevelt's own son could have carried." [24]

This statement must be evaluated in conjunction with that of the editor himself regarding the quality of the labor exerted by Joseph P. Lash, whose name appears on the title page of the volumes covering 1928-1945 as assistant to the editor. Elliott Roosevelt repeatedly wrote of the "editors" in his Introduction, and stated:

> In preparing these volumes I found that my time was rather limited. For that reason I availed myself of the assistance of Mr. Joseph P. Lash. It was Mr. Lash who performed all of the research for the information contained in the footnotes. For more than a year he has devoted his full time to this work and I am indeed grateful to him for his unflagging energy and the ability and scholarship he has shown in completing this exhaustive study. My contribution to these volumes has been limited principally to securing as wide an assortment of correspondence as possible, and acting in an advisory capacity. The principal burden of the job has rested on the shoulders of Mr. Lash.

Responsibility for the accuracy, completeness, genuineness, and editorial matters concerned with the routine of reproducing the assembled letters in book form seems to have been shared, however, with a Mr. Louis Eisner, who "handled from the outset the transcription of all the letters gathered and of all the footnote material. His job involved more hours of labor than that undertaken by any other member of the staff."

A Note on Style explains the editorial practice, which was to retain original punctuation, capitalization, and spelling, in general, although where sense "would have been distorted" punctuation was changed.

Of the 1,868 selections contained in the *Personal Letters, 1928-1945* (2 volumes), nearly all are outgoing letters from "F.D.R." By years the distribution is as follows:

---

[24] P. xvii.

1928—*16*	1932—*107*	1936—*115*	1940—*132*	1944—*116*
1929—*85*	1933— *72*	1937—*105*	1941—*209*	1945— *26*
1930—*80*	1934— *70*	1938—*113*	1942—*156*	
1931—*95*	1935—*100*	1939—*155*	1943—*106*	

The number of pages devoted to each year roughly follows the item totals; thus 1941 has the most pages, 1933 and 1934, relatively fewer. One vital fact to be drawn from these figures is this: These two volumes of 1,581 pages in all, containing "personal" letters of one of the world's busiest executives of all time, give an average of only *one* letter for every 3.2 days, or just *two* letters per working week. It can readily be seen that this tiny sample of the correspondence of the Governor of the nation's most populous state for four years and President of the United States for twelve years is but a small part of the typewritten and handwritten sheets to which he affixed his signature.

Under these circumstances, the manner in which Roosevelt's son and his assistants selected their tiny sample takes on added interest. Those who feel that here they have the personality and character of Franklin Roosevelt spread out before them, must seek the facts about the special selectivity of this particular sample.

Elliott Roosevelt in his Introduction makes the following points: First, the volumes contain "whatever family letters are available," and their small quantity is attributed to Franklin Roosevelt's decreased time for considering family matters.

Second, it is noted that the volumes contain correspondence with "those people with whom he established a close personal relationship, whether because of the nature of their duties or because he went out of his way to keep in close contact." However, it is indicated that most of the people "occupied positions of public importance." Repetitious items and those which did not seem to contribute "additional perspective" to Roosevelt's relationships were excluded.

The editors felt that taken as a whole the letters showed "the full scope of Franklin Roosevelt's thinking, the versatility of his mind, and the almost incredible range of information which he had constantly available to him." They also showed "the sweep and dimension of the great events of the Roosevelt era" and a "movement of events toward their great climaxes." These phrases indicate directional, historical, and biographical concern on the part of the editor(s).

Third, correspondence which the editors deliberately and quite openly excluded from their pages falls into several categories. (A) Material which it is stated that the "General Services Administration" of the government has not opened to outsiders. The restriction is understandable and affects all searchers with apparent equality. (B) Letters in what Mr. Roosevelt calls "a few voluminous files" at the Roosevelt Library. The editors admit that they "did not undertake to search through these particular files," but they nevertheless assert that those files "contain only scattered and occasional personal material." (C) Going into more detail on letters which were excluded, they say that those which would be prejudicial to the maintenance of friendly relations with foreign nations were "restricted for the time being," apparently by the government.

Letters relating to patronage, and to both applications for and recommendations to government positions were kept out of the pages. The story of how the President and Governor built his Cabinets and filled top administrative jobs, both civilian and military, must be considered almost wholly without any help from the *Personal Letters.* The editors excluded "the major part . . . of the material in which F.D.R. spoke candidly of his political opponents and enemies. . . ." Some such documents were extracted and printed with deletions. For this policy, too, they blame restrictions. Yet whatever the nature of the case, this latter basis for selection sounds distinctly like censorship of Rooseveltian words which could only result in giving a false impression of the temperament of the President.

In this connection the care that Mr. Roosevelt's advisors felt they had to exercise in censoring his utterances is described by Mr. Moley:

> Above everything else, I wanted to be certain that the picture of gallantry, of friendliness, of statesmanship was not blotted out by demagogic attacks, by adolescent personalizings [by Roosevelt].[25]

It was Elliott Roosevelt's hope that his volumes would "provide historians of the future with material which will ease their job of assessment of Franklin D. Roosevelt as a very human person." As in the case of the *Public Papers,* this concern for the historians of the future, expressed so often by the Roosevelt family and their close associates, evokes skepticism on the part of the historian.

The sixteen yearly surveys of events which occupy about three pages each, are unsigned and may have been written either by Mr. Elliott Roosevelt or Mr. Lash or by some other person or persons. Intelligently partisan statements concerning the Governor and President, they include few errors of fact.

Students of the human mind, who so often admit to ignorance

---

[25] *After Seven Years,* p. 64.

on human motivation, will want to reserve judgment on the certainty with which the unknown author of these surveys operates within the mind of Franklin Roosevelt. Thus in the sketch of the year 1938 the following appear: "F.D.R. had been determined . . . had been convinced . . . was won over . . . was confirmed in this determination . . . did not interpret . . . major objective remained. . . ."

When all of these details have been taken into consideration, it may be said that the notes which accompany many of the letters are helpful, although at times it seems that the space might have been filled with extensive quotations from the incoming letters themselves. If the user of these volumes is fully conversant with the original purpose of publication and the natural problems of execution of so technical a task in the hands of persons lacking editorial experience, he can profit immensely from them.

Many letters appear which do not show the President in what some may consider a particularly flattering light, and there is ample ammunition in the 1,868 items of these two volumes to refute innumerable generalizations on Roosevelt's personality and character circulated in article and book form since his death in 1945.

The astonishing informality of many of the letters included will stimulate historians to seek out those letters in the files at the Roosevelt Library which were not, and doubtless in many cases could not be, included. There must be agreement with the judgment of Frank Freidel in reviewing these volumes for the *American Historical Review*, LVI (July, 1951), 925, "The *Personal Letters* do serve as a starting point for research on Roosevelt."

Franklin Roosevelt's name is attached to six books as their author. A lecture he delivered at Milton Academy in May, 1926, was printed under the title *Whither Bound?* [26] It is chiefly notable for its contention that the state is just "people." Other remarks show the trend of his political thinking at that time.

His speech at the Houston Convention in 1928 was printed, together with a brief biography of candidate Alfred E. Smith, under the title *The Happy Warrior: Alfred E. Smith*. The Houston speech should be compared with Roosevelt's similar speech, using the same famous designation for Smith in 1924 in the New York City Democratic Convention.

Under the title "On Your Own Heads" Mr. Roosevelt had earlier

---

[26] The handwritten manuscript of an address, "The Social Age," delivered at Harvard University before the Phi Beta Kappa Society on June 19, 1929, is to be found in the Scrap Book prepared by Miss LeHand and deposited in the Roosevelt Library.

published in *Scribner's Magazine,* LXI (April, 1917), 413-416, his plea for universal military training.

Roosevelt tried his hand at writing newspaper columns in the 1920's, and these have been assembled from their printed versions in the *Macon* [Ga.] *Telegraph* and *Beacon* [N.Y.] *Standard* by Donald Scott Carmichael, a founder of a group of "Rooseveltiana" collectors, as *FDR Columnist* (Chicago, 1947). Mr. Carmichael has performed useful bibliographical services from time to time. Those seriously interested in the writings of Franklin Roosevelt will find this book more helpful if used in conjunction with original drafts and the correspondence of the columnist with his editor regarding complaints about his printed words. These are available at the Roosevelt Library.

During the course of the 1932 campaign there appeared *Government—Not Politics* (Covici-Friede, 1932), a reprinting of various magazine articles which appeared under Mr. Roosevelt's name in *Liberty, American Magazine,* and *Country Home.* A strange feature of the book is the dating of only the initial article and the final article, and the omission of the credit line to another article. There is no Introduction or other new material in the book.

Following his inauguration, after recalling the initial edition for corrections, Roosevelt issued *Looking Forward* (John Day, 1933), a compilation from his addresses delivered in the 1932 campaign, to which were added "parts which bind the material together as a whole." The Introduction was dated March 1, 1933, at Hyde Park. The text of the inaugural address, beginning on page 261, contains the initial sentence which is absent from the version in the *Public Papers.*

The chapter entitled "Expenditure and Taxation" is important for the presence of such sentiments as these:

> No man in public office today can fail to realize the demand and the need for lower taxes. He knows that business, industry and agriculture are straining under a tax load heavier than they can safely bear. He knows that high taxes are one of the contributive causes of unemployment. . . .
>
> Not only must government income meet prospective expenditures but this income must be secured on the principle of ability to pay. . . .
>
> It is obvious that sound money is an international necessity, not a domestic consideration for one nation alone. Nothing is more needed than such exchanges of opinion; nothing could do more to create a stable condition in which trade could once more be resumed.

Throughout the text, however, there was the sentiment that not only was government increasing its services, but that this was both right and inevitable; and whatever the cost, it was worth it. Certain statements now read strangely in perspective of New Deal legislation, for example, "Government regulation of the holding companies needs no new machinery of government." [27]

A year later the President issued *On Our Way* (John Day, 1934). "This book," wrote Roosevelt, "without argument and without extended explanation, seeks to set forth simply the many significant events of a very busy year." The remainder of the Foreword is one of the most significant of Franklin Roosevelt's defenses of the early New Deal legislation. "With regard to the individual excellence of each one of them [the alphabetical agencies], I can only repeat what I have often said—that the individual parts in this planned program are by no means inflexible or infallible. In some respects we may have to change the method; in others, we may not have gone far enough. Time and experience will teach us many things."

The inaugural address was again printed, together with a notation that there had been "a number of variations in texts" published, and the assertion that "the text here given is the correct one." Numerous other addresses or parts of speeches delivered in 1933 were printed together with comments of explanation or defense.

The book is one of the most important for the study of the New Deal, a fact the reviewer for the *Catholic World* [28] noted when he wrote, "It is a book whose value in the field of history and of political science will increase with the passing of time." Norman Thomas found in its pages "a president who has courage, political shrewdness, a liberal point of view, and a willingness to act." [29] Cheaply bound and printed on inexpensive paper, the book was widely reviewed and must have had a considerable impact on the contemporary mind.

In 1946 there appeared in *The True Woodrow Wilson* by Harold Garnet Black a three-page Introduction which had been prepared in 1930 and sent by Mr. Roosevelt to Mr. Black for inclusion in his biography of Wilson. This estimate of Wilson, attributed to Roosevelt, has been of considerable interest and has been reprinted in *The Roosevelt Treasury*, edited by James N. Rosenau, and elsewhere.[30] Examination of the photostatic copies of the exchange

---

[27] P. 236.
[28] October, 1934, p. 127.
[29] *Saturday Review of Literature*, April 14, 1934, p. 625.
[30] Mr. Roosevelt kept the manuscript submitted to him by the author, Mr. Black, for a year. Finally, under repeated urging from Mr. Black, Mr. Roosevelt

of telegrams between Governor Roosevelt, his secretary, Louis Howe, and Mr. Black leads to the conclusion that the essay was probably written by Mr. Howe with few if any alterations by Mr. Roosevelt.

Mention should be made of a number of compilations of miscellaneous writings, speeches, and messages by President Roosevelt which have appeared since 1933. John A. Lapp compiled *The First Chapter of the New Deal* (Chicago; J. A. Prescott, 1933). The Preface was dated August 1 and Introduction by Raymond Moley dated August 24, the latter being important for its forthright assignment of credit or responsibility for different items of the New Deal legislation to that date. The book contains the texts of laws and some speeches, and a certain amount of summarizing commentary.

Numerous writers have referred to the usefulness of the document *Development of United States Foreign Policy. Addresses and Messages of Franklin D. Roosevelt* (Government Printing Office, 1942, pp. 150), which contains thirty-six items. Few apparently realize the partisan origins of this publication, or the fact that it was not compiled from the original manuscripts. Democratic Senator John Overton of Louisiana asked in the Senate on March 17, 1942, that it be printed as a government document, stating that the compilation contained "certain outstanding addresses and papers of Franklin D. Roosevelt relating to peace and war covering the period 1933-41 inclusive." The documents, he assured a questioning colleague, "have been very carefully selected as representing the most important utterances of the President. . . ." And he continued, "I have requested that they be published because I think they will be of great historical value." Questioned pointedly by Senator Homer T. Bone (D) of Washington as to whether documents had been included containing specific information on Presidential requests for defense appropriations through the years, a part of the record he thought vitally relevant, Senator Overton replied that they had not been.[31]

Specialists will want to know that the thirty-six documents were

---

telegraphed from Warm Springs to Louis Howe in New York City, May 5, 1930, "Do please send me the Woodrow Wilson book preface." And on May 19, from Warm Springs, Mr. Roosevelt telegraphed Black: "At last I am sending you the suggested introduction and I hope that you will like it, for I have liked the way in which you have handled President Wilson in your book." The manuscript was sent to Mr. Black, and he incorporated it in his book as the contribution of Mr. Roosevelt. (Correspondence in Personal Papers, Franklin D. Roosevelt, Roosevelt Library.) The Wilson Papers so far have failed to reveal the letter of Wilson incorporated in the Introduction ascribed to Roosevelt.

[31] *Cong. Rec.*, 77 Cong., 2 Sess. (1942), vol. 88, pp. 2537.

compiled from the first nine volumes of the Rosenman-edited *Public Papers*, the *Congressional Record, Department of State Bulletin*, White House releases, and what Senator Overton termed "other official sources."

There also appeared in 1942 a publication entitled *Roosevelt's Foreign Policy, 1933-1941: Franklin D. Roosevelt's Unedited Speeches and Messages* (Wilfred Funk, 1942). An Introduction, signed "The Publishers" appears to be a summary of the Foreword by Samuel I. Rosenman in the *1928-32* volume of the *Public Papers*. The initial sentence, however, is strikingly similar to that on the title page of the government document just discussed. That the addresses and messages from 1933 to 1940 (items 1 to 207) were taken from the *Public Papers* is perfectly apparent, as a detailed check of minute points will show. The occasional notes in that section of the book are deeply indebted to the notes in the Rosenman set. The existence of its nine volumes goes unmentioned, however, as "The Publishers" assert, "Nowhere else is there one or many volumes containing such a complete story of the transition of the United States from a state of peace to a nation involved in the greatest war of history." That statement may have had some justification at the time, however, for the 144 final items illustrative of the year 1941. Apparently it is for that section only that the publishers were "indebted to executives and others in numerous government departments for access to original public records and particularly to Douglas Lurton for the compilation and collation of these papers and letters, and to Leslie Erhardt, editor of Congressional Intelligence, Incorporated, and his associate, Stephen P. Smith, for their painstaking search of various government archives in assisting in the assembly of this material."

A small book of quotations was edited by Dagobert D. Runes, under the title, *The American Way* (Philosophical Library, 1944). The subtitle was "Selections from The Public Addresses and Papers of Franklin D. Roosevelt." It should be pointed out at this time, perhaps, that the copyright on the Rosenman-edited *Public Papers* covers only "any introduction, note or title" but not, of course, texts of any of the documents. This fact clearly has been known to a variety of compilers and editors through the years.

J. B. S. Hardman edited thirty-seven addresses from the period 1932 through 1943 and added some historical material, arranging the whole by subject, under the epic title, *Rendezvous with Destiny: Addresses and Opinions of Franklin D. Roosevelt* (Dryden Press, 1944), thereby adding to the number of those who have found Tom Corcoran's phrase expressive of their philosophy of modern history.

The "fear" phrase from the first inaugural was chosen by B. D. Zevin for his compilation of sixty-two speeches, arranged chronologically, entitled *Nothing to Fear: The Selected Addresses of Franklin Delano Roosevelt, 1932-1945* (Houghton Mifflin, 1946). Harry Hopkins wrote the Foreword. In a perceptive review, R. L. Duffus said he found through the years a gradual loss of Roosevelt's buoyancy and lightheartedness, wit and pungency. Had not the war burden worn down his physical and nervous resistance?

> In his first addresses he appeared to have enough vitality to reassure a whole sick nation. In his later ones, reread, one senses an appeal, as though he were restating fundamentals in the hope that they would be remembered after his voice was silent.[32]

The chain of uncritical compilations was broken, but only briefly, in 1947 with the issuance of the beautiful volume *Wartime Correspondence Between President Roosevelt and Pope Pius XII* (Macmillan, 1947). An Introduction and Notes prepared in the State Department were ascribed to Myron C. Taylor, the personal representative of President Roosevelt to His Holiness Pope Pius XII, and Prefaces were contributed by President Truman and Pope Pius XII. No effort is made to pass judgment on the significance of this correspondence to American diplomacy or to world politics. The book can be used profitably by students of the era.

Frank Kingdon edited *As FDR Said: A Treasury of His Speeches, Conversations, and Writings* (Duell, Sloan & Pearce, 1950), a book issued by the same publishing house that put out the Elliott Roosevelt *Personal Letters* set.

Maxwell Meyersohn and Adele Archer combined to produce *Wit and Wisdom of Franklin D. Roosevelt* (Beacon Press, 1950).

The following year saw the publication of Donald Day's *Franklin D. Roosevelt's Own Story: Told in His Own Words from His Private and Public Papers* (Little, Brown, 1951) which drew from Martin P. Claussen, formerly a member of the staff of the Roosevelt Library, a definitively critical review.[33] Of the book's 650 items, he found, 388 were

> wholly unidentified and unevaluated, whether in a heading or an editorial note, as to the circumstances, the place, the person, the institution, or the other context in which FDR was prompted to speak out. Similarly, most of the other 262 documents are only casually identified. In addition, Mr. Day fails to cite the physical location of a single item by even a routine file reference or a book page, and

---

[32] *New York Times Book Review*, September 29, 1946.
[33] *Mississippi Valley Historical Review*, XXXIX (June, 1952), 150-153.

thus he surely guarantees frustration to any of the serious students
to whom he says he is appealing.

Mr. Claussen properly concluded that the Day book was "an almost
unusable item of Roosevelt literature and one that will be dis-
carded as just another potboiler on the FDR theme." The *New
York Times* reviewer observed that "Day's book makes F.D.R. a
saint and a Messiah." The *Library Journal* reviewer endorsed the
book "Recommended" for library purchase, finding the editorial
work "apparently well done."

Carroll Kilpatrick edited *Roosevelt and Daniels, A Friendship in
Politics* (University of North Carolina Press, 1952), a compilation of
correspondence between Franklin Roosevelt and his superior of
Navy Department days, carried on over a period of many years. It
will be noted that not all of the letters have been printed, nor the
full texts of many others. "Unimportant detail" was often excluded.
Like the *Personal Letters* set, this one excludes those letters which
"refer adversely to a living person."

Individual addresses of President Roosevelt have been printed on
occasion by the Government Printing Office, as well as by various
private organizations. Such publications are of more interest to
collectors than to historians. Mention may be made of the following
publications: *The World Situation: President Roosevelt's Address
of October 5 on the World Political Situation* (New York; Carnegie,
1937); *Developments in the European Situation: Peace Appeal of
President Roosevelt on April 14* (1939); *Freedom of the Seas; Address by President Roosevelt, September 11, 1941* (1941); *Address
of President Roosevelt, December 29, 1940* (1941); and *Last Address
of President Franklin Delano Roosevelt. . . . Prepared for Delivery
on April 13, 1945* (1945.) [!] The above publications were distributed
by the Carnegie Foundation to International Relations Clubs for
their libraries in colleges and universities.

In considering the speeches of the President—wherever published
—it is well to remember that the immediate situation was of course
very much in his mind, and certainly in the minds of his aides in
preparation of the speech to be made. But there is every reason to
consider and ponder at length upon the statement of one of them:

> The work that was put in on these speeches was prodigious, for
> Roosevelt with his acute sense of history knew that all of those words
> would constitute the bulk of the estate that he would leave to posterity
> and that his ultimate measure would depend upon the reconciliation
> of what he said, and what he did.[34]

---

[34] Sherwood, *Roosevelt and Hopkins*, p. 212.

Recordings of Roosevelt addresses, including those broadcast by radio, can be obtained by the determined investigator through the co-operation of network officials, private collectors, and officials of the Roosevelt Library. The Library has a mimeographed list of over five hundred such recordings that are owned by the Library, but this is of course not a complete list of all recordings in existence.

Most of these should be reproductions of what was actually said and, within the limits of equipment, a reasonable facsimile of how it was said, provided the speech was not reread for the purpose. In the case of tape recordings, it may be well to remember the ease with which tape may be cut, spliced, edited, and rerun, so that words, phrases, and whole sections may be removed from an address without leaving any trace whatsoever. For this reason, a recording may not be an exact rendition of the original.

Experts in the field of mass communications have been creating a new kind of historical story for sale to the public: the long-playing recorded compilation of words and sounds associated with important events. Editing and splicing, "dubbing in" of music, and adding commentary of more or less accuracy, these untrained historians but imaginative persons have been giving thousands who seldom read serious works an illusion of reality in reliving the past.

Franklin Roosevelt has been the subject of several long-playing recordings offered for commercial sale. Arthur Lane wrote and produced "The Voice of FDR . . . Excerpts of His Speeches During the Presidential Years (1932-1945)." Narrative by Quentin Reynolds. (Decca 33 1/3 RPM Record, 1952.) Behind the First Inaugural Address is appealing music, and the words of the President are frequently hushed to give opportunity for the comments of the narrator. Continuity is entirely lacking, as extracts from the Address of March 4, 1933, give way to the cheery tones of "Marching Along Together," followed by "I see one-third of the nation . . .", words of four years later. The entire reverse of the LP record jacket is given over to an inaccurate version of the "Eulogy to F.D.R." written by Robert Sherwood at the request of CBS network the night and early morning following Roosevelt's death, and read over the radio the following day at 11:40 A.M. by Thomas Chalmers.

James Fleming edited and narrated " 'Mr. President' from FDR to Eisenhower" (RCA Victor, 33 1/3 RPM Record, 1952), obtaining his material from tape recordings in NBC archives. He was substantially aided in his searches by a number of trained engineers and experts in the cutting and splicing of tape. The result is that he has assembled a sentence here, a humorous phrase there, a slip of the tongue, and now and then a paragraph of more significance

—the whole amounting to an interesting continuity. Yet the lifting of material out of context has seriously distorted the Roosevelt story, and the historical record in general is treated lightheartedly.

4. The Official Record, 1933-1945

All official utterances of Franklin Roosevelt as President of the United States may be found in the Public Documents of the United States Government. For example, the Public Proclamations are published in the *United States Statutes-at-Large*.

In the Public Documents are recorded all the public Acts of the President. Search in the endless array of such documents is facilitated by indices and calendars by years and by subject.

Included in the Public Documents are important publications of the various departments of the government. Those of the State Department are of the utmost importance. For example, in the publications of that department (1949) is *Post War Foreign Policy Preparation* (1939-1945), Publication 3580 in General Foreign Policy Series 15. No understanding of the President's plans for peace can be reached without a use of this volume. The basic work of the State Department is to be traced in *Peace and War: United States Foreign Policy 1931-1941* (Publication 1983).

Of increasing interest are the published hearings of committees of the Senate and the House; for example, *Hearings before the Committee on Armed Services and the Committee on Foreign Relations, United States Senate, Eighty-second Congress, First Session, to Conduct an Inquiry into the Military Situation in the Far East and the Facts Surrounding the Relief of General of the Army Douglas MacArthur from His Assignments in that Area.* Parts 1, 2, 3, 4, 5, including Appendix and Index, August 17, 1951. In this publication may be found important testimony concerning United States relations with China during the war.

Congressional hearings contain much vital information on such topics as farm tenancy, communism in government, the attack on Pearl Harbor, neutrality legislation, and similar matters. Such printed and mimeographed reports may be easily located through guides to government documents or through consulting the bibliographies of textbooks or specialized monographs.

5. Contemporary Commentators

Rewarding sources of information on the Roosevelt leadership are to be found in contemporary newspapers, magazines and news summaries broadcast by radio. Never was stronger evidence available of the conflict between truth and error in the makeup of contemporary history. Despite the valiant attempt of the conscientious columnist and news analyst to present "the facts," rumor, supposition and downright falsehood were repeatedly presented as "history." Inasmuch as the interest of the citizen was very real, much of this presentation made permanent impression and must be considered as a definite part of the record.

The *New York Times* and its *Index* provided indispensable information contained in feature articles, editorials on economic, political and international affairs, and in standard news summaries.

The commentary of Arthur Krock, blended with his straight news reporting, generally provided the most evenly balanced contemporary treatment of President Roosevelt's relation to the events of the period 1933-1945 to be found.

Editorial comment from such papers of diverse viewpoint as the *Chicago Tribune,* the *San Francisco Examiner,* and *New York Herald-Tribune* was profitably consulted, and on occasion their columns proved helpful.

If this were a study of public opinion, editorials from coast to coast in metropolitan and country newspapers would have been searched for reactions to every move of Mr. Roosevelt. Polls, despite their shortcomings, would have been subjected to exacting scrutiny. The compilation of Hadley Cantril and Milder Strunk (eds.), *Public Opinion, 1935-1946* (Princeton University Press, 1951), proved a satisfactory summary of polls, while *Fortune* magazine surveys retain their usefulness.

Few "columnists," other than Walter Lippmann, Arthur Krock, and David Lawrence were consulted for information on Mr. Roosevelt. Columns of Mr. Lippmann appeared in several compilations, and Mr. Lawrence published *Diary of a Washington Correspondent* (New York: Kinsey, 1942), covering his comments written "on or about the dates mentioned," for the period from July, 1940 to July, 1942.

While some radio commentators have published brief collections of their broadcasts, notably H. V. Kaltenborn, William L. Shirer, Cecil Brown, and D. F. Fleming, most of that which went over the air during the Roosevelt years is not now available.

The three thousand listings of books, articles, reviews, and editorial and commentator opinion—which were gathered in this investigation—were arranged *in chronological order* rather than alphabetically. This provided a constant source of fact and opinion in the stream of time and proved invaluable. In particular was this true of editorial comment and propaganda presentation. The listing included not only leading newspaper sources such as the *New York Times* and *Christian Science Monitor,* and opinion journals such as the *New Republic* and *Wall Street Journal,* but as well, magazines of wide circulation including *Life, Time, Newsweek, Collier's,* and *The Saturday Evening Post,* which inform and influence millions of people.

Examples will illustrate the material of this kind which could be consulted.

The period between election day, 1932, and March 4, 1933, brought sketches of the victorious President-elect, including the serialization of his mother's *My Boy Franklin* in *Good Housekeeping.* Louis Howe drew a partisan character sketch in "Winner," *Saturday Evening Post,* 205 (February 25, 1933). An article by Drew Pearson which strongly stressed the personal courage of the paralysis victim, "President-Elect," *Harper's,* 166 (February, 1933), was widely quoted by writers and editors when the dramatic assassination-attempt headlines of February made its theme of intense interest.

The First Inaugural Address stimulated innumerable articles. The uncertainties of the banking crisis and the "100 days" gave rise to efforts to explain the nature of Presidential leadership. These included: a review article by Edmund Wilson, "Hudson River Progressive," *New Republic,* 74 (April 5, 1933); Anne O'Hare McCormick, "Road Away From Here," *New Outlook,* 161 (May, 1933), intelligent and penetrating; an English appraisal by S. K. Ratcliffe, "President Roosevelt in Command," *Contemporary Review,* 143 (May, 1933); nearly the entire issue of *Nation's Business* for June, 1933; and George Creel, "Kitchen Cabinet," *Collier's,* 91 (June 17, 1933). Foreign appraisals of Roosevelt's early weeks in office noted the parallels and differences between the positions occupied by Mussolini and Hitler, and the strong executive in power across the Atlantic.

By 1935 it was clear that each important radio address by the Chief Executive would be the occasion for articles in popular magazines, as editors surmised an interest by their readers in the direct approach being made to them from the White House. Already there were articles looking forward to 1936.

Presidential messages always gave critical writers a chance to be heard. Innumerable articles on the election of 1936 added to the normal interest in Presidential activities. Several journals published strongly partisan post-nomination articles as the issues clarified, following them up on occasion with equally strong articles of rebuttal.

As in 1932-1933, post-election guessing on the new national direction occupied magazine writers. Chief among the articles forthcoming was one in which Roosevelt co-operated with George Creel, who produced "Roosevelt's Plans and Purposes," *Collier's*, 98 (December 26, 1936).

The battle over the President's Judiciary Bill was the stimulus for countless articles in the spring of 1937, as writers discussed the Constitution and recent Supreme Court decisions. Numerous articles in law journals treated the theme from various viewpoints. As these reactions of the day were not indexed under the name of the President in law journal indices, only those willing to explore under general headings can find the product of professional writers on this subject. The close of the Court fight brought a summing up and a tendency to view the battle in longer perspective. The Quarantine Speech of early fall, however, turned writers on Roosevelt to foreign themes, a tendency broken momentarily as economic recession set off articles such as John T. Flynn's "Has One Short Year Upset the Apple Cart?" *New Republic*, 93 (December 29, 1937).

With 1939, writers increasingly noted the Presidential tendency to intervene in European affairs, but when worried eyes turned to the war abroad later in the year the Roosevelt personality almost ceased for a time to be a matter of magazine concern. A new array of third-term articles had appeared in the summer, and early 1940 saw these increase sharply in quantity and emotionalism.

At the dawn of fateful 1941, a *Life* article entitled "Roosevelt Thinks Up Plan to Make America a Non-Fighting Ally of Britain," December 30, 1940, may have been the opening shot in a new war of words to come.

On January 8, 1941, the *Christian Century* editorialized in "President's War." Whether it would be that or not was a bone of contention for the ensuing eleven months. In the *New York Times Magazine* for March 9, 1941, Anne O'Hare McCormick wrote on another theme of the times, "Roosevelt of the World Crisis; New Dealer Submerged in the Defense Leader." An interesting exchange of early spring was "F. D. R.; President of the World," *New Republic*, March 31, 1941, and a response by O. G. Villard in *Christian Century*, April 9, 1941. By September, Raymond Moley could write "War, Limited," for *Newsweek*, September 22, 1941, and J. M. Gillis, long-time editor of *Catholic World*, declared in the pages of his journal, "President Declares War," October, 1941.

After the attack on Pearl Harbor, articles about the President dropped off sharply as writers turned to more immediately dramatic and demanding themes.

Commander-in-Chief Roosevelt, like Wilson and Lincoln before him, played a dual role which did not escape the attention of professional writers. "Presidency; Its Tradition Is Leadership in Freedom; Will Franklin Roosevelt Preserve That Tradition?" asked *Fortune*, January, 1942. Yet critical articles were rare in 1942 as Roosevelt took constant action as Commander-in-Chief. Even the *New Republic* and the *Christian Century*, persistent foes of the Roosevelt foreign policy of 1941, recognized the temporary end of an argument. Prematurely, yet perhaps inevitably, *Time* expressed a question in some minds in mid-summer, "Term IV?", August 31, 1942. The Congressional election of autumn brought few articles linking Roosevelt to issues of the moment.

In the year 1943 an increase in political treatment was apparent. E. Blair pointed out the "political aspects" of the State of the Union message in *Barron's*, January 11, 1943, and after several writers had reflected in March on the meaning of the first Roosevelt decade, the *New Republic* raised the question of the fourth term. By June the popular magazines of the nation were full of the question.

Mention should be made of the significant and officially inspired Forrest Davis article, "Roosevelt's World Blueprint," *Saturday Evening Post*, April 10, 1943; a reply appeared in *Christian Century*, May 5, 1943.

The year of the fourth-term election brought more articles on Franklin Roosevelt than either 1934, the year of summing up, or 1936, the year the New Deal stood its important electoral testing. The apparent shelving of that New Deal by the President in his well-known January, 1944, press conference brought much magazine commentary.

The Barkley incident, with its challenge of the political leadership of the President, invited thought on the role of the Presidential office and the Congress in the American system. The health of the President, the nature of the future peace, and the wartime trip into the Pacific were subjects for varied comment.

After the votes had been counted, and *Newsweek* had written "Four Years More of Mighty Tasks Face Roosevelt After Close Race," November 13, 1944, there appeared a number of articles on Franklin Roosevelt. Sharply significant was George Creel's analysis, "President's Health," *Collier's*, March 3, 1945. The Yalta Conference was the occasion for articles about the President as negotiator. Finally, came the fateful news from Warm Springs.

The call to write obituaries came to innumerable writers, and in the first weeks brought a flood of evaluations. Like Washington and Lincoln, the real man who had lived and breathed, made mistakes, had enemies as well as friends, and maintained a private as well as a public life, was submerged under a sea of eulogizing print. "Not Since Lincoln," rhapsodized Harold Laski in *Nation,* April 21, 1945. Quickly the necessity of fighting on in unity moved the theme forward. *Newsweek* noted, for example, "U.S. Closes Ranks Under Truman After Shock of Roosevelt's Death," April 23, 1945. The *Saturday Evening Post* a month later published what many were saying in private, "Everybody Knew It but the People; Roosevelt's Health," May 19, 1945. With the arrival of summer more serious efforts at appraisal were notable at home and abroad. Yet by the close of the year, with the war over, the new Truman administration seized more and more space in American journals, and articles on Roosevelt were fewer and more particularized.

6. *Contemporary Interpretations*

It may be that Franklin Roosevelt has already attracted more printed words from his contemporaries than anyone who ever lived. Those words which have appeared in published books are here arranged in the chronological order of their first appearance.

This form of presentation may seem irksome to specialists in quick search of a particular title, but chronological arrangement tends to contribute further interpretation of the Roosevelt era.

With the election of Franklin D. Roosevelt as President of the United States and his inauguration on March 4, 1933, specialized volumes of many kinds began to flow from the presses of the nation.

The first two publications of the era following March 4, 1933, were symbolic. The third national exhibition of newspaper typography, sponsored by the Ayer Galleries, resulted in the reproduction of *Front Pages from 1314 Newspapers . . . [dated March 4, 1933]* (Philadelphia, 1933); and equally concentrated was *Ten Days, A Crisis in American History* (New York: Duffield & Green, 1933), whose pseudonymous author, "George Grey," claimed for his fifty-eight page tract the designation of "first book on Roosevelt's administration." Of moderate interest is the reproduction of newspaper headlines by Benjamin Duffy for the period February 14 to May 23, entitled *The World's Greatest 99 Days* (Harper, 1933).

The dramatic banking crisis attracted writers in 1933 and later, including Marcus Nadler, Lawrence Sullivan, J. F. T. O'Conner, C. C. Colt and N. S. Keith, and staff members of the National Industrial Conference Board and the American Institute of Banking.

The legislation and the aggressive exercise of Presidential leadership which marked the "one hundred days" inspired numerous writers to attempt evaluations. For student use was Julia Emily Johnsen's compilation of essays, *Increasing the President's Power* (Wilson, The Reference Shelf, IX, No. 2, 1933), while Cleveland Rodgers, editor of the *Brooklyn Daily Eagle,* produced a running account of the first six months under the title *The Roosevelt Program* (Putnam's, 1933). A compilation on its indicated theme is *Foreign Problems Confronting the New Administration* (Foreign Policy Association, 1933); it contained related views of R. L. Buell, Walter Millis, and others.

Appearing late in 1933 were two substantial volumes, Earle Looker, *The American Way: Franklin Roosevelt in Action* (John Day, 1933) and a new book by Ernest K. Lindley, written from a Washington perspective, *The Roosevelt Revolution: First Phase* (Viking, 1933). Both have continuing value as contemporary appraisals of the early days of the New Deal. Both were reviewed by John Corbin, a former *New York Times* editorial writer, in a review article *Saturday Review of Literature,* November 18, 1933 (pp. 265ff). He found each book "casual and fragmentary" in matters "historic and economic," but noted that both authors were close to "their hero" and gave first-hand pictures of the Roosevelt mind in moments of political decision.

Lindley wrote from his own knowledge and from several newspaper and periodical files including *Newsweek* and *Literary Digest.* "The Roosevelt Revolution," concluded Lindley, "is democracy trying to create out of American materials an economic system which will work with reasonable satisfaction to the great majority of citizens. The nomenclature of political science has been ransacked for a suitable name for the economic system which is the apparent goal of the Roosevelt Revolution. Regulated capitalism, state capitalism, disciplined democracy, a co-operative state, guild socialism—these and many other names have been suggested. Henry A. Wallace has used 'a balanced social state.' As good a phrase as any is Mr. Roosevelt's, 'an economic constitutional order.'" (Pp. 322-323.)

The initial year of the New Deal continued to pre-empt the attention of contributors to political and economic literature in 1934. A social treatment of the first twelve months, Pare Lorentz, editor, *The Roosevelt Year, A Photographic Record* (Funk & Wagnalls, 1934), with over four hundred photographs illustrative of life on farm and factory, does much to recreate the times. A bit overdramatic and sensational in its approach ("Tear gas fell like rain that summer," p. 127) and containing some textual errors, the book can still be used with profit; Mark Sullivan thought its compiler judicial in his selection of pictures.

Charles A. Beard and George H. E. Smith summarized the initial recovery program of the administration in *The Future Comes: A Study of the New Deal* (Macmillan, 1933).

Less objective were: George H. Soule, *The Coming American Revolution* (Macmillan, 1934); Alfred M. Bingham, *Challenge to the New Deal* (New York: Falcon Press, 1934), a collection of criticisms from the left; Glenn Frank, *America's Hour of Decision* (McGraw-Hill, 1934); and Ralph Robey, *Roosevelt Versus Recovery* (Harper, 1934), a strong and well-reasoned attack on New Deal economics by a member of the business administration faculty of Columbia University.

Other skillful challenges to the Roosevelt program of 1933 were David Lawrence, *Beyond the New Deal* (McGraw-Hill, 1934), William MacDonald, *The Menace of Recovery: What the New Deal Means* (Macmillan, 1934), James P. Warburg, *It's Up to Us* (Knopf, 1934), and the two volumes of Roger W. Babson, *Washington and the Revolutionists* (Harper, 1934) and *The New Dilemma* (Revell, 1934). To Harold L. Ickes, however, the first year had ushered in what he termed *The New Democracy* (Norton, 1934), as seen from his position in the Cabinet.

Serious contemporary evaluations of permanent value are: the collected essays of Leo Wolman, Rexford Tugwell, A. A. Berle, Jr., and others in *America's Recovery Program* (Oxford University Press, 1934). Joseph B. Hubbard edited *Current Economic Policies* (Holt, 1934).

The early appraisal by Louis M. Hacker, *A Short History of the New Deal* (Crofts, 1934), may not reflect the author's later judgments. *See* John F. Gerstung, "Louis M. Hacker's Reappraisal of Recent American History," *The Historian*, XII (Spring, 1950).

Of some significance are: American Management Association, *Management Policies in the Light of the New Deal* (New York, 1934), collected addresses; Schuyler C. Wallace, *The New Deal in Action* (Harper, 1934); Charles Merz, "Roosevelt's First Year: 12 Epochal Months," *Essay Annual, 1934* (pp. 1-15); and two journalistic accounts, Unofficial Observer [John Franklin Carter], *The New Dealers* (Simon & Schuster, 1934) and Frank Kent, *Without Gloves* (Morrow, 1934), the latter covering what its author termed "the great federal experiments, their operations and operators" with such detail as what he called "the perpetual motion" of the administration would allow. "It never slows down sufficiently to give either the public or the administrators a chance to see clearly where we are. There is no opporunity to take stock," Kent complained. (P. 299.)

Also important, not alone for the message it conveyed about "changing the rules of the game," but for the increased public attention it brought to its author, was *New Frontiers* (Reynal & Hitchcock, 1934). Henry A. Wallace urged in his pages an "unwritten constitution" of "guiding principles" to mold a different and assertedly better social and economic future.

Herbert Hoover, meanwhile, declared in *The Challenge to Liberty* (Scribner's, 1934), "For the first time in two generations the American people are faced with the primary issue of humanity and all government—the issue of human liberty." Liberalism, Hoover thought, was being overthrown, and he warned, "We cannot extend the mastery of government over the daily life of a people without somewhere making it master of people's souls and thoughts." (P. 203.)

By 1935 opposition books of substance appeared regularly. Ogden L. Mills, Hoover's Secretary of the Treasury, asked *What of Tomorrow?* (Macmillan, 1935); David Lawrence issued *Stumbling into Socialism* (Appleton-Century, 1935), declaring, "The main issue which supersedes all others is whether we shall change our form of government." The "would-be spokesmen for the common man," Lawrence thought, were in fact his most dangerous enemies.

James P. Warburg, a prolific author on economic subjects, who had been a Roosevelt appointee to the London Conference in 1933, charged the President with effectuating the Socialist rather than the Democratic platform, in his little book *Hell Bent for Election* (Doubleday, 1935). *Still Hell Bent* (Doubleday, 1936), he decided a year later.

George Michael's *Handout* (Putnam's, 1935) charged the administration with violations of good public relations practices. Huey Long, persistent critic, in addition to reading into the *Congressional Record* the texts of his violent radio castigations of Franklin "Rousezevelt," prepared an odd volume of self-serving opposition, *My First Days in the White House* (Harrisburg, Pa.: Telegraph Press, 1935), having already declared *Every Man a King* (New Orleans: National Book Co., 1933).

Serious productions of 1935 were: Ernest Minor Patterson (ed.), *Increasing Government Control in Economic Life*, Annals, 178 (March, 1935); Walter Earl Spahr, *An Economic Appraisal of the New Deal* (Farrar & Rinehart, 1935); Roy V. Peel and Thomas

C. Donnelly, *The 1932 Campaign* (Farrar & Rinehart, 1935); Alonzo E. Taylor, *The New Deal and Foreign Trade* (Macmillan, 1935); and Walter Lippmann, *The New Imperative* (Macmillan, 1935). Also published were Gertrude and John V. C. Southworth, *The New Deal; an Impartial History . . .* (Syracuse: Iroquois Publishing Co., 1935); Frank Bohn and Richard T. Ely, *The Great Change: Work and Wealth in the New Age* (Nelson, 1935); and the vigorous volume largely composed of articles reprinted from *Today*, Rexford G. Tugwell's *The Battle for Democracy* (Columbia University Press, 1935). Reviewers disagreed sharply on its content, its message, and its significance.

Many of the authors of 1935 doubtless wrote with one eye on the 1936 Presidential campaign and election. Certainly the battle lines of that year, with Roosevelt, his policies, and his practices the issue, appear even more clearly in books published after January 1, 1936. On the Republican, or anti-Roosevelt side there were, for example: *Facts: the New Deal Versus the American System* (Republican Nat'l Com., 1936); John S. Cannon, *Billions for Boondoggling: Vetoes for Veterans* (Kansas City, Mo.: Empire, 1936); Herbert Hoover, *American Ideals vs. the New Deal* (Scribner's, 1936), a series of ten addresses; Howard E. Kershner, *The Menace of Roosevelt and His Policies* (Greenberg, 1936); another Ogden L. Mills book, *Liberalism Fights On* (Macmillan, 1936); Earl Reeves (ed.), *Truth About the New Deal* (Longmans, Green, 1936), a collection of interviews with confirmed opponents like Robert L. Lund of the Nat'l Association of Manufacturers; Ira L. Reeves, *Is All Well on the Potomac?* (Chicago: American Forum Publishing Co., 1936); Joseph L. Stackpole, *Rosie in Squanderland; or, Billions for Votes* (New York: Paisley Press, 1936); Charles P. Taft, *You and I—and Roosevelt* (Farrar & Rinehart, 1936); and Norman Thomas, *After the New Deal, What?* (Macmillan, 1936).

Democratic partisans replied or affirmed their beliefs with vigor. *I'm for Roosevelt* (Reynal & Hitchcock, 1936) asserted Joseph P. Kennedy. Roosevelt termed it a step in "sane education" of the country, a "splendid" piece of work. Typical of lesser efforts was Edward Lee Spruell, *Forward with Roosevelt* (Richmond: Spruell Publishing Co., 1936). Far less influential than its author intended was *Guilty! The Confession of F. D. R., Written by a Friend* (Doubleday, 1936), in which the President was permitted by the writer to "confess" to charges against him in such a way as to try to refute the charges. An attempt by the anonymous author, Donald Richberg, to gain a reading by the Chief Executive before publication seems to have failed. (See *Personal Letters, 1928-1945*, p. 597.)

Journalists continued the practice of assembling columns into books. The following appeared in 1936: Boake Carter, *"Johnny Q. Public" Speaks! The Nation Appraises the New Deal* (New York: Dodge Publishing Co., 1936); Marquis W. Childs, *They Hate Roosevelt!* (Harper, 1936); Frank Kent, *Without Grease: Political Behavior, 1934-1936* . . . (New York: W. Morrow, 1936); Walter Lippmann, *Interpretations, 1933-1936* (Macmillan, 1936), selected and edited by Allan Nevins.

The year 1936 also saw the first trickle of the later flood of books on the Supreme Court, samples being: Robert K. Carr, *Democracy and the Supreme Court* (University of Oklahoma Press, 1936); Frederic R. Coudert, *The New Deal and the United States Supreme Court* (Clarendon Press, Oxford, 1936), a lecture; Drew Pearson and Robert S. Allen, *Nine Old Men* (Doubleday, 1936) and David Lawrence, *Nine Honest Men* (Appleton-Century, 1936).

Other publications of political, social, or economic note were: Herbert Agar, *What Is America?* (London: Eyre and Spottiswoode, 1936); Charles A. Beard (ed.), *Current Problems of Public Policy* (Macmillan, 1936), a compilation of platforms and similar political materials; Nicholas Roosevelt, *The Townsend Plan: Taxing for Sixty* (Doubleday, 1936); and Walter Lippmann and Allan Nevins (eds.), *A Modern Reader: Essays on Present-Day Life and Culture* (Heath, 1936), a collection of essays above the average in insight, on the whole, with the extreme left and extreme right excluded.

For contemporaries as well as for posterity, the year 1937 was the year of the Supreme Court controversy. Books on the theme appeared at many levels and at many hands. Only volumes dedicated exclusively to the judicial problem can be listed. Probably the most important were: William R. Barnes and A. W. Littlefield (eds.), *The Supreme Court Issue and the Constitution* (Barnes & Noble, 1937), useful for quoted comments of the day; Julie E. Johnsen (compiler), *Reorganization of the Supreme Court* (Wilson, The Reference Shelf, 1937); Merlo J. Pusey, *The Supreme Court Crisis* (Macmillan, 1937), a volume prepared, it appears, with co-operation from the opposition to the Judiciary Bill in the Congress; Walter Lippmann, *The Supreme Court, Independent or Controlled?* (Harper, 1937). A hastily written tract by columnists Drew Pearson and Robert S. Allen, *Nine Old Men at the Crossroads* (Doubleday, 1937) and a newspaper supplement containing summaries of opposition comment, "The Constitution, the Supreme Court, and President Roosevelt," Supplement to the *St. Louis Post-Dispatch,* March 30, 1937, show conflicting viewpoints of the day.

Specialists will want to see, in addition, the contemporary or subsequent books and articles by Alpheus T. Mason and Edward S. Corwin (both tending toward the Roosevelt point of view) and books by and about Justices Roberts and Sutherland, together with the two-volume intimate biography of Charles Evans Hughes by Merlo J. Pusey which continues the author's earlier efforts to forestall criticisms of the Court and its Chief Justice. Bar association and law school journals of 1937 remain most important sources of opinion and fact on both sides of the Supreme Court issue. Robert K. Carr, *The Supreme Court and Judicial Review* (Farrar & Rinehart, 1942) and H. Arthur Steiner (ed.), *Significant Supreme Court Decisions, 1934-37* (Student's Co-op, U.C.L.A., 1936) are helpful.

Books on other themes published in 1937 which bear on Franklin Roosevelt are: Marion L. Ramsay, then director of a division of the Rural Electrification Administration, *Pyramids of Power* (Bobbs-Merrill, 1937), subtitled *The Story of Roosevelt, Insull and the Utility Wars;* a small book of analysis and appraisal by the editors of the London *Economist* entitled *The New Deal* (Knopf, 1937); Stanley High, *Roosevelt—And Then?* (Harper, 1937), the contribution of a former speechwriter of Roosevelt's 1936 campaign; Albert S. J. Baster, *The Twilight of American Capitalism* (London: King, 1937); and Frank W. Fetter, *The New Deal and Tariff Policy* (University of Chicago Press, 1937).

A further statement in determined opposition was Ogden L. Mills, *The Seventeen Million* (Macmillan, 1937), its title a reference to the votes cast for the 1936 Republican candidate.

In 1937 came the third of the Ernest K. Lindley volumes, *Half Way with Roosevelt* (Viking, 1937). The book contained 449 pages of discussion and analysis of the New Deal and the first term which were initially published in August, 1936, but is better viewed in the revised edition of January, 1937. Lindley wrote prematurely in that edition, "A decisive election has been followed by a period of calm." (P. 3.) Worthy of close attention is his considered judgment, following a discussion of words, epithets, and labels, "The New Deal is not a doctrine, nor a system, but the result of a mingling of doctrines, ideas, influences, political groups, and pressures." (P. 36.) To this he added, "Mr. Roosevelt not only operates by the trial-and-error method, but openly avows that he does." (P. 47.) Like the other Lindley books, this one has a special value derived from the friendly contact the author enjoyed with Roosevelt and his advisers. Its plain intimation of a quick and open conflict between the President and the Supreme Court (chapter XIII and pp. 439-440) has special interest for that reason.

The appearance of Walter Lippmann's *The Good Society* (Little, Brown, 1937), was apparently an intellectual event of 1937. Reviewers thought it his finest book, especially the parts which indicted collectivism both of the right and of the left. It was persuasively written in "the language of principle," wrote a reviewer.

Old political battles were revived in 1938 as journalistic writers rallied around the figure of Franklin Roosevelt or, often disillusioned by the economic and Constitutional blows of 1937, expressed their fears with increasing vigor. A thoughtful critical statement very well received by reviewers was that by Nicholas Roosevelt, distant cousin of the President, *A New Birth of Freedom* (Scribner's, 1938). It stressed the dangers to traditional democratic freedoms in accelerating centralization of executive or governmental power. Joseph Alsop and Turner Catledge attempted a first appraisal of the Court fight in *168 Days* (Doubleday, 1938). Thirteen *New York Times* correspondents produced *We Saw It Happen* (Simon & Schuster, 1938).

Eleanor Roosevelt expressed her views on world peace and international co-operation in *This Troubled World* (New York: Kinsey, 1938).

Other books of special interest were: Eleanor Roosevelt, *My Days* (Dodge Publishing Co., 1938); Dorothy Thompson, *Dorothy Thompson's Political Guide* (Stackpole, 1938), subtitled "A Study of American Liberalism and its Relationship to Modern Totalitarian States"; American Council on Public Affairs, M. B. Schnapper (ed.), *The Federal Government Today* (New York, 1938); Betty Lindley, *A New Deal for Youth: The Story of the National Youth Administration* (Viking, 1938); and a book by Communist chief Earl Browder, *Social and National Security* (New York: Workers Library, 1938).

Scribner's began in 1938 the publication of the speeches of Herbert Hoover under the title *Addresses Upon the American Road,* some volumes of which would later appear from the Stanford University Press. The book published in 1938 covered the years 1933 to 1938. When examined as a set, these volumes constitute a chronological critique of the Roosevelt policies and the New Deal.

The timing of Lawrence A. Nixon in editing *What Will Happen and What to Do When War Comes* (Greystone, 1939) was matched by the forecast of H. E. Russell, Jr., its *Boston Transcript* reviewer (September 9, 1939), who wrote, "When war breaks out, there is little doubt that we will be drawn into it. No citizen or his resources will be spared. It is best for all to know just what to expect beforehand."

Rixy Smith and Norman Beasley conveyed an unflattering picture of Franklin Roosevelt in their *Carter Glass: A Biography* (Longmans, Green, 1939); other unfavorable items appeared in Robert A. Taft, *A Republican Program: Speeches and Broadcasts* (Cleveland: Ingalls, 1939); A. W. Rosinia, *New Deal Under the Micro-scope* (Chicago: Arkin, 1939), and a small collection of 1938 and 1939 speeches by Herbert Hoover, *America's Way Forward* (New York: Constitutional Publications, 1939).

Other books of some significance were: René Vincent, *L'expéri-ence Roosevelt: La politique et monétaire postérieure à 1934* (Paris, 1939); Carl B. Swisher (ed.), *Selected Papers of Homer Cummings* (Scribner's, 1939); Joseph Alsop and Robert Kintner, *Men Around the President* (Doubleday, 1939), an excellent account of the rapid changes in advisers.

The following books touching on Franklin Roosevelt directly or indirectly en route to their separate goals appeared in 1940 and 1941: Charles A. Beard and George H. E. Smith, *The Old Deal and the New* (Macmillan, 1940); John Chamberlain, *The American Stakes* (Carrick & Evans, 1940), virtually a repudiation of the author's viewpoint in his earlier *Farewell to Reform* (1932); Arthur Whipple Crawford, *Monetary Management Under the New Deal* (Washington, D.C.: American Council on Public Affairs, 1940), with a helpful bibliography; Shelby C. Davis, *America Faces the Forties* (Dorrance, 1940), an appraisal and forecast by a business-man-economist who served as Thomas E. Dewey's economic adviser in the pre-convention campaign; Peter H. Odegard, *Prologue to November, 1940* (Harper, 1940); Arthur M. Schlesinger, *The New Deal in Action, 1933-1939* (Macmillan, 1940), a brief summary and appraisal which enlarged on an edition issued in 1939, both de-signed to further the usefulness of a widely used textbook; George C. S. Benson, *The New Centralization* (Farrar & Rinehart, 1941); Robert H. Jackson, *The Struggle for Judicial Supremacy* (Knopf, 1941), which portrayed American "power politics" as in a state of crisis; and Eugene Lyons, *The Red Decade* (Bobbs-Merrill, 1941), a book which, twelve years after its publication, still drew the irritated fire of those who had sought during the 1930's to solve American problems with foreign solutions (see Granville Hicks, "How Red Was the Red Decade?" *Harper's,* September, 1953, an attempt to minimize what Lyons had called "The Stalinist Penetra-tion of America").

Only a specialized monograph could list the whole literature of Presidential campaign years, but the following attacks on Roosevelt or his policies should be mentioned: Thomas E. Dewey, *The Case Against the New Deal* (Harper, 1940); Harrison E. Fryberger, *No Third Term for Roosevelt!* (New York: Advance, 1940); *The Roose-velt Record in Red!* (Washington, D. C., 1940), an attempt by the research division of the Republican National Committee to hold the President personally responsible for United Front collaborators holding office under his administration. A new volume of "American Road" addresses by former President Hoover, delivered from 1938 to 1940, appeared in 1940. Other books of 1940 were: Eleanor Roosevelt, *Moral Basis of Democracy* (Howell, Soskin, 1940); S. E. Edmunds, *The Roosevelt Coup d'Etat of 1933-40* (Charlottesville, Va.: Michie Co., 1940); and Joseph F. Guffey, *Roosevelt Again!* (Philadelphia: Franklin, 1940); John T. Flynn, *Country Squire in the White House* (Doubleday, 1940).

Flynn, in earlier years a writer for the *New Republic,* attempted "to explain the New Deal in terms of the man who sponsored it." Acid reviews greeted this volume written, as he admitted at once, in "a year of campaign books." Flynn charged that Roosevelt had held back on reforms like social security, had reached the close of his second term without licking unemployment although spending billions of dollars trying, and was "the recognized leader of the war party" deeply occupied in "meddling" in European affairs. Flynn in the nature of things was unable to document his assertions, although students of the era know that numerous facts can be marshaled to support them.

Frederick Lewis Allen's *Since Yesterday* (Harper, 1940) was an attempt to repeat the author's earlier venture into social history which suffered in this case because the era of which he wrote had not really ended in 1940. The readers of 1940 were not yet in the mood to look back at the depression years as something over and gone.

The excerpts from the diary of Roosevelt's choice for "eyes and ears" in Berlin, published as *Ambassador Dodd's Diary, 1933-1938* (Harcourt, Brace, 1941) after editing by his children, William E. Dodd, Jr. and Martha Dodd, do not tell the whole story of German-American diplomatic relations in those years. Important additions of fact for part of that period were made by H. L. Trefousse in *Germany and American Neutrality, 1939-1941* (New York: Bookman Associates, 1951), although certain of the major premises on which he based his pro-administration conclusions can be questioned.

The dramatic attack at Pearl Harbor and the compulsion felt by most Americans to strive for visible unity of action seems to have kept professional writers from attempts to explore the diplomacy of 1937 to 1941. The critical, anti-British, and isolationist note struck by P. E. Sargent in *Getting U S into War* (Boston: Sargent Press, 1941), 640 pages of quotations and pamphleteering prose, failed to gain its author a large audience then or later.

Far more nearly in line with the mood of the day was the friendly and patriotic *How War Came* (Simon & Schuster, 1942), in which Forrest Davis and Ernest K. Lindley codified contemporary opinion on foreign relations from the fall of France to the Pearl Harbor attack.

Other volumes of the war years pursued various themes: speeches delivered over a three year period comprised Sumner Welles, *World of the Four Freedoms* (Columbia University Press, 1943); the Bureau of Special Services of Time, Inc., issued *The United States in a New World* (1943); Michael W. Straight urged *Make This the Last War: The Future of the United Nations* (Harcourt, Brace, 1943). Of academic interest is an appraisal from the enemy camp, Paul Osthold, *Roosevelt Zwischen Spekulation und Wirklichkeit* (Berlin, 1943). Henry Morton, *Atlantic Meeting* (Dodd, Mead, 1943) recorded the Atlantic Charter Conference. Sumner Welles produced *The Time for Decision* (Harper, 1944).

A Columbia dissertation, Louis W. Koenig's *The Presidency and the Crisis: Powers of the Office from the Invasion of Poland to Pearl Harbor* (King's Crown, 1944), was largely a documented approval of the extension of executive powers.

Walter Johnson, *The Battle Against Isolation* (University of Chicago Press, 1944), was an important contribution, presenting the work of the Committee to Aid the Allies, and based upon wide use of manuscript sources. Dexter Perkins, *America and Two Wars* (Little, Brown, 1944), by the authority on the Monroe Doctrine, was a penetrating critique of views, policies, and problems.

Carl Becker's *How New Will the Better World Be?* (Knopf, 1944) was an intelligent appraisal offering little comfort to those who, reading Wendell Willkie's *One World* (Simon & Schuster, 1943, or in any of six or more foreign editions), had bid a premature farewell to power politics. Becker declared: ". . . I think that it is quite futile to discuss post-war reconstruction on the assumption that the sentiment of nationalism will be any less strong than it has been, or that nations will cherish their sovereign independence any less than they have, or be less disposed to defend and promote their real or supposed national interests, or be less concerned with a balance of power that is advantageous to them." And, he predicted, "Making a new and better world is a difficult business and will prove to be a slow one."

Walter Lippmann in *U. S. Foreign Policy: Shield of the Republic* (Little, Brown, 1943) sought to find "the American policy which will most adequately and surely make this republic solvent in its foreign relations." The Lippmann view of Russian-American relations in the post-war era was not immune to the ideologically blind wishful thinking which characterized American expectations at the time, and the quick fall of Nationalist China to the Communists was not anticipated in his penetrating pages.

By 1944 such works as those of Becker, Lippmann, and Straight commanded an audience of thoughtful persons concerned over the future. Indeed, it was in that year that the Twentieth Century Fund issued its directory of nearly two hundred organizations in and out of the government which were carrying on continuing post-war planning programs. (See The Twentieth Century Fund, *Postwar Planning in the United States*, 1944.)

Some writers continued to address themselves to domestic themes with which the President, by then serving his third term, was intimately concerned. Journalistic were: John Franklin Carter, writing as Jay Franklin, *Remaking America* (Houghton Mifflin, 1942) which summed up in 287 pages everything good he thought the New Deal had done to mid-1941; Marquis W. Childs, *I Write from Washington* (Harper, 1942); Raymond Clapper, *Watching the World* (McGraw-Hill, 1944), selections made posthumously from columns published 1933-1944; John T. Flynn, *As We Go Marching* (Doubleday, 1944); Garet Garrett, *The Revolution Was* (Caldwell, Idaho: Caxton, 1944); and Merlo John Pusey, *Big Government: Can We Control It?* (Harper, 1945), a critical treatise by the *Washington Post* editorial writer with a foreword by Charles A. Beard.

Criticisms of the Roosevelt administration during the war years were: Samuel Crowther, *Time to Inquire* (John Day, 1943), a defense of private enterprise; Wallace N. Jewett, *The Crucifixion of Democracy* (Cynthiana, Ky.: Hobson Press, 1944); Wendell L. Willkie, *An American Program* (Simon & Schuster, 1944); and Ann M. Wolf, *No Fourth Term* (n.p.: Blackhawk Printing Co., 1944). Of some interest is the brief *UE-CIO Looks at FDR* (New York, 1944), an Electrical Workers tract.

Russell Lord edited under several titles in 1944-1945 for a joint British and American audience various writings of Henry Wallace. Robert A. Taft attacked the economics of the Wallace book *Sixty Million Jobs* (Simon & Schuster, 1945), while remarking in passing, "Mr. Wallace states well the ideal conditions which we would all like to see brought about in America." (*New York Times*, September 9, 1945.)

Substantial books which appeared during the war were: Wesley C. Clark, *Economic Aspects of a President's Popularity* (Philadelphia: 1943), a doctoral thesis; William F. Ogburn (ed.), *American Society in Wartime* (University of Chicago Press, 1943); Giovanni Ortolani, *Le Responsabilità di F. Delano Roosevelt, 1936-1942* (Milan, 1943), a blast from Fascist Italy; Henry M. Wriston, *Challenge to Freedom* (Harper, 1943), in which the president of

Brown University launched an attack on the idea of the state as an end in itself; George Fort Milton, *The Use of Presidential Power, 1789-1943* (Little, Brown, 1944); Scholastic Magazine, *1944: America Votes. A Non-Partisan Handbook of the 1944 Presidential Election* (New York, 1944); Thomas Paul Jenkins, *Reactions of Major Groups to Positive Government in the U. S., 1930-1940* (University of California Press, 1945), a particularly able introduction to a subject deserving additional monographic treatment; and Max Lerner, *Public Journal—Marginal Notes on Wartime America* (Viking, 1945), one hundred editorials written by the author for the provocative newspaper *PM* during 1943 and 1944.

An interpretative book under the able authorship of Basil Rauch in 1944, *The History of the New Deal, 1933-1938* (Creative Age Press, 1944) ranked with formal Roosevelt biographies in importance, for its interpretation was widely noticed. Rauch saw two New Deals, the first stressing recovery, the second reform. The first he saw trying to aid business (NIRA) and large farm producers (AAA), while the second was aimed at union labor and, presumably, small farmers. "The shift . . . from the First to the Second New Deals, the first stressing recovery, the second reform. The first most practical justification for the change was the failure of the First New Deal, particularly NRA, to produce sound economic recovery, and the security program of 1935 was launched only after thorough experiment with the more conservative methods of achieving recovery." The book's chief significance lies in the heavy use made of it by later textbook writers.

Books on international matters of interest to students of Franklin Roosevelt appearing in 1945 were: Henry Steele Commager, *The Story of the Second World War* (Little, Brown, 1945), published in November and in a Pocket Book edition in December; General George C. Marshall, *Selected Speeches and Statements* (Washington, D. C.: Infantry Journal, 1945), a handy source book for the years 1938 to 1945, edited by H. A. De Weerd; also General Marshall's *The Winning of the War in Europe and the Pacific: Biennial Report, 1943-1945* (Simon & Schuster, 1945); Kenneth Pendar, *Adventures in Diplomacy* (Dodd, Mead, 1945); and James P. Warburg, *Foreign Policy Begins at Home* (Harcourt, Brace, 1945), a book endorsing a "planned" but not a "managed" economy for the postwar United States while searching hopefully for solutions to future world problems.

Donald M. Nelson was ostensibly the author of *Arsenal of Democracy* (Harcourt, Brace, 1946), but Eliot Janeway has stated that the book was in fact written by Bruce Catton. (See *Saturday Review of Literature*, October 23, 1948, p. 10.) Two small volumes interpreting aspects of New Deal years were: Edward S. Corwin, *Constitutional Revolution, Ltd.* (Claremont, Calif., 1946), a revision of lectures delivered in 1941; and David Mitrany, *American Interpretations* (London: Contact Publications, 1946), subtitled "four political essays." Journalistic in character were: Olive Ewing Clapper, *Washington Tapestry* (Whittlesey House, 1946); Jonathan Daniels, *Frontier on the Potomac* (Macmillan, 1946), a facile description of wartime Washington; Eleanor Roosevelt, *If You Ask Me* (Appleton-Century, 1946); and A. Merriman Smith, *Thank You, Mr. President* (Harper, 1946), the latter particularly revealing on the President's health.

Cortez A. M. Ewing, *Congressional Elections, 1896-1944* (University of Oklahoma, 1947), presented an important statistical study stressing sectionalism. Leo Gurko, *The Angry Decade* (Dodd, Mead, 1947), is a highly debatable social and literary account of the 1930's; Broadus Mitchell, *Depression Decade: From New Era Through New Deal, 1929-1941* (Rinehart, 1947), an economic textbook account by a Socialist scholar which must be used, despite the labor bestowed on it by its outspoken author, with great care. Edgar E. Robinson, *They Voted For Roosevelt: The Presidential Vote, 1932-1944* (Stanford University Press, 1947), provided a complete presentation of the popular vote by counties from original manuscript and/or printed sources together with a brief interpretation.

In 1948 appeared C. Herman Pritchett, *The Roosevelt Court: A Study in Judicial Politics and Values, 1937-47* (Macmillan, 1948); Dixon Wecter, *The Age of the Great Depression, 1929-1941* (Macmillan, 1948), Volume 13 in the "History of American Life" series; Sumner Welles, *We Need Not Fail* (Houghton Mifflin, 1948); Charles A. Beard, *President Roosevelt and the Coming of the War, 1941: A Study in Appearances and Realities* (Yale University Press, 1948); Floyd A. Cave and associates, *The Origins and Consequences of World War II* (Dryden Press, 1948); Thomas A. Bailey, *The Man in the Street: The Impact of American Public Opinion on Foreign Policy* (Macmillan, 1948).

The year after Harry Truman's election to the Presidency by the American voters little was published on the Roosevelt theme, but in the year 1950 there commenced a stream of books interpretative of the war years in particular, which will be discussed below in a separate section, "Toward Understanding."

7. Memoirs of Contemporaries

The first of the memoirs appeared in the bookstores even before inauguration day. Sara Delano Roosevelt's account of her famous son as a small boy in the 115 pages of *My Boy Franklin* (New York: Long & Smith, 1933) was prepared by writers from information supplied by Franklin Roosevelt's mother.

Hugh S. Johnson, who served as National Industrial Recovery Act Administrator from June 16, 1933, to October 15, 1934, described *The Blue Eagle from Egg to Earth* (Doubleday, 1935). This volume excited comment because of the aggressive personality of its author and his obvious knowledge of one phase of early New Deal developments.

A friendly reception was given *This Is My Story* (Harper, 1937), in which the wife of the President, writing as Eleanor Roosevelt, described less partisan years than she was to set forth in a volume in 1949.

Openly political was James A. Farley's memoir, *Behind the Ballots* (Harcourt, Brace, 1938), in which the Chairman of the Democratic National Committee (after 1932) told "the personal history of a politician." Clifton Fadiman observed of this inside story of organization politics at work that it demonstrated "the complete divorce that may exist in our democracy between the leaders who have genuine social and political ideas and those other leaders whose function is simply to get the first kind elected." A successor volume in 1949 was to present a far more vigorous appraisal of Roosevelt.

The only memoir of consequence in 1939 proved to be Raymond Moley's scorching *After Seven Years* (Harper, 1939). This volume by so respected a critic who at the same time had been so close to Franklin Roosevelt during the first term, marked the beginning of the end of full acceptance of the President's leadership by a considerable number of his earlier advisors. As a member of candidate Roosevelt's speechwriting team in 1932, Assistant Secretary of State in 1933, and editor of *Today* from 1933 to 1937, Moley wrote from the inside. A notebook aided his memory in the preparation of *After Seven Years*. Some reviewers thought this book as unflattering to its author as to Franklin Roosevelt. The volume has risen in public appreciation with the passing of time.

Another memoir of 1939 was William H. (Alfalfa Bill) Murray, *The Presidency, the Supreme Court and Seven Senators* (Boston: Meador, 1939), which was prepared with the aid of Anson B. Campbell.

Few memoirs of the first two terms appeared in book form. Daniel C. Roper, Secretary of Commerce, in his *Fifty Years of Public Life* (Duke University Press, 1941), gave some details of his administration of the Department of Commerce. Harold L. Ickes produced some vigorous controversy with his *Autobiography of a Curmudgeon* (Reynal and Hitchcock, 1943).

Charles Michelson, a reporter who served the Democratic National Committee and the NRA effectively, turned out a book of gossip in *The Ghost Talks* (Putnam's, 1944). As an insider Michelson was able to reveal some facts of value.

A career diplomat, Joseph Grew, selected by Roosevelt to serve as Ambassador to Japan, where his career was to end abruptly on December 8, 1941, issued in 1944 a volume *Ten Years in Japan* (Simon & Schuster, 1944). It was to be supplemented later by the two-volume *Turbulent Era* (Houghton Mifflin, 1952). The works have their chief value in their recitals of events, small in themselves but cumulatively important, which were drawn from the author's diaries and personal papers.

Contrasting sharply with these memoirs of ten and then forty years, is the portrayal of a single evening by Louis Adamic, *Dinner at the White House* (Harper, 1946). Invited to dine with the Roosevelts on January 13, 1942, he was surprised to find Churchill a guest at the dinner. The author has been termed tasteless, bitter, radical, and naïve. But Adamic, prior to his tragic death, was a professional writer, a former Guggenheim fellow, and on this occasion claims to have recorded his (and his wife's) observations almost immediately on arriving home. Carroll Kirkpatrick has well stated the place this strange book holds in Roosevelt literature: "Louis Adamic has captured the spirit and personality of Roosevelt . . . as well as, if not better than anyone else I have read. It is far from the final picture, but it comes as close to the truth, I believe, as any yet drawn." *New Republic,* 115 (September 16, 1946), 331.

The years immediately following the death of Roosevelt and the ending of the war were fruitful in memoirs. Some material of importance on the Vice-Presidential candidate of 1920 and events of succeeding decades, including the London Economic Conference of 1933, appear in James M. Cox, *Journey Through My Years* (Simon & Schuster, 1946). Vice-Admiral Ross T. McIntire chose George Creel to collaborate with him in telling the clinical story of the President in *White House Physician* (Putnam's, 1946). Medical consultant to Roosevelt from 1933, he apparently wrote to silence rumors about the health of his "charge" during the 1944 campaign.

Both professional and popular reviewers have acclaimed the memoir of Roosevelt's Secretary of Labor, Frances Perkins [Mrs. Paul Wilson], *The Roosevelt I Knew* (Viking, 1946), despite the fact that it constitutes only a summary of what its author must have known about the President. Howard Taubman of the *New York Times* lent editorial and critical aid to the author in the preparation of the book. Her complete loyalty to first Governor and then President Roosevelt must be considered in weighing key evaluations of his conduct. The book gives every appearance of general factual accuracy. It had wide reading in England. A German translation appeared in 1947.

Exasperating to the historian is the account of Elliott Roosevelt, *As He Saw It* (Duell, Sloan & Pearce, 1946) which quickly won translation into at least six other languages because of immense world interest in the wartime conferences of the President of the United States. It was written in anger, was anti-British and kindly toward the Soviet Union. Many reviewers agreed with Erwin D. Canham of the *Christian Science Monitor*, "The extensive direct quotations from private conversations with his father are not convincing to this reviewer. They have a synthetic sound." The author was reticent about his utilization of notes. Yet the book cannot be dismissed. With all its faults it remains an account with which each student of Roosevelt must make his peace. Also published in 1946 was Jonathan M. Wainwright, *General Wainwright's Story* (Doubleday, 1946) and Harry C. Butcher, *My Three Years with Eisenhower* (Simon & Schuster, 1946).

A book of unique value in revealing the press conference as an instrument of great importance is Merriman Smith, *Thank You, Mr. President* (Harper, 1946).

Memoirs of less significance appeared in 1947: Ruth Butts Stevens' account of Warm Springs social life, *"Hi-ya, Neighbor,"* (Atlanta: Tupper and Love, 1947); and Michael Francis Reilly, *Reilly of the White House* (Simon & Schuster, 1947), a protector of the President's person. This book was published in a London edition in 1946 as *I Was Roosevelt's Shadow*.

Of greater value, but limited because of lack of intimate contact with the President were: John G. Winant, *Letter from Grosvenor Square* (Houghton Mifflin, 1947), by the Republican from New Hampshire appointed Ambassador to Great Britain in 1941; William F. Halsey's martial reminiscence of the Pacific war, *Admiral Halsey's Story* (Whittlesey House, 1947); and General George S. Patton, *War As I Knew It* (Houghton Mifflin, 1947).

James F. Byrnes, *Speaking Frankly* (Harper, 1947) rated news column space on publication because of its blunt recital of the difficulties of negotiating with the post-war Soviet diplomats. Byrnes, who became successively Congressman, Senator, Supreme Court Justice, director of major war agencies, and Secretary of State (July, 1945-January, 1947) then returned to his native South Carolina to serve as state governor, gives important information about Yalta and also on domestic affairs during the war.

Edward J. Flynn, in *You're the Boss* (Viking, 1947), kept Roosevelt in the forefront of his narrative of machine and organizational Democratic party politics. The details furnished on the 1928 New York State gubernatorial campaign, the 1932 and subsequent Roosevelt election efforts, especially the third-term nomination and the Wallace and Truman Vice-Presidential selections, cannot be ignored. The book defends "good" bosses forthrightly, thus, "My hope in writing this book has been to show that, while bosses are inevitable under our system of government, bad bosses are not." (P. 235.) The character and personality sketch of Roosevelt in Chapter XVI is penetrating and deserves serious attention.

The third major memoir of 1947 was contributed by George Creel, master propagandist of the Wilson administration and journalistic ghost writer extraordinary during the 1930's and 1940's, in *Rebel At Large* (Putnam's, 1947). From his chapter 34, "Franklin Roosevelt Takes Over," to the end of the book, there appear a succession of sidelights on the New Deal, New Dealers, and President Roosevelt which have great value. The role Creel played in writing authoritative "revelations" of Roosevelt's plans for *Collier's* in order to facilitate the Presidential estimation of public opinion, was a major one which has had too little publicity. The book as a whole is better for its hypotheses than for its too brief description of important events.

Winston Churchill published in 1948 the first of his detailed volumes on the British war effort in *The Gathering Storm* (Houghton Mifflin, 1948), in this and in the subsequent volumes providing hitherto little known information about his extensive contacts with President Roosevelt.

Other books which illuminated phases of world events and included anecdotes about the Commander-in-Chief of United States forces, or the President, were: Arthur Bliss Lane, *I Saw Poland Betrayed* (Bobbs-Merrill, 1948); Dwight D. Eisenhower, *Crusade in Europe* (Doubleday, 1948); and Joseph W. Stilwell, *The Stilwell Papers* (Wm. Sloane Associates, 1948), which treated a long career in China (1920-23, 1926-29, 1932-39), and as commander of Chinese and American armies during the war.

A book carefully prepared by McGeorge Bundy from materials furnished by Henry L. Stimson, Secretary of War in the Roosevelt

Cabinet, was *On Active Service in Peace and War* (Harper, 1948). Stimson was strongly critical of the administrative habits of the President.

In 1948 came two large volumes by Cordell Hull, *Memoirs* (Macmillan, 1948). Full and revealing on the Economic Conference of 1933 and various diplomatic maneuverings in Latin America, the account of the Secretary of State from 1933 to 1944 was less comprehensive on matters touching the diplomacy of World War II. Reviewers, fully admitting the honesty, sincerity, and capabilities of Hull, nevertheless deplored omissions in the record. The Hull *Memoirs* have by no means obviated the need for a thoroughgoing biography of the man or a minute study of his often unsatisfactory relations with his chief.

White House Diary (Doubleday, 1948) by Henrietta Nesbitt, "F. D. R.'s housekeeper," provided a routine account, its tone well indicated by a reviewer who commented, "Americans who didn't like the Roosevelts and their gregarious mode of living, will certainly find its pages aggravating."

Important was the second volume of the Farley memoirs, entitled *Jim Farley's Story; the Roosevelt Years* (Whittlesey House, 1948), in which he carried his account of the Democratic party and its chief to the accession of Truman. The accuracy of conversations between Roosevelt and his manager of patronage contained in the book was challenged by some readers, accepted by others. James A. Hagerty noted that Farley had written from memoranda of conversations made at the time. Indeed, those who had rhapsodized over the fabulous Farley memory, were much embarrassed when that memory was turned against parts of the Roosevelt tradition. Reviewers tended to suggest that "historians of the future" would have to verify or contradict the icy anecdotes.

The year 1949 brought another of the Churchill volumes, *Their Finest Hour* (Houghton Mifflin, 1949); two more military memoirs, General Clair L. Chennault, *Way of a Fighter* (Putnam's, 1949), and General H. H. Arnold, *Global Mission* (Harper, 1949); as well as *Roosevelt and the Russians: The Yalta Conference* (Doubleday, 1949) in which the story of Edward R. Stettinius, then Secretary of State, was unfolded through the editing of Walter Johnson, a professional historian. The President was pictured as mentally alert, the Russians were shown to have conceded more points in round numbers than the United States, but again part of the Yalta picture was missing.

Three memoirs which derived from positions of greater intimacy appeared in 1949. Rambling, intertwined with history which its author did not see at first hand, yet significant on a few points, was the memoir of the White House mail clerk, Ira R. T. Smith, *"Dear Mr. President . . ."* (Messner, 1949).

The President's secretary, Grace G. Tully, had a Foreword by William O. Douglas, a Supreme Court Justice, for her *F. D. R., My Boss* (Scribner's, 1949). One reviewer thought it "the most personal account of Roosevelt as a human being that is likely to be written," while a publication for the guidance of librarians in book purchasing found it "A gossipy book, not recommended." Always conscious of the point of view of the Democratic party, past and present, and discursive on personal matters of no consequence, nevertheless the author unconsciously presented readers with a portrayal of "the Boss" at daily work over a seventeen-year period which cannot be ignored. It is a book which repays repeated consultation.

Eleanor Roosevelt treated the gubernatorial and Presidential years in *This I Remember* (Harper, 1949). Occasional admissions of imperfection in her husband give the casual reader an impression of impartiality and frankness of utterances. Yet what the writer of the "My Day" columns chose to remember about the New Deal and the war years does little damage to her husband's memory. How could it be otherwise? Her personal influence in the partisan politics of those years will long be a subject of debate, in which her own disclaimer will have to be discounted at the outset.

Winston Churchill produced both *The Hinge of Fate* and *The Grand Alliance* in 1950, quoting messages passing between the White House and Downing Street of which neither the English nor the American public at the time had inkling.

General Mark W. Clark treated the highly controversial Italian campaign in his *Calculated Risk* (Harper, 1950), but failed to silence critics.

Closer to the person of the Commander-in-Chief was Admiral William D. Leahy, his personal Chief of Staff, who reminded readers five years after the death of the President, *I Was There* (Whittlesey House, 1950). This is a good, plain, and unadorned record drawn from daily notes, at least in part, but a partisan imprimature was clearly stamped on it in a Foreword by President Harry S. Truman. Named chief of the Bureau of Navigation in 1933 and Chief of Naval Operations in 1937 and retired on August 1, 1939, Leahy later served as Governor of Puerto Rico and Ambassador to France. His memoir is extremely valuable on the Yalta Conference.

Marriner S. Eccles published his "public and personal recollections," *Beckoning Frontiers,* under the editorship of Sidney Hyman (Knopf, 1951).

Walter Millis, an experienced popular writer on the origins of American entry into three wars, edited *The Forrestal Diaries* (Viking, 1951). With much paraphrasing of original materials which, when available at Princeton University in later years will become an all-important source, the Millis-Forrestal account of the years from 1944 to the death of the conscientious Cabinet member filled some gaps in the record.

The same may be said of the manuscripts of Arthur H. Vandenberg, a portion of which have been edited by his son, Arthur H. Vandenberg, Jr., under the title *The Private Papers of Senator Vandenberg* (Houghton Mifflin, 1952).

The Commander-in-Chief, United States Fleet, and Chief of Naval Operations (1941-45), Ernest J. King, presented in 1952 with the aid of Walter Muir Whitehill, *Fleet Admiral King: A Naval Record* (Norton, 1952).

More important by far to the student of Roosevelt the man is the autobiography of William L. Chenery, editor of *Collier's* for eighteen years and its publisher for seven, entitled *So It Seemed* (Harcourt, Brace, 1952). Revealing on the third-term decision, on the role of Roosevelt as author, and on changing thought during his Presidential years, Chenery's book must not be missed by close students of Franklin Roosevelt.

Samuel I. Rosenman, *Working with Roosevelt* (Harper, 1952) is a lengthy memoir born of intimate service to the Governor and the President. While no serious study of Roosevelt as speaker can be considered adequate without full consideration of its detailed recital of behind-the-scenes drafting and redrafting, writing and rewriting, this book is not definitive. The story of a contemplated new liberal party formation by the President with Wendell Willkie seems most improbable and has been challenged by some reviewers. Rosenman did not *invent* the term "New Deal," nor is it certain that his recital of the origin of its first use by Roosevelt in an address is the whole story. As has been pointed out above, the amount of Rosenman and the amount of Roosevelt in the introductions and annotations to the published *Public Papers* series provide a nice question for methodological study. The loyalty of Rosenman to Roosevelt and his memory seems complete and all encompassing, and his book, for all its often dispassionate phrasing, is partisan to the core.

After an initial volume of *The Memoirs of Herbert Hoover, Years of Adventure, 1874-1920* (Macmillan, 1951), Mr. Hoover published *The Cabinet and the Presidency, 1920-1933* (Macmillan, 1952) and *The Great Depression, 1929-1941* (Macmillan, 1952). Historians and political scientists reviewing the volumes readily accepted many points of the Hoover indictment of the New Deal, some of his barbs directed at Roosevelt as candidate for public office and as economist, and much of his defense of the Hoover administration. Few reviewers enjoyed sufficient space to pass judgment on the many faceted attack made by Hoover on New Deal policies on the domestic front, nor did they fully appreciate the deep significance of his method of drawing most heavily for ammunition from the books written by close associates of President Roosevelt. It should be said that these volumes must be carefully analyzed by all students of the period.

An important source of personal as well as official and professional judgment on the Roosevelt years was published in September, 1953: *A Front Row Seat*, "an exciting personal narrative," by Nicholas Roosevelt (University of Oklahoma Press).

As an outgrowth of a contribution to the Columbia University oral history project, Louis B. Wehle published in 1953 *Hidden Threads of History* (Macmillan), including an extremely valuable account of his conversations with Franklin Roosevelt, contributing hitherto unknown details of pre-convention discussions in 1920, of steps taken by the President-elect during the interregnum in 1932-1933, and of President Roosevelt's attitude on his candidacy in 1944. This book, attempting an appraisal, struck a general point of view somewhere between the "eulogistic memoirs" and those written with determination to destroy legend and myth.

The first volume of a series of outstanding importance is *The Secret Diary of Harold L. Ickes: The First Thousand Days, 1933-1936* (edited by Jane D. Ickes), published late in 1953 by Simon & Schuster.

Beginning with the June, 1948, issue of *The Western Political Quarterly*, R. G. Tugwell published a succession of articles of the greatest value in presenting President Roosevelt as he was seen by one who worked closely with him for a number of years. These include the following: "The Preparation of a President," *The Western Political Quarterly*, I (June, 1948); "The New Deal in Retrospect," (December, 1948); "The New Deal; the Available Instruments of Governmental Power," (December, 1949); "The New Deal; the Progressive Tradition," (September, 1950); "The Two Great Roosevelts," (June, 1951); "The Compromising Roosevelt," (June, 1953); also: "The Protagonists; Roosevelt and Hoover," in *The Antioch Review*, XIII (winter, 1953-1954); "The Experimental Roosevelt," in *The Political Quarterly* (July, 1950); and "The Progressive Orthodoxy of Franklin D. Roosevelt," in *Ethics* (October, 1953).

8. Biographies of the President

Ernest K. Lindley, reporter for the *New York Herald-Tribune,* was the able author of the pioneer biography, *Franklin D. Roosevelt, A Career in Progressive Democracy* (Bobbs-Merrill, 1931). This volume served as a point of departure for a long list of successors. A fellow journalist noted its appearance on the eve of a Presidential election year, and wrote, "On the whole, the book is an intelligent and effective campaign document. And, quite unlike other books of which this may be said, it is accurate enough to guide future and more critical biographers." Still, said Arthur Krock in the *New York Times* of November 29, 1931, the book was "frankly, propaganda." The Lindley book has acquired a special value in the perspective of years, as a portrayal of the Governor in the light he and his closest advisors sought just before pre-convention campaigning for delegates would begin in earnest.

Favorable pictures of candidate Roosevelt were also offered by Leland M. Ross and Allen W. Grobin, *This Democratic Roosevelt: The Life Story of "F.D.": An Authentic Biography* (Dutton, 1932); and by Earle Looker, *This Man Roosevelt* (New York: Brewer, Warren & Putnam, 1932). A reviewer found the former "laudatory, almost theatric" and little more than a "success" story; this was an adequate commentary. The Looker volume is less eulogistic and more informative.

The "biographies" of 1933 require little comment. They included: Alvin P. Johnson, *Franklin D. Roosevelt's Colonial Ancestors* (Boston: Lothrop, Lee & Shepard, 1933), an account of their part in the making of American history; the fifty-eight-page treatment by Joseph Lasky, *Our President, Franklin Delano Roosevelt* (New York: Walter & Mahon, 1933); Armando Roa, *Roosevelt, the Executive Dictator* (Havana: Cultural, 1933), possibly the first appraisal from outside the United States; the breezy juvenile, the first of many uncritical treatments of the Roosevelt theme for youngsters, by Mrs. Sadyebeth Lowitz, *Young America's Story of Franklin D. Roosevelt, Man of Action* (Doubleday, 1933); and Bernard Faÿ, *Roosevelt and His America* (Little, Brown, 1933), also issued in a French edition. The book by Faÿ bore the marks of hasty writing, was superficial in spots, and pictured its hero in epic proportions. There are flashes of insight that have stood the test of time. Belle Moses enjoyed some Roosevelt family assistance in the preparation of her book for youngsters, *Franklin Delano Roosevelt, The Minute Man of '33* (Appleton-Century, 1933). A foreign view was that of

François de Tessan, *Franklin D. Roosevelt* (Paris: Editions Baudin-iere, 1933).

One compilation of 1934 edited by Don Wharton, *The Roosevelt Omnibus* (Knopf, 1934), retains value for its articles, cartoons, and brief critical bibliography. The book stressed Roosevelt the human being, of course, without any detailed treatment of the President in office. Other publications of the year were Nick L. Hogan, *The Roosevelt Cabinet; Biographies of the President and His Official Advisors* (Philadelphia: c. by author, 1934); Samuel Nisenson, *From Boyhood to President with Franklin Delano Roosevelt* (Cleveland: World Syndicate, 1934); Elisabeth Vernon Quinn, *Picture Story of Franklin D. Roosevelt* (Stokes, 1934); and Wayne Whipple, *The Story of Young Franklin Roosevelt* (Chicago: Goldsmith, 1934).

A biography of the President's mother, Sara Delano Roosevelt, written by Mrs. Rita Kleeman, appeared in 1935 under the title, *Gracious Lady* (Appleton-Century, 1935).

The most penetrating study of the year was written by a *Nation* editor, Mauritz A. Hallgren, entitled, *The Gay Reformer: Profits Before Plenty Under Franklin D. Roosevelt* (Knopf, 1935). Re-viewers accorded it surprised respect, for the former newspaperman had written an attack on the President for his renunciation of radicalism. It contained, moreover, perhaps the first unfavorable interpretation in book form of the Roosevelt boyhood, early career, and governorship. In the Presidency, there had been "demogogism" rather than "collectivism" or "socialism," and, continued Hallgren, "He has erred, not because he has not meant well, not because he has not tried to do right, but largely because of his economic illiteracy and his class prejudices. His emotions run deep, but his thinking skips lightly over the surface, affected only by the more concrete experiences and more obvious facts of life." (P. 310.) He had benefited the profit system by strengthening industrial and finance monopolism while winning the confidence of the masses to himself. (P. 312.) War would be not unlikely under him for Roose-velt, lofty patriot, ardent navalist, eager to please, will prove ready to do or die to save the capitalist system. (Pp. 315-16.) The Marxian bias of Hallgren was clearly displayed, but, reported Elmer Davis, "Nevertheless, his bias does not affect his accuracy as a reporter, and where it colors his interpretation the coloring may easily be dis-counted." (*Saturday Review of Literature,* September 23, 1933, p. 125.)

The year of the Roosevelt-Landon campaign, 1936, was fertile in biographical treatments of the Democratic candidate for re-election. These included Bellamy Partridge, *An Imperial Saga; The Rosse-velt* [*sic*] *Family in America* (New York: Hillman-Curl, 1936), a

325-page genealogical study, which had the virtue of presenting facts about T.R. and F.D.R. in parallel; and James C. Young, *Roosevelt Revealed* (Farrar & Rinehart, 1935). Some extracts from writings and speeches were included in a book by Patrick Joseph O'Brien which was otherwise chiefly notable for its electioneering title, *Forward with Roosevelt: An Authentic Narrative of His Life, Aims, and Ambitions, and a Graphic Story of His Endeavors for Social Security* . . . (Winston, 1936).

Brief and ephemeral were: Archibald C. Knoles, *Franklin Delano Roosevelt, the Great Liberal* (Burlington, N. J.: Enterprise, 1936); Erich Brandeis, *Franklin D. Roosevelt, the Man* (New York: American Offset, 1936); Paul Haber, *The House of Roosevelt* (Brooklyn: Author's Publishing Co., 1936); and R. M. Arundel, *Roosevelt Riddles* (Doubleday, 1936), published under the pseudonym Russell Moore. None of these short books deserve to be called a biography in the usual sense of the word.

Interpretations of the President from abroad appeared in 1938. Few Americans noted the appearance of Stephen K. Bailey, *Roosevelt and His New Deal* (London: Fact, 1938), Juan Guixe, *L'expérience Roosevelt* (Paris: Editions contemporaines, 1938), or the printed Fourth of July address of José Manuel Cortina in English and Spanish editions, *Franklin Delano Roosevelt and the New Democracy* (Havana: P. Fernandez, 1938).

The appraisal of Emil Ludwig, *Roosevelt: A Study in Fortune and Power* (Viking, 1938), translated from the German, reissued by Garden City Publishing Company in 1941, and gaining publication in a Buenos Aires edition in Spanish, created more of a stir. A careless psychological study, it must be examined because of its author's assertion that Roosevelt co-operated to some extent in its preparation and read the sections quoting him directly previous to publication. The book grossly overworked the theme of the great leader of the upper class descending to champion the cause of the oppressed masses, an idea which particularly appealed to the author.

Popular in nature was Dr. William L. Stidger, *These Amazing Roosevelts* (New York: Macfadden Book Co., 1938).

Two unusual studies of Franklin Roosevelt appeared in 1940. One, by Surat Singh Batra, *Men or Miracles* (Lahore: National Publishing Society, 1940) was an essay comparing Mussolini, Hitler, De Valera, Stalin, and Roosevelt.

Unpublished, but now microfilmed, was a doctoral dissertation by Turner Christian Cameron, Jr., prepared in 1940 at Princeton University, *The Political Philosophy of Franklin Delano Roosevelt*

(Microfilm #2926, University Microfilms, Ann Arbor, Mich., 324 pp.).

The years of World War II naturally brought immense interest throughout the world to the person of Franklin Roosevelt. This was reflected clearly in the large number of studies of his personality and leadership published in foreign countries. In a variety of languages and written all too often to "sell" rather than to penetrate the surface through detailed research and investigation, few were examined for this study. They are listed here for the information of specialists. Mario Neves, *Roosevelt* (Lisbon: Parceria A. M. Pereira, 1941. Pp. 66.); Alfred Oste, *Franklin Roosevelt* (Stockholm: A. Bonnier, 1941. Pp. 274.); Luigi Barzini, *Roosevelt e la guerra all'Inghilterra, commenti e spiegazioni* (Milan: A. Mondador, 1942. Pp. 337.); Antonio Bulcao, *Roosevelt* (Rio de Janeiro: Norte editora 1942. Pp. 168.); Gerard Chevalier, *Connaissez-vous . . . Roosevelt?* (Montreal: Editions Fides, 1942. Pp. 28.); Giselher Wirsing, *El continente sin limite; programa de Roosevelt para un dominio americano del mundo* (Madrid: Afrodisio Aguado, 1942. Pp. 484.); Basil D. Moon, *Roosevelt, World Statesman,* (London: P. Davies, 1942. Pp. 192.); another edition, *Franklin Roosevelt, His Life and Achievement* (London: Nicholson & Watson, 1942. Pp. 192.); Heinrich Dietz, *F. D. Roosevelt, gesicht und methode eines volksverführers* (Berlin: Junker und Dünnhaupt, 1943. Pp. 152.); Frederico de Madrid, *Franklin Roosevelt, el presidente extraordinario* (Madrid: Editorial Pace, 1944 Pp. 472.); Diego Abad de Santillan, *El pensamiento politico de Roosevelt* (Buenos Aires: J. Toryho, 1944. Pp. 288.); Walter Philip Carman, *Roosevelt: Franklin Delano Roosevelt, 1882-1945* (Wellington: A. H. & A. W. Reed, 1945. Pp. 41.); Congreso, Camara de diputados, Chile, *Homenaje a la memoria del excmo. senor Franklin Delano Roosevelt, abril 13 de 1945* (Santiago de Chile, 1945. Pp. 43.); Peretz Cornfeld, *Ruzwelt* (Tel-Aviv, 1945. Pp. 146.); Raymond Las Vergnas, *F. D. Roosevelt; ou, La dictature de la liberté* (Paris: Editions universelles, 1945. Pp. 126.); Alfred Oste, *Franklin Roosevelt* (Stockholm: Kooperative förbundets bokförlag, 1945. Pp. 32.); Université catholique, Louvain, *In memorian Franklin Delano Roosevelt, Lovanii, die 16a Mai 1945* (Louvain, 1945. Pp. 30.), part French, part English, part Flemish, part Latin; Jean Revel, *Roosevelt* (Paris: Bonne Presse, 1945. Pp. 93.).

In 1946, the first post-war year, there appeared the following foreign biographical treatments: American Institute in Czechoslovakia, *In Memoriam, Franklin Delano Roosevelt, 1882-1945* (Prague? 1946? Pp. 14.); Cor Dommelshuizen (ed.), *Leven en werken van Franklin Delano Roosevelt . . .* (West-Friesland, 1946. Pp. 36.);

Alberto Giordano, *Roosevelt y los EE. UU.; biografía del hombre y del país* (Buenos Aires: Editorial Sophos, 1946. Pp. 252.); Kees Hazelzet, *Franklin Delano Roosevelt, de aristocrat, die vocht voor den kleinen man* (Wageningen: Gebr. Zomer & Keuning, 1946. Pp. 63.); Alfred Oste, *Franklin D. Roosevelt* (Copenhagen: Samlerens forlag, 1946. Pp. 319.).

While these evidences of the power of the United States and the drama surrounding its leader were appearing in foreign lands, biographers at home were not idle. A book by Gerald W. Johnson, *Roosevelt: Dictator or Democrat?* (Harper, 1941) was reprinted with notes and an introduction by D. W. Brogan under the title *Roosevelt: An American Study* (London: H. Hamilton, 1942) for a British audience and was translated into German. Radio biographies of Roosevelt, Stalin, Churchill, and Hitler were subsequently issued by NBC under the title, *These Four Men* (New York: Wm. E. Rudge's, 1941). *Current Biography, 1942*, prepared and printed a sketch of the bare details of the President's life. Karl Schriftgiesser, *The Amazing Roosevelt Family, 1613-1942* (Wilfred Funk, 1942) had, in addition to genealogical data, what amounted to a brief biography of Franklin Roosevelt on pages 304-354.

In 1944, Noel F. Busch, a *Life* editor and war correspondent, asked *What Manner of Man?* (Harper, 1944), and answered, "a good but not very wise man; vain, captious, over-confident, and warmhearted; no more honest than most, but friendlier than the average; courageous but . . . not totally without a certain somewhat meretricious grandeur." (P. 184.) Allan Nevins found some value in the preliminary comment and analysis in the book, despite major flaws in its historical and psychoanalytical aspects.

Frank Kingdon wrote the brief campaign biography *"That Man" in the White House* (Arco, 1944). He would later compile extracts from Roosevelt's speeches under the title *As FDR Said*.

A biography by the English author of thirty-five novels and twenty-nine other previous works, Compton Mackenzie, *Mr. Roosevelt* (Dutton, 1944), did not deserve its publication on the continent or in this country on the basis of any real originality. There were one hundred illustrations, however, a quarter of them in color.

Another book of 1944 was Frank B. Ober, *Is President Roosevelt Indispensable?* (Baltimore: Daily Record Co., 1944).

The death of President Roosevelt was the signal in 1945 and 1946 for volumes of tribute of special interest as sources. On sale just *six* days after the news from Warm Springs was the paperbound Donald Porter Geddes (ed.), *Franklin Delano Roosevelt, A Memorial* (Pocket Books, 1945), issued seven months later in hard covers (Dial, 1945). The final page of the first edition bore the single sentence, "All royalties from this book have been donated to a charitable cause that was close to the heart of the President." The extraordinary sentimentality of the volume is matched only by its extravagance. An unfortunate editorial choice, but a revealing one, was the caption under the picture of a happy Stalin and delighted Roosevelt, " 'We leave here friends in fact, in spirit and in purpose.' "

Clark Kinnaird edited, with an introduction by Philip S. Foner, *The Real F. D. R.: An Intimate Close-up in Pictures and Anecdotes, with a Factual Record of His Life and Works* (Citadel Press, 1945). It is chiefly of interest for its two hundred pictures. Mrs. Rita Kleeman wrote *Young Franklin Roosevelt* (Messner, 1946) for children.

Three of the books that appeared in 1947 are Aage Heinberg, *To Statsmenn, Theodore og Franklin D. Roosevelt* (Oslo: S. Dahl, 1947); Frank Kingdon, *Architects of the Republic* (New York: Alliance, 1947), an unusual attempt at a spiritual evaluation of Washington, Jefferson, Lincoln, and Roosevelt; and a treatment for children, Ann Weil, *Franklin Roosevelt, Boy of the Four Freedoms* (Bobbs-Merrill, 1947).

Another volume of the year was produced by biographer Alden Hatch, who had freely admitted in an earlier book on Wilson that he had never written about a man for whom he did not feel sympathy and admiration. The book, *Franklin D. Roosevelt: An Informal Biography* (Holt, 1947), English edition (London: Skeffington, 1948), drew from Gerald W. Johnson the observation: "The great revelation of the book is the way in which Roosevelt's career lends itself to dramatic treatment. Without doubt, this is a book destined to have a long line of successors. The material is too perfect to be ignored. One cannot read this book without being sure that novelists and playwrights will be busy with Roosevelt for a long time to come, and probably poets, too." (*New York Herald-Tribune Book Review*, February 9, 1947, p. 6.)

An election year, 1948, witnessed the appearance of a controversial book by John T. Flynn, *The Roosevelt Myth* (Devin-Adair, 1948). Reviewers were unwilling to swallow this bitter pill without vigorous protest. They agreed that it was too strong, too extreme, too black and white. Even so, the book marks a turning point in Roosevelt biography, since after its appearance in 1948 biographers began to give more attention to opposing points of view.

The sensitive study by Robert E. Sherwood, *Roosevelt and Hopkins: An Intimate History* (Harper, 1948, 1950), was issued in various editions. For the 1950 revision in pocket book size, 2 volumes, the Notes were increased from twenty-five to forty-seven pages. Because this book provided a guide to numerous actions of the President which were hitherto unsuspected by the public, it has enjoyed much attention since its publication. Test of the validity of its portrayal of the Roosevelt-Hopkins relationship, and more important, its description of Roosevelt's dealings with foreign powers during the war years, will come at a later time. Sherwood was close to both men, as the Rosenman memoir shows: "For the last five years of the President's life—the most important years—Hopkins was unquestionably the most influential of those who worked with him." Sherwood's *Roosevelt and Hopkins* gives the story of this influence, how it was developed, how it was exercised, and how it waned.

The Government Printing Office issued in 1948 the memorial address delivered by John G. Winant on July 1, 1946, before the joint meeting of the House and Senate, entitled simply *Franklin Delano Roosevelt* (House Document no. 770, 79 Cong., 2 Sess., 83 pp.).

Possibly the first of the sensational books about the late President was Emanuel Mann Josephson, *The Strange Death of Franklin D. Roosevelt: History of the Roosevelt-Delano Dynasty, America's Royal Family* (New York: Chedney Press, 1948).

Other books of the year were: Reginald Hugh Kiernan, *President Roosevelt* (London: G. G. Harrap, 1948); Firmin Roz, *Roosevelt* (Paris: Dunod, 1948); Walter Tittle, *Roosevelt as an Artist Saw Him* (New York: McBride, 1948); and Per Vogt, *Franklin D. Roosevelt* (Oslo: J. G. Tanum, 1948).

The brief interpretative study of Roosevelt which comprises Chapter XII of Richard Hofstadter, *The American Political Tradition and the Men Who Made It* (Knopf, 1948), entitled "The Patrician as Opportunist," should be read in conjunction with other chapters in the book, especially the one on Hoover. The book, skillfully written, is the result of an ambitious research project.

Raymond Moley wrote a perceptive and valuable book in *Twenty-Seven Masters of Politics, In a Personal Perspective* (Funk & Wagnalls, 1949), which included, in addition to that of Roosevelt, analyses of Smith, Hoover, Willkie, Dewey, Garner, Wallace, Farley, Ed Flynn, Howe, Michelson, Frankfurter, Hugh Johnson, Woodin, Long, Rayburn, and Byrnes.

More than 170 drawings and a simple text comprised Olin Dows, *Franklin Roosevelt at Hyde Park* (New York: American Artists Group, 1949), a country squire treatment by a close friend and author.

Cyril Clemens pursued his hobby with *F. D. Roosevelt and Mark Twain*, "overrun from *The Dalhousie Review* (October, 1945)" and republished as *Mark Twain and Franklin D. Roosevelt* (International Mark Twain Society, 1949), the latter an account of an interview given Clemens by Roosevelt on the occasion of the presentation of a Mark Twain Gold Medal. Eleanor Roosevelt wrote the Foreword.

Another of the books for children was Marcus Rosenblum, *The Story of Franklin Roosevelt* (Simon & Schuster, 1949).

Stefan Lorant gathered together many well known and a few new pictures in his *FDR: A Pictorial Biography* (Simon & Schuster, 1950). Two sketches of Roosevelt's career which, though brief, are professionally written are: George E. Mowry, "Franklin Delano Roosevelt," *Collier's Encyclopedia* (1950), XVII, 131-135, and Allan Nevins, "Franklin Delano Roosevelt," *Chambers' Encyclopaedia*, XI, 827-830. A doctoral dissertation completed at Columbia University in 1950 by Bernard Bellush, which is based on research in gubernatorial manuscripts is entitled *Apprenticeship for the Presidency, Franklin D. Roosevelt as Governor of New York* (Microfilm #2521, University Microfilm, Ann Arbor, Mich., 1951). The virtue of this study is its reproduction of important paragraphs from the personal and official correspondence of Governor Roosevelt in the Roosevelt Library.

John Gunther, writer of "inside" books on geographic areas, turned biographer for *Roosevelt in Retrospect: A Profile in History* (Harper, 1950). "What I have written," Gunther said, "sizeable as it may seem, is little more than a preliminary sketch, an estimate, a survey, an appraisal, moreover an appraisal from a personal as well as a political point of view." The book is, of course, neither Roosevelt nor retrospect, but, as Basil Rauch put it, "a fabulous collection of anecdotes." Those who already know the memoir literature on Roosevelt will find the book familiar. Historians will do well to bypass the book as a source of stories about the President and re-examine the original Gunther sources, since he seems to have been unable to resist the interesting, regardless of its possibly apocryphal standing. "The testimony of a servant at Hyde Park was often as illuminating as that of a member of the Cabinet," he asserts. The author writes on matters of immense importance armed with the slightest hint of evidence. That a book of this character could attain wide circulation in mid-century without the barest use of historical method in the evaluation of sharply conflicting factual evidence, and without even a partial use of the Roosevelt Library, is itself a tribute to the extent of the continuing Roosevelt legend five years after the President's death.

Other studies of 1950 were Hugh Anthony Allen, *Roosevelt and the Will of God* (New York: Lifetime Editions, 1950); Argentine Francis Alington, *Franklin Roosevelt* (London: SCM Press, 1950), issued under the pseudonym of Hugh Talbot; Clara and Hardy Steeholm, *The House at Hyde Park* (Viking, 1950), which contributes some new details in the family picture; and Gene Schoor, *The Picture Story of Franklin Delano Roosevelt* (Fell, 1950).

In 1951 Mabel Montgomery, *A Courageous Conquest: The Life Story of Franklin Delano Roosevelt* (New York: Globe Book Co., 1951) appeared with editing by Henry I. Christ. An important compilation of more than one hundred extracts from memoirs and biographies with interspersed commentary, is James N. Rosenau (ed.), *The Roosevelt Treasury* (Doubleday, 1951). The editor gained experience previous to the work on this volume by serving as research assistant to Elliott Roosevelt on the second volume of the *Personal Letters* series.

The first volume in a multi-volume biography of Franklin Roosevelt was published in 1952 with the appearance of Frank Freidel, *Franklin D. Roosevelt: The Apprenticeship* (Little, Brown, 1952). The author made extensive use of manuscript sources. The study is invaluable for this alone, as well as for careful weighing of the evidence. This volume carried the Roosevelt story from birth through the close of World War I. The reviewers, almost without exception, hailed it as the "definitive biography."

Eve Merriam, *The Real Book About Franklin D. Roosevelt* (New York: Garden City Books, 1952) appeared at the time; also David E. Weingast, *Franklin D. Roosevelt: Man of Destiny* (Messner, 1952).

Harold Gosnell, in his *Champion Campaigner, Franklin D. Roosevelt* (Macmillan, 1952), found that as a campaigner for office Roosevelt had "charm, optimism, confidence, generosity, faith, a vibrant voice, a handsome physique, a good memory, courage, a fine sense of humor, an excellent digestion, freedom from worry, a great gift for words, calmness, poise and patience." Gosnell gives too little weight to such aids to the Roosevelt campaigning as economic depression, 1932; inept opposition; federal relief funds; and New Deal legislation.

Roosevelt and the Warm Springs Story, by Turnley Walker (A. A. Wyn, 1953), was said by Eleanor Roosevelt to be "one of the most delightful books written about my husband."

The second volume in the series by Frank Freidel, *Franklin D. Roosevelt: The Ordeal* (Little, Brown, 1954), covered the period 1919-1928. It is marked by the same characteristics of method and style that appeared in the first volume two years earlier. There is every reason to accept the judgment of one reviewer that "this is the definitive biography of Roosevelt's emergence." It is written with an amazing grasp of detail, and a growing power of interpretation.

9. *Toward Understanding*

The years following the death of President Roosevelt were marked by the appearance in books, articles, and monographs of increasingly critical treatment of the events of the years 1933 to 1945. The steady stream of memoir and biography which had concentrated on the President's person did not cease with his death. The year 1945 included a heavy response, of course. With short lapses the stream has flowed on without sign of diminution.

Somehow symbolic was the title of Roger Butterfield's reflections, "What Will the Historians Say?" *Saturday Review of Literature,* April 21, 1945.

Charles A. Beard produced *American Foreign Policy in the Making, 1932-1940: A Study in Responsibilities* (Yale University Press, 1946). Orderly in chronology and containing no concluding chapter, the book's careful documentation aroused critical response. Walter P. Hall presented in *Iron Out of Calvary* (Appleton-Century, 1946) "an interpretative history of the Second World War."

George E. Morgenstern, *Pearl Harbor* (Devin-Adair, 1947) conveyed a far less favorable picture of the role of Roosevelt in the coming of the war than Walter Millis in his *This is Pearl!* (Morrow, 1947). Less noticed at the time was Herbert Feis, *Seen From E.A.; Three International Episodes* (Knopf, 1947). The "Morgenthau Diaries" appeared in small part in *Collier's,* September 27-October 25, 1947, and aroused intense interest among writers on political themes. Notable was the detailed review by J. M. Gillis in *Catholic World,* November, 1947. Hamilton Basso tried to delineate a "Roosevelt Legend" in *Life,* November 3. 1947.

Close associates of the President in their own writings did little to weaken the growing legend, valuable to the future fortunes of the political party of which Franklin Roosevelt had been the central power for so many years. Robert E. Sherwood, former speechwriter for the President, serialized his "Secret Papers of Harry L. Hopkins" in *Collier's,* May 29-September 18, 1948, and Harold L. Ickes published in the *Saturday Evening Post,* June 5-July 24, 1948, "My Twelve Years with F.D.R."

Also published in 1948 were Sumner Welles, *We Need Not Fail* (Houghton Mifflin, 1948); Thomas A. Bailey, *The Man in the*

Street: The Impact of American Public Opinion on Foreign Policy (Macmillan, 1948); Bruce Catton, *War Lords of Washington* (Harcourt, Brace, 1948); and Richard Hofstadter, "The Roosevelt Reputation," in *The Progressive,* November, 1948. The appearance of the more outspoken second volume of his series by Charles A. Beard, *President Roosevelt and the Coming of the War, 1941: A Study in Appearances and Realities* (Yale University Press, 1948) did the Roosevelt reputation no good. Defenders seized quickly on what may have been the most influential immediate criticism, which depended partly on ridicule, Samuel Eliot Morison's "Did Roosevelt Start the War? History Through a Beard," *Atlantic,* August, 1948. In October, 1948, the Foundation for Public Affairs published in their *Monthly Analysis of Foreign Policy* a paper by Thomas A. Bailey entitled "The Dilemma of Democracy," which was a succinct discussion of the role of President Roosevelt in the events leading to the Japanese attack upon the United States.

As American relations with Soviet Russia deteriorated, William C. Bullitt wrote, "How We Won the War and Lost the Peace," *Life,* August 30-September 6, 1948, and Karl Schriftgiesser noted certain aspects of what he chose to call the "Battle Over the Bones of F.D.R." for *United Nations World,* November, 1948. The following year C. L. Rossiter wrote "Political Philosophy of F. D. Roosevelt: A Challenge to Scholarship," in the *British Review of Politics,* 11 (January, 1949). Articles of interest were R. K. White, "Hitler, Roosevelt, and the Nature of War Propaganda," *Journal of Abnormal Psychology,* 44 (April, 1949) and David M. Potter, "Sketches for the Roosevelt Portrait," *Yale Review,* September, 1949. Also published at this time was W. H. Hale's "Roosevelt, the Myths and the Man," *American Scholar,* 18 (October, 1949).

Publication of the second volume of Winston S. Churchill's memoirs on World War II (partly serialized in *Life*) *Their Finest Hour* (Houghton Mifflin, 1949), revealed that President Roosevelt had corresponded with the British Prime Minister in a manner to attract the abiding interest of Americans, as has been previously noted.

The year 1949 was singularly barren in publication of material relevant to the life and influence of President Roosevelt. Attention was centered on President Truman, by then confirmed in office by the people.

With the opening of 1950, however, came a fresh stream of volumes on public affairs which touched the Roosevelt theme. Among them were some which were touched with growing revisionism and some which were not. Basil Rauch, *Roosevelt: From Munich to Pearl Harbor, A Study in the Creation of a Foreign Policy*

(Creative Age Press, 1950) did not follow the lead of Beard, nor did Herbert Feis, *The Road to Pearl Harbor* (Princeton University Press, 1950), the latter a quietly written narrative account. William Henry Chamberlin, *America's Second Crusade* (Regnery, 1950) tried to revalue the story, which Hanson W. Baldwin, experienced writer on military affairs for the *New York Times,* addressed himself to in *Great Mistakes of the War* (Harper, 1950).

Allan Nevins, *The New Deal and World Affairs . . . 1933-1945* and D. W. Brogan, *The Era of Franklin D. Roosevelt* were among several new volumes in the Chronicles of America Series issued by the Yale University Press in 1950. Other books of varying value were: James K. Eyre, *The Roosevelt-MacArthur Conflict* (Chambersburg, Pa.: Craft Press, 1950); Ralph E. Flanders, *The American Century* (Harvard University Press, 1950); and Herbert L. Marx (ed.), *The Welfare State* (Wilson, The Reference Shelf, 1950).

Thomas A. Bailey in *America Faces Russia* (Cornell University Press, 1950) offered a scholarly and realistic account of Russian-American relations in the nineteenth and twentieth centuries which was based on detailed research in contemporary journals of opinion and related sources. Admiral William D. Leahy's memoir, *I Was There* was serialized in the *Saturday Evening Post* in 1950. John Gunther's *Roosevelt in Retrospect: A Profile in History* (Harper, 1950), widely read, gave long-time journalistic friends of Franklin Roosevelt a chance to recreate old enthusiasms in lengthy and largely uncritical reviews. Important for thoughtful analysis was R. W. Van Alstyne's "United States and Russia in World War II," *Current History,* November and December, 1950. Harold Gosnell defended a theme vital to a forthcoming book in his article, "Does Campaigning Make a Difference?" *Public Opinion Quarterly* (No. 3, 1950).

Growing dissent was brought to the attention of many who had not been following the revisionist literature on the coming of the war, when A. M. Schlesinger, Jr. wrote the widely noticed "Roosevelt and His Detracters," *Harper's* June, 1950.

A thoroughly scholarly treatment of a controversial problem was Jeannette P. Nichols, "Roosevelt's Monetary Diplomacy in 1933," *American Historical Review,* 56 (January, 1951).

Published in 1951 were Sumner Welles, *Seven Decisions That Shaped History* (Harper, 1951), following serialization in *Harper's;* Frederic R. Sanborn, *Design for War: A Study of Secret Power Politics, 1937-1941* (Devin-Adair, 1951) which advanced conspiratorial interpretations; and Eliot Janeway, *The Struggle for Survival* (Yale University Press, 1951). Skillful in research method was F. H. Sanford's statistical "Public Orientation to Roosevelt," *Public Opin-*

ion Quarterly (No. 2, 1951). An outstanding critique was Samuel Lubell, *The Future of American Politics* (Harper, 1952).

The year 1952 brought Australian journalist Chester Wilmot's invaluable and outspoken study, *The Struggle for Europe* (Harper, 1952) and Charles C. Tansill, *Back Door to War* (Regnery, 1952), an attempt by a professionally trained historian to document a Machiavellian version of events.

The first volume in a projected series on "The World Crisis and American Foreign Policy" was *The Challenge to Isolation, 1937-1940* (Harper, 1952). The authors, William L. Langer and S. Everett Gleason, have placed all workers in this field in their debt. Their first volume is based upon a mastery of all materials in print and wide use of unpublished materials, including much State Department matter and some of the papers of President Roosevelt.

Paul H. Appleby mixed personal opinion with use of published memoirs to reach his conclusions in "Roosevelt's Third Term Decision," *American Political Science Review*, XLVI (September, 1952). Matthew Josephson, *Sidney Hillman: Statesman of American Labor* (Doubleday, 1952) was an intimately researched biography written within a frame of reference which many, even within the labor movement, would question.

Leland D. Baldwin, *The Stream of American History* (American Book Company, 1952), a two-volume textbook for college use, was a thoughtful production whose section on the Presidency of Franklin Roosevelt was outspoken and often critical, a fact setting it somewhat apart from many of its fellows in the textbook field.

10. *The Continuing Stream*

As the end of the first decade following the death of Franklin Roosevelt approached, it appeared that the stream of publication concerning him and his era would not diminish for many years.

Already in view are publications of extreme value to those who would come to an understanding of the Roosevelt years. In the professional journals is this particularly the case. Books tend to reflect the dominant interests of the more serious members of society, and consequently deal currently for the most part with foreign affairs.

Certain to emerge are clinical studies by specialists on every aspect of the New Deal. It is already obvious that month by month will appear re-examination and re-evaluation of the critical events of the war years.

One example of increasing interest in the health—and illness—of the President is found in W. G. Eliasberg, "How Long Was Roosevelt Ill Before His Death?" in *Diseases of the Nervous System,* XIV (November, 1953), 323-328.

In the *Journal of the History of Ideas,* XIV (June, 1953), 421-438, Whitney R. Cross writes of "Conservation Ideas of the Two Roosevelts."

W. H. Shannon's study of "Roosevelt, De Gaulle and Our Vichy Policy" may be found in *Social Studies,* 44 (October-November, 1953), 203-208, 247-254.

William L. Neumann published "Franklin D. Roosevelt and Japan, 1913-1933," in *Pacific Historical Review,* XXII (May, 1953).

The *American Magazine* financed the travels of Clarence Woodbury to make possible a lengthy report on the evolution of Franklin Roosevelt's family tree, "Will There Always Be a Roosevelt?" in their issue for January, 1953. The article sheds much light on the careers of the Roosevelt children and indirectly, therefore, on their father.

Wayne S. Cole provides extremely valuable evidence, based on manuscript materials in the Hoover Library, upon *America First; the Battle Against Intervention* (University of Wisconsin Press, 1953).

Robert Paul Browder, in *The Origins of Soviet-American Diplomacy* (Princeton University Press, 1953), writes from the point of view shown in his chapter entitled "Roosevelt Takes the Initiative." In his Preface, Browder states, "So far as I have been able to discover, the Department of State had little to do with recognition, although several of its officers played important roles in the event. and the decision to recognize Soviet Russia was taken and the subsequent negotiations were conducted by the White House." The steps in the negotiations have been carefully and clearly stated by Browder.

Harry Elmer Barnes edited *Perpetual War for Perpetual Peace* (Caldwell, Idaho: Caxton, 1953), a "critical examination of the foreign policy of Franklin Delano Roosevelt."

The Yalta Betrayal, by Felix Wittner (Caxton Press, 1953), presents data—much of it quoted from accounts of participants—on "the decline and fall of Franklin Delano Roosevelt."

Beyond Containment, by William Henry Chamberlin (Regnery, 1953), pointed out that the victory of 1945 left arrayed against the United States a mass of power more menacing than any in American history.

Herbert Feis, in *The China Tangle* (Princeton University Press, 1953), produced a valuable book marked by extensive research and judicial statement. The spirit is best seen in the chapter on Yalta. The book received wide praise, but some condemnation as another example of "official history," which it definitely was not.

Robert C. North in *Moscow and the Chinese Communists* (Stanford University Press, 1953) maintained that the policies of the United States in China were not the result of subversion. These policies, asserts Mr. North, grew out of lack of information, bad judgment, and sometimes out of a false idealism. They produced a disintegration and uncertainty that led to the loss of China to the Communists.

William L. Langer and S. Everett Gleason published the second volume in the series on "The World Crisis and American Foreign Policy" as *The Undeclared War, 1940-1941* (Harper, 1953). The narrative of events of vast complexity has been presented with great clarity. The authors acquit the President of deliberately encouraging a Japanese attack at Pearl Harbor.

Winston Churchill completed his massive series on World War II by the publication of the sixth volume, *Triumph and Tragedy* (Houghton Mifflin, 1953). It appeared to be the most informative of all sources yet revealed on the closing months of the war.

Including the struggle of Robert A. Taft as Senator against the leadership of Franklin D. Roosevelt 1939-1945, *The Taft Story* by William S. White (Harper, 1954) sheds further light on the war policies of the President.

An exceedingly valuable contribution on the making of the foreign policies of President Roosevelt is found in Richard N. Current's *Secretary Stimson, A Study in Statecraft* (Rutgers University Press, 1954), based in large part on diaries of Secretary Stimson and William R. Castle. Current's article on "The Stimson Doctrine and the Hoover Doctrine" in the *American Historical Review*, LIX (April, 1954), 513-542, is also illuminating.

A survey by "the noted correspondent of the *Chicago Tribune*," Chesley Manly, was published as *The Twenty-Year Revolution from Roosevelt to Eisenhower* (Regnery, 1954).

In *The Web of Subversion* (John Day, 1954), James Burnham tells the story of the revelations brought in Congressional hearings —and otherwise—of Communists in the American government in the 1930's and after. The author defines subversion as "influencing or attempting to influence, actions and policies of the United States Government in such a way as to injure United States interests and to serve Soviet (or international Communist) interests."

Rear Admiral Robert A. Theobald, U. S. N. (retired), in *The Final Secret of Pearl Harbor* (Devin-Adair, 1954) described the Japanese attack from the point of view of a naval officer presenting a lawyer's brief in attack upon the official version. The story, with some additional documentation, is on the whole the same that has been presented several times since 1945. This story was published in entirety in *U. S. News and World Report*, April 2, 1954.

Further light on "Pearl Harbor" was shed in "More About Pearl Harbor," in *U. S. News and World Report*, April 16, 1954, a chapter of a forthcoming book, *Admiral Ambassador to Russia*, by Admiral William H. Standley, U. S. N. (retired). Admiral Standley, Chief of Naval Operations, 1933-1937, was a member of the Presidential Commission headed by Associate Justice Owen J. Roberts to investigate the circumstances of the Pearl Harbor attack.

In *The Man Behind Roosevelt: The Story of Louis McHenry Howe* (World Publishing Company, 1954), Lela Stiles presents interesting material on the minutiae of daily politics as seen by a secretary to Mr. Howe.

Pertinent in its discussion of the historical development of the Presidency in the light of the crises of the Roosevelt years is Sidney Hyman, *The American President* (Harper, 1954).

W. A. Eddy published *F. D. R. Meets Ibn Saud: West Met East in the Suez Canal* (New York: American Friends of the Middle East, 1954), "a first-hand documentary account."

The second volume of *The Secret Diary of Harold L. Ickes: Inside Struggle* (Simon & Schuster, 1954) covers the period from the election of 1936 to September, 1939. As in the case of the first volume, it is to be noted that this is not the full record as the author wrote the diary.

In the *Virginia Quarterly* (Summer, 1954), Dexter Perkins discusses the whole question of responsibility for American entrance into World War II in answering the query, "Was Roosevelt Wrong?" This is an excellent critique of "revisionist" literature.

A moving autobiography by Jonathan Daniels entitled *The End of Innocence* (Lippincott, 1954), presents a great deal of new material on Franklin Roosevelt in the years 1913 to 1921. But there are important contributions on the later years, as well, notably on the last year of the President's life, when Daniels served as Administrative Assistant and Press Secretary to the President.

The autobiography of Donald Richberg, *My Hero* (Putnam's, 1954), included important testimony on the New Deal, particularly the period 1933-1937.

In writing on "Some Contributions of Harold L. Ickes" in *The Western Political Quarterly*, VII (June 1954), pp. 238-252, M. J. Harmon states that "In 1937, Ickes gave President Roosevelt the idea for his controversial 'quarantine' speech in Chicago." (P. 244.)

In the *U. S. News and World Report*, August 20 and 27, 1954, is reported a sharp interchange between Mrs. Eleanor Roosevelt and Martin Dies concerning the nature and extent of radicalism among a considerable number of the younger members serving in the Roosevelt administration. The controversy involved particularly the activities and the testimony of Mr. Joseph Lash before the House Un-American Activities Committee. Mr. Lash subsequently served as assistant to Elliott Roosevelt in editing *The Personal Letters, 1928-1945.*

Vital as revelations of Roosevelt policy in the Pacific war, two books on the career of General Douglas MacArthur were published in 1954. *MacArthur 1941-1951* (McGraw-Hill) was the joint product of Major General Charles A. Willoughby, who was MacArthur's Intelligence officer for ten years, and John Chamberlain. Hanson Baldwin, in reviewing this book, cautions that it is "not balanced history, and that its numerous significant contributions and interesting narrative are marred by generalities, distortions, omissions and inaccuracies." The second book, *The Untold Story of Douglas MacArthur* (Devin-Adair), was written by Frazier Hunt, described as a "veteran war correspondent." Not "an inspired or authorized biography," it claims to be "a newspaperman's report after a thorough examination of the records and after many interviews with persons concerned in the events described."

Japan's Decision to Surrender, by Robert J. C. Butow (Stanford University Press, 1954), is the definitive story of the struggle within Japan (1941-1945), based upon primary sources, Japanese in particular, and the result of research in Japan.

The third volume of *The Secret Diary of Harold L. Ickes: The Lowering Clouds,* was issued by Simon and Schuster on December 3, 1954, too late for use in the preparation of this volume.

An able summary of "The Muddle Before Pearl Harbor," which does not solve the "mystery," was presented by Naval Historian Captain T. B. Kittredge, U.S.N.R. (retired), in *U. S. News and World Report,* December 3, 1954.

INDEX

INDEX